QUICK FIXES

FOR YOUR HOME

Walter Curtis

Publications International, Ltd.

Walter Curtis is the author of numerous how-to books on home maintenance, repair, and remodeling.

Illustrations: Ilene Robinette; Clarence A. Moberg

Photography: Dave Szarzak/White Eagle Studio

Louis Weber, CEO
Publications International, Ltd.
7373 North Cicero Avenue
Lincolnwood, Illinois 60712

Permission is never granted for commercial purposes.

Manufactured in China.

8 7 6 5 4 3 2 1

ISBN: 0-7853-8366-2

Library of Congress Control Number: 2003101563

CONTENTS

INTRODUCTION

Use your quick fix notebook to keep track of the make, model number, and part numbers for all your major appliances. You'll be glad you did when it's time to tackle a quick fix!

THE *ONE* BOOK YOU NEED FOR YOUR HOME

With all the dozens of home repair books available today, why is *this* book the first and most important one you should own? Because it gets you off to the right start!

Things break, with a little help or on their own. Light switches quit working. A window gets broken. The furnace quits. A faucet leaks. A wall crack appears. A table surface is damaged. And on and on. We all have a list of things we really should fix if we had the time *and* know-how. Fortunately, most home repairs are really quick fixes!

ABOUT QUICK FIXES A quick fix is a repair you can finish in a short time (five minutes to a couple of hours) with basic tools and practically no prior experience. You don't have to be an electrician, for example, to replace a broken switch. And you don't need to be a plumber to unstop a drain. All you need is a little time plus a few tools and some clear instructions.

FINDING THE TIME When? Whenever! The fixes in this book are relatively easy to complete once you know what you're going to be doing and have gathered the needed parts and tools. (Don't worry, this book will show you how to find and choose them, too.) So whenever you have some free time, you can grab the parts and tools and make quick work of it.

You may be surprised at how much extra time you can find if you have instructions, tools, and parts standing by. You can tackle these quick fixes just about any time. Set aside an hour or two each week to take on the next task in your quick fix notebook. You might get a few of them done every week.

What's a quick fix notebook? It's your handy record of what needs to be fixed, the page number in this book where you'll find instructions, and a list of the parts you'll need in advance—parts you can pick up and put in your toolbox until you're ready to do the job. The record can be a small notebook you keep with you or on a desk or kitchen counter where it's handy. As you think of a job, just write it down. Then, when you have a moment, you look it up in this book and determine what you'll need in advance, such as parts and tools. Take the notebook to the hardware store and pick up the parts you need for many fixes all at once, saving you time. And maybe even buy a new handy tool for your toolbox.

WORKING SMART Here's the secret to quick fixes: Getting ready is half the job. Gathering the parts and tools and knowing what you need to do is typically as time consuming as actually making the repair. Fortunately, you can get ready for quick fixes by simply reading this book and following the instructions. It may take you less time to do it than to read about it!

GETTING HELP Fortunately, you can call on help when you need it. Besides this book, you can get useful information on small repairs from the manufacturer of the problem item or a professional repair person.

The first tip to keep in mind is to never *ever* throw away the owner's manual that comes with any gadget you get (until you throw the product itself away). Instead, keep it in a place where you can find it easily. Why? Because not only do the manuals typically include troubleshooting and repair information, but they also usually tell you where to get parts and may even show you which parts to get. Using the make, model number, and part number, you can get a replacement part for virtually anything made in the past 10 years. Even if the manufacturer is long gone and the warranty is a yellowed piece of paper, you often can find replacement parts.

FINDING PARTS WHEN YOU NEED THEM

Where can you find replacement parts? For many quick fixes, parts are as near as your local hardware store. If you haven't visited one before, do so soon. Each of the rows should have signs above to point you in the right direction: Plumbing, Electrical, Fasteners, etc. Once in the electrical aisle, for example, you'll find electrical wire, switches, receptacles, boxes, wire nuts, and scads of other parts. The fastener department will have bins and boxes of nails, screws, bolts, nuts, and maybe adhesives.

How can you make sure you are getting the correct part? If you've already removed the problem part, take it with you to the hardware store. If you don't have the broken part yet, find a knowledgeable clerk to help you. If you can't find a helpful clerk, shop another store. Better hardware stores will have clerks with electrical experience hovering around the electrical parts aisles, for example. If you go on a weekend you may be talking to someone who works as an electrician during the week. Or you can turn to nearby customers who look like they know what they're buying and ask for help.

That's another important tip: Ask for help. It's okay. You won't be annoying most folks. In fact, most customers and clerks *enjoy* helping you get the right part. Also, if in doubt, buy both. If it's an expensive part, you may be able to return the unused, uninstalled part. If it's cheap (less than the cost of your time to return it), put the part in your toolbox because you may need it for another job.

What about hard-to-find parts? If you have access to the Internet, you can find one or more resources for just about any replacement part imaginable. Otherwise, check the telephone book for companies that sell the product you're fixing, call them, and ask about replacement parts. Using a model and part number, you can find just about anything.

ENJOYING QUICK FIXES

Yes, you actually can enjoy quick fixes. Unlike everything else in life, quick fixes come with instructions, are typically easy to solve, and are inexpensive. Most important, finishing a quick fix and scratching it off your list is a pleasant experience. You've learned something. You've fixed something. And, even if it isn't fixed, you can save money by telling the repair person what's been unsuccessfully tried.

After awhile you'll start looking at quick fixes as challenges rather than problems. You'll see a faulty light switch as a 15-minute fix that will make you feel proud every time you turn on the light.

USING THIS BOOK

Quick Fixes for Your Home is organized to help you get the most from your time and efforts. Before starting your first quick fix, read Chapter 1 on tools and materials. You'll learn what tools you'll need for various fixes as well as how to safely use them. This chapter will also help you select and fill your own quick fix tool box to make all repairs easier.

The succeeding chapters each cover a part of your house that has common components and similar fixes:

- Chapter 2 addresses rooms (walls, floors, ceilings, doors, windows).

- Chapter 3 tells you about electrical things (receptacles, switches, lighting, fans, doorbells, garage door openers).

- Chapter 4 handles plumbing fixes (faucets, toilets, pipes).

- Chapter 5 covers quick heating and cooling system fixes.

- Chapter 6 offers interior painting, wallpaper, and furniture fixes plus tips on resolving pest problems.

- Chapter 7 tackles exterior fixes (paint, fences, decks, roofs, gutters).

- Chapter 8 shows you how to clean most anything in your home with simple-to-make cleaning solutions and clear instructions.

- The Glossary defines more than 100 household terms for clarity and easy reference.

This really is the *one* book you need for your home!

From electrical fixes to plumbing repair to interior updating, quick fixes can be completed by the do-it-yourself novice in hardly any time at all.

CHAPTER 1

QUICK FIX TOOLBOX

Quick fixes mean having the right tools and materials on hand so you can get right at the job and on with your life. In this first chapter you'll learn to select and gather what you'll need for your toolbox as well as choose materials and fasteners to make the job go smoothly. You'll refer back to this chapter many times as you learn about the various quick fixes featured in this book. So don't skip this chapter: Knowing about the basics will help you in the long run.

QUICK FIX TOOLS

What tools will you need? In the coming pages you'll learn about tools that measure, cut, drill, nail, tighten and loosen, hold, clamp, test, paint, and more. Most important, you'll learn which ones you really need and how to use them safely.

First, let's talk about quality. The smartest rule about buying tools is to buy good quality. High-quality tools are not only safer to use, but most will last a lifetime with proper care. You can usually identify a quality tool by its machining: The metal parts are smooth and shiny, and the tool is well balanced—it fits comfortably in your hand. Inferior tools, on the other hand, have defects or rough metal (often hidden by paint) and exhibit crude machining. Most important, however, is that good tools are safer to use. Cheap tools can break and cause accidents.

You can expect to pay an average of 25 percent more for high-quality equipment, but cheap tools are no bargain—you get what you pay for, so you may have to replace them more often. Besides, the money you save on your very first do-it-yourself repair may pay for the tools you needed. And, after that, the tools are yours to keep!

Useful tools for your quick fix toolbox include measuring tools, saws, drills, and fastener tools. You may also want tools for specific tasks, such as electrical or plumbing repairs.

Common measuring tools for quick fixes.

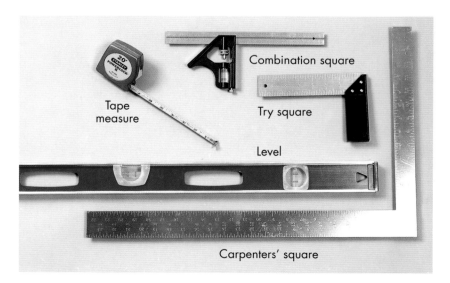

Tape measure

Combination square

Try square

Level

Carpenters' square

MEASURING AND MARKING TOOLS

Just about every quick fix project calls for accurate measurements. Not only do you have to know precisely how many feet and inches are involved, but you also need to ensure everything comes out plumb, level, and square. The following are basic devices for measuring and marking.

TAPE MEASURE Flexible tape measures are available in lengths of up to 50 feet; a tape that is 12 to 25 feet is usually considered adequate. You should buy a tape at least ⅝-inch wide so it will stay rigid when extended. Most tapes have an automatic power return that is useful but not necessary.

SQUARE The standard size for a carpenters' square is 18 to 24 inches (body) by 12 or 18 inches (tongue). The size is important for cutting straight edges on plywood and hardboard.

For small jobs, a combination square is easier to use than a carpenters' square because the combination square is smaller—typically only 12 inches long. The body of the square slides along the blade and can be set at any point with a thumb-screw. The square's body may incorporate a small bubble level or a scratch awl that can be used for leveling and marking your work. This type of square can also be used as a depth gauge, a miter square, and, with the blade removed, a straightedge and ruler.

A try square looks like a small carpenters' square with a wood or plastic handle. The measurements go across the metal blade, not the handle. This type of square is used to test the squareness of edges in planing and sawing work. It can also be used to check right-angle layouts. Its tongue has a maximum length of 12 inches; it is wide, but it can be used as a straightedge, ruler, and depth gauge.

LEVEL Two- and three-bubble levels are standard for most leveling needs. The edges of a level can be used as a straightedge. Laid flat against a vertical surface, a level can determine both horizontal and vertical levels—often needed when hanging pictures. Levels are made of either wood or lightweight metal, such as aluminum. Lengths range to 6 feet, with 30 inches being the most popular size.

CHALK LINE A chalk line is used for marking a straight line over long distances, such as for replacing wallpaper or flooring tiles.

STUD FINDER A stud finder comes in handy if you need to find the studs behind walls to hang a heavy item, for example.

HANDSAWS

Once measurements are made, materials can be cut using a saw. A wide selection of handsaws and power saws are available to match the needs of various cutting jobs.

CROSSCUT SAW A crosscut saw, as its name implies, cuts across the grain of wood. A crosscut saw has five to ten or more teeth per inch to produce a smooth cut in the wood. It is used for cutting plywood and hardboard panels and for cutting miters (angles).

RIPSAW A ripsaw cuts along the grain of wood, called "ripping." Its teeth are spaced three to five teeth per inch. Because a ripsaw's teeth are wider set than those of the crosscut saw, it can slice through wood like a chisel. The final cut of a ripsaw is rough, and the wood usually has to be sanded to its final measurement.

BACKSAW A backsaw has a reinforced back to stiffen the blade. Its teeth are closely spaced— like those of a crosscut saw—so the cut is smooth. A backsaw is used for making angle cuts and for trimming molding. It's designed for use in a miter box; the reinforced back serves as a guide.

KEYHOLE SAW A keyhole saw has a 10- to 12-inch tapered blade. It's used to cut openings for pipes, electrical boxes, and almost any straight or curved internal cuts that are too large for an auger bit, a drill, or a hole saw. A quality keyhole saw has removable blades with a variety of tooth spacings for cutting such materials as wood, plastic, metal, and hardboard.

COPING SAW A coping saw has a thin blade that is secured with two pins at the ends of the saw. A variety of blades are available, with both ripsaw and crosscut tooth spacing.

HACKSAW A hacksaw is used to cut metal, plastic, and pipe.

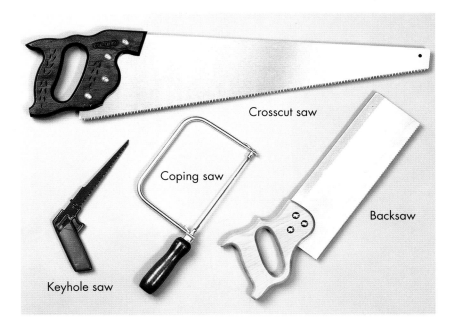

Crosscut saw

Coping saw

Backsaw

Keyhole saw

Common types of handsaws.

POWER SAWS

Power saws can be intimidating at first, and they should be! Improperly used, they can do damage in a hurry. You should always observe the proper safety precautions. Once you make a few practice cuts, however, you'll soon become comfortable with it. (Turn to page 27–28 for tool safety.)

CIRCULAR SAW A portable electric tool, the circular saw is the power version of a crosscut saw or ripsaw. The guide on the saw can be adjusted to cut miters and pockets in most building materials. Several blades are available: crosscut, rip, masonry, metal, and plastic. A table is one of the accessories available for a circular saw so it can be mounted to work as a table saw.

SABER SAW A saber saw, also called a jigsaw, consists of a 4-inch blade driven in an up-and-down or reciprocating motion. This portable power tool uses many blade designs for a variety of materials, including wood, metal, plastic, masonry, ceramic, and high-pressure laminate. This is the power counterpart to a keyhole and coping saw; it will make smooth fine-line or contour cuts either with or across the grain.

DRILLS

Three sizes of chuck to hold drill bits in place are available for power drills: ¼-inch, ⅜-inch, and ½-inch capacity. The two most popular sizes are ¼ and ⅜ inch. The ¼-inch chuck has a capacity of ¼-inch drills in metal and ½-inch drills in wood. A ¼-inch drill can handle only a limited range of drilling operations and shouldn't be used for difficult jobs, but it's the least expensive type of electric drill.

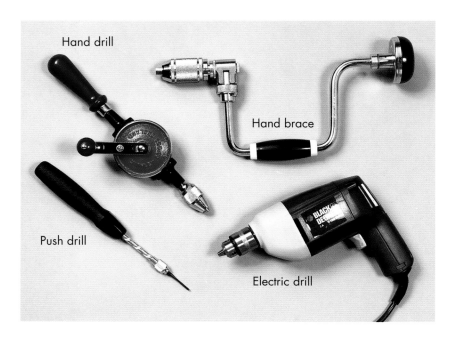

Hand drill

Hand brace

Push drill

Electric drill

Hand and power drills.

tools that help you apply fasteners, such as nails, bolts, and adhesives. Fastener tools include hammers, screwdrivers, pliers, and clamps.

HAMMERS The most popular hammer is the carpenters' curved-claw nail hammer; 16 ounces is a good size for men and 14 ounces for women. It is steel-headed, wood- or steel-handled, and used for driving nails and other fasteners. The claw at one end of the head is a two-pronged arch used to pull nails out of wood. The other parts of the head are the eye and the face. A flat-face, or plane-face, hammer is good for beginners to use, but it is more difficult to drive a nail flush to the work surface with this hammer.

A rubber mallet comes in handy when you're trying to unstick painted windows or have to do light hammering on surfaces that can be damaged. Other specialty hammers include a ball-peen hammer for working with metal and a mason's hammer for brick and concrete projects.

SCREWDRIVERS Every toolbox should have one set of high-quality screwdrivers that are only used for tightening and loosening screws. There are many types of screwdrivers, which vary depending on the screw head each is designed to fit. Following are the most popular screw heads:

- **Standard head.** Also known as a flat, slotted, or straight screwdriver. Make sure the tip is the correct width and thickness to snugly fit the screw-head slot.

- **Phillips head.** Also called cross or X-head screwdrivers, Phillips heads fit into a cross-shape recess in the screw or bolt head.

- **Torx head.** Torx head (or similar designs called Robertson) screwdrivers fit into a square or hexagonal hole, which allows more torque for tightening or loosening the fastener.

WRENCHES The purpose of a wrench is to turn a bolt head or nut. Selecting the appropriate wrench depends on the fastener's design and size. It can also depend on how difficult the fastener is

The ⅜-inch drill can make ⅜-inch holes in metal and ¾-inch holes in wood; a hole saw can also be used with this tool to cut holes up to 3 inches in diameter. Many ⅜-inch drills have a hammer mode that permits drilling in concrete along with a reversing feature that is handy for removing screws. A variable-speed drill is also a handy tool to own; the rotation can be started slowly and then sped up. A variety of attachments and accessories are available, including wire brushes, paint mixers, and even a circular saw attachment.

Power drills come in corded and cordless models. Cordless drills, which use an onboard battery and typically include a recharger, are becoming increasingly popular.

The two main types of hand drills used are the push drill and the hand brace. Push drills are good for making pilot holes and for setting hinges. A hand brace is particularly handy when working in restricted areas because of its ratcheting mechanism.

FASTENER TOOLS

Fastener tools are often the first to be selected for the quick fixer's toolbox. They are simply

BITS		
Drill Bit	**Drill Type**	**Use**
Twist	Hand, power, or drill press	Small-diameter holes in wood and metal
Spade	Power or drill press	Holes up to 1½ inches in wood
Auger	Brace	Holes up to 1½ inches in wood
Expansion	Brace	Holes up to 3 inches in wood
Fly cutter	Drill press	Holes up to 6 inches in wood; smaller holes in other materials
Hole saw	Power or drill press	Holes up to 3 inches in wood

to reach. Wrench types include open end, combination, adjustable, and Allen. **Tip:** When using a wrench, pull it toward you rather than pushing it away. This gives you more control and reduces the chance of injury if the wrench slips.

- **Box end.** A box, or closed, end wrench is used where there is room to place the wrench mouth around the fastener. Box end wrenches are available in 6- and 12-point versions to match the number of sides on the fastener. Hexagon fasteners have 6 sides, or points, and are the most popular.

- **Open end.** This type of wrench is used for turning fasteners in locations where a box end wrench cannot encompass the fastener.

- **Combination.** A combination wrench has ends that perform specific tasks. One end may be open and the other closed, one may be offset and the other straight, or the two ends might be of fractionally different sizes.

- **Adjustable.** An adjustable wrench can be used on a variety of fastener sizes. The disadvantage is that it is less stable than a fixed-size wrench and can easily injure you or damage the fastener. An adjustable wrench should be used only if the correct size wrench is not available.

- **Socket.** Socket wrenches fit over the fastener, making removal easier and safer than with other wrenches. Sockets come in standard and extended depth; extensions are available to make removing fasteners easier. They are often purchased in sets by drive size.

- **Allen.** Called by the Allen brand name, these are used on fasteners with a hexagonal hole in the head. Allen wrenches are available with L- or T-shape handles.

PLIERS Think of pliers as an extension of your fingers, only stronger. They are used to grasp and hold a part. Pliers should not be used as wrenches to tighten or loosen fasteners. Common types of pliers include slip-joint, groove-joint, needle-nose, and locking.

- **Slip-joint.** This type of pliers has two settings in the handle to allow for two widths. Once the correct width is selected, the handles are closed together to force the jaw around the part and hold it securely.

- **Groove-joint.** Groove-joint pliers are similar to slip-joint except they use an elongated hole in the handle with grooves that allow multiple widths.

- **Needle-nose.** This type has jaws that come to a point for securely grasping small parts or wires, especially in tight locations.

- **Locking.** Sometimes called by the Vise Grip brand name, locking pliers are adjustable and can be locked to hold a part in place.

CLAMPS Clamps are essential for some quick fixes, like holding parts together while glue dries. Spring clamps, which look like large metal clothespins, are inexpensive and are used for clamping small jobs, such as gluing veneers to core material. C-clamps are also useful and come in a wide range of sizes. They are made from cast iron or aluminum and have a C-shape body. A screw with a metal pad applies tension on the material being clamped. Because C-clamps can exert a lot of pressure, buffer blocks of scrap wood should be inserted between the jaws of the clamps and the material being clamped. Screw, bar, and strap clamps are used by woodworkers.

Various types of clamps.

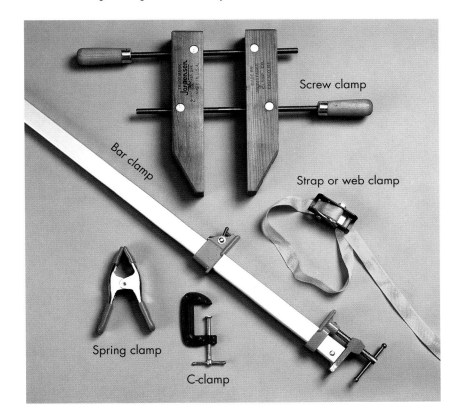

Screw clamp

Bar clamp

Strap or web clamp

Spring clamp

C-clamp

ELECTRICAL TOOLS

Chapter 3 will show you how to make quick electrical fixes using basic tools. Most are inexpensive and can be found in your local hardware store.

How does electricity work? It must have a continuous path, or circuit, in order to flow. Think of it as a two-lane road from point A to point B and back. If one or both lanes are blocked, traffic stops. The flow of auto traffic over a highway is measured with a traffic counter placed across the road. The flow of electrical current is measured by placing an electrical tester at two points in the circuit. Most electrical problems can be solved by using a voltage tester, a continuity tester, or a volt-ohm-milliammeter (VOM), also known as a multimeter or multitester.

VOLTAGE TESTER A voltage tester is the simplest of these tools. It consists of a small neon bulb with two insulated wires attached to the bottom of the bulb housing; each wire ends in a metal test probe. This type of tester is always used with the current turned on to determine whether there is current flowing through a wire and to test for proper grounding. It is also used to determine whether adequate voltage is present in a wire. Look for a tester rated for up to 500 volts.

To use a voltage tester, touch one probe to one wire or connection and the other probe to the opposite wire or connection. If the component is receiving electricity, the light in the housing will glow. If the light doesn't glow, the trouble is at this point. For example, if you suspect an electrical outlet is faulty, insert one probe of the tester into one slot in the outlet and the other probe into the other slot. The light in the tester should light. If it doesn't, the outlet may be bad. To further test the outlet, pull it out of the wall. Place one probe of the tester on one terminal screw connection and the other probe on the other terminal screw. If the tester bulb lights, you know the outlet is malfunctioning—there is current flowing to the outlet, but it isn't flowing through the outlet to provide power to the appliance plugged into it. If the test bulb doesn't light, there is no current coming into the outlet. The problem may be a blown fuse or tripped circuit breaker, or the wire may be disconnected or broken behind the outlet.

CONTINUITY TESTER A continuity tester consists of a battery in a housing, with a test probe connected to one end of the battery housing and a test wire with an alligator clip connected to the other end. It is used with the current turned off to determine whether a particular electrical component is carrying electricity and to pinpoint the cause of a problem.

To use a continuity tester, unplug the appliance and disassemble it to get at the component you want to test. Fasten the clip of the tester to one wire or connection of the component, and touch the probe to the other wire or connection. If the component is receiving electricity and transmitting it, the tester will light or buzz; this indicates

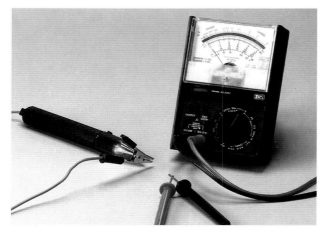

Continuity tester (left) and VOM, or multitester (right).

that the circuit is continuous. If the tester doesn't light or buzz or it reacts only slightly, the component is faulty. **Caution:** Do not use a continuity tester unless the appliance is unplugged or the power to the circuit is turned off.

VOLT-OHM-MILLIAMMETER (VOM) A voltage tester and a continuity tester are adequate for many diagnostic jobs, and they are relatively inexpensive. But for more serious electrical and appliance troubleshooting and repairs, invest in a volt-ohm-milliammeter, or volt-ohm meter (VOM). A VOM is battery powered and is used with the current turned off. It's used to check continuity in a wire or component and to measure the electrical current—from 0 to 250 volts, AC (alternating current, as in houses) or DC (direct current, as in batteries)—flowing through the wire or component. A multitester is used with plug-in test leads, which may have probes at both ends or a probe at one end and an alligator clip at the other. An adjustment knob or switch is set to measure current on the scale desired, usually ohms. The dial indicates the current flowing through the item being tested. **Caution:** Do not use a VOM unless the appliance you want to test is unplugged or the power to the circuit is turned off.

A VOM is useful for testing appliances because it is used while the power is turned off, so there's no danger of electric shock. It provides more precise information than the continuity tester and, therefore, is preferable for testing many components. Learning to read a VOM is very easy, and manufacturers provide complete operating instructions with the meters.

COMPRESSED AIR A can of compressed air, sold under a variety of names and brands, is very useful for cleaning appliances and electrical fixtures. Compressed air can remove particles of food or even help dislodge loose parts from a toaster, for example. Some compressed air cans come with an extension tube that fits in the can's nozzle to precisely direct the air. If you cannot find canned compressed air at your hardware or home supply store, try a computer shop where it's sold as a dust remover for keyboards and other electronics.

ELECTRICAL CONTACT CLEANER Electrical contact cleaner is simply compressed air with a cleaning agent that evaporates, such as isopropyl alcohol. It is useful for cleaning electric components that have food, grease, or oils on them. It can dislodge foreign elements and clean components. Several brands of electrical contact cleaner are available at larger hardware stores, electronics dealers, and hobby shops.

PLUMBING TOOLS

Chapter 4 will show you how to make quick fixes to plumbing. You may already have many of the tools necessary for most plumbing jobs because they are the same tools used for other do-it-yourself projects. Other special tools include pipe wrenches and various plumbing aids.

PIPE WRENCHES You'll need a medium-size adjustable pipe wrench to tighten and loosen pipes and other plumbing connections. You can purchase one at hardware stores and plumbing-supply houses.

A basin wrench is a specialized tool that allows you to reach tight spots under sinks and basins. The jaws of a basin wrench not only adjust to accommodate nuts of different sizes, but they also flip over to the opposite side so you can keep turning without removing the wrench.

A socket wrench set is useful for removing recessed packing nuts and for use on tub and shower fixtures as well as other do-it-yourself household repairs.

For changing a toilet seat, you'll need a wrench, or perhaps a deep socket wrench. If you need to remove a toilet for replacement or repair, you may need a spud wrench. Older toilets frequently have a large pipe—called a spud—that connects the tank to the bowl. The spud is held to the bowl and tank by extra-large hexagonal slip nuts. A spud wrench is designed to remove these slip nuts. The adjustable type of spud wrench is far more versatile than the nonadjustable type, which has a fixed opening at each end.

PLUMBING AIDS Plumbers' snakes, or drain-and-trap augers, come in various lengths. A short snake is all that's necessary for most plumbing repairs. A closet auger is a version of the plumbers' snake designed specifically for clearing clogs in toilets. The closet auger is shorter than a regular snake, and it comes encased in a plastic or metal housing with an easy-to-use crank.

PAINTING TOOLS

You will tackle quick painting fixes in Chapters 6 and 7. A good paint job depends as much on selecting the right tools as on selecting the right paint. With the proper equipment, even inexperienced do-it-yourselfers can do a professional-quality job.

PAINTBRUSHES With few exceptions, paintbrushes fall into two camps: natural bristle brushes, made of animal hair, and synthetic bristle brushes, usually made of nylon. At one time, the naturals were considered the best, but today the synthetics are every bit as good. Besides, you can't use a natural bristle brush with waterbase latex paints because water makes the bristles limp. Consequently, if you're painting with a water-thinned paint, your brush selection is already 50 percent easier.

Buy the best brushes you can afford. If you have to spend a

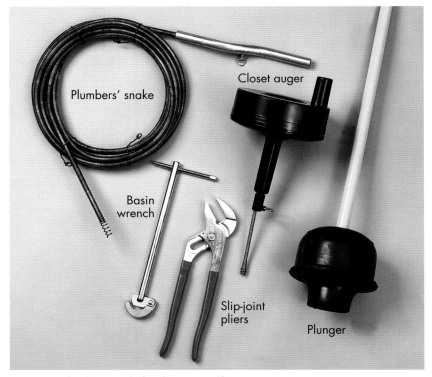

Common plumbing tools for do-it-yourselfers.

Plumbers' snake
Closet auger
Basin wrench
Slip-joint pliers
Plunger

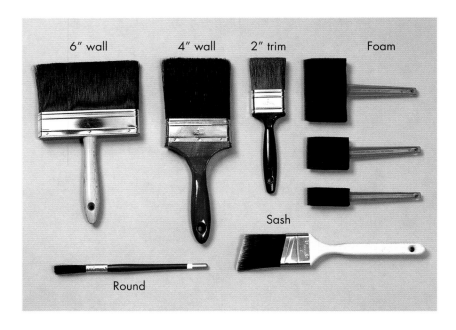

6" wall   4" wall   2" trim   Foam

Sash

Round

Common bristle and foam paintbrushes.

few dollars more for top quality brushes, it will be worth it in the long run. Quality brushes make any painting task go more easily and quickly, and they can be thoroughly cleaned to look like new for the next job. With a little care, good paintbrushes will last for many years of home maintenance.

Regardless of price, you can distinguish between a good brush and a bad one by examining them closely at the store. Spread the bristles and inspect the tips. The more flags, or split ends, the better the brush and its paint-spreading capabilities. Rap the brush on the edge of a counter; a good brush may lose a few bristles, but a bad one will lose many. Find a brush with long, tapered bristles, particularly on narrow brushes. As a general rule, the bristle length should be about one-and-a-half times as long as the width of the brush (the exception is with wider brushes, often called wall brushes). A 1½-inch-wide brush, for example, should have bristles about 2¼ inches long. Bristle length gives you flexibility to paint into corners and around trim. Finally, choose smooth, well-shaped handles of wood or plastic that fit in your hand comfortably.

Paintbrushes come in a wide variety of sizes and types and are necessary for those hard-to-reach spots a paint roller can't reach. Here are some of the main types of paintbrushes:

- **Wall.** This type spreads the most paint over the most surface. A 4-inch-wide brush is a good choice, though 3½- and 3-inch wall brushes may be easier to use.

- **Trim.** A 2-inch-wide trim brush is ideal for woodwork and for "cutting in" around windows, doors, and corners before painting walls with a roller.

- **Sash.** A sash brush has an angled bristle end. Available in 1-, 1½-, or 2-inch widths, the angled sash brush makes close work easier—especially when you're painting around windows. Used carefully, it reduces the need to use tape to protect window panes.

The same size brushes are also available in foamed urethane. Instead of bristles, they have spongelike heads. They are increasingly popular among do-it-yourselfers, particularly in smaller sizes used for interior or exterior trim painting. Disposable foam brushes come in widths up to 3 inches and are cheap enough to toss out after one use.

PAINT ROLLERS For large, flat surface areas like walls and ceilings, paint rollers will help you get the job done in about half the amount of time it would take with a paintbrush. Most painters use brushes for trim work and around windows and doors, then turn to rollers to fill in the big blank spaces. Rollers for painting flat areas come in varying widths—from 4 to 18 inches—but the two most common sizes for interior jobs are 7 inches and 9 inches wide.

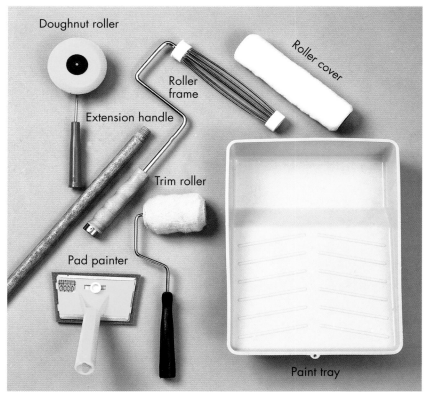

Doughnut roller

Roller cover

Roller frame

Extension handle

Trim roller

Pad painter

Paint tray

Paint rollers, pad, and tray.

Paint rollers intended for wall or ceiling painting have handles made of plastic or wood that may have been hollowed out and machined to accept an extension handle. They also have a metal or plastic frame that is slipped inside a roller cover. Of the two types, the metal-rib version (also known as a bird cage or spring-metal frame) is best because it's easier to clean and less likely to stick to the inside of the roller cover.

The type of roller cover you should buy is largely determined by the kind of paint you'll be using, but they are all fiber-covered or urethane-foam-covered cylinders that soak up paint from a tray and then release it when rolled over a flat surface. The rolling action creates a vacuum that actually pulls the paint off the roller. Made of lamb's wool, mohair, Dynel, acetate, or polyurethane foam, most rollers are labeled with the kind of paint for which they are intended to be used. Choose your roller cover accordingly. The roller package will also identify the length of the roller cover's nap, or pile, which can vary from 1/16 inch to 1½ inches. For rough surfaces, use the long naps; choose short ones for smooth surfaces. The pile is attached to a tube that slips over the roller's plastic or cardboard frame.

Paint trays are made of aluminum or plastic and come in standard 7-inch and 9-inch versions. The 9-inch size is most popular because you can then use either a 7- or 9-inch roller. Some trays come with hooks that allow you to attach them directly to a ladder. The trays, of course, are washable and durable. But to make cleanup even easier, buy some disposable plastic tray liners or line the tray with aluminum foil.

OTHER QUICK FIX TOOLS

PLANES Need to shave the edge of a sticking door? Use a jack plane to remove excess wood and bring the surface of the wood to trueness and smoothness; a smoothing plane brings wood to a final finish. A block plane can do both, plus it is used to smooth and cut the end grain of wood. All are relatively inexpensive and can be found at most hardware stores.

ELECTRIC SANDER Need to sand a surface but don't have all day? An orbital sander is the handiest for most small projects.

QUICK FIX MATERIALS

To make a quick fix you need to know what materials to select and how to use them. This section offers basic information on selecting

---

FINDING THE RIGHT QUICK FIX TOOL

So how can you choose the right tool for a quick fix? Actually, it's relatively easy. Simply ask:

- What material am I working with (lumber, plywood, drywall, paint, plastic, ceramic, etc.)?
- What do I need to do (fasten, attach, remove, resurface, etc.)?
- Which tools described in this chapter best fit the job?
—Hammers fasten wood
—Brushes and rollers resurface drywall with paint
—Glues attach parts and materials together
—VOMs test electrical devices
—Screwdrivers, wrenches, and pliers remove and replace parts
- You can build your own basic toolbox to include common repair tools:
—14- or 16-ounce hammer
—Standard and Phillips screwdrivers
—Pliers
—Adjustable wrench
—Basin wrench
—2-inch paintbrush
—Handsaw or power saw
—Hand drill or power drill
—Assorted fasteners
—Glues and adhesives for wood and plastic

---

lumber, plywood, drywall, and other materials for common do-it-yourself projects.

LUMBER

Maybe you've noticed that lumber sizes are often misleading. The "nominal" cross-section dimensions of a piece of lumber, such as 2×4 or 1×6, are always somewhat larger than the actual, or dressed, dimensions. The reason is that dressed lumber has been surfaced or planed smooth on four sides (called S4S). The nominal measurement is made before the lumber is surfaced.

Board measure is a method of measuring lumber in which the basic unit is 1 foot long by 1 foot wide by 1 inch thick, called a board foot. It is calculated by nominal, not actual, dimensions of lumber. The easiest formula for figuring nominal board feet is:

$$\frac{\text{Thickness} \times \text{Width} \times \text{Length}}{12}$$

The answer is in board feet. Lumber is often priced in board feet. However, most building material retailers and lumberyards also price

One-by (1×) lumber is called board:

Nominal Size	Dressed Dimensions (inches)
1×6	¾×5½
1×8	¾×7¼
1×10	¾×9¼

Two-by (2×) and four-by (4×) lumber is called dimension lumber:

Nominal Size	Dressed Dimensions (inches)
2×2	1½×1½
2×4	1½×3½
2×6	1½×5½
2×8	1½×7¼
2×10	1½×9¼
2×12	1½×11¼
4×4	3½×3½

lumber by the running foot for easier calculation. That is, a 2×4×8 is priced at eight times the running foot cost rather than as 5.333 board feet.

PLYWOOD

Some quick fixes require that you use or at least understand plywood. Knowing about plywood can save you money and may mean the difference between a successful project and one that fails.

For example, you don't need to buy an expensive piece of plywood that's perfect on both sides if only one side will be seen. Similarly, there's no sense in paying for ⅝-inch thickness when ¼-inch plywood is really all you need. Plywood also comes with different glues, veneers, and degrees of finish. By knowing these characteristics you may be able to save money as well as do a better job.

Available at home centers, hardware stores, and lumberyards, plywood is better than lumber for some jobs. It is strong, lightweight, and rigid. Its high-impact resistance means plywood doesn't split, chip, crack all the way through, or crumble; the cross-laminate construction restricts expansion and contraction within the individual plies. Moreover, you never get "green" wood with plywood. When you buy a sheet of plywood, you know exactly what size you're getting, unlike with other types of lumber that have nominal and actual measurements. For example, a 4×8-foot sheet of ¾-inch plywood measures exactly 4 by 8 feet and is exactly ¾ inch thick.

Plywood is broadly categorized into two types: exterior and interior. Exterior plywood is made with nothing but waterproof glue and should always be used for any exposed application. Interior plywood, made with highly resistant glues, can actually withstand quite a bit of mois-

PLYWOOD GRADES

Interior Grade	Face	Back	Inner Plies	Common Uses
A-A	A	A	D	Cabinet doors, built-ins, and furniture where both sides show.
A-B	A	B	D	Alternate for A-A. Face is finish grade; back is solid and smooth.
A-D	A	D	D	Finish grade face for paneling, built-ins, and backing.
B-D	B	D	D	Utility grade. One paintable side. Used for backing, cabinet sides, etc.
C-D	C	D	D	Sheathing and structural uses such as temporary enclosures, subfloor. Unsanded.
Underlayment	C-plugged	D	C, D	For underlayment or combination subfloor-underlayment under tile and carpeting.

Exterior Grade	Face	Back	Inner Plies	Common Uses
A-A	A	A	C	Outdoors, where appearance of both sides is important.
A-B	A	B	C	Alternate for A-A, where appearance of one side is less important. Face is finish grade.
A-C	A	C	C	Soffits, fences, base for coatings.
B-C	B	C	C	For utility uses such as farm buildings, some kinds of fences, base for coatings.
C-C plugged	C plugged	C	C	Excellent base for tile, backing for wallcoverings, high-performance coatings.
C-C	C	C	C	Unsanded, for backing and rough construction exposed to weather.

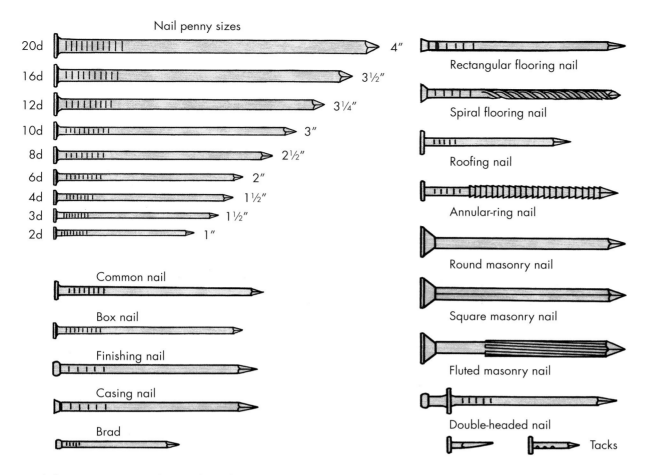

Nail penny sizes

20d	4"
16d	3½"
12d	3¼"
10d	3"
8d	2½"
6d	2"
4d	1½"
3d	1½"
2d	1"

Common nail

Box nail

Finishing nail

Casing nail

Brad

Rectangular flooring nail

Spiral flooring nail

Roofing nail

Annular-ring nail

Round masonry nail

Square masonry nail

Fluted masonry nail

Double-headed nail

Tacks

ture. There is interior plywood made with IMG (intermediate glue), which is resistant to bacteria, mold, and moisture, but no interior plywood is made for use outdoors.

When purchasing plywood, look for a back stamp or edge marking bearing the initials APA or DFPA. APA stands for American Plywood Association, while DFPA is the Douglas Fir Plywood Association. These two organizations represent most of the plywood manufacturers, and they inspect and test all plywood to ensure quality is high and grading is accurate. The most critical plywood grading category for most home projects is the appearance grade of the panel faces. Check the Plywood Grades table on page 16 before you buy any plywood. The table indicates the various uses for each grade. The first letter indicates the face grade, while the second indicates the back grade.

DRYWALL

Quick fixes to drywall typically mean patching rather than replacing. However, you should know something about it. Drywall, also known as gypsum wallboard, has all but replaced plaster in modern homes. Its rocklike gypsum core makes drywall as fire-resistant as plaster, and its heavy paper facing eliminates the cracking problems that plague plaster walls. Best of all, drywall is far easier to work with than plaster.

The standard-size sheets for walls measure 4×8 feet. All drywall sheets are 4 feet wide, but many building material outlets offer 10-foot and even 12-foot lengths. The most popular thicknesses of drywall are ½ inch (typically for walls) and ⅝ inch (ceilings).

QUICK FIX FASTENERS

Most quick fix projects require such fasteners as nails, screws, glues, and bolts. And there are many of each type to choose from! The following are some of the most common types of fasteners and advice on how to select the right one for your fix.

NAILS

The easiest way to fasten two pieces of wood together is with nails. They are manufactured in a variety of shapes, sizes, and metals to complete almost any fastening job. Most commonly, nails are made of steel, but other types—aluminum, brass, nickel, bronze, copper, and stainless steel—are available for use where corrosion could occur. In addition, nails are manufactured with coatings—galvanized, blued, or cemented—to prevent rusting and to increase their holding power.

Nail size is designated by penny size, originally the price per hundred nails. Penny size, almost always referred to as "d," ranges from 2 penny, or 2d (1 inch long), to 60 penny, or 60d (6 inches long). Nails shorter than 1 inch are called brads; nails longer than 6 inches are called spikes. The length of the nail is important, because at least two-thirds of the nail should be driven into the base, or thicker, material. For example, a 1×3 nailed to a 4×4 beam should be fastened with an 8 penny, or 8d, nail. An 8d nail is 2½ inches long; ¾ inch of its length will go through the 1×3, and the remaining 1¾ inches will go into the beam.

Nails are usually sold by the pound; the smaller the nail, the more nails to the pound. You can buy bulk nails out of a nail keg; the nails are weighed and then priced by the retailer. Or you can buy packaged nails, sold in boxes ranging from 1 pound to 50 pounds. For most quick fixes, a few 1-pound boxes of popular nail sizes will last a long time. What follows are some of the most common nail types.

COMMON NAILS Used for most medium to heavy construction work, this type of nail has a thick head and can be driven into tough materials. Common nails are made from wire and cut to the proper length and are available in sizes 2d through 60d.

BOX NAILS Lighter and smaller in diameter than common nails, box nails are designed for light construction and household use.

FINISHING NAILS Finishing nails are lighter than common nails and have a small head. They

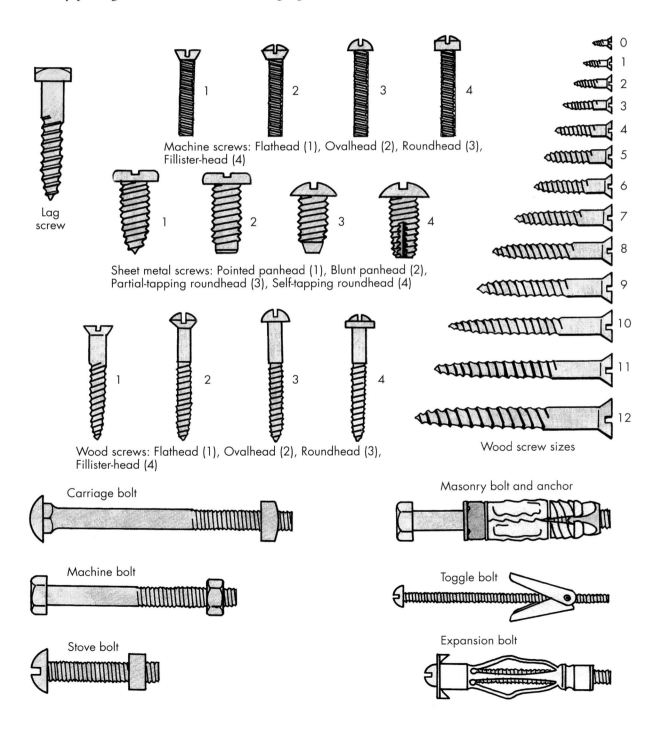

Lag screw

Machine screws: Flathead (1), Ovalhead (2), Roundhead (3), Fillister-head (4)

Sheet metal screws: Pointed panhead (1), Blunt panhead (2), Partial-tapping roundhead (3), Self-tapping roundhead (4)

Wood screws: Flathead (1), Ovalhead (2), Roundhead (3), Fillister-head (4)

Wood screw sizes

Carriage bolt

Machine bolt

Stove bolt

Masonry bolt and anchor

Toggle bolt

Expansion bolt

DRILLING FOR WOOD SCREWS

Gauge Number	Decimal Diameter	Fractional Diameter	Shank Hole Twist Bit	Shank Hole Drill Gauge	Pilot Hole Hardwood Twist Bit s	Pilot Hole Hardwood Twist Bit p	Pilot Hole Hardwood Drill Gauge s	Pilot Hole Hardwood Drill Gauge p	Pilot Hole Softwood Twist Bit s	Pilot Hole Softwood Twist Bit p	Pilot Hole Softwood Drill Gauge s	Pilot Hole Softwood Drill Gauge p	Auger Bit Number	Threads per Inch
0	.060	1/16−	1/16	52	1/32	–	70	–	1/64	–	75	–	–	32
1	.073	5/64	5/64	47	1/32	–	66	–	1/32	–	71	–	–	28
2	.086	5/64+	3/32	42	3/64	1/32	56	70	1/32	1/64	65	75	3	26
3	.099	3/32+	7/64	37	1/16	1/32	54	66	3/64	1/32	58	71	4	24
4	.112	6/64+	7/64	32	1/16	3/64	52	56	3/64	1/32	55	65	4	22
5	.125	1/8−	1/8	30	5/64	1/16	49	54	1/16	3/64	53	58	4	20
6	.138	9/64	9/64	27	5/64	1/16	47	52	1/16	3/64	52	55	5	18
7	.151	5/32−	5/32	22	3/32	5/64	44	49	1/16	3/64	51	53	5	16
8	.164	5/32+	11/64	18	3/32	5/64	40	47	5/64	1/16	48	52	6	15
9	.177	11/64+	3/16	14	7/64	3/32	37	44	5/64	1/16	45	51	6	14
10	.190	3/16+	3/16	10	7/64	3/32	33	40	3/32	5/64	43	48	6	13
11	.203	13/64−	13/64	4	1/8	7/64	31	37	3/32	5/64	40	45	7	12
12	.216	7/32−	7/32	2	1/8	7/64	30	33	7/64	3/32	38	43	7	11
14	.242	15/64+	1/4	D	9/64	1/8	25	31	7/64	3/32	32	40	8	10
16	.268	17/64+	17/64	I	5/32	1/8	18	30	9/64	7/64	29	38	9	9
18	.294	19/64−	19/64	N	3/16	9/64	13	25	9/64	7/64	26	32	10	8
20	.320	21/64−	21/64	P	13/64	5/32	4	18	1/64	9/64	19	29	11	8
24	.372	3/8	3/8	V	7/32	3/16	1	13	3/16	9/64	15	26	12	7

s = Slotted head   p = Phillips head

are often used for installing paneling and trim where you do not want the nail head to show.

ROOFING NAILS Usually galvanized, roofing nails have a much larger head than common nails. This helps to prevent damage to asphalt shingles.

DRYWALL NAILS Nails made for drywall installation are often ringed and have an indented head. Annular-ring nails have sharp ridges all along the nail shaft, providing greater holding power.

MASONRY NAILS There are three types of masonry nails designed for use with concrete and concrete block: round, square, and fluted. Masonry nails should not be used where high strength is required. Fastening to brick, stone, or reinforced concrete should be made with screws or lag bolts.

TACKS Available in both round and cut forms, tacks are used to hold carpet or fabric to wood. Upholstery tacks have decorative heads.

CORRUGATED FASTENERS Corrugated fasteners, also called wiggly nails, are used for light-duty joints where strength is not important. The fasteners are set at right angles to the joint.

SCREWS

Screws provide more strength and holding power than nails. Additionally, if something needs to be disassembled, screws can easily be removed. Like nails, screws are available with different coatings to deter rust. They are manufactured with four basic heads and different kinds of slots. Flathead screws are almost always countersunk into the material being fastened so the head of the screw is flush with (or lower than) the surface. Oval-head screws are partially countersunk, with about half the screw head above the surface. Round-head screws are not countersunk; the entire screw head lies above the surface. Fillister-head screws are raised above the surface on a flat base to keep the screwdriver from damaging the surface as the screw is tightened.

Most screws have slot heads and are driven with slotted, or standard, screwdrivers. Phillips-head screws have crossed slots and are driven with Phillips screwdrivers. Screws are measured in both length and diameter at the shank, which is designated by gauge number from 0 to 24. Length is measured in inches. The length of a screw is important because at least half the length of the screw should extend into the base material. **Tip:** To prevent screws from splitting the material, pilot holes must be made with a drill before the screws are driven.

For most home repair purposes, wood screws will suffice. Sheet metal screws, machine screws, and lag screws also come in various types. If you're trying to replace one of these screws, take an old screw with you to the hardware store.

WOOD SCREWS Wood screws are usually made of steel, although brass, nickel, bronze, and copper screws should be used if there is potential for corrosion.

SHEET METAL SCREWS Use this type of screw to fasten pieces of metal together. Sheet metal screws form threads in the metal as they are installed. There are several different types of sheet metal screws. Pointed panhead screws are coarse-threaded; they are available in gauges from 4 to 14 and lengths from $\frac{1}{4}$ inch to 2 inches. Pointed panheads are used in light sheet metal. Blunt panhead screws are used for heavier sheet metal; they are available in gauges from 4 to 14 and lengths from $\frac{1}{4}$ inch to 2 inches. Both types of panhead screws are available with either plain or Phillips-head slots.

ROUNDHEAD SCREWS Partial-tapping round-head screws have finer threads; they can be used in soft or hard metals. They are available in diameters from $\frac{3}{16}$ inch to $1\frac{1}{4}$ inches. Self-tapping roundhead screws are used for heavy-duty work with thick sheet metal and are available in diameters from $\frac{1}{4}$ inch to 2 inches and in lengths from $\frac{1}{8}$ to $\frac{3}{4}$ inch. Both types of roundhead screws are available with either plain or Phillips-head slots.

MACHINE SCREWS Machine screws are blunt-ended screws used to fasten metal parts together. They are commonly made of steel or brass. Like other fasteners, they are also made with coatings—brass, copper, nickel, zinc, cadmium, and galvanized—that help deter rust. Machine screws are manufactured with each of the four basic types of heads—flathead, ovalhead, roundhead, and fillister-head—and with both plain and Phillips-head slots. They are typically available in gauges 2 to 12 and diameters from $\frac{1}{4}$ inch to $\frac{1}{2}$ inch and in lengths from $\frac{1}{4}$ inch to 3 inches.

LAG SCREWS For light work, lead, plastic, or fiber plugs (called anchors) can be used to hold screws. But for larger jobs and more holding power, lead expansion anchors and lag screws are used. Lag screws are heavy-duty fasteners. They are driven with a wrench and are used primarily for fastening to masonry or wood framing. The anchors are inserted into holes drilled in the masonry, and the lag screws are driven firmly into the anchors.

BOLTS

Bolts are used with nuts and often with washers. The three basic types are carriage bolts, stove bolts, and machine bolts. Other types include the masonry bolt and anchor, toggle bolt, and expansion bolt, which are used to distribute weight when fastening something to a hollow wall. Machine bolts are manufactured in two gauges: fine-threaded and coarse. Carriage and stove bolts are coarse-threaded. Bolt size is measured by shank diameter and by threads per inch, expressed as diameter by threads (for example, $\frac{1}{4}\times20$). Carriage bolts are available up to 10 inches long, stove bolts up to 6 inches, and machine bolts up to 30 inches. Larger sizes usually must be special ordered.

CARRIAGE BOLTS Carriage bolts are used mainly in making furniture. They have a round head with a square collar and are tightened into place with a nut and wrench. The collar fits into a prebored hole or twists into the wood, preventing the bolt from turning as the nut is tightened. Carriage bolts are coarse-threaded and are available in diameters from $\frac{3}{16}$ to $\frac{1}{4}$ inch and lengths from $\frac{1}{2}$ inch to 10 inches.

STOVE BOLTS Stove bolts aren't just for stoves; they are quite versatile and can be used for almost any fastening job. They are available in a wide range of sizes, have a slotted head—flat, oval, or round, like screws—and are driven with a screwdriver or tightened into place with a nut and wrench. Most stove bolts are completely threaded, but the larger ones may have a smooth shank near the bolt head. Stove bolts are coarse-threaded and are available in diameters from $\frac{5}{32}$ to $\frac{1}{2}$ inch and lengths from $\frac{3}{8}$ inch to 6 inches.

MACHINE BOLTS Machine bolts have either a square head or a hexagonal head. They are fastened with square nuts or hex nuts and are wrench-driven. Machine bolts are manufactured in very large sizes; the bolt diameter increases with length. They are either coarse-threaded or fine-threaded and are available in diameters from ¼ inch to 2 inches and lengths from ½ inch to 30 inches.

MASONRY BOLTS AND ANCHORS These work on the same principle as the lag bolt or screw; a plastic sleeve expands inside a predrilled hole as the bolt is tightened.

HOLLOW WALL BOLTS Toggle bolts and expansion bolts are used for fastening lightweight objects, such as picture frames, to hollow walls. Toggle bolt wings are opened inside the wall by a spring. Expansion bolts are inserted into an expansion jacket, which expands as the bolt is tightened. The bolts are available in diameters from ⅛ to ½ inch and lengths up to 8 inches for walls as thick as 1¾ inches.

ADHESIVES

Adhesives chemically attach two or more surfaces together. The right adhesive can make any fix quicker and longer lasting. Here's some information on adhesives frequently used by do-it-yourselfers.

MULTIPURPOSE ADHESIVES If you keep a small assortment of multipurpose adhesives in stock you will be able to make a wide variety of repairs. The following are the most common types of multipurpose adhesives.

- **White glue** (polyvinyl acetate, or PVA). PVA glue is a white liquid, usually sold in plastic bottles. It is recommended for use on porous materials—wood, paper, cloth, porous pottery, and nonstructural wood-to-wood bonds. It is not water resistant. Clamping is required for 30 minutes to 1 hour to set the glue; curing time is 18 to 24 hours. School glue, a type of white glue, dries more slowly. Inexpensive and nonflammable, PVA glue dries clear.

- **Epoxy.** Epoxies are sold in tubes or in cans. They consist of two parts—resin and hardener—that must be thoroughly mixed just before use. They are very strong, very durable, and very water resistant. Epoxies are recommended for use on metal, ceramics, some plastics, and rubber; they aren't recommended for flexible surfaces. Clamping is required for about 2 hours for most epoxies. Drying time is about 12 hours; curing time is one to two days. Epoxy dries clear or amber and is more expensive than other adhesives.

- **Cyanoacrylate.** Also called super or instant glue, cyanoacrylate is similar to epoxy but is a one-part glue. These glues form a very strong bond and are recommended for use on materials such as metal, ceramics, glass, some plastics, and rubber; they aren't recommended for flexible surfaces. Apply sparingly. Clamping is not required; curing time is one to two days. Cyanoacrylates dry clear.

- **Contact cement.** A rubber-base liquid sold in bottles and cans, contact cement is recommended for bonding laminates, veneers, and other large areas and for repairs. It can also be used on paper, leather, cloth, rubber, metal, glass, and some plastics because it remains flexible when it dries. It is not recommended for repairs where strength is necessary. Contact cement should be applied to both surfaces and allowed to set; the surfaces are then pressed together for an instant bond. No repositioning is possible once contact has been made. Clamping isn't required; curing is complete on drying. Contact cement is usually very flammable.

- **Polyurethane glue.** This high-strength glue is an amber paste and is sold in tubes. It forms a very strong bond similar to that of epoxy. Polyurethane glue is recommended for use on wood, metal, ceramics, glass, most plastics, and fiberglass. It dries flexible and can also be used on leather, cloth, rubber, and vinyl. Clamping is required for about 2 hours; curing time is about 24 hours. Polyurethane glue dries translucent and can be painted or stained. Its shelf life is short, and it is expensive.

- **Silicone rubber adhesive or sealant.** Silicone rubber glues and sealants are sold in tubes and are similar to silicone rubber caulk. They form very strong, very durable waterproof bonds, with excellent resistance to high and low temperatures. They're recommended for use on gutters and on building materials, including metal, glass, fiberglass, rubber, and wood. They can also be used on fabrics, some plastics, and ceramics. Clamping is usually not required; curing time is about 24 hours, but the adhesive skins over in less than 1 hour. Silicone rubber adhesives dry flexible and are available in clear, black, and metal colors.

- **Household cement.** The various adhesives sold in tubes as household cement are fast-setting, low-strength glues. They are recommended for use on wood, ceramics, glass, paper, and some plastics. Some household cements dry flexible and can be used on fabric, leather, and vinyl. Clamping is usually not required; setting time is 10 to 20 minutes, curing time is up to 24 hours.

- **Hot-melt adhesive.** Hot-melt glues are sold in stick form and are used with glue guns. A glue gun heats the adhesive above 200°F. For the best bond, the surfaces to be joined should also be preheated. Because hot-melt adhesives are only moderately strong and bonds will come apart if exposed to high temperatures, this type of glue is recommended for temporary bonds of wood, metal, paper, and some plastics and composition materials. Clamping isn't required; setting time is 10 to 45 seconds, and curing time is 24 hours.

WOOD GLUES Wood glues are specifically made for wood repair projects. Here are your main choices:

- **Yellow glue** (aliphatic resin or carpenters' glue). Aliphatic resin glue is a yellow liquid, usually sold in plastic squeeze bottles and often labeled as carpenters' glue. Yellow glue is very similar to white glue but forms a slightly stronger bond. It is also slightly more water resistant than white glue. Clamping is required for about 30 minutes until the glue sets; curing time is 12 to 18 hours. Yellow glue dries clear but does not accept wood stains.

- **Plastic resin glue** (urea formaldehyde). Plastic resin glue is recommended for laminating layers of wood and for gluing structural joints. It is water resistant but not waterproof and isn't recommended for use on outdoor furniture. This glue is resistant to paint and lacquer thinners. Clamping is required for up to 8 hours; curing time is 18 to 24 hours.

- **Resorcinol glue.** This glue is waterproof and forms strong and durable bonds. It is recommended for use on outdoor furniture, kitchen counters, structural bonding, boats, and sporting gear. It can also be used on concrete, cork, fabrics, leather, and some plastics. Resorcinol glue has excellent resistance to temperature extremes, chemicals, and fungus. Clamping is required; curing time is 8 to 24 hours, depending on humidity and temperature.

ADHESIVES FOR GLASS AND CERAMICS Most multipurpose adhesives will bond glass and ceramics, but specialized versions often bond them more securely.

- **China and glass cement.** Many cements are sold for mending china and glass. These cements usually come in tubes. Acrylic latex-base cements have good resistance to water and heat. Clamping is usually required.

- **Silicone rubber adhesives.** Only silicone adhesives made specifically for glass and china are recommended. They form very strong bonds, with excellent resistance to water and temperature extremes. Clamping is usually required.

METAL ADHESIVES AND FILLERS Need to make a repair in metal? Here are some popular adhesives that can make a strong bond with metal:

- **Steel epoxy.** A two-part compound sold in tubes, steel epoxy is quite similar to regular epoxy. It forms a very strong, durable, heat- and water-resistant bond and is recommended for patching gutters and gas tanks, sealing pipes, and filling rust holes. Drying time is about 12 hours; curing time is one to two days.

- **Steel putty.** This metal putty consists of two putty-consistency parts that are kneaded together before use. It forms a strong, water-resistant bond and is recommended for patching and sealing pipes that aren't under pressure. It can also be used for ceramic and masonry. Curing time is about 30 minutes; when dry, it can be sanded or painted.

- **Plastic metal cement.** Plastic metal is one-part adhesive and filler. It is moisture resistant but cannot withstand temperature extremes. This type of adhesive is recommended for use on metal, glass, concrete, and wood, where strength is not required. Curing time is about four hours; when dry, plastic metal cement can be sanded or painted.

PLASTIC ADHESIVES Plastics present a special problem with some adhesives because solvents in the adhesives can dissolve plastic. Here are some popular plastic adhesives.

- **Model cement.** Usually sold in tubes as "model maker" glues, model cement forms a strong bond on acrylics and polystyrenes and can be used on most plastics, except plastic foam. Clamping is usually required until the cement has set (about 10 minutes); curing time is about 24 hours. Model cement dries clear.

- **Vinyl adhesive.** Vinyl adhesives, sold in tubes, form a strong, waterproof bond on vinyl and on many plastics, but don't use them on plastic foam. Clamping is usually not required. Vinyl adhesive dries flexible and clear; curing time is 10 to 20 minutes.

- **Acrylic solvent.** Solvents are not adhesives as such; they act by melting the acrylic bonding surfaces, fusing them together at the joint. They are recommended for use on acrylics and polycarbonates. Clamping is required; the bonding surfaces are clamped or taped together, and the solvent is injected into the joint with a syringe. Setting time is about five minutes.

OTHER QUICK FIX SUPPLIES

As you tackle the quick fixes in this book you'll need other supplies, such as paint and abrasives. Because there is such a difference between various paints, let's take a look at them first.

INTERIOR PAINTS

Quick fixes inside your home (see Chapter 6) include painting small areas or making touch-ups. Although paints are available for every possible surface, there is no such thing as an all-surface paint. The wrong paint can damage a surface and often not adhere well, so it's crucial to know in advance what goes where and when. Fortunately, modern paint technology has taken a lot of the risk out of choosing the proper paint. Formulas for so-called "latex paints" have been improved to withstand dirt, moisture, and daily wear and tear, so these paints are no longer reserved exclusively for low-traffic areas. They are as washable and durable as the old oilbase paints, so you no longer have to think in terms of latex paints for walls and oilbase enamels for woodwork, windows, and doors.

Still, an important factor in paint selection—aside from personal color preference—is gloss. Regardless of the type of coating you choose, the gloss of the one you buy will affect both its appearance and its durability. High-gloss paints are the most durable because they contain more resin than either semigloss or flat paints. Resin is an ingredient that hardens as the paint dries. The more resin, the harder the surface. Consequently, for kitchens, bathrooms, utility rooms, doors, windows, and trim, high-gloss paints are ideal. Semigloss paints, with less resin and a reduced surface shine, are slightly less wear-resistant but still suitable for most woodwork. Finally, flat paints are the coatings of choice for most interior walls and ceilings because they provide an attractive, low-glare finish for surfaces that take little abuse and require only infre-

quent washings. Here's a paint primer to help you decide what kind of paint you need for the quick fix at hand.

LATEX PAINT The word "latex" originally referred to the use of rubber in one form or another as the resin, or solid, in paint. The solvent or thinner, called the "vehicle," was water. Today, many paints are made with water as the thinner but with resins that are not latex, and the industry is leaning toward such terms as "water-thinned" or "water-reducible." If the paints are called latex at all, the term often used is "acrylic latex" because they contain a plastic resin made of acrylics or polyvinyls rather than rubber.

In addition to the speed of drying, new opacity (the ability to completely cover one color with another), and washability of acrylic latex paints, the greatest advantage of water-thinned paints is you can clean up with water. The higher expense—as well as the potential fire hazard—of volatile thinners and brush cleaners is gone. If you wash the brush or roller immediately after the painting session is over, it comes clean in just a few minutes.

Latex paint works well on surfaces previously painted with latex or flat oilbase paints. It can even be used on unprimed drywall or unpainted masonry. However, latex usually does not adhere well to high-gloss finishes and, even though it can be used on wallpaper, there is a risk that the water in the paint may cause the paper to peel away from the wall. Because of its water content, latex will cause bare steel to rust and will raise the grain on raw wood.

ALKYD RESIN PAINT The use of synthetic alkyd resin for solvent-thinned (oilbase) paints has brought several advantages. One of the most useful is a special formula that makes the paint yogurt-thick. A brush dipped in it carries more paint to the surface than previous versions. Yet, under the friction of application, the paint spreads and smooths readily.

In most gloss and semigloss (or satin) paints, alkyd materials are still preferred for trim, doors, and even heavy-traffic hallways. Many homeowners still like them best for bathrooms and kitchens, where they feel more confident of washability despite the availability of water-thinned enamels in satin or gloss that can be safely cleaned with standard household cleaners.

The opacity of alkyd paints has improved with the addition of a material that diffuses and evaporates, which leaves minute bubbles that reflect

INTERIOR PAINTS		
Type	**Characteristics/Use**	**Application**
Acoustic	For acoustic ceiling tile. Water-thinned, water cleanup.	Spray (preferable) or roller.
Alkyd	Solvent-thinned, solvent cleanup. Don't apply over unprimed drywall.	Brush, roller, pad.
Cement	For concrete, brick, stucco. Some contain waterproofing agents. Must be mixed just before use.	Brush.
Dripless	For ceilings. More costly than ordinary paints.	Brush or roller.
Epoxy	For metal, glass, tile, floors, woodwork: high-stress areas. Expensive. May require special mixing; tricky to use.	Brush.
Latex	Most popular. Water-thinned, water cleanup. Gloss, semigloss, flat. May be used over most surfaces but not on wallpaper, wood, or metal.	Brush, roller, pad.
Metal	For bare or primed metal or as a primer for other types of paint. Some water-thinned, most solvent-thinned.	Brush or spray.
Oil	Slow-drying, strong odor. Coverage may not be as good as synthetic paints. Solvent-thinned, solvent cleanup.	Brush, roller, spray.
One-coat	Water- or solvent-thinned. Costs more than regular latex or alkyd. Surface must be sealed first. Excellent covering power.	Brush, roller, pad.
Polyurethane/Urethane	Expensive. Can be used over most finishes, porous surfaces. Extreme durability. Solvents, primers vary.	Brush.
Textured	Good for covering surface defects. Premixed or mix-at-home types. Application slow. Permits surface design of choice.	Brush, roller, pad, trowel, sponge.

and scatter light and makes the paint look thicker than it really is. With paints of this formula, one coat of white will completely cover black or bright yellow.

While alkyds should not be used on unprimed drywall (they can raise the nap of its paper coating) or unprimed masonry, they are suitable for raw wood and almost any previously painted or papered surface. The most durable of interior paints, alkyds are dry enough for a second coat within four to six hours. Solvents must be used for thinning and cleanup. Check the label to find which solvent is recommended by the manufacturer. And, while the solvents may be almost odorless, they're still toxic and flammable, so you should work in a well-ventilated room.

RUBBERBASE PAINT Available only in a limited number of colors and in flat or low-gloss finishes, this paint contains a liquefied rubber. It is expensive and has a potent aroma, but, because rubberbase paint is waterproof and durable, it's an excellent coating for concrete. It can be applied directly to unprimed masonry. When used on brick, rubberbase paint should be preceded by a sealing coat of clear varnish. Before putting it on new concrete, wash the concrete with a 10 percent solution of muriatic acid, rinse thoroughly, and let dry completely. (Wear goggles and gloves when working with muriatic acid,

and work in a well-ventilated space.) Like alkyds, rubberbase paints require special solvents; check the label for specifications.

TEXTURED PAINT If you're after a finish that looks like stucco, or if you want an effective cover-up for flawed surfaces, textured-surface paint will do the job. Some varieties come premixed with sandlike particles suspended in the paint. Because of their grittiness, these paints are usually used on ceilings. With other varieties, you have to add the particles and stir thoroughly. Another form of textured paint has no granules. Thick and smooth, it's applied to the surface and then textured with special tools. Textured paints are available in either flat-finish latex or alkyd formulations. Latex versions are frequently used on bare drywall ceilings because they can be used without a primer and they help to camouflage the seams between sheets of drywall.

One of the problems with textured paint becomes evident when the time comes to paint over it. All those peaks and valleys created by the texturing actually increase the surface area of the wall. The rough surface will require 15 to 25 percent more paint the second time around.

DRIPLESS PAINT Quite a bit more expensive than conventional alkyd paint, dripless paint is ideal for ceilings because it's so thick it won't run off a roller or brush. It will usually cover any surface in a single coat, but, because it's so dense, it won't go as far as its more spreadable relatives.

ONE-COAT PAINT With additional pigment to improve their covering capabilities, true one-coats are otherwise just more expensive versions of ordinary latex or alkyd paints. For best results, reserve them for use on flawless, same-color surfaces that have been previously sealed. **Tip:** Not all paints advertised as "one-coat" really are. Read the warranty.

ACOUSTIC PAINT Designed for use on acoustic ceiling tile, this paint covers without impairing the tile's acoustic qualities. It can be applied with a roller, but a paint sprayer is more efficient and less likely to affect the sound-deadening properties of the tile.

PRIMERS Primers are inexpensive undercoatings that smooth out uneven surfaces, provide a barrier between porous surfaces and certain finishing coats, and allow you to use an otherwise incompatible paint on a bare or previously painted surface. For flat paint finishes, the primer can be a thinned-out version of the paint itself. But that's often more expensive than using a premixed primer, which contains less-expensive pigment, dries quickly, and provides a firm foundation or "tooth" for the final coat of paint. Latex primer has all the advantages of latex paint—almost odor-free, quick drying, and easy to clean up—and is the best undercoat for drywall, plaster, and concrete. Don't use it on bare wood, though, because the water in it may raise the grain. For raw wood, it's best to use an alkyd primer.

EXTERIOR PAINTS

You'll learn about quick exterior fixes, including painting, in Chapter 7. One of the major differences between indoor and outdoor painting is, with outdoor painting, there is a wider range of exterior surfaces to consider. These surfaces include clapboard and aluminum siding, wood shingles, tar shingles, cedar shakes, brick, concrete block, stucco, and, of course, old paint. On many older homes, you'll find a combination of these surfaces. Fortunately, there is a paint for every type of surface, and some paints are suitable for more than one surface.

Like interior paints, exterior paints are available in either water-thinned or solvent-thinned formulas and in three lusters: flat, semigloss, and gloss. There are, however, several characteristics that distinguish exterior coatings from those used inside the house. For one thing, exterior paints are more expensive. They also contain more resin (for moisture resistance and durability) and more pigment (for color).

You may want to choose your paint based on what was used before. As with interior paints, latex works best over latex and alkyd works best over alkyd. If you can't tell or are unsure about what type of paint is on the house, use an alkyd-base paint.

Latex paints are easier to apply, dry quickly, and can help minimize moisture problems because they "breathe." Cleaning up is a matter of soap and water. These paints do not adhere as well to oilbase or alkyd-base paints or to poorly prepared surfaces, however. Alkyds, on the other hand, are extremely durable, but they are more difficult to work with and they dry slowly. Also, solvents must be used with alkyds to clean brushes, rollers, paint trays, and drips.

One of the alkyd types of exterior paint may be especially appealing because of its regulated, self-cleaning property. It's called "chalking," and that's exactly what it does. Over a period of years, the paint surface slowly oxidizes. Each rainfall washes off a minute quantity of the paint—along with dirt. As a result of this shedding, the paint surface is constantly renewing itself. The price of this convenience used to be chalky residue on foundations and shrubs, but the newest formulas control the shedding so it doesn't stain adjacent surfaces. Chalking paint is not recommended for every house. In areas with little rainfall, for example, the powder tends to remain on the surface, dulling the paint. In wet regions, chalking paint may not be worth the extra expense because frequent rainfalls will keep the outside of the house clean no matter what kind of paint is used. If you live in or near either of these climatic extremes, ask your paint dealer if the chalking type is suitable for your area.

ABRASIVES

Choosing the proper abrasive for a given job usually means the difference between mediocre results and a truly professional appearance. Depending on the job, you'll choose between sandpaper, steel wool, and a file.

SANDPAPER Most do-it-yourselfers still refer to various grades of "sandpaper," but the proper term for these sanding sheets is "coated abrasives." There are four factors to consider when selecting any coated abrasive: the abrasive mineral, or

SELECTING THE RIGHT EXTERIOR COATING

Most of the coatings listed below can be applied with an airless sprayer as well as a brush, roller, or painting pad. But if you want to spray, read the labels carefully or ask your paint dealer if you're buying a sprayable coating. Latex paints require only water to thin them enough for spraying. With alkyds, oils, and other types of paints, you'll have to purchase the appropriate solvents to dilute them.

Type	Characteristics/Use	Application
Acrylic	A type of latex; water-thinned and water cleanup. Fast-drying and suitable for any building material, including masonry and primed metal.	Brush, roller, pad, spray. Comparable to regular latex paint.
Alkyd	Similar to oilbase paints, but dries faster. Solvent-thinned, solvent cleanup. Use over oil and alkyd coatings.	Brush, roller, pad, spray. Smooths out more readily than latex, but more difficult to apply.
Latex	Most popular exterior paint. Excellent durability. Water-thinned, water cleanup. Mildew-proof; may even be applied over damp surfaces. Do not use over oil paints unless specified by the manufacturer.	Brush, roller, pad, spray. Except when spraying, don't thin; apply thickly with little spreadout.
Oil	Extremely durable, but dries slowly. Solvents must be used for cleanup. Least popular.	Brush, roller, pad, spray on very dry surfaces. Insects and rain are dangers because of lengthy drying time.
Marine	Excellent durability on wood, some metals. Expensive. Solvent cleanup.	Brush recommended due to thick, gooey consistency.
Masonry	May be latex, alkyd, epoxy, Portland cement, or rubber. Some contain their own primers.	Brush, roller. Latex types easiest to apply.
Metal	Water-thinned or solvent-thinned, usually with rust-resistant ingredients.	Brush, roller, pad, spray. Prime bare metals first.
Primers	Seals raw wood, bare metal. Also use over old, worn finishes. Provides good bonding for top coating. Use primer formulated for top coat.	Brush, roller, pad, spray. Easier than top-coat painting. Porous surfaces may drink up lots of primer.
Porch/Deck	Alkyd, latex, epoxy, rubber, oil, or polyurethane types. Synthetics dry quickly; oilbase types dry slowly but are very durable. Limited color selection.	Brush, roller, pad, or wax applicator. For floors, pour on, smooth out. For decks, dip applicator and apply.
Shingle	Alkyd-base, oilbase, or latex-base. For wood siding shingles. Permits escape of moisture behind shingles.	Brush, roller, pad, spray. Do not use on creosote-treated wood less than eight years old.
Stains	Water- or solvent-thinned; both types durable. Choice of transparent, semi-transparent, solid-stain pigmentation. May contain preservatives.	Brush, roller, pad, spray.
Preservatives	Moisture-, rot-, and insect-resistant for decks, fences, wood siding, and shingles.	Brush, spray.
Varnish	Acrylic for metal; moisture-cured urethane, alkyd, or spar types for exterior wood.	Brush, roller, or pad. Limited durability; one to two years. Won't dramatically alter natural appearance and color of woods.

which type of rough material; the grade, or the coarseness or fineness of the mineral; the backing (paper or cloth); and the coating, or the nature and extent of the mineral on the surface.

Paper backing for coated abrasives comes in four weights: *A*, *C*, *D*, and *E*. *A* (also referred to as "Finishing") is the lightest weight and is designed for light sanding work. *C* and *D* (also called "Cabinet") are for heavier work, while *E* is

for the toughest jobs. The coating can be either open or closed. Open coated means the grains are spaced to only cover a portion of the surface. An open-coated abrasive is best used on gummy or soft woods, soft metals, or on painted surfaces. Closed coated means the abrasive covers the entire area. They provide maximum cutting, but they also clog faster and are best used on hard woods and metals.

SELECTING SANDPAPER

Grit	Number	Grade	Coating[1]	Common Uses
Very coarse	30	2½	F,G,S	Rust removal on rough-finished metal.
	36	2	F,G,S	
Coarse	40	1½	F,G,S	Rough sanding of wood; paint removal.
	50	1	F,G,S	
	60	½	F,G,A,S	
Medium	80	0(1/0)	F,G,A,S	General wood sanding; plaster smoothing; preliminary smoothing of previously painted surface.
	100	00(2/0)	F,G,A,S	
	120	3/0	F,G,A,S	
Fine	150	4/0	F,G,A,S	Final sanding of bare wood or previously painted surface.
	180	5/0	F,G,A,S	
Very fine	220	6/0	F,G,A,S	Light sanding between finish coats; dry sanding.
	240	7/0	F,A,S	
	280	8/0	F,A,S	
Extra fine	320	9/0	F,A,S	High finish on lacquer, varnish, or shellac; wet sanding.
	360	—[2]	S	High-satinized finishes; wet sanding.
	600	—[2]	S	

[1] F = flint; G = garnet; A = aluminum oxide; S = silicon carbide. Silicon carbide is used dry or wet, with water or oil.
[2] No grade designation.

There are three popular ways to grade coated abrasives. Simplified markings (coarse, medium, fine, very fine, etc.) provide a general description of the grade. The grit refers to the number of mineral grains that, when set end to end, equal 1 inch. The commonly used O symbols are more or less arbitrary. The coarsest grading under this system is 4½, and the finest is 10/0, or 0000000000.

STEEL WOOL Steel wool comes in many grades of coarseness. Always apply the correct grade of steel wool to the work you have at hand, as shown in the chart below.

FILES A wood rasp, with a rasp and/or curved-tooth cut, is used to remove excess wood. The piece of wood is final-smoothed with a single-cut or double-cut file. You may not need files for most quick fixes. If you do decide to add some to your quick fix toolbox, buy an assortment of flat files—wood rasp, bastard, second-cut, and smooth.

QUICK FIX SAFETY

Performing quick fixes around your home should be satisfying and safe. (You won't feel satisfied if you have to visit the emergency room because of a cut or fall!) Choose safe tools, learn how to use them correctly, and employ safety equipment to avoid injuries.

SAFE TOOLS

The first rule of tool safety is to buy good quality, as suggested at the beginning of this chapter. You don't have to buy the best, but lowest cost can often mean lowest value. The best value is typically higher-quality tools and equipment

SELECTING STEEL WOOL

Grade	Number	Common Uses
Coarse	3	Paint and varnish removal; removing paint spots from resilient floors.
Medium coarse	2	Removing scratches from brass; removing paint spots from ceramic tile; rubbing floors between finish coats.
Medium	1	Rust removal; cleaning glazed tiles; removing marks from wood floors; with paint and varnish remover, removing finishes.
Medium fine	0	Brass finishing; cleaning tile; with paint and varnish remover, removing stubborn finishes.
Fine	00	With linseed oil, satinizing high-gloss finishes.
Extra fine	000	Removing paint spots or stains from wood; cleaning polished metals; rubbing between finish coats.
Super fine	0000	Final rubbing of finish; stain removal.

purchased at a discount. It's also important to use your tools correctly. It may be tempting to use a screwdriver as a chisel, but doing so can damage the tool and, more important, damage you. Also, never remove the safety guards installed on power equipment, and always wear safety goggles when working with power equipment. Safety glasses should also be worn when sanding, filing, or doing any other job that produces flying particles. Make sure your safety glasses wrap around the sides to keep deflected particles from reaching your eyes from any angle.

Once you've purchased high-quality tools and learned how to use them properly, you're good to go—right? Not quite. The most dangerous tool is one that isn't well maintained. A dull saw is less safe than a sharp one. A hammer with a loose handle can do more damage than one in good repair. A power tool with a frayed cord can electrocute you. So, be diligent about tightening loose parts, fixing damaged cords, and sharpening dull blades.

SAFE LADDERS

A sturdy stepladder will make lots of quick fixes easier, from changing lightbulbs to painting a room to cleaning gutters to replacing a smoke alarm battery. If you don't already own one, get one. Invest in a good ladder, and use it for all those out-of-reach projects.

Most home-use ladders are made of wood or aluminum. Depending on quality, both types are reliable. Aluminum, however, weighs only 20 to 50 percent as much as wood, which means it's easier to take it in and out of storage or move it around. On most good ladders you'll find labels that indicate a rated strength. For example, a Type I industrial-grade ladder, rated at 250 pounds, is the strongest. A Type II commercial-grade ladder is rated at 225 pounds; Type III is rated at 200 pounds. Fortunately, each type has actually been successfully tested at four times its rated load. For around-the-house purposes, invest in security and durability and buy a Type II ladder. One that's 6 feet tall will do for most homeowners, but taller ones—8, 10, 12, and all the way up to 16 feet—are available. For an extra measure of safety, get one with rubber or plastic feet so your ladder won't skid on hard floors.

If you're painting a ceiling from a single stepladder, you'll find yourself going up and down like a yo yo, constantly moving the ladder to reach unpainted areas. A safer alternative is to buy a second ladder of the same size. Then, using a pair of 2×8-foot boards, make a scaffold between them—a platform from which you can paint for longer periods of time by moving from one end of the bridge to the other. For stability, don't make your scaffold higher than is absolutely necessary and no longer than 6 to 8 feet in length. Use C-clamps to fasten each end of the 2×8s to a rung of each ladder.

USING LADDERS SAFELY There's no such thing as an absolutely safe ladder. Gravity is always an unrelenting enemy. However, there are ways to greatly reduce your risk of accidents and injury.

- Always open a stepladder to its fullest position, lock the spreader braces on each side in place, and pull down the bucket shelf.

- Whether you are going up or coming down, always face the ladder head-on, and use both hands to hold onto the side rails or rungs.

- Don't climb higher than two rungs from the top; don't sit or stand on the top or the bucket shelf.

- To keep yourself from overreaching and getting off balance, never let your navel go beyond either of the ladder's side rails.

QUICK FIX TOOL CARE

Quality tools aren't cheap. Fortunately, with care, they can last many years and be a better long-term investment than cheap tools. Here are some useful tips on tool care.

- Protect your tools from moisture. Keep a thin coating of oil on metal parts, wrap them in plastic wrap, or keep carpenters' chalk or mothballs (both of which absorb moisture) in your toolbox.

- A piece of garden hose slit open is a handy protective cover for the teeth of a handsaw between projects. Circular saw blades store conveniently in heavy shipping envelopes.

- To remind yourself to unplug an electric drill when changing accessories, fasten the chuck key near the plug end of the cord.

- Tack rags will last longer if they're stored in an airtight container to keep them from drying out. Airtight storage also prevents spontaneous combustion, which can be very dangerous. (This safety tip applies equally well to other rags, coveralls, work gloves, and any other clothes that might absorb flammable oils and solvents.)

- Don't take a chance of hitting a thumb or finger when hammering a small brad, tack, or nail. Slip the fastener between the teeth of a pocket comb; the comb holds the nail while you hold the comb. A bobby pin or a paper clip can be used the same way as a comb.

- If you must work on a ladder in front of a door, lock the door.

- Put the paint can or tray on the bucket shelf before you climb the ladder. And don't go up the ladder with tools in your hand or in your pockets.

ELECTRICAL SAFETY

Electricity can help you—or it can hurt you. An appliance can make your coffee in the morning. A frayed cord can electrocute you. Here are some rules for working safely with electricity.

- Never work on an electrical circuit that is live or attached to an electrical source. Unplug the circuit, trip the circuit breaker, or unscrew the fuse before you begin working.

- Use only equivalent replacement parts. That is, replace a controller with one that has the same function and rating. Don't replace a 10-amp appliance cord with one that is rated for 5 amps.

- Some appliances use capacitors, which are electrical components that store high voltage. Touching a charged capacitor, such as those in a microwave oven, can electrocute or burn you.

- Carefully check all loose wires for related damage or stress, and reconnect them using electrical tape, wire nuts, or other enclosing fasteners. Not only can a loose wire break an electrical circuit, it can also injure you if you touch it while it is energized or hot. Loose wires are caused by vibration or other factors.

- Most important, think before you act. Electricity follows strict laws. You must follow the same laws in order to repair electrical systems safely.

OTHER SAFETY TIPS

Need some more safety tips? Sure you do. Fortunately, most of them are built on good old common sense.

- Quick doesn't mean work as fast as you can move. It means planning out the task in advance and doing it safely and well.

- Don't change a power-saw blade or bit without first unplugging the cord or disconnecting the battery pack.

- Before you embark on any quick plumbing fixes, always turn off the water supply to the fixture or the main shutoff.

Tips for ladder safety.

- Wear latex gloves when working with adhesives so you don't bond your fingers together.

- Before you replace or repair any electrical fixture, deenergize electrical circuit by pulling appropriate fuse or tripping proper circuit breaker.

- Wear a painter's mask, particularly if you are using alkyd paints indoors. When painting overhead, wear goggles to keep paint out of your eyes.

- Wear safety glasses when sanding, filing, or doing any job that produces flying particles.

As you gain experience fixing things you can add more tools to your toolbox, paying for them with the savings you've earned by not calling a repair person.

CHAPTER 2

QUICK ROOM FIXES

You have various rooms in your home for living, dining, sleeping, and other necessities. Some of these rooms have plumbing, electrical, and heating and cooling systems that sometimes require quick fixes. These are covered in later chapters. What all these rooms do have in common are walls, floors, ceilings, doors, and windows.

QUICK WALL FIXES

Walls and ceilings make up about 80 percent of a home's interior surfaces, so knowing how to make repairs to them can be very helpful to a homeowner. Best of all, you can make many of these repairs more quickly and easily than you might think. Whether your home's walls are made of drywall, plaster, or paneling, here are some quick fixes you can tackle on your own.

FIXING POPPED NAILS

In most newer homes, the walls are surfaced with gypsum wallboard, also known as drywall. Chapter 1 offers an overview of this popular building material. Drywall, like all building materials, has its own characteristics and problems. One of the most common problems results from shrinking or warping in the framing behind the drywall. As the wood studs age and shrink, nails loosen and pop out of the wood, producing an unsightly bump or hole in the surface. No matter how many times you drive the nails back in, the problem is likely to recur, so it's better to fix it permanently the first time around. Here's how:

1. Redrive popped nails. If nails are sticking out far enough to get claw of hammer around them, pull them out first. To redrive them, hold nail set over nail head and hammer nail as far as you can into stud. Nail head will punch through drywall's outside layer of paper and into drywall itself.

2. To make sure nail stays in place (and to take pressure off it), drive another drywall nail through wallboard and into stud about 2 inches above or below old nail. Pound nail flush with wall and then give it one more light hammer whack to "dimple" drywall surface around nail head.

3. Using putty knife, cover new nail head and fill hole over old one with spackling compound.

4. Let dry, then lightly sand area. Since spackling compound shrinks as it dries, you may need to repeat process once or twice more. Touch up patches with paint or primer.

What You'll Need
Hammer
Nail set
Drywall nails
Putty knife
Spackling compound
Sandpaper
Paint or primer
Paintbrushes

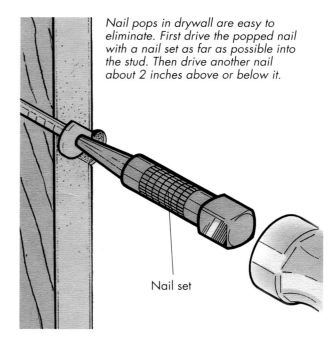

Nail pops in drywall are easy to eliminate. First drive the popped nail with a nail set as far as possible into the stud. Then drive another nail about 2 inches above or below it.

Nail set

FIXING HOLES IN DRYWALL

Tough as it is, drywall can withstand only limited abuse. A door flung open with too much force can produce a doorknob-size hole in the wall. This kind of damage looks bad, but even large holes are easy to fix. The easiest way is to purchase a drywall repair kit. Measure the hole, and visit your local hardware store or home improvement center for a kit. There are various sizes and types for different applications. For example, a drywall patch for a ceiling is thicker than one for a wall. Before you use the kit, remove any loose paper or plaster around the edges of the hole. Then apply drywall patch, following the manufacturer's instructions.

SMALL DRYWALL HOLE

To make a repair to a small drywall hole without a kit:

1. Prepare tin can lid that is at least 1½ inches more in diameter than hole in drywall for backing piece. Use keyhole saw to cut out narrow horizontal slit in wall on each side of hole (see illustration on page 31). Measurement of hole plus both narrow slits should equal

What You'll Need
Clean tin can lid
Tape measure
Keyhole saw
Awl
Thin wire or string
Scissors or wire
    cutters
Scrap wood
Putty knife
Drywall patching
    compound
Sandpaper
Primer and paint
Paintbrushes

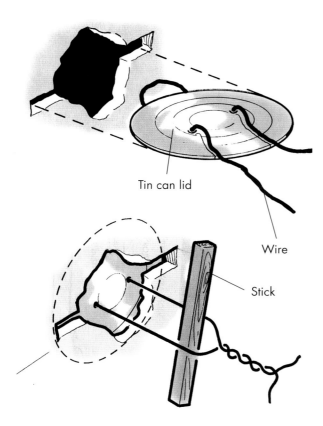

Tin can lid

Wire

Stick

Cut slits from the sides of the hole, then thread a wire through a tin can lid and slide it in. Pull the lid flat on the inside of the wall, and hold it in place with a stick.

diameter of lid so you can insert lid sideways into hole.

2. Use awl to punch two holes in center of lid. Thread 12-inch piece of wire or string through holes.

3. Holding ends of wire, slide lid through slit. Still holding wire, pull lid toward you until it's flat against inside of wall. To hold in place, set stick of scrap wood over hole on outside of wall and twist wire tightly over stick. Can lid should be held firmly against inside of wall.

4. Use putty knife to apply premixed drywall patching compound over patch following manufacturer's instructions. (Don't use spackling compound because it shrinks as it dries.) You can also mix plaster of paris with water to make thick paste. Pack compound or plaster into hole against backing and behind stick. Keep compound inside hole, cover backing, and fill slits, but don't spread it on wall surface. Leave patch slightly low, and don't try to level it. Let patch dry until it turns bright white, typically at least 24 hours. When dry, cut string or wire and remove stick.

5. To finish patch, fill it completely with more plaster of paris or drywall patching compound to make patch level with wall surface. Let dry, lightly sand area, prime, and paint.

LARGE DRYWALL HOLE Sometimes a wall can get a large hole or a section can be damaged by water or other causes. Here's how to fix it without a drywall repair kit:

1. Cut scrap piece of drywall with utility knife into square or rectangle. Scrap piece should be a little bigger than hole or damaged area. If you don't have piece of drywall, purchase drywall patch from hardware store. Set patch against damaged area, and lightly trace around it with pencil. Cut out outlined area with keyhole saw. Keep saw cut on inside of traced line so hole in drywall will be exactly the same size as patch.

2. To hold wallboard patch in place, install small board about 6 inches longer than long dimension of hole. Put board into hole, center it horizontally, and hold it firmly against inside of wallboard. To help keep it there, fasten ends of board to drywall with flathead screws driven through wall at sides of hole; countersink screws below surface of drywall.

What You'll Need
Scrap piece of
   drywall
Utility knife
Pencil
Keyhole saw
Small board
Flathead screws
Screwdriver
Spackling or
   wallboard joint
   compound
Putty knife
Sandpaper
Primer and paint
Paintbrushes

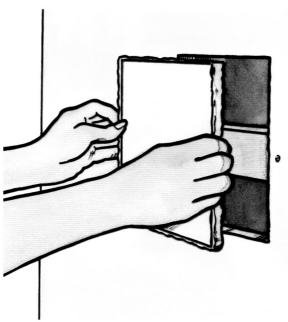

Secure a backing board on the inside of the wall to brace the patch; then coat the edges of the patch with spackling compound and set it into place in the hole.

3. Use spackling compound or wallboard joint compound as glue to hold patch in place. Spread compound on back of drywall patch and around edges. Set patch into hole and adjust it so it's exactly even with surrounding wall. Hold it in place until compound starts to set. Let compound dry at least overnight.

4. Once compound is dry, fill patch outline and cover exposed screw heads with spackling or joint compound. Let dry, lightly sand area, prime, and paint.

FIXING CRACKED PLASTER

Older homes often have lath-and-plaster walls. Latex paint will hide hairline cracks in plaster, at least temporarily. The coverup, though, may last only a few hours or a few months. Small plaster cracks have an annoying way of showing up again and again. It may be smarter to enlarge them and fix them properly once and for all. Making a small flaw bigger may sound like reverse logic, but it's easier to fix big cracks in plaster than small ones. Use plaster of paris, which doesn't shrink as it dries, or purchase premixed plaster repair compound. To repair:

What You'll Need
Utility knife
Vacuum cleaner
Plaster of paris or premixed plaster repair compound
Paintbrushes
Scraper or trowel
Wood block
Medium- or fine-grade sandpaper
Primer and paint

1. Cut away loose plaster with utility knife. Turn knife to make opening wider and more clean-lined. Remove debris while preserving structural integrity of surface around it. Clean away loose plaster and dust with vacuum cleaner.

2. Mix thick paste of plaster of paris and water, and wet crack thoroughly with paintbrush dipped in water. Pack plaster of paris (or repair compound) into wet crack to its full depth, and smooth surface with scraper or trowel. Let filled crack dry at least 24 hours.

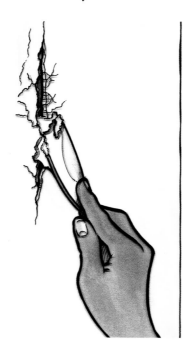

To fill a large crack in a plaster wall, remove loose plaster, then wet the crack and pack in plaster of paris to its full depth. Smooth the surface with a scraper.

3. Lightly sand patch when plaster is dry with medium- or fine-grade sandpaper wrapped around wood block. If crack was wide, replaster it at least once more to make surface smooth, rewetting plastered area each time. Let area dry for at least 24 hours after final plastering.

4. Lightly sand patch again, and prime it with thinned coat of paint or primer. When primer is dry, paint entire wall.

REPLACING PANELING

Many walls have been covered with wood or simulated wood paneling. However, like most things, paneling can deteriorate, stain, or otherwise need replacement. You can buy plywood paneling that is either finished or ready-to-finish. Or, you can buy hardboard panels that simulate various finishes. Paneling can be a quick fix in small areas, but be aware that paneling a large room may be more than a quick fix. To install paneling on existing walls:

What You'll Need	3d finishing nails and hammer or panel adhesive
Long, straight board	
Drywall joint compound	Large sheet of paper
Sandpaper	Masking tape
Replacement paneling	Scissors
1×1 boards	Drill
Pencil	Keyhole saw
Handsaw or electric saw	Nail set
Tape measure	Wood putty

1. Remove molding and trim, and check for high or low spots by moving long, straight board against wall and watching for any gaps as you draw it along. Build up any low spots with drywall joint compound, and sand down any high spots.

Note: If the walls are cracked or very uneven, attach paneling to furring strips (see page 33). Masonry walls must always be furred and water-proofed before paneling is installed.

2. Stack panels in room to be paneled with 1×1 boards between each one. Leave them there for at least 48 hours before installing them to allow panels to adjust to moisture content of room.

3. Once panels are stabilized, lean them against walls, matching wood grain as best you can. When you have panels arranged the way you want them, number panels on back side.

4. As necessary, cut panels to fit their position on wall. If you are using trim molding, the fit at floor and ceiling does not have to be as tight as it does for panels without trim molding. Also, make sure panels at room's corners are cut to fit well, as most corners are not perfectly plumb, or vertically level.

5. If you plan to nail panels in place, use 3d finishing nails to attach panels to furring strips or wall studs. Drive nails about every 6 inches along edges of panel and about every 12 inches through its center. If you are using panel

adhesive, run ribbon of adhesive across all furring strips or in similar pattern on wall surface. Place panel against wall or furring strips, press down, then pull panel away from wall and reset it to distribute adhesive for a better bond.

6. To cut paneling for door or window, use large sheet of paper to make pattern. Tape paper in place, press it against door or window frame, mark it with pencil, and use scissors to cut it to size. Use this pattern to transfer marks to panel.

7. To make cutouts for electrical outlets or switches, trace outline of switch or outlet box onto panel, and drill pilot, or starter, holes at opposite corners. Then use keyhole saw to cut straight lines between corners.

8. Finally, apply finish molding as described on page 34. Be sure to countersink nails and fill holes with matching wood putty.

INSTALLING FURRING STRIPS Many walls, especially those in a basement, require thin wood strips, called furring strips, behind paneling being installed or replaced. Furring strips are 1×2s or 1×3s that are nailed or glued to the wall, with small wood wedges under them as needed to even up low spots. The 1×3s tend to provide a better bearing surface and are easy to install.

The amount of furring depends on how uneven your walls are. If they're smooth, with a variation of only ½ inch or so between high and low spots, you only need to put up vertical strips, nailing or gluing them over studs and compensating for low spots by wedging wood shims under the strips. Then cut short horizontal pieces to fit between them at floor and ceiling level.

ESTIMATING WALL PANELING

It's easy to estimate how many 4×8-foot panels you need if you know the dimensions of the room you plan to panel. Use this table:

Perimeter of Room	Panels Needed
20 feet	5
24 feet	6
28 feet	7
32 feet	8
60 feet	15
64 feet	16
68 feet	17
72 feet	18
92 feet	23

If your walls are very uneven, you may need to double-fur them. With double-furring, you create a grid with two layers of strips. Start by nailing up vertical strips, spaced 16 inches on center from floor to ceiling. Even these up as best you can with shims, and note any problem spots. Next, install horizontal strips, spaced 16 inches from center to center. Nail these to the vertical strips, further shimming as necessary to smooth the grid.

At electrical wall switches and outlets, you'll need to compensate for the increased thickness of the wall. Remove the cover plates and reset the electrical boxes out the necessary distance. **Caution:** Turn off the electrical power to the circuits you are working on before removing the cover plates.

REPLACING MOLDING Moldings are wood trim around doors, windows, and wall perimeters, such as between a wall and floor or wall and ceiling. Moldings not only make your rooms look finished, but they also protect your walls and doorways, absorbing bumps and scrapes before they get to the walls, kind of like car bumpers. Because baseboards are at floor level where they can be struck by all sorts of objects, they are the most easily damaged moldings. Read on to learn how to replace baseboard molding; you can apply the same techniques to other types of moldings as well.

REMOVING MOLDING Before you install fresh molding, you must remove the old molding. Here's how:

1. Remove any shoe molding (quarter-round piece of wood that fits against both baseboard and floor). Because it's nailed to subfloor, gently pry with putty knife at one end of shoe molding to get it started. Then, use short pry bar and wood block for leverage. Once started, shoe molding should come up easily.

To remove shoe molding, first pry it gently with a putty knife, then use a small pry bar.

What You'll Need
Putty knife
Short pry bar
Wood block
Small cedar shingle wedges
Hammer

2. Pry off damaged baseboard. To do this, start at one end and insert small, flat pry bar between baseboard and wall. Pry gently, and move farther down molding whenever you can, slipping small cedar shingle wedges into any

gaps. Work all the way along baseboard, prying and wedging. Then work back between wedges, tapping wedges in deeper as baseboard comes out. Continue until molding comes off.

3. Check to see if any nails have been pulled through either shoe molding or baseboard. If so, pull out nails completely.

To remove a baseboard, pry it with a pry bar, then use a wedge.

USING MITER BOX If the old baseboard came off intact, you can use it as a pattern for cutting the new one. If part of it is missing or badly damaged, however, you will have to use a miter box to cut the new moldings without the aid of a pattern. An inexpensive wooden or plastic miter box is adequate for this work. Slots in the box allow you to cut molding at 45° angles. Use either a backsaw or a fine-tooth blade in a hacksaw to do the sawing. Before sawing, place the molding you are about to cut next to the molding it will rest against to be sure the cut is the correct one. The following steps instruct you on how to make two 45° cuts and to join two pieces of molding so they form a right angle:

What You'll Need
Replacement
   molding
Miter box
Backsaw or hacksaw

1. Place length of molding in miter box, making sure lip of miter box presses against edge of table or bench so you can keep it steady.

2. Hold molding tightly against side of miter box to prevent it from slipping as you saw 45° cut at one end.

3. Repeat procedure for other length of molding. Two lengths should form a perfect right angle.

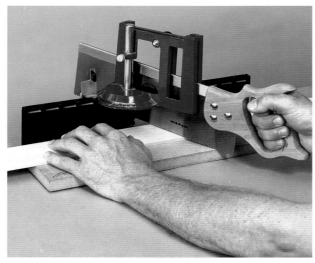

Use a miter box and a backsaw to make 45° miter cuts.

INSTALLING MOLDING When you finish all the mitered joints, you are ready to install the new baseboard molding and reinstall the shoe molding.

1. Cut molding to size, then paint or stain it. To make sure you don't damage finish, you may want to paint or stain moldings after you've installed them on your walls.

What You'll Need
Finish molding
Miter box
Backsaw
Paint or stain
Paintbrushes
Stud finder
Finishing nails
Hammer
Nail set

2. Fit all pieces together before nailing to ensure you cut molding correctly.

3. Locate wall studs. If you're replacing molding, they should be where old molding was nailed.

4. Nail baseboard in place with finishing nails, then use nail set to drive nail heads below surface of molding.

5. Install shoe molding with finishing nails. Shoe molding, however, must be nailed to floor and not to baseboard. Drive nail heads below surface of shoe molding with nail set.

QUICK FLOOR AND STAIR FIXES

When you consider the punishment caused by everyday foot traffic, it's surprising that floors and stairs hold up as well as they do. Eventually, though, wear and tear take their toll. Squeaks develop, minor damage afflicts resilient tile and sheet flooring, or entire surfaces begin to show their age and need replacing or refinishing. Fortunately, there are quick fixes for most floor and stair problems.

REMOVING FLOOR SQUEAKS

Squeaky floors and stairs aren't serious structural problems, but they can be annoying. If your floors are exposed hardwood, you may be able to stop the squeak by sprinkling talcum powder over the noisy boards and sweeping it back and forth to force it down into the cracks. On stairs, use packaged graphite powder or talcum powder in a squeeze bottle; apply along all the joints in the problem area. The powder will lubricate the edges of the boards, eliminating the noise. Following are some more permanent ways to solve squeaky problems.

If there's a basement or crawl space under the noisy floor, work from this area to locate the problem. You'll need a helper upstairs to walk on

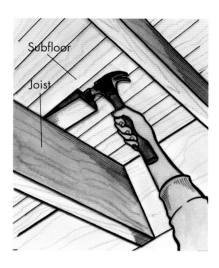

From under the floor, drive wedges into gaps between the subflooring and the joists to stop squeaks.

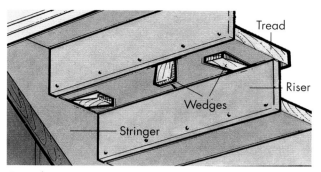

Squeaks in stairs can sometimes be eliminated by installing wedges between the moving components.

the squeaky spot while you work. Watch the subfloor under the noisy boards while your helper steps on the floor above. If the subfloor moves visibly or if you can pinpoint the noise, outline the affected areas with chalk. At the joists closest to your outlines, look for gaps between the joist and the subfloor; wherever there's a gap, the floorboards can move. To stop squeaks here, install shingles or wood shims into the gaps to reduce movement.

If there are no gaps along the joists, or if the squeaks are coming from an area between joists, there's probably a gap between the floorboards and the subfloor. To pull the two layers together, install wood screws up through the subflooring in the squeaky areas. Make sure you drill pilot holes before inserting the screws so you don't crack the wood. The wood screws must be long enough to penetrate into the floor above you but not so long that they go all the way through the boards and stick up through your floor.

If you can't get at the floor from underneath, you'll have to work from the top with spiral flooring nails. First, locate the squeak and try to determine whether it's at a joist or between joists. To eliminate the squeak, drive two spiral flooring nails, angled toward each other in a V,

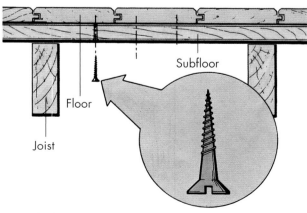

Squeaks between subflooring and flooring can often be eliminated using wood screws to pull the layers together.

through the floorboards and the subfloor. If the squeak is at a joist, use longer spiral flooring nails, driving them through the floorboards and the subfloor and into the joist. Drill pilot holes first to keep the boards from splitting.

If the floor is tiled or carpeted and you can't get at the floorboards from above or below, you probably won't be able to eliminate the squeak without removing the floor covering. Before you do this, try to reset the loose boards by pounding. Using a hammer and a block of scrap wood as a buffer, pound the floor firmly in an area about 2 or 3 feet square over the squeaky boards. The pressure of the pounding may force loose nails back into place.

REMOVING STAIR SQUEAKS

Stairs are put together with three basic components: the tread, the riser, and the stringer (the side piece). In most cases, squeaks are caused by the tread rubbing against the riser or the stringer. If you can, work from under the stairs to fix the squeak. You'll need a helper to walk up and down the stairs while you work.

While your helper walks on the stairs, watch them from below, looking for movement and for cracks in the wood, loose nails, or other problems. The simplest way to fix a squeak is to wedge the components that are moving. Cut small wedges from wood shingles or shims. To install a wedge, apply carpenters' glue to the side that will lie against the stairs. Drive the wedge into the squeaking joints, either tread-riser or tread-stringer. When the wedge is tight, secure it with small nails, being careful not to split the wedge. The nails must be long enough to hold the wedge securely, but make sure they don't go all the way through the stair component and stick out on the other side.

If the joints aren't wide enough to take wedges, use 1×2-inch wood braces to stop the movement of the boards. Use one long or two or more short

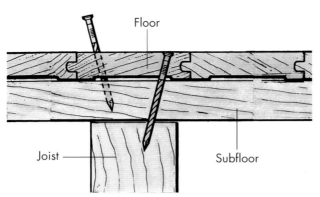

If you cannot access the underside of the floor, angle flooring nails from above into a joist, then fill nail holes with wood putty.

1×2 blocks for each stair-width joint. Apply carpenters' glue to the sides of the block that will lie against the stairs, then set the block into the squeaking joint and nail it into place.

If you can't get at the stairs from underneath, work from the top. For squeaks at the front of a tread, where it meets the riser below it, drive pairs of spiral flooring nails, angled toward each other in a V, across the tread and into the top of the riser. Countersink the nail heads with a nail set, and cover them with wood filler. For squeaks at the back of a tread, where it meets the riser above, apply carpenters' glue to thin wedges, and use a hammer and a wood buffer block to pound them in. Then carefully trim the wide ends of the wedges flush with the riser. If the wedges are noticeable, cover the joint with quarter round or other trim molding; treat all other joints the same way so they match.

FIXING TILE FLOORS

Tile repairs are very simple to make because only the affected tiles must be repaired. If a tile is loose, it can be reglued with floor tile adhesive. If it's just loose at one edge or corner, there may be enough old adhesive left on the tile to reattach it. Cover the tile with aluminum foil and then with a clean cloth. Heat the loose edges with an iron, set to medium heat, to soften the old adhesive and rebond it. When the adhesive has softened, put weights over the entire tile and let the adhesive cure for several hours or overnight.

If the old adhesive isn't strong enough to reattach the tile, use a floor tile adhesive made for that type of tile. Heat the tile as described above, and carefully lift the loose edges with a paint scraper or a putty knife. Scrape the old adhesive off the edges of the tile, and apply a thin coat of new adhesive, using a notched spreader or trowel. Smooth the tile firmly from center to edges, and put weight on the entire tile. Let the adhesive cure as directed by the manufacturer before removing the weights.

For a damaged tile, you can easily replace it. Carefully pry the damaged tile up with a paint scraper or a putty knife. After removing the tile, scrape all the old adhesive off the floor to make a clean base for the new tile. Fill any gouges in the tile base with wood filler, and let the filler dry completely.

Check the fit of the new tile in the prepared opening, even if you are using the same standard size as the old tile. If the new tile doesn't fit exactly, sand the edges or carefully slice off the excess with a sharp utility knife and a straight-edge. When the tile fits perfectly, spread a thin coat of floor tile adhesive in the opening, using a notched trowel or spreader. Warm the new tile with an iron to make it flexible, then carefully set it into place in the opening, pressing it firmly onto the adhesive. Weight the entire tile firmly, and let the adhesive cure as directed by the manufacturer. Remove the weights when the adhesive is completely cured.

FIXING SHEET FLOORS

When a floor is badly worn or damaged, use scrap flooring to patch it. You'll need a piece of flooring a little bigger than the bad spot, with the same pattern.

1. Position flooring scrap over bad spot so it covers damaged area completely and align pattern exactly with floor pattern. You'll be using this piece of scrap flooring as a patch for damaged flooring.

2. Affix scrap firmly in place on floor, using package sealing tape all around edges. Then, with straight edge and sharp utility knife, cut rectangle through scrap piece and through flooring below it to make patch bigger than damaged area. Cut along joints or lines in pattern, if possible, to make patch harder to see. Be sure corners are cleanly cut.

3. Once flooring is cut through, untape scrap piece and push out rectangular patch. Soften old flooring inside cut lines by heating it with iron, set to medium heat. Cover patch area with aluminum foil and then with clean cloth;

> **What You'll Need**
> Matching flooring
>   for patching
> Package sealing tape
> Utility knife
> Straight edge
> Iron
> Aluminum foil
> Clean cloth
> Paint scraper or
>   putty knife
> Water putty
> Medium- or fine-
>   grade sandpaper
> Floor tile adhesive
> Notched trowel or
>   spreader
> Weights

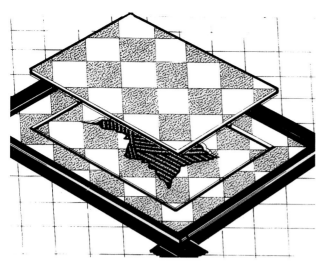

Use a piece of scrap flooring to cut a patch for damaged flooring.

press until adhesive underneath has softened. Carefully pry up damaged piece with paint scraper or putty knife. Scrape all old adhesive off floor to make clean base for patch. If there are any gouges in floor, fill them with water putty. Let dry completely.

4. Install patch in opening. If it binds a little, you can sand edges slightly to adjust the fit. When patch fits exactly, spread thin coat of floor tile adhesive in opening with notched trowel or spreader. Then set patch into gap, press in firmly, and wipe off any excess adhesive around edges.

5. Heat-seal edges to main sheet of flooring. Protect floor with aluminum foil and clean cloth, as above; press edges firmly but quickly with hot iron.

6. After bonding edges, place weight over entire patch and let adhesive cure as directed by manufacturer. Remove weights when adhesive is completely cured. Don't wash floor for at least a week.

FIXING BURNS IN CARPETING

Professional carpet repair can be expensive. But what else can you do when your carpeting is damaged by cigarette or other burns? Actually, with a little patience, you can usually fix the damage just as well yourself. Here are some quick fix tips.

When only the tips of the carpet fibers are burned, carefully cut off the charred fiber with a pair of small sharp scissors. Lightly sponge the area with a mild detergent solution and again with clean water. The low spot won't be noticeable when the carpet dries.

If a large area of carpet is damaged, you'll have to replace the burned area with a patch cut from a piece of scrap carpet. Here's how:

1. From scraps, cut out rectangle or square of carpet a little larger than burned area. In order for patch to blend in with existing carpet without being highly noticeable, it must match pattern in carpet or pile must run in same direction.

2. Press scrap firmly over damaged area. Holding it carefully in place, use utility knife to cut around edges and through carpet under it. Cut completely through backing, but don't cut into carpet padding.

3. When entire damaged area is cut out, lift burned piece out of hole. Check patch for fit, and, if necessary, slightly trim edges so it fits opening exactly.

4. To install patch, stick piece of double-face carpet tape or apply adhesive to padding on each side of hole. Position patch, and firmly press edges onto padding. Let adhesive dry for several hours before walking on patch.

Use a pair of small, sharp scissors to cut off burnt carpet fibers.

What You'll Need
Carpet scraps
Small sharp scissors
Utility knife
Double-face carpet
  tape or latex
  carpet adhesive

FIXING CERAMIC TILE

Ceramic tile is a popular surface for floors, countertops, and shower stalls. Although it is very durable, it can eventually show signs of wear. Tiles crack or loosen, and the grout between tiles wears down and crumbles. These are more than simple cosmetic problems, because unless you fix the damage, water can seep behind the tiles and cause more serious trouble. To keep the problem from getting worse, make the repairs as soon as you can.

REPLACING TILE The hardest part of this job may be finding a tile to match the broken one. If you can't find a tile that matches, try salvage yards for an old one. To replace a tile:

1. First, remove old tile by putting piece of masking tape at its center. Then, wearing safety goggles, drill hole into taped spot with carbide bit. Peel off tape, and score an *X* across tile with glass cutter. Break up tile with chisel and hammer; remove pieces.

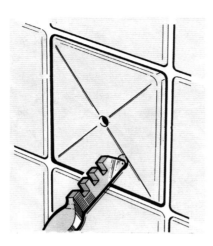

Remove the damaged ceramic tile by drilling a hole in the center and cutting it with a glass cutter. Chisel out the pieces.

2. Use scraper or chisel to remove old adhesive and grout from wall. Make sure there's no loose grout around opening.

3. Spread ceramic mastic on back of new tile with putty knife or notched spreader, leaving tile edges clean.

4. Carefully set new tile into opening on wall. Press tile in firmly, moving it slightly from side to side to distribute mastic, until it's flush with surrounding surface. Space around tile should be even, and tile should be perfectly aligned. Use tape or toothpicks around edge of tile to hold it in place. Let mastic cure according to manufacturer's instructions.

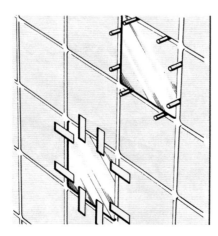

Hold the new tile in place with tape or toothpicks.

5. Remove tape holding tile in place. Wear rubber gloves as you mix ceramic tile grout to fill joints around tile, following manufacturer's instructions. Use damp sponge to apply grout all around new tile, filling gaps completely.

6. Let grout set for 15 minutes, then wipe wall with clean damp sponge or towel to remove any excess grout. Be careful not to disturb grout around new tile. After removing excess, let grout dry completely—at least 12 hours. Do not let tile get wet during this drying period.

7. Once grout is dry, firmly rub tile with damp towel to remove any remaining grout from wall.

Loose ceramic tiles can be removed and then reattached with the same procedure. Scrape out the old grout around the loose tile with the corner of a putty knife, and carefully pry out the tile. If it cracks, it will have to be replaced with a new one, as explained above. You can locate loose tiles by tapping across the wall with the handle of a putty knife.

REGROUTING TILE Grout is the cementlike material used to fill in spaces between tiles. Crumbling grout should be replaced as soon as possible to prevent mildew and water damage. To regrout tile:

1. Scrub tile thoroughly with strong household cleaner. Rinse well. If old grout is mildewed, you must remove mildew before you regrout. To do this, scrub tile joints with old toothbrush dipped in chlorine bleach. Rinse wall thoroughly.

2. Remove all crumbling grout you can with edge of putty knife, then vacuum.

3. Rinse wall to make sure it's absolutely clean, but don't dry it. Wall should be damp when new grout is applied.

4. Wearing rubber gloves, mix ceramic tile grout according to manufacturer's instructions. Apply grout with damp sponge, firmly wiping it in areas that need grouting to fill joints. Smooth newly grouted joints with clean damp sponge. As necessary, add more grout, and smooth it again, filling tile joints completely.

5. Let grout dry for at least 12 hours. Don't let wall get wet during this period. Then scrub wall firmly with clean dry towel to remove any grout that's left on tiles.

6. To protect new grout, seal tile joints with silicone tile grout spray.

QUICK CEILING FIXES

Ceilings are subject to various damages, including water spots from leaks and grease and other food stains. If the ceiling is drywall, follow the instructions in the section on fixing drywall (see pages 30–31). The process is the same whether the repair is on a wall or ceiling, with the exception of making sure any patch you purchase for your drywall ceiling is specifically designed for ceiling repair. If the ceiling is made up of tile, try these quick fixes.

REPLACING DAMAGED CEILING TILES

To remove and replace one or more damaged interlocking ceiling tiles:

1. If tile is applied to furring, use keyhole saw to cut hole large enough to stick your hand through center of damaged tile. Carefully remove damaged tile with your fingers. If tile is glued directly to plaster or drywall ceiling, make hole in tile with chisel, and carefully pry off pieces.

What You'll Need
Keyhole saw
Chisel
Replacement ceiling tile
Utility knife
Ceiling tile adhesive

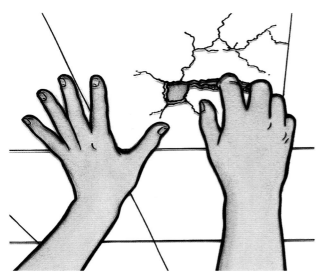

Remove as much of the damaged ceiling tile as possible with your fingers.

2. Cut tongue or grooved edges from replacement tile with utility knife. The edges you should remove can be determined by holding replacement tile in position over opening in ceiling. Match cut tile to opening (it may need trimming to fit). Remove any old staples or adhesive from furring strips or ceiling. Be careful not to damage edges of adjoining tiles.

3. Place ceiling tile adhesive at each corner of new tile, and press tile into opening. If it is not aligned with surrounding tiles, you can slip it into proper position before adhesive dries. Then hold tile in position for several minutes until adhesive sets.

QUICK DOOR FIXES

Doors are great—when they work. But what if a door is sticking or won't entirely close? Or perhaps you want to replace a door with a different style or type. Fixing or replacing a door is relatively easy and usually requires only a few common tools and a couple hours of your time.

UNSTICKING DOORS

Doors, like windows, stick for a number of reasons—from poor construction to extreme humidity. In most cases, it's easy to unstick a stubborn door. To diagnose the problem, close the door, watching it carefully to locate the binding point. If there's a gap between the door and the frame opposite the binding edge, the hinges probably need adjustment. If you can't see a gap anywhere between the door and the frame and you had to slam the door to close it, the wood has probably swollen from extreme humidity. If the hinges and the wood are both in good shape, the door frame itself may be out of alignment; check the frame with a carpenters' square.

To fix a door with poorly adjusted hinges, examine the hinges for loose screws, both on the door and on the frame. Securely tighten any loose screws. If a screw doesn't tighten, the screw hole has become enlarged. When the hole is only slightly enlarged, you may be able to correct the problem by replacing the screw with a longer one, but make sure the head is the same size.

Another option is to use a hollow fiber plug with the old screw. To do this, spread carpenters' glue on the outside of the plug, and insert the fiber plug into the enlarged screw hole. Then drive the screw into the hole. If the screw hole is badly enlarged, you can use wood toothpicks to fill it in. Loose hinge screws can also be tightened by filling the hole with wooden toothpicks dipped in glue and trimmed flush. Dip the toothpicks into carpenters' glue and insert them around the screw hole. Let the glue dry, then trim the toothpicks flush with the surface. When you drive the screw into the filled-in hole, it should hold securely.

If the screws are not loose, the hinges may have to be readjusted on the door frame. Close the door, watching to see where it sticks and where it gaps. If the door is tilted in the frame, it will stick at the top on one side and at the bottom on the other, and there will be a gap between the door and the frame opposite each binding point.

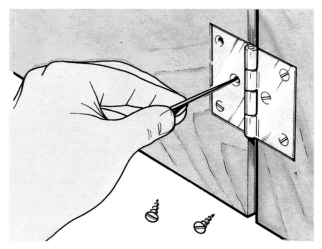

Loose hinge screws can be tightened by filling the hole with wooden toothpicks dipped in glue and trimmed flush.

If the door hinges need shimming, open the door as far as it will go. Push a wedge under it to hold it firmly. At the hinge to be adjusted, loosen the screws from the hinge leaf on the door frame, but don't touch the screws in the door itself. Cut a piece of thin cardboard to the same size as the hinge leaf, and mark the location of the hinge screws on it. Cut horizontal slots in the shim to fit over the screws; slide the shim over the screws behind the loosened hinge leaf. Keeping the shim in place, tighten the screws to resecure the hinge. Remove the wedge holding the door and close the door. If the door still sticks, but not as much as it did before, add another shim under the hinge.

If the door sticks even after shimming, or if there is no gap anywhere around the frame, you'll have to remove some wood at the binding points. Use a block plane on the top or bottom of the door or a jack plane to work on the side. If the door sticks at the sides, try to plane only on the hinge side; the latch side is beveled slightly, and planing could damage the bevel. Use the plane carefully, removing only a little wood at a time. Keep your cuts even across the entire binding edge.

If the door sticks because the frame is out of alignment, there's not much you can do to fix it. At the binding point, set a piece of 2×4 flat against the frame, and give it several firm hammer blows. This may move the frame just enough to solve the problem. If this doesn't work, you'll have to adjust the hinges or plane the edges to allow for the unevenness of the frame. The door may end up slightly crooked, but it won't stick.

REPLACING INTERIOR DOORS

Hanging or installing a door isn't as difficult as it may seem. Replacing an existing door is easy if the new door core is the same size. Installing a door in a new partition wall is also very easy if you buy a prehung door so you don't have to build the door frame yourself. In fact, you probably can tackle this quick fix in an hour or two if you have the necessary materials and tools ready.

INSTALLING PREHUNG DOORS Prehung doors are the easiest to install. These doors come already set in a frame, and one side of the frame has been trimmed with molding. Usually, the hardware has been installed, too, making the process even easier. To buy a prehung door, you need to know the size of the rough door opening. There are approximately 3 inches at the side

Measure the old door and opening before buying a new door or prehung door system.

jambs and 1½ inches at the head jamb for fitting purposes. To install a prehung door:

1. Set door into rough opening and vertically level, or plumb, door jamb sides, filling any gaps at top and sides with cedar shingle shims.

2. Nail head and side jambs to rough framing, using 16d finishing nails. Countersink nail heads into face of jambs with nail set. Fill holes with wood putty.

3. Nail finished casing or molding to doorway with 10d finishing nails. Countersink nail heads, and fill with wood putty.

4. Apply wood sealer to both sides of door and top, bottom, and side edges. Seal casing and door moldings, too.

What You'll Need
Prehung door
Level
Cedar shingle shims
Hammer
16d finishing nails
Nail set
Wood putty
10d finishing nails
Wood sealer

INSTALLING LOCKSETS Once you've hung a new door, you need to fit it with a lockset. Some doors come predrilled for standard-size locksets. Other doors require you to drill the holes yourself, using a template provided by the lock manufacturer. With any door, you need to cut mortises, or holes, in the door edge for the lockset and in the frame for the strike plate that engages the lock's bolt. Here's how:

1. Wrap paper or cardboard template that comes with new lockset around edge of door according to manufacturer's instructions. If necessary, use tape to secure template. Template will be used to locate two holes: one hole for lock cylinder and the other for edge of door for bolt. Mark centers for these two holes on door.

What You'll Need
Lockset
Tape
Pencil
Power drill with hole-saw attachment
Combination square
Sandpaper
Chisel
Screwdriver

2. Use power drill with hole-saw attachment to drill hole the size specified for lock cylinder. Be careful not to damage veneer on opposite side of door. When you see point of drill coming through, stop and finish boring from other side.

3. Drill hole the appropriate size for bolt into edge of door until you reach cylinder hole. Use combination square against edge of door and drill bit to keep bit at right angle to door. Smooth edges of holes with sandpaper.

4. Insert bolt into hole, and place bolt plate in position over it. Trace bolt plate's outline on edge of door. Follow manufacturer's instruc-

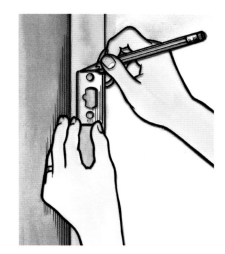

Insert the bolt assembly and trace its outline over the edge of the door; remove excess wood to mount the assembly.

tions to remove bolt and mortise edge for bolt plate so it will be flush with surface.

5. Use chisel to cut mortise. Insert bolt and plate in mortise, and drill pilot holes for mounting screws. Install screws to secure bolt in place.

6. Insert outside lock cylinder so stems or connecting bar fits into bolt assembly. Attach interior lock cylinder, and secure it with screws.

Install the outside lock cylinder so the stems or connecting bar fits into the bolt assembly.

7. Locate proper spot for strike plate on jamb, and drill proper-size hole in jamb. Using strike plate as pattern, mark jamb for mortising, and cut mortise. Install strike plate with screws so it fits flush with jamb.

OTHER QUICK DOOR FIX TIPS

- If you're trying to remove a door's hinge pin and the pin won't budge, press a nail against the hinge bottom and tap upward against the nail with a hammer.

- For better control when lifting a door off its hinges, remove the bottom pin first. When replacing a door on its hinges, insert the top pin first.

- You do not need to worry about oil dripping on the floor if you quiet a squeaky hinge by lubricating its pin with petroleum jelly rather than oil.

- If you need to plane the bottom of a door because it scrapes the threshold or the floor, you can do so without removing the door. Place sandpaper on the threshold or floor, then move the door back and forth over this abrasive surface. Slide a newspaper or magazine under the sandpaper if it needs to be raised in order to make contact.

- To remove ¼ inch or more from a door, score with a utility knife to prevent chipping, and finish with a circular saw.

- When you've fashioned a door to the exact size for hanging, bevel the latch edge backward to let it clear the jamb as it swings open and shut.

- Before you replace a door that you have planed, seal the planed edges with wood sealer. If you don't, the door will swell and stick again.

QUICK WINDOW FIXES

Windows are often trouble spots. Along with doors, windows are the major source of heat-loss in most homes. They also may stick shut when they're painted or swell shut from humidity. Inside, shades and venetian blinds may not work right, glass gets broken, and screens get torn. Fortunately, there's a lot you can do to keep your windows working properly.

UNSTICKING WINDOWS

Double-hung wood-frame windows, especially in older homes, often stick. The most common cause of this problem is that the window has been painted shut and the paint has sealed it closed. The solution is usually simple: Break the seal, and clear and lubricate the sash tracks. Unsticking a window takes strength, but it isn't difficult. Here's how:

What You'll Need
Stiff putty knife or
   paint scraper
Hammer
Chisel
Medium-grade
   sandpaper
Sanding block
Silicone lubricant
Block of scrap wood
Small pry bar

1. Before you start to work, make sure window is unlocked.

2. Look for evidence of a paint seal between sash and window frame. To break seal, push blade of stiff putty knife or paint scraper into joint, cutting straight in through paint. If necessary, lightly tap knife with hammer to force blade in. If window was painted on outside, repeat procedure to break seal on outside.

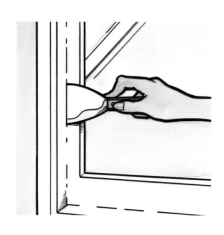
Use a putty knife to free a window that's been painted shut.

3. If window still doesn't open, check tracks in window frame above sash; they're probably blocked with built-up paint. Using hammer and chisel, carefully clean excess paint out of tracks. Cut out thickened paint, but be careful not to gouge the wood of the tracks. Smooth cleaned-out tracks with sandpaper on a narrow sanding block, then spray them with silicone lubricant.

4. If window still sticks, the paint in lower part of tracks is probably holding it. Set block of scrap wood against sash at window frame. Gently tap block of wood with hammer to force sash back from frame. Move block of wood all around window sash, tapping sash back from frame; then try window again. If it opens, clean and sand tracks, and lubricate them with silicone spray.

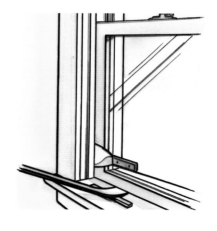
A really stuck window may require using a small pry bar to open it.

5. If window still doesn't open, use small pry bar on it, preferably from outside. Insert flat end of pry bar under sash; set block of scrap wood under it for better leverage. Pry gently at corners of sash and then from corners in toward center. Use pry bar very carefully; too much pressure could damage both sash and frame. If window opens, clean and lubricate tracks with silicone spray. If it still doesn't open, sticking may be caused by extreme humidity, poor construction, or uneven settling. Call carpenter to fix window rather than trying to force it open.

REPLACING BROKEN OR CRACKED GLASS

A broken windowpane not only allows the weather into your home, it is also a security hazard. Luckily, broken glass is one of the easiest problems to fix. You can buy replacement glass, cut to measure, at lumberyards and hardware stores. Here's how to replace a broken pane in a single pane (one thickness of glass) window:

1. Wearing safety goggles, remove broken or cracked glass from window frame. To remove glass without excessive splintering, crisscross pane on both sides with masking tape, then rap it with a hammer. Most of the pane will be held together. Wearing gloves, work any remaining pieces of glass back and forth until they're loose enough to pull out. Knock out any stubborn pieces with hammer.

2. Remove all old putty from frame, using chisel or scraper to pry it out. As you work, look for fasteners that held glass in place—metal tabs called glaziers' points in wood-frame windows; spring clips in metal frames. If putty doesn't come out easily, apply linseed oil to it, and let oil soak in. Then scrape out softened putty, being careful not to gouge out window frame.

3. Apply linseed oil on raw wood around pane to prevent new putty from drying out too fast. If frame is metal, apply rust-resistant paint.

4. Measure frame for new glass. It should be just smaller than opening to allow for expansion and contraction and to allow for imperfections in frame or glass. Measure both ways across opening, from inside edge to inside edge, and subtract $\frac{1}{16}$ to $\frac{1}{8}$ inch each way. Have double-strength glass cut to these precise dimensions. Purchase enough new glaziers' points or clips to be installed every 6 inches or so around pane.

5. Install new glass using glaziers' compound or putty. Roll large chunk of compound between your palms to make long cord (about diameter of pencil). Starting at a corner, press compound into outside corner of window frame, where glass will rest. Cover entire diameter of frame. With compound in place, carefully set

What You'll Need
Safety goggles
Masking tape
Hammer
Heavy gloves
Chisel or scraper
Linseed oil
Clean cloth
Tape measure
Replacement glass
Glaziers' points or spring clips
Putty knife
Glaziers' compound or putty
Single-edge razor blade or glass scraper
Rust-resistant paint and paintbrush

new pane of glass into frame, pressing it firmly against compound. Press hard enough to flatten, squeezing out air bubbles and forcing some of the compound out around frame. Then, to hold glass in place, install new glaziers' points or spring clips every 6 inches or so around pane. Push points partway into wood with blade of putty knife held flat against glass; if the frame is metal, snap spring clips into holes in frame.

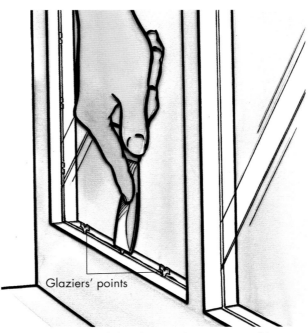

Glaziers' points hold the glass in place in a wood-frame window. Push the points in with a putty knife.

6. To seal new pane with glaziers' compound all around outside edge, roll another cord of glaziers' compound, and press it firmly into the glass-frame joint, all around pane. Use putty knife to smooth compound all along

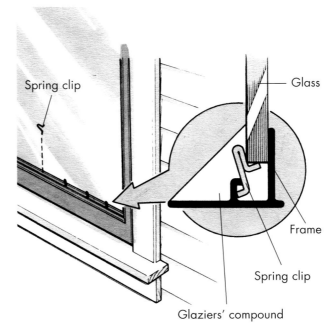

Metal-frame windows often use clips to hold glass in place.

joint around pane, matching putty to other nearby windows. Hold putty knife at an angle to lip of frame, so knife cuts compound off cleanly and evenly along glass. If putty knife sticks or pulls at glaziers' compound, dip blade into linseed oil, and shake off excess. Use long, smooth strokes to keep joint even around pane.

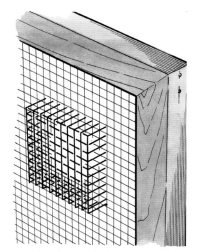 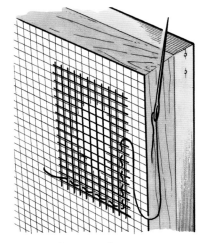

Patch a larger hole in a metal screen using a small piece of screening.

7. With razor blade or glass scraper, carefully remove excess glaziers' compound from both sides of new glass and frame. Let compound dry for about three days.

8. Paint new compound and frame to match rest of frame. Lap paint slightly over edge of compound and onto glass to seal pane completely. Make sure paint is dry before you clean glass.

FIXING SCREENS

Pinholes in screening are very simple to fix. If the screening is metal, use a sharply pointed tool to push the strands of wire back toward the hole; you may be able to close the hole completely. If there's still a hole, apply clear nail polish or household cement over it. Let the sealer dry. Apply additional coats until the opening is filled.

If the screening is vinyl or fiberglass, move the threads back into place. Otherwise, fill tiny holes with clear nail polish or household cement. Be careful not to let any sealer run down the screen. Nail polish may dissolve some types of screen materials.

To close a large hole, cut a patch from a scrap piece of screening, the same type (vinyl, fiberglass, or metal) as the damaged screening. Don't use metal screening made of a different metal; placing two metals together—steel to copper, for instance—can cause corrosion.

A vinyl patch is very easy to install, if you can lay the screen flat. Cut a patch about ½ inch bigger all around than the hole, and set it over the hole. Place a sheet of aluminum foil over the patch area, shiny side down, and press the patch firmly with a hot iron, being careful not to touch the screen directly with the iron. The heat will fuse the patch onto the screening. If you can't lay the screen flat, sew the patch into place with a needle and nylon thread using a firm running stitch, but don't pull the thread too tight. Apply clear nail polish over the edges of the patch to keep it from fraying.

To patch metal screening, cut a square or rectangle about 1 inch bigger all around than hole. Pull out the wires on all four sides to make a wire fringe about ½ inch deep around the patch. Bend the fringe wires down sharply at a right angle; use a wood block to make a clean bend on each side of the patch. When the fringe wires are evenly bent, set the patch over the hole in the screen, and press to insert the bent fringe wires through the screening around the hole. The patch should be flat against the screen, covering the hole completely. Fold fringe wires down flat toward the patch's center on the other side of the screen. Then stitch around the entire patch with a needle and nylon thread or with fine wire.

REPLACING SCREENS

When a screen has many holes or when metal screening becomes bulged and rusted, consider replacing the screening entirely. As long as the frame is in good condition, this isn't as difficult as it sounds. You may be able to buy the screening cut to size. If not, use scissors to cut it about 1½ inches larger all around than the opening. An aluminum-frame screen will require plastic splining, a few inches longer than the diameter of the screen, to replace the old spline.

WOOD FRAMES

1. Use stiff putty knife to carefully pry up molding around edges of screen. Pry out tacks or staples that held screening in place, and remove screening. Pull out any staples or tacks left in frame.

2. Lay new screen fabric over frame, and trace outline of opening on it with chalk.

What You'll Need
Stiff putty knife
Chalk
Scissors
Tape measure
Sawhorses
Weights or clamps
Rope
Scrap boards
Staple gun and
    heavy-duty
    staples
Screening

Then cut screening to size, 1½ inches larger all around than traced outline.

3. Bow or arch frame for easier installation by weighting or clamping frame. To use the weight method, set frame the long way across two sawhorses, and hang 10-pound weight from rope around center of frame. To clamp frame into bow, set it on workbench or wide board across two sawhorses. Place C-clamp at center of each long side, holding frame to work surface, and set long piece of scrap wood, such as a 2×4, between frame and work surface at each end. As you tighten C-clamps, frame will bow.

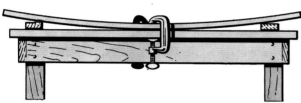

Use a C-clamp, a table, and two 2×4s to bow a screen frame.

4. Set screening across frame, aligned along one unclamped end. Use staple gun loaded with heavy-duty staples to attach screening to wooden frame, placing staples at right angles to frame, about 2 to 3 inches apart. If you're using fiberglass screening, turn cut edge under about 1 inch before stapling it down. When first end is securely stapled, pull loose screening over clamped frame, and stretch it firmly and evenly across to the opposite end. Holding it firmly as you work, staple second end into place, setting staples 2 to 3 inches apart at right angles to frame. Then unclamp or unweight frame; screening should be pulled very tight as it straightens out. Staple two sides into place; trim off any excess screening.

5. Replace molding to cover stapled edges of screening.

ALUMINUM FRAMES

1. With screwdriver or putty knife, pry up plastic spline that holds old screening in place; remove old screening.

2. Lay frame flat, and position new screening over it. Trim edges so screening extends just to outside edges of frame. If necessary, set scrap boards the same thickness as frame under screening to help keep them on same level.

3. Position screening so one end and one side are lined up on outside edge of splining groove in

> **What You'll Need**
> Screwdriver or
>   putty knife
> Screening
> Scissors
> Scrap boards
> Splining tool

frame. Hold screening carefully in place and, with convex roller of splining tool, force edge of screening into splining groove. Secure other two sides the same way, stretching screening taut as you work.

4. When all four sides of screening are in place, cut off any excess screening. Using concave end of splining tool, drive spline into groove to hold screening in place. Start installing spline at one corner, and work around frame. Cut off excess splining where ends meet.

On metal-frame screens, a plastic spline holds the screening in a groove. To install the screening, roll the spline into the groove with a splining tool.

FIXING WINDOW SHADES

Every homeowner and apartment-dweller who has ever used window shades is familiar with the many problems that beset them. There's the shade that's so tightly wound it snaps all the way up, the one that's so loose it won't go up at all, and the one that binds at the edges or falls out of its brackets. In most cases, only a simple adjustment is needed to get shades working properly.

A shade that binds is being pinched by brackets set too close together. If the brackets are mounted on the wall or on the outside of the window frame, this is easy to remedy: Tap the brackets slightly outward with a hammer. This technique also may work on brackets mounted inside the window frame. If the shade still sticks, take it down. You'll have to remove some wood from the roller. Remove the round pin and the metal cap on the round-pin end of the roller. Then sand the end of the roller down with medium-grade sandpaper. Badly binding shades may require further adjustment. If the brackets are mounted on the outside of the frame, you can move one bracket out slightly. Fill the old screw holes with wood plastic. If brackets are inside-mounted, shade will have to be cut down professionally to fit the frame or be replaced.

The opposite problem occurs when the mounting brackets are set too far apart. In extreme cases, the shade may even fall when you try to use it. If the brackets are mounted outside the frame, tap them gently together with a hammer, or move one bracket in closer to the other. If the brackets are mounted inside the frame, you'll have to adjust the space with shims. Take the shade down, and cut a piece of thin cardboard a

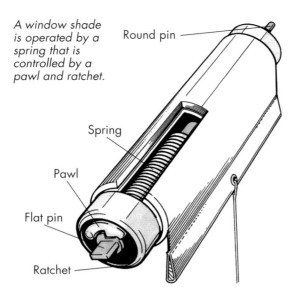

A window shade is operated by a spring that is controlled by a pawl and ratchet.

Round pin

Spring

Pawl

Flat pin

Ratchet

little smaller than one bracket. Unscrew the bracket, set the shim behind it, and screw the bracket on over the shim. If necessary, add one or more shims to both brackets.

When the shade won't go up or down properly, the roller mechanism is probably at fault. Shades are operated by a strong coil spring inside one end of the roller. The pin that holds the shade up at this end of the roller is flat; this flat pin tightens or loosens the spring when you roll the shade up or down. At the flat-pin end of the roller, the spring is controlled by a pawl and ratchet that stop the movement of the spring when the shade is released. If the shade is too tight or too loose, or if it doesn't stay in place when you release it, there is usually a problem with the spring or with the pawl-and-ratchet mechanism. Unless the spring is broken, this is easy to fix.

If the shade won't stay up, the spring is too loose. Pull the shade down enough to turn the roller a few times; if it's extremely loose, pull it down about halfway. Lift the flat-pin end of the roller out of its bracket. Then roll the shade up by hand, keeping it tightly rolled. Set the roller back on the bracket and try the shade again. If it still doesn't stay up, repeat the procedure.

If the shade snaps up and is hard to pull down, the spring is too tight. With the shade rolled up, lift the flat-pin end of the roller out of its bracket and unroll the shade two or three turns by hand. Replace the roller on the bracket, and test its operation. Adjust it further if necessary.

If the shade won't stay down, the pawl-and-ratchet mechanism may need cleaning. Take the shade down and remove the cap at the flat-pin end of the roller. Vacuum out any obvious dust, and clean the mechanism with a soft cloth. Spray silicone lubricant into the mechanism. Replace the metal cap and rehang the shade.

FIXING VENETIAN BLINDS

Venetian blinds are one of the most practical and long-lasting window treatments around, but they can develop problems. When the cords break or the tapes look frayed and shabby, you can give your blinds new life by installing replacement cords and tapes, often sold in kits.

REPLACING LIFT CORD If the blind is clean and otherwise in good condition and the old lift cord is not broken, you can install a new lift cord without removing the unit from the window. Here's how:

1. With blinds down, tilt slats horizontally. Ends of cord are secured to underside of bottom rail. If bottom rail is wood, knotted ends of cord are simply stapled under ends of tapes. If bottom rail is metal, remove end caps and clamps from rail to expose knotted cords. Untie knot on side opposite lift cord, and butt end of new cord to this end. Tape two ends firmly together with adhesive tape.

> **What You'll Need**
> Replacement lift cord
> Adhesive tape
> Scissors

2. Pull gently on old lift cord to draw new cord up through slats on this side, across top, and through control pulleys. Leave a loop of excess cord for new lift cord, and continue to draw cord down through slats on lift cord side.

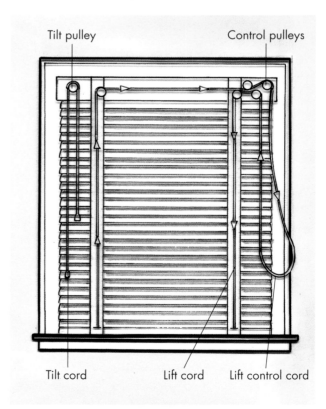

Tilt pulley   Control pulleys

Tilt cord   Lift cord   Lift control cord

The lift cord is threaded up one side of the blind, over a pulley, across the top and through the control pulley, and then down the other side. A loop of cord from the control pulleys forms the lift control.

3. When taped end of new cord reaches bottom rail, untape old cord, discard it, and cut off any excess cord at starting end. Knot both ends of new cord, and secure them the same way old cord was secured. Replace end caps on bottom rail, and slide equalizer clip off old lift cord and onto new one. Adjust cord with equalizer until blind works smoothly.

An equalizer clip allows for adjustment of the lift cord.

REPLACING TILT CORD Here's how to replace a venetian blind's tilt cord:

1. Untie or cut off knots at ends of tilt cord, and remove pulls. Tilt cord is simply threaded over pulley and out again; it doesn't connect with lift cord. Remove old tilt cord by pulling it out. Then thread one end of new cord over pulley and feed it in until it comes out over other side of pulley.

2. Slip cord pulls over ends of cord, and knot ends to hold the pulls on.

CLEANING SLATS AND REPLACING TAPES Use the following steps to replace a lift cord that is broken:

1. Take blind down and lay it out flat, all the way open. Untie both ends of lift cord, as above. Pull cord out of blind, and set equalizer clip aside.

2. Remove slats one by one, stacking them in order. If they're dirty, soak them in detergent solution, then rinse and dry them thoroughly on both sides.

4. Pull out hooks that hold tapes in place at the top of blind. (One hook holds tapes on each side.) Position new tapes in top box and slide hook into each pair of tapes, front and back, at sides of box. Slide slats into place between tapes; make sure they're all right side up, facing the right way. Fold ends of tapes under, and fasten them to bottom rail under last slat.

5. Thread lift cord into blind, starting at tilt cord side and working up that side, across top, through control pulley, and down other side. Tapes have woven strips, or ladders, connecting front and back pieces on alternating sides.

Insert new cord right at center of tapes, so these ladders are placed on alternate sides of cord. At control pulley, leave long loop of cord for new lift cord, and keep threading cord down through slats on that side.

6. Cut off any excess cord, knot both ends of the cord, and secure ends to bottom rail.

7. Slide equalizer clip onto lift cord, and install new tilt cord, as described previously.

Before rehanging blind, check the control pulley mechanism to make sure it's working properly. If you can see dirt or lint in the pulleys, vacuum it out, and wipe the mechanism clean with a soft cloth. Then spray a little silicone lubricant into the pulleys to keep them working smoothly.

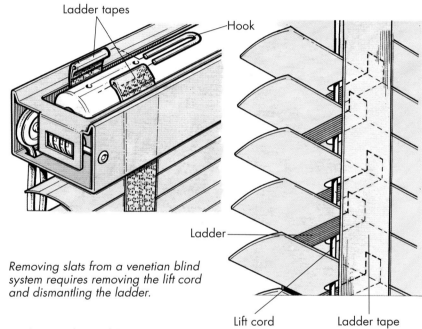

Ladder tapes
Hook
Ladder
Lift cord
Ladder tape

Removing slats from a venetian blind system requires removing the lift cord and dismantling the ladder.

MORE QUICK WINDOW REPAIR TIPS

• To prevent a windowpane crack from spreading, score a small arc with a glass cutter just beyond the crack, curving around it. Most of the time crack will travel only as far as the arc.

• Before trying to chisel hardened putty from a wooden window frame, brush raw linseed oil over putty. Let it soak in to soften the putty.

• Fill a pellet gun hole in a windowpane with clear nail polish or shellac. Dab at the hole; when the application dries, dab again and reapply until the hole is filled. The pane will appear clear.

• To cover a clear bathroom window without putting up curtains, make the glass opaque by brushing on a mixture of 4 tablespoons of Epsom salts and ½ pint of stale beer.

CHAPTER 3

QUICK ELECTRICAL FIXES

Electricity isn't rocket science. In fact, it's quite simple and logical. Obviously, you won't become as skilled as a professional electrician by reading this chapter, but you will learn about the workings of your home's electrical system and how to easily make safe electrical improvements. You should still call in an electrician for the tough jobs, but you certainly don't need to pay out big bucks for simple repairs that you can do yourself in just a short time. This chapter will show you how!

ABOUT ELECTRICITY

Your home's plumbing and electrical systems may seem as different as any two things could be. But there are significant parallels. Water enters your home through a pipe under pressure, and, when you turn on a tap, the water flows at a certain rate (gallons per minute). Electricity enters your home through wires, also under pressure (called voltage, measured in volts). When you turn on an electrical device, the electricity flows at a certain rate (current, measured in amperes, or amps).

Unlike water, which is used as it comes from the tap, electricity is meant to do work: It is converted from energy to power, measured in watts. Since household electrical consumption is relatively high, the unit of measure most often used is the kilowatt, which is equal to 1,000 watts. The total amount of electrical energy you use in any period is measured in terms of kilowatt-hours (kwh).

The instrument that records how much electricity you use is called an electric meter. This meter tells the power company how much electricity they need to charge you for. There are two types of electric meters in general use. One type displays a row of small dials on its face with individual indicators. Each meter dial registers the kilowatt-hours of electrical energy. For example, if you leave a 100-watt bulb burning for 10 hours, the meter will register 1 kilowatt-hour ($10 \times 100 =$ 1,000 watt-hours, or 1 kwh). Each dial registers a certain number of kilowatt-hours of electrical energy. From right to left on most meter faces, the far right is the one that counts individual kilowatt-hours from 1 to 10; the next one counts the electricity from 10 to 100 kilowatt-hours; the third dial counts up to 1,000; the fourth counts up to 10,000; and the dial at the extreme left counts kilowatt-hours up to 100,000. If the arrow on a dial is between two numbers, the lower number should always be read.

The second type of electric meter performs the same function, but, instead of having individual dials, it has numerals in slots on the meter face, much like an odometer in a car. This meter is read from left to right, and the numbers indicate total electrical consumption. Some meters also use a multiplying factor—the number that appears must be multiplied by ten, for instance, for a true figure in kilowatt-hours. Once you know how to read your meter, you can verify the charges on your electric bill and become a better watchdog of electrical energy consumption in your home.

Three main lines (older houses may have two) are responsible for supplying 110–120/220–240 volts AC (alternating current) to your home. The exact voltage varies depending on several

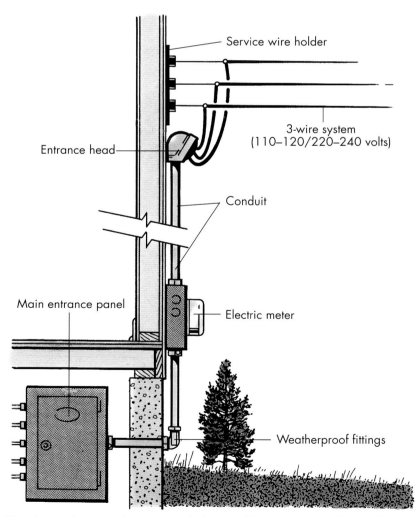

The electrical service drop, or supply line, and the meter are as far as the local utility company is involved in your home's electrical system. From that point on, the system is your responsibility.

external factors. This three-wire system provides you with 110–120-volt power for lighting, receptacles, and small appliances as well as 220–240-volt power for air conditioning, an electric range, a clothes dryer, a water heater, and, in some homes, electric heating.

ELECTRICAL SERVICE ENTRANCE

Electricity enters your home through the power company's service equipment, which is simply a disconnect device mounted in an approved enclosure. It's used to disconnect the service from the interior wiring system. Usually called a main fuse, main breaker, main disconnect, or often just "the main," this disconnect might be a set of pull-out fuses, a circuit breaker, or a large switch.

Although main disconnects can be mounted outdoors in a weatherproof box, they are nearly always inside the house in a large enclosure that also contains the fuses or circuit breakers, which handle the distribution of power throughout the building. This is called a main entrance panel, a main box, or an entrance box. The three wires from the meter enter this box. Two of them—the heavily insulated black and red lines—are attached to the tops of a parallel pair of exposed heavy copper bars, called buses, at the center of the box. These two lines are the "live," or "hot," wires. The third wire, generally bare, is the "neutral." It is attached to a separate grounding bar, or bus, that is a silver-color strip in the main box. In most homes this ground bus is actually connected to the ground—the earth—by a heavy solid copper wire clamped to a cold water pipe or to an underground bar or plate.

OVERLOAD PROTECTION

Power is distributed through your house through various electrical circuits that start in the main entrance panel. The 110–120-volt circuits have two conductors—one neutral (white) wire and one hot (black) wire. The 220–240-volt circuits may have two hot wires alone or a third, neutral wire may be added. In all cases, the hot lines are attached directly to the hot main buses. The neutral wire is always connected to the ground bus and never, under any circumstances, should it pass through a fuse or circuit breaker.

Fuses and circuit breakers are safety devices built into your electrical system. If there were no fuses or circuit breakers and you operated too many appliances on a single circuit, the cable carrying the power for that circuit would get extremely hot, short circuit, and possibly start a fire. To

Circuit breaker panel

Circuit breakers do not blow like fuses. They are switches that automatically trip open to interrupt the flow of electrical current when it overloads the circuit.

Main circuit breaker

Single circuit breaker

Double circuit breaker

Push tripped circuit breaker to ON to restore power

prevent electrical overloads, circuit breakers and fuses are designed to trip or blow, stopping the flow of current to the overloaded cable. For example, a 15-ampere circuit breaker should trip when the current through it exceeds 15 amperes. A 20-ampere fuse should blow when the current through it exceeds 20 amps. A fuse that blows or a circuit breaker that trips is not faulty; it is doing its job properly, indicating that there is trouble somewhere in the circuit. A blown fuse or tripped circuit breaker usually means there are too many appliances plugged in to that circuit or some malfunctioning device, like an appliance with an internal short, is connected to the circuit. Locate and eliminate the cause of the trouble before replacing a blown fuse or resetting a tripped circuit breaker.

Caution: Never try to defeat this built-in safety system by replacing a fuse with one of a higher current-carrying capacity. The fuse or circuit breaker capacity should be equal to or less than the current-carrying capacity of the conductors. For example, don't replace a 15-ampere fuse with a 25-ampere fuse. Replace fuses and breakers only with ones of the same size and amperage.

Circuit breakers do not blow like fuses; they are switches that automatically trip open to interrupt the flow of electrical current when it overloads the circuit. To reset a tripped breaker, turn it fully off and then back on.

BRANCH AND FEEDER CIRCUITS

Circuits to all the devices in your home that require electrical power start from the fuses or circuit breakers. There are two types of circuits: feeder and branch. Feeder circuits use thicker cables that travel from the main entrance panel to smaller distribution panels called subpanels, or load centers. These auxiliary panels are located in remote parts of a house or in outbuildings, and they are used for redistribution of power, such as in a garage. Feeder circuits aren't found in all houses.

All of the circuits in a home that run from either the main entrance panel or from other smaller panels to the various points of use are branch circuits. For 110–120-volt needs, a circuit branches out through a circuit breaker from one of the main buses and from the ground bus. For 220–240 volts, many circuits use only the two main buses. But all three wires are needed for devices that operate on both 110–120 volts and 220–240 volts.

The 110–120-volt branch circuits go through fuses or breakers, which are labeled either 15 or 20 amps. The 15-amp branches go to ceiling lamps and wall receptacles in rooms where less energy-demanding devices, such as table lamps, are found. The larger 20-amp circuits go to receptacles in the kitchen, dining, and laundry areas where heavy-duty appliances are used.

A 15-amp circuit can handle a total of 1,800 watts, while a 20-amp circuit can handle a total of 2,400 watts, but these figures represent circuits that are fully loaded. In practice, you should limit the load on a 15-amp circuit to no more than 1,440 watts, and the load on a 20-amp line should exceed no more than 1,920 watts.

How can you know the load on a circuit? Add up the individual wattages for all lamps and appliances plugged into each circuit. When computing the load on each branch circuit, allow for motor-driven appliances that draw more current when the motor is just starting up than when it's running. A refrigerator, for example, might draw up to 15 amps initially but will quickly settle down to around 4 amps. Suppose the refrigerator is plugged into a 20-amp branch circuit and a 1,000-watt electric toaster (which draws a little more than 8 amps) is also plugged into that circuit. If the refrigerator motor starts while the toaster is toasting, the total current load will exceed the current-carrying capacity of the circuit, and the fuse will blow or the circuit breaker will trip.

Newer homes have three incoming power lines that supply 110–120/220–240 volts AC. This provides 110–120 volts for lighting, outlets, and small appliances and 220–240 volts for heavier appliances.

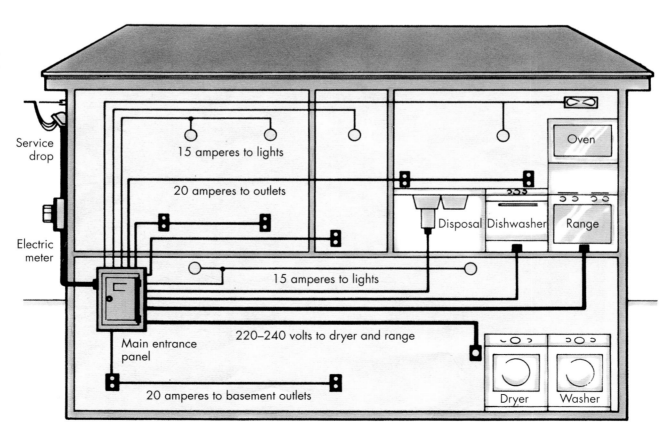

ELECTRICAL SAFETY

Some electrical repairs require a licensed electrician, but the repair or replacement of many electrical components can be done by a do-it-yourselfer. In this chapter, you'll learn what quick fixes you can do yourself as well as how to do them. Make safety your first priority, and you'll be amazed at what you can do to maintain and upgrade the electrical devices in your home.

All electrical devices and electrical wires are designed to provide the greatest measure of safety, but you can defeat any built-in safeguards with carelessness and ignorance. To work safely with electricity, be aware of the following hazards and precautions.

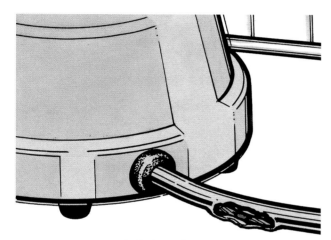

Examine wiring regularly for safety reasons. Replace cords that have brittle or damaged insulation.

- Never do anything that would break the conductor's insulation. Do not, for example, staple an extension cord to a baseboard or wall. The staple can cut through the insulation and create a short circuit, which, in turn, can start a fire. Moreover, you should examine all wiring regularly and discard any cord with brittle insulation. Replace the old cord with a new one that has good insulation.

- Turn the power off before replacing a receptacle or a switch or doing any other work on a circuit. If your system operates with fuses, remove the fuse for the circuit you're working on and slip it into your pocket or toolbox. If you leave it nearby, someone might put the fuse back in while you're working on the circuit. If your home's electrical system uses circuit breakers, trip the appropriate circuit breaker to its OFF position. Then, to make sure no one accidentally flips the circuit breaker back on while you're working, put a piece of tape and a sign over the circuit breaker's handle telling people what you're doing.

- When you work on an electrical circuit, make all wire joints and connections inside an approved electrical box. There are several ways to join wires, but the best way is to use solderless connectors of either the crimp-on or screw-on wirenut kind. Never connect wires together in a behind-the-wall or in-the-ceiling location that is not accessible by simply opening an electrical box. In addition, when joining insulated wires to one another or when fastening them under terminal screws, make sure no uninsulated or bare wire extends beyond the connection. The insulation should go right up to the solderless connector or terminal screw.

- Everyone in the family should know where and how to throw the master switch that cuts off all electrical current.

- If there's a chance of contact between water and electricity, do not wade in water until the master switch has been shut off.

- Always assume an electrical receptacle or apparatus is energized until you prove otherwise with a circuit tester or by pulling a fuse or tripping the disconnect plug.

- Use only insulated pliers when working with electricity.

- Stand on a dry board or wooden platform when working with a fuse box or circuit breaker box. Also, use a wooden rather than an aluminum stepladder to minimize the risk of shock when working with electrical wiring.

- You can save time by determining which circuits activate which receptacles in your home and then diagramming or printing the information inside the circuit breaker or fuse box.

One of the best ways to join wires is to use solderless connectors called wirenuts. Twist the conductor ends together, and screw the wirenut into the twisted ends. Make sure no bare conductor is exposed.

ELECTRICAL GROUNDING

Proper grounding of your electrical system is essential to your safety. Electricity always follows the path of least resistance, and that path could be you whenever an appliance or another electrical component is not grounded.

Grounding directs electrical energy into the earth by providing a conductor that is less resistant than you are. This is accomplished by attaching one end of the wire to the frame of an appliance and fastening the other end to a cold-water pipe. Most plastic-coated electrical cable contains a bare wire, which carries the grounded connection to every electrical box, receptacle, and appliance in your home. You can usually tell whether your electrical system is grounded by checking the receptacles. If you have the kind that accepts plugs with two blades and one prong, your system should have three wires, one of which is a grounding wire. The prong carries the safety ground to the metal frame of any appliance that has a three-wire plug and cord.

An appliance's metal frame can pose a safety hazard to you and your family. If a power cord's insulation wears away just at the point where the cord enters the metal frame, contact between the metal current conductor and the metal frame could make the whole appliance alive with electricity. Touching a charged metal frame of the appliance while simultaneously touching a water faucet or a radiator will make the current surge through *you*.

There are other places throughout the electrical system where conductor/metal contact is a distinct possibility and a safety hazard. Be sure to inspect, maintain, and make repairs wherever wires enter a metal pipe (conduit), where the cord enters a lamp or lamp socket, and where in-wall cable enters an electrical box. Surfaces at these points must be free of burrs that could chafe the wire and damage its insulation. Washers and grommets protect the wire at these various points of entry. However, the best thing you can do to ensure a safe electrical system is to make sure the whole system is grounded and the ground circuit is electrically continuous, without any breaks.

RESTORING A CIRCUIT

The fuses or circuit breakers in your electrical system are there for a purpose: to blow or trip if the circuit is overloaded. When that happens, as

it does from time to time in almost every home, what do you do?

The first step should be taken even before a circuit trips. If you haven't already done so, make a list of all the branch circuits in your home by number and by what area each one controls. Then you can figure out which receptacles and fixtures are on each branch circuit. If you aren't sure the list is accurate and complete, you can verify it with a very simple procedure. Remove a fuse or trip a circuit breaker to its OFF position, then check to see what equipment or devices are deenergized. Of course, it's easy to see when a ceiling light goes out, but you can check a receptacle just as easily by plugging in a lamp. A small night-light is an ideal indicator. Once you know exactly which receptacles, fixtures, and appliances are connected to each branch circuit, write all the information on a card, and attach the card inside the door of the main entrance panel.

When a circuit goes off, there may be some visual or audible indication of the trouble spot, such as a bright flare from a lamp or a sputtering, sparking sound from an appliance, that will immediately lead you to the source of the trouble. If so, disconnect the faulty equipment. Take a flashlight, and go to the main entrance panel. Check to see which fuse is blown or which breaker has tripped, and determine from your information card which receptacles, appliances, and lighting fixtures are on the circuit. Then disconnect everything on that circuit you can, and inspect those fixtures you can't easily disconnect for signs (or smells) of malfunction.

Replace the fuse, or reset the breaker. If the circuit holds, it's possible something you disconnected is faulty. Check for short circuits or other problems. If there's no evidence of electrical fault in the fixtures, the problem may be too much current draw for the circuit to handle. In this case, remove some of the load from the circuit.

If the new fuse blows or the circuit breaker refuses to reset, the problem lies in either the equipment that's still connected or in the circuit cable itself. Check the still-connected items, examining each for faults until you find the offending equipment. If the circuit still goes out when there are no loads connected to it, the wiring is faulty, probably due to a short in a junction or receptacle box or in the cable itself. If you suspect faulty electrical wiring, call an electrician.

A circuit breaker is a remarkably trouble-free device, but once in a while a breaker does fail. The result is the circuit will not energize, even when it's fault-free. When a circuit goes out, if the circuit breaker itself has a distinctive burnt plastic smell, if the trip handle is loose and wobbly, or if the breaker rattles when you move it, the breaker has probably failed. Turn off the circuit, check the breaker with a continuity tester, and replace it as needed.

COPING WITH A POWER OUTAGE

What do you do when all the power in the house goes off? Usually this is due to a general power outage in an entire neighborhood or district, but sometimes the problem lies in an individual residential wiring system.

The first step is to see whether the outage is a general power outage or restricted to your home. If it's nighttime, look around the neighborhood to see if everyone else's lights are off. During the day, call a neighbor to see if others are affected. Or, if you have a circuit breaker main disconnect, check to see whether it has tripped to the OFF position. If the main entrance is wired with fuses, pull the fuse block out and slip the fuses free. Check them with a continuity tester to see if they are still good. With a probe lead touched to each end of the fuse, the tester light will come on if the fuse is good.

If the trouble is a general power outage, all you can do is call the power company. If your main breaker is still in the ON position or both main fuses are good but your neighbors have power and you don't, the fault lies between your main entrance panel and the power transmission lines. The reason could be a downed service drop, a faulty or overloaded pole transformer, or some similar problem. Call the power company; this part of your system is their responsibility.

If you find a tripped main breaker or blown main fuses in your main entrance panel, the problem lies within the house and may be serious. Do not attempt to reset the breaker or replace the fuses. The difficulty may be a system overload, using more total current than the main breaker can pass. Or there may be a dead short somewhere in the house.

The first step is to go back through the house and turn off everything you can. Then, if you have a circuit breaker panel, flip all the breakers to the OFF position. Once the breakers are off, reset the main breaker to the ON position. One by one, trip the branch circuit breakers back on.

If one of them fails to reset, or if the main breaker trips off again as you trip the branch breaker on, the source of the trouble lies in that circuit. The circuit will have to be cleared of the fault.

If all the breakers go back on and the main breaker stays on, you're faced with two possibilities. One is that something you disconnected earlier is faulty. Go back along the line, inspect each item for possible fault, and plug each one back in. Sooner or later you'll discover which one is causing the problem, either visually or by noticing that a breaker trips off when you reconnect it. The other possibility is systemwide overloading. This is characterized by recurrent tripping out of the main breaker when practically everything in the house is running but there are no electrical faults to be found. To solve this problem, you can either lessen the total electrical load or install a new larger main entrance panel with new branch circuits to serve areas of heavy electrical usage and help share the total load. This job requires a licensed electrician.

The troubleshooting approach is similar if the main panel has fuses, except you'll need a supply of fuses on hand. First, pull all the cartridge fuses and unscrew all the plug fuses in the panel. Replace the main fuses, and put the fuse block back into place. Then, one by one, replace each fuse or set of fuses until the one that's causing the outage blows out again. This is the circuit that must be cleared. General overloading, however, will cause the main fuses to go out again. If this happens, call in an electrician, who can test for overloading and suggest remedies.

EMERGENCY BLACKOUT KIT

Is your home susceptible to power outages due to the local utility company, wind storms, or other problems? Here's a quick fix: Make an emergency blackout kit that includes the following items:

- Candles or oil lamps and matches for area lighting

- Flashlight, battery lantern, or other auxiliary light source for troubleshooting

- Correct and up-to-date circuit directory posted on main entrance panel door

- Tool kit with appropriate tools for making electrical repairs

- Circuit tester, preferably the voltage-readout type

Items for an emergency blackout kit.

- Two replacement plug fuses of each amperage rating in use, preferably Type S

- Four replacement cartridge fuses, including main fuses, of each amperage rating in use

- One replacement pull circuit breaker of a rating equal to the smallest size in use or one of each size in use

- One replacement double-pull circuit breaker of each amperage rating in use

- Selection of lightbulbs

- One replacement duplex receptacle to match existing units

- One replacement single-pole switch to match existing units

- One replacement three-way or other special switches to match existing units

- Wirenuts and electrical tape

CHECKING RECEPTACLE POLARITY

Residential wiring systems installed in older homes use a two-wire system in the 110–120-volt branch circuits. One conductor is hot, and the other is neutral. The neutral may also serve as a ground, but, unfortunately, it usually does not. When this is the case, the system is ungrounded and the situation is potentially hazardous.

You can easily tell if your circuits are of this type by looking at receptacles. There are only two slots for each plug in ungrounded receptacles. Modern wiring calls for the installation of a third conductor. Receptacles used with this system have three openings: two vertical slots and a third, rounded hole centered below or above them. Either two-prong or three-prong plugs can be plugged into these receptacles, but only the three-prong kind will carry the equipment grounding line to the electrical equipment. Also, one of the vertical slots is different in size from the other, so the newer types of two-pronged plugs can be inserted in only one direction. This ensures that the equipment being connected will be properly polarized, hot side to hot side and neutral to neutral.

For proper operation and safety, make sure all receptacles on each circuit are installed with the individual conductors going to the correct terminals so there are no polarity reversals along the line. Unfortunately, receptacles are not always connected this way, even in new wiring systems installed by professional electricians. Check out your receptacles with a small inexpensive tester called a polarity checker, designed for this purpose. It looks like a fancy three-pronged plug and contains three neon bulb indicators.

To check your receptacles for polarity, plug a polarity checker into a receptacle. The lights will tell you if the polarity is correct and, if not, which lines are reversed. If there is a reversal, turn the circuit off, pull the receptacle out of the electrical box, and switch the wires to the proper terminals (see page 55). If the equipment-grounding circuit is open (discontinuous), trace the circuit with a continuity tester until you find the disconnection or missing link; reconnect it to restore the effectiveness of the circuit.

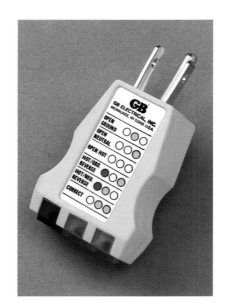

To make sure outlets are installed properly—with the individual conductors going to the correct terminals—you can use a plug-in analyzer to check polarity.

QUICK RECEPTACLE FIXES

Nearly everyone has come across a receptacle that doesn't work as well as it should or one that doesn't work at all. How does it happen that a receptacle fails to do its job efficiently and safely? There are two possible explanations.

An electrical receptacle can be permanently damaged through improper use. Sticking a hairpin or a paper clip in it, for example, can shorten a receptacle's—and your—life. You may never do anything as foolish as sticking a paper clip in a receptacle, but you can do the same damage when you plug in an appliance with a short circuit. Regardless of how the damage occurred, the damaged receptacle must be replaced.

Another possible explanation for a receptacle that doesn't work efficiently and safely is that it is just so old and has been used so often that it's worn out. There are two clear indications of a worn-out receptacle: the cord's weight pulls the plug out of the receptacle or the plug blades do not make constant electrical contact within the receptacle slots. At that point, the old receptacle should be replaced. This is not difficult, but you must follow the correct installation procedures precisely.

REPLACING RECEPTACLES

1. Before working on receptacle, deenergize circuit that controls it. Inspect old receptacle to see whether it can take a plug with a round prong (for grounding) in addition to two flat blades. Buy new receptacle with 20-amp rating of same type—grounded or ungrounded—as one you're replacing.

What You'll Need
Replacement receptacle
Screwdriver
Single-edge razor blade or utility knife
Grounding screws or clips
Wire stripper with cutting blade

2. Take off plate that covers receptacle by removing center screw with screwdriver. If cover doesn't come off easily, it's probably being held in place by several coats of paint. Carefully cut paint closely around edge of cover plate with razor blade or utility knife.

3. Remove two screws holding receptacle in electrical box. Carefully pull receptacle out of box as far as attached line wires allow. Loosen terminal screws on receptacle and remove line wires. **Caution:** If wires or insulation is brittle or frayed, that part of circuit should be professionally rewired.

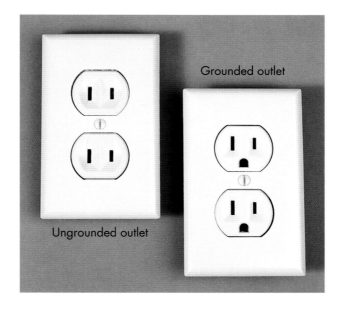

Ungrounded outlet

Grounded outlet

When replacing a receptacle, see whether it accepts only plugs with two flat blades or whether it can take plugs that have a rounded ground prong (see caption below).

4. Connect wires to new electrical receptacle with white wire under silver-color screw and black wire under dark-color screw. If you discover a green wire or a bare wire in box, fasten wire under screw that has dab of green color on it, then fasten it to box with grounding screw or clip. Make sure to loop line wires in clockwise direction under heads of terminal screws so screw heads will pull wire loops tighter. Also take care to connect wires so all wire without any insulation is secured safely under screw heads. Clip off any excess uninsulated wire.

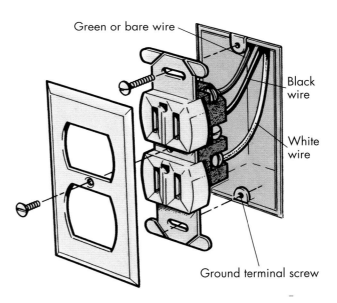

Green or bare wire

Black wire

White wire

Ground terminal screw

A replacement receptacle must match the one you are removing. If you have the grounded type, you must buy a receptacle that has a ground terminal screw and slots for three-prong grounded plugs.

5. Carefully fold wires into space in electrical box behind receptacle, then push receptacle into box. Although there's no such thing as right side up for a two-blade receptacle, there is a correct position for receptacles designed to handle three-prong grounding plugs. Grounding plugs often attach to their cords at a right angle, so you should position receptacle so cord will hang down without a loop.

6. Tighten the two screws that hold receptacle in receptacle box, then replace cover plate. Restore fuse or trip circuit breaker.

Slots in some receptacles are not identical; one is wider than the other. The wider one connects to the white or neutral wire, while the narrower slot connects to the black or hot wire. Some plugs, in fact, are designed with one wide and one narrow blade, and these plugs will fit into the receptacle in only one way. The idea behind such a polarized plug is to continue the hot and neutral wire identity from the circuit to the appliance.

REPLACING WALL SWITCH

Sometimes a light fixture that's in perfect operating condition doesn't work because the wall switch to the receptacle is faulty. There are several primary symptoms of switch failure:

- the switch loses its snap or there is no clear distinction between the ON/OFF positions

- flipping the switch no longer turns the light on or off

- flipping the switch makes the light flicker, but the light will not stay on or off

- the switch may work occasionally, but you have to jiggle it back and forth several times to keep the light on

If you spot any of these symptoms of switch failure, install a replacement wall switch as soon as possible. Here's how:

1. Deenergize electrical circuit that controls switch.

2. Remove switch cover plate. If cover plate doesn't come off easily, it is probably being held in place by several layers of paint. Use razor blade or utility knife to cut paint closely around edge of plate to free it.

3. Inspect old switch to determine type of replacement model you need. (Replace cover until you return with new switch.) You must use the same type, but, in most cases, you can install a better grade of switch than the one you had before.

4. Prepare new switch for installation. Some kinds of wall switches have no terminal screws for conductor attachments. Instead, switch has small holes that are only slightly larger than bare copper conductors. Remove about ½ inch of insulation from ends of wires, then push bare ends into holes. Locking tabs make electrical connection and grip wires so they can't

What You'll Need
Screwdriver
Single-edge razor blade or utility knife
Replacement receptacle or switch
Wire stripper with cutting blade
Grounding screws or clips

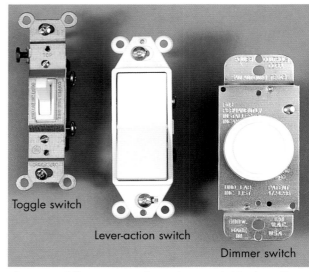

There are different types of switches available, but all work on the same general principles. Usually, you can base your selection of a replacement switch on the features you like best.

Toggle switch
Lever-action switch
Dimmer switch

pull out. If necessary, release wires from old switch by inserting narrow-blade screwdriver in slots next to wire-grip holes.

5. Remove mounting screws on switch cover plate and take off plate. With cover plate removed, you'll see two screws holding switch in switch box. If necessary, remove screws, and carefully pull switch out of box as far as attached wires allow. If there are two screws with wires attached, switch is a simple ON/OFF (single-pole) type. If there are three screws with wires attached, you're working with a more complicated type called a three-way switch. Replacement switch must be the same type as old one, either single-pole or three-way. Three-way switches allow you to turn light on and off from two different loca-

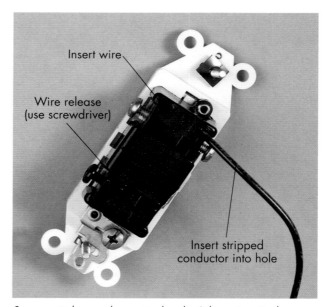

Insert wire
Wire release (use screwdriver)
Insert stripped conductor into hole

Some switches and receptacles don't have terminal screws. They have holes into which the stripped wire ends are inserted. Other types, like this one, have both holes and terminal screws.

tions, such as at top and bottom of stairway. Look carefully at three terminal screws; you'll see that two are one color while the third is a different color. Do not disconnect any wires until you compare old switch with replacement switch so you know which wire goes to which terminal screw.

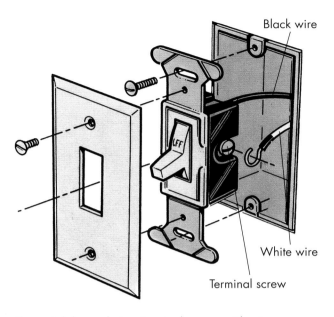

If a switch has only two terminal screws with wires attached, it's a simple ON/OFF (single-pole) switch. This type of switch is very easy to install. Connect the line wires to the screws, secure the switch, and replace cover plate.

Black wire

White wire

Terminal screw

6. Loosen one of the old terminal screws, remove wire, and attach wire to corresponding terminal screw on new switch. Repeat with remaining wires. Take care to connect wires so all bare wire is safely under screw heads; clip off any excess uninsulated wire. Procedure is the same whether you're working with simple ON/OFF switch or three-way switch, but you must be more careful with the latter. Verify wiring by comparing it with manufacturer's diagram on packaging of new switch.

7. If you're installing modern wire-grip type of wall switch, cut off end of each wire to leave only ½ inch of bare wire. Push one bare end of wire into each wire-grip hole, and check that wires have caught properly by tugging gently on them. **Caution:** If wires or insulation going into electrical box are brittle or frayed, that part of circuit should be professionally rewired.

8. Replace switch in wall electrical box. Push switch into box carefully, and make sure wires fit neatly into box behind switch. There are small tabs extending from switch's mounting bracket; these tabs should lie flat against wall outside electrical box. They hold switch flush with wall no matter how electrical box is angled inside.

9. Put switch back into place, using two mounting screws provided with new switch. Oval holes in mounting bracket allow you to fasten switch so it's straight up and down even when screw holes in electrical box are tilted.

10. Attach cover plate with screws you took out earlier, and replace circuit fuse or trip circuit breaker back on.

All switches work on the same general principles, and you can usually choose a switch with features you like best. The single-pole toggle switch is still the most popular. When the toggle switch is mounted properly, the words ON and OFF are upright on the toggle lever, and the light goes on when you flip the switch up. A variation of the traditional toggle switch is the lever-action switch, which lies almost flush with the wall. It turns the fixture on when someone pushes the top of the switch in. The push-button switch has a single button that turns the light on when pressed and off when pressed again. Some switches are available with the extra feature of a built-in neon lamp that glows when the switch is off, making it easy to locate the switch in the dark. Dimmer switches, with a dial to control the brightness, turn the light off when the dial is turned all the way down or pushed in. Some dimmer switches are like toggle types. Sliding the toggle upward increases the light's intensity; sliding it all the way down turns off the light. You can install these switches as replacements for nearly any type of switch.

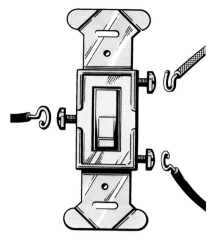

Three-way switches allow you to turn a light on and off from two different locations, such as at the top or the bottom of a stairway.

QUICK LIGHTING FIXES

REWIRING LAMPS

You can easily repair household lamps that don't work properly. Available at any well-stocked hardware or electrical store, the plug and cord are simple and inexpensive to replace. You can install a new socket just as easily. Replacement sockets come in various finishes so you should be able to find a socket that is similar to the color tone of the existing socket.

The most common lamp and small appliances cord is Type SPT, often called zip cord. The conductor sheath is plastic; it splits easily along a molded groove.

LAMP TROUBLESHOOTING CHART

Problem	Possible Cause	Solution
Lamp does not light	1. Lamp unplugged.	1. Plug lamp in.
	2. Circuit dead.	2. Restore circuit.
	3. Bulb loose.	3. Tighten bulb.
	4. Bulb burned out.	4. Replace bulb.
	5. Loose connection at plug or socket.	5. Trace and repair.
	6. Defective wall switch.	6. Replace switch.
	7. Defective socket switch.	7. Replace socket.
	8. Defective center contact in socket.	8. Pry contact up or replace socket.
	9. Broken conductor in line cord.	9. Replace line cord.
Lamp blows fuse or trips circuit breaker	1. Overloaded circuit.	1. Check total load on circuit. If overloaded, transfer some equipment to different circuit.
	2. Short circuit in socket, in cord, or in lamp wiring.	2. Replace socket and cord. Rewire carefully to make sure no bare wires touch each other or any metal parts of lamp.
Lamp flickers when moved or touched	1. Lamp bulb loose in socket.	1. Tighten bulb.
	2. Loose connection, usually where line cord wires are fastened under terminal screws on lamp socket.	2. First make sure lamp is unplugged; then take socket apart and inspect wire connections under screws. Tighten screws or, if necessary, cut off a short piece of cord and reattach wire ends.
	3. Defective contacts or faulty switch in socket.	3. First make sure lamp is unplugged; then remove socket and replace it with new one.
	4. Defective lamp cord.	4. Replace cord. Rewire so no bare wires touch each other or any metal parts of lamp.

Lamp cord is known as Type SPT, or zip cord. The #18 size is satisfactory for most lamp applications. Zip cord is available in many colors, the most common being black, brown, white, and transparent. Match the cord color to the lamp stand or the wall that holds the receptacle. The customary length is 6 feet, but you can use as much cord as you need to reach from the lamp to the receptacle. To figure out how much cord to buy, calculate the length of the cord (including cord that is hidden in the lamp), and add 1 foot for attachments to socket and plug and for slack. In terms of safety and appearance, it's better to have an adequate length of cord than to compensate for a short one with an extension cord. To rewire a lamp:

1. Pull plug out of wall socket. You should never do any work while lamp is connected.

2. Remove shade, unscrew bulb, and squeeze socket shell at switch to separate shell and cardboard insulator from socket cap. If you plan to reuse socket, do not use screwdriver to pry socket apart. Pull socket out of shell as far as attached wire permits. If this doesn't give you enough wire to work with, push cord up from bottom of lamp for additional slack.

3. Loosen socket's terminal screws, and remove cord wires from under them. If lamp is small and cord goes through in straight path, slide old wire out, and feed new wire through from either end to the other. If old cord offers any resistance at all, don't tug on it. Check to see if you can disassemble lamp to make removal easier. Also, make sure cord is tied in knot to keep it from being pulled out at its base.

4. To remove tight cord, cut wire off about 12 inches from lamp's base, slit cord's two conductors apart, and strip about an inch of insulation off ends. Do the same to one end of new length of cord. Twist bare new and old conductor ends together, and fold twists flat along cord. Wrap electrical tape around splice. Pull on old cord from top of fixture, and work new cord through; at same time, push on new cord from bottom. When you have sufficient length of new cord through top, clip off old cord.

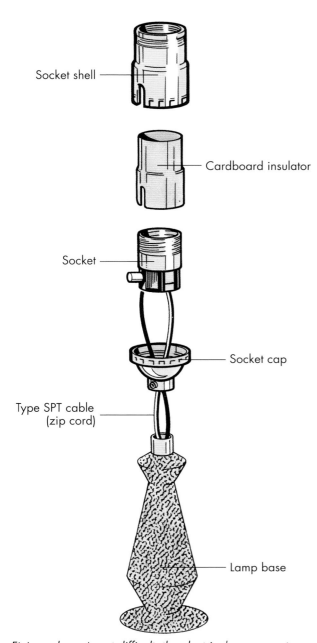

Socket shell

Cardboard insulator

Socket

Socket cap

Type SPT cable
(zip cord)

Lamp base

Fixing a lamp is not difficult; the electrical components are inexpensive and easy to replace. The parts that are most often responsible for lamp failure are the socket, the cord, and the plug.

5. Once you pass new cord through lamp, split end so you have about 3 inches of separated conductors. Use wire stripper tool to strip about ¾ inch of insulation from end of each conductor, then twist strands of each together. Be careful not to nick strands when you strip insulation.

6. Bend twisted end of each wire into clockwise loop, and place each loop under terminal screw on socket with loop curled clockwise around screw. Tighten terminal screws. As each screw is tightened, clockwise loop will pull wire tighter under screw head. (A counterclockwise loop would tend to loosen wire.) Clip off excess bare wire with diagonal cutters. All uninsulated wire must be under screw heads, with no loose strands or exposed bare

wire. If bare wire is visible beyond screw heads, unscrew terminals, remove wires, and make connection again.

7. Slide socket shell over insulator, and slip shell and insulator over socket. Then snap shell and socket into cap.

8. Install quick-clamp plug on other end of cord. Stick end of cord into slot on side of plug, and push down on lever at top. Metal prongs inside plug will bite through cord's insulation, piercing copper wires to make electrical connection. If you use screw-type plug, prepare wire ends just as you did when making socket screw connections, then knot them together. Loop each wire around prong of plug before tightening bare end under screw head. Knots and loops keep wires from accidentally touching each other and also make it more difficult to loosen connections by pulling on cord.

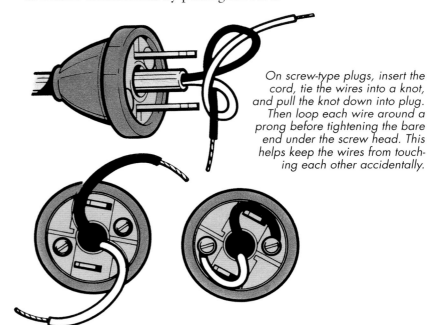

Quick-clamp plug

Insulation
not stripped

A quick-clamp plug is very easy to install. Metal prongs inside the plug bite through the cord's insulation and pierce the copper wires inside to make the electrical connection.

On screw-type plugs, insert the cord, tie the wires into a knot, and pull the knot down into plug. Then loop each wire around a prong before tightening the bare end under the screw head. This helps keep the wires from touching each other accidentally.

9. Tighten wires under screw heads, and clip off any excess uninsulated conductor before you plug in lamp.

REPLACING INCANDESCENT LIGHT FIXTURES

Replacing a light fixture is relatively simple. In fact, the biggest problem you'll probably encounter is the mechanical complexities of attaching a new fixture to older mounting hardware.

Here's how to replace an incandescent light fixture. The simplest fixture installation uses a fixture strap secured to the electrical box. Connect white wire to white and black to black.

1. Before you replace or repair any light fixture, deenergize electrical circuit by pulling appropriate fuse or by tripping proper circuit breaker.

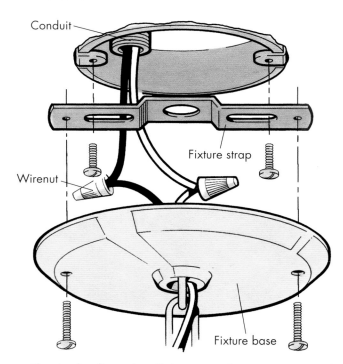

The simplest fixture installation uses a fixture strap secured to the electrical box. Connect white wire to white and black to black.

2. Take off light cover, unscrew bulb(s), and disassemble all mounting hardware. Usually there are just screws holding fixture against wall or ceiling. If light fixture has no visible mounting hardware, it could have a decorative feature that doubles as a fastener. Take off mounting hardware and withdraw fixture from electrical box.

3. Disconnect lamp fixture wires from circuit wires. If wire joint is fused together with old insulating tape, cut wires close to tape. **Caution:** If wires or insulation coming into electrical box are brittle or frayed, that part of circuit should be professionally rewired. Once you remove old fixture, examine electrical box and new fixture to determine which of the following installation procedures you should use for additional steps.

For fixture installation in standard electrical box:

Make sure you have about ¾ inch of bare copper conductor on end of each line wire before you start to connect wires of your new lighting fixture. If necessary, remove enough insulation from line wires so you can twist each line wire end together with end of each light fixture wire, white wire to white wire and black to black. Screw wirenut tightly over each pair of twisted ends. Hold onto fixture to support its weight until you attach mounting screws; otherwise, you might break a connection or damage fixture wires.

If fixture has more than one socket:

Connect black wire from each socket to black line wire and white wire from each socket to white line wire. When three or four socket wires are joined to line, use larger wirenut.

4. Mounting screws of proper length are typically included with your new lamp fixture. Screws 2 or 2½ inches long are sufficient for most fixtures. Insert screws into attachment screw holes in electrical box, and tighten each screw four or five turns to hold it in place. Mount fixture by passing fixture's keyhole slots over screw heads. Then rotate fixture enough so screws are forced into narrow parts of keyhole slots.

5. Tighten screws, being careful not to overtighten them; they should be just snug enough to hold fixture firmly in place. If you tighten mounting screws too much, you may distort and misalign fixture. With fixture mounted properly, screw in bulbs and attach globe or cover.

6. Replace fuse or trip circuit breaker back on.

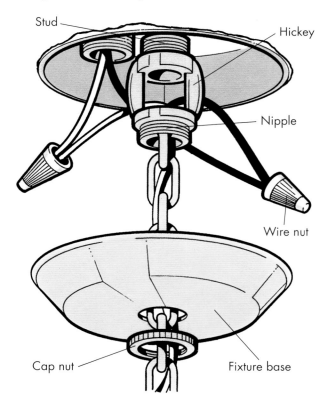

Some fixtures don't use a mounting strap; the fixture is secured to the stud with a "hickey," or reducing nut.

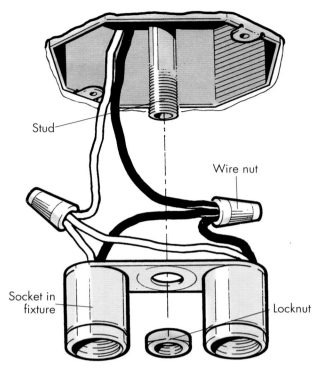

If there is more than one socket, connect the white wire from each socket to the white line wire and the black wire to the black line wire.

Some fixtures are mounted with a short piece of threaded pipe, called a nipple. To mount this type of fixture, screw the nipple into the center hole of the strap, and set the fixture onto the nipple. Screw a cap nut onto the nipple to hold the fixture in place.

Other light fixtures are not strap-mounted. Instead, a nipple is connected to the box stud with a reducing nut or an adapter called a "hickey." A reducing nut is threaded at one end to fit the stud and at the other end to fit the nipple. To mount a fixture that uses a reducing nut, screw the nut onto the stud and the nipple onto the nut. Set the fixture onto the nipple, set the fixture into place, and screw a cap nut onto the nipple to hold the fixture in place. To mount a fixture with a hickey, screw the hickey onto the stud, and then mount the fixture the same way.

INSTALLING FLUORESCENT LAMPS

You might consider replacing some of your old incandescent fixtures with fluorescent lamps. Fluorescent light provides even and shadow-free illumination, but, best of all, fluorescent bulbs are more efficient than incandescent bulbs. In an incandescent bulb, much of the electric power is discharged as heat instead of light. The fluorescent bulb, in contrast, remains cool.

How does a fluorescent lamp work? In a fluorescent circuit, beginning at the left-hand prong of

the plug, current goes through the ballast, through one of the lamp filaments, through the closed switch in the starter, through the other filament in the lamp, and out the right-hand prong of the plug. The current heats the two small elements in the ends of the fluorescent tube; then the starter opens and current flows through the lamp.

The ballast is a magnetic coil that adjusts the current through the tube. It makes a surge of current arc through the tube when the starter opens, and then it keeps the current flowing at the right rate once the tube is glowing. In most fluorescent fixtures, the starter is an automatic switch. Once it senses that the lamp is glowing, it stays open. The starter closes whenever you deenergize the fixture.

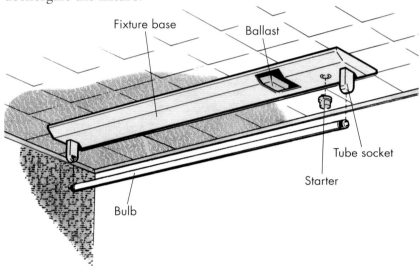

A fluorescent fixture has three main parts—bulb, ballast, and starter. When one of these components malfunctions, replacement is usually the answer.

Many fluorescent fixtures have more than one tube in order to provide more light. These lamps must have individual starters and ballasts for each tube. The fixture may appear to have two tubes working off one ballast, but actually there are two ballasts built into one case. Fixtures with four tubes, similarly, have four starters and four ballasts. In some kinds of fixtures, the starters are built in and cannot be individually replaced.

Since there are only three primary parts in a fluorescent lamp, you can usually take care of any repairs yourself. All fluorescent lamps grow dimmer with age, and they may even begin to flicker or flash on and off. These are warning signals, and you should make the necessary repairs as soon as you notice any change in the lamp's normal performance. A dim tube usually requires replacement, and failure to replace it can strain other parts of the fixture. Likewise, repeated flickering or flashing will wear out the starter, causing the insulation at the starter to deteriorate.

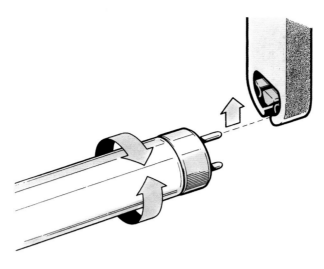

To install a new fluorescent tube, insert the tube's prongs into the holder and twist the tube to lock it into place. Change the tube when it dims, flickers, or flashes on and off.

sure the tube is burned out, test the old tube in another fluorescent fixture. Remove the old tube by twisting it out of its sockets in the fixture. Install the new tube the same way—insert the tube's prongs into the socket and twist the tube to lock it into place.

If the problem is not in the tube, try changing the starter. Fluorescent lamp starters are rated by wattage, and it's important you use the right starter for the tube in your fixture. Remove the old starter the same way you removed the old tube, by twisting it out of its socket in the fixture. Install a new one by inserting it into the socket and twisting it to lock it into place.

Fluorescent fixtures can be serviced quite simply by the replacement method. If you suspect that a part may be defective, replace the part with a new one. Start with the fluorescent tube or bulb. You can either install a new one or, if you're not

The ballast is also rated according to wattage, and a replacement ballast—like a replacement starter—must match the wattage of the tube and the type of fixture. The ballast is the least likely part to fail and most difficult to replace, so leave the ballast for last when you start replacing parts. If neither the tube nor the starter is defective, the problem must be the ballast. To replace a

FLUORESCENT LAMP TROUBLESHOOTING CHART

Problem	Possible Cause	Solution
Lamp will not light	1. Burned-out tube.	1. Replace with new fluorescent tube of correct dimensions and wattage.
	2. Defective starter.	2. Replace starter with new one of appropriate wattage.
	3. Defective ballast, sometimes accompanied by the odor of burning insulation.	3. Replace ballast; before replacing, consider cost of new ballast in comparison to value of lamp fixture.
	4. Defective switch.	4. Replace switch.
	5. Tube not seated correctly in sockets.	5. Reseat tube in sockets.
	6. No power to lamp.	6. Check power circuit.
Lamp glows dimly	1. Defective tube.	1. Replace tube. If lamp has been flashing on and off for extended period, also replace starter.
	2. Defective starter.	2. Replace starter with one of correct wattage.
Tube ends lit but middle dim or dark	1. Wiring incorrect.	1. Check wiring.
	2. Shorted starter.	2. Replace starter with new one of appropriate wattage.
	3. Tube burned out.	3. Replace tube.
Spiraling or flickering lamp	1. Tube burned out.	1. Replace with new fluorescent tube of correct dimensions and wattage.
	2. Defective or wrong starter.	2. Replace starter with one of appropriate wattage.
	3. Low line voltage.	3. Check voltage; it must be within 10 percent of 120 volts.
	4. Wrong ballast.	4. Replace ballast.
Lamp flashes on and off repeatedly	1. Defective tube.	1. Replace tube and starter.
	2. Defective starter.	2. Replace starter with one of appropriate wattage.

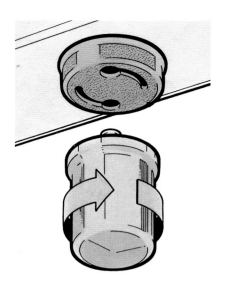

To install a starter in a fluorescent fixture, simply insert the starter and twist it to secure it in its socket.

faulty ballast, deenergize the circuit, disassemble the fixture, transfer wires from the old ballast to the new one—one at a time, to avoid an incorrect connection—and, finally, reassemble the fixture.

If the tube, the starter, and the ballast are all working properly but the lamp still doesn't light, check for a defective switch. If the lamp is controlled by a wall switch, replace the switch, as detailed in the next section. If the lamp has a push-button switch, the old switch can be replaced by a new one of the same type. To deenergize the circuit before working on the switch, remove the circuit's fuse or trip the circuit breaker.

In most cases, the switch screws into a threaded mounting nut on the inside of the lamp. Two wires from the switch are connected, usually with wirenuts, to four wires from the fluorescent tube. Disassemble the fixture as far as necessary to gain access to the back of the switch, then screw

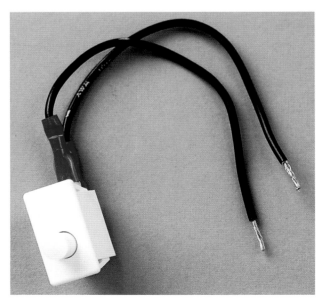

If the lamp is controlled by a push-button switch, the switch can also be replaced. Transfer the wires one at a time from the old switch to the new one.

in the new switch and transfer wires from the old switch to the new one, one at a time to avoid an incorrect connection. Reassemble the fixture, and reenergize the circuit.

If you're considering installing a new ballast or a new switch, consider putting in an entirely new fixture. An old fluorescent fixture suffers the same aging effects that an incandescent fixture does. Of course, you can also replace an old incandescent lamp with a new fluorescent model. Either replacement is well within the capabilities of the do-it-yourselfer. Here's how to install a new fluorescent fixture:

1. Deenergize old fixture. Note that simply turning off wall switch may not deenergize fixture, so be sure to remove circuit's fuse or trip circuit breaker.

2. Remove old hardware that holds existing lamp fixture in place, and disconnect lamp wires from circuit line wires. Then disassemble new fluorescent lamp as far as necessary to gain access to fixture wires.

3. Connect fixture wires to line wires with wirenuts or crimp-type solderless connectors. Match wires by color: white wire to white, black to black.

4. Position fixture against ceiling, and fasten it with screws packaged with new lamp. You may have to reassemble fixture, either before or after mounting it, depending on its style. Restore power.

QUICK DOORBELL FIXES

When your doorbell or door chime doesn't ring, the fault could be in any part of the circuitry—the button, the bell or chime, or the transformer. The transformer is the electrical component that steps down the 110–120-volt current to the 10 to 18 volts at which doorbells and chimes operate. You can work safely on all parts of a doorbell circuit except the transformer without disconnecting the power. If you don't know which part of the circuit is faulty:

1. Remove screws that hold doorbell push button to your house.

2. Pull out button as far as circuit wires allow, then detach wires by loosening terminal screws on button. Bring the two bare wire ends together. If bell rings, you know fault is in button. Install new one by connecting the two wires to terminal screws of new button and reattaching button to your house. Door-

What You'll Need
Screwdriver
Wire stripper with cutting blade
Wirenuts or solderless connectors
Replacement fluorescent fixture

What You'll Need
Screwdriver
Replacement button, bell or chime, or transformer
12-volt circuit tester
110–120-volt circuit tester or continuity tester
Wirenuts or crimp-on connectors

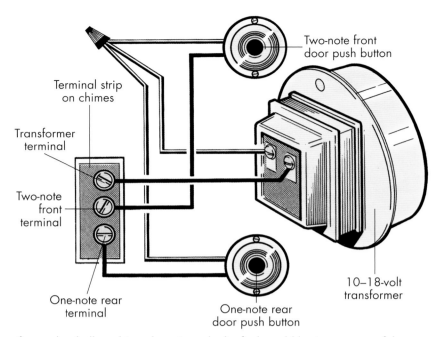

Terminal strip on chimes

Transformer terminal

Two-note front terminal

One-note rear terminal

Two-note front door push button

Two-note front door push button

One-note rear door push button

10–18-volt transformer

If your doorbell or chime doesn't work, the fault could be in any part of the circuitry—from a push button to the bell or chimes to the transformer. Before removing any wires at the terminal strip, it's a good idea to tag them so they can be replaced correctly.

bell button is a single-pole switch (two wires attached), and you can place either wire under either screw.

3. If bell doesn't ring when you bring the two bare wire ends together, fault lies elsewhere—in bell or chime assembly, wiring, or transformer. Remove snap-on cover of bell or chime. Removal may be harder than you expect; there are several different types of covers, and you may have to try several procedures. Try lifting cover slightly upward and then pulling it out. If this doesn't work, pull it straight out without first lifting it up. Or look to see whether snap-on cover is held to bell or

chime assembly with prongs; if so, depress prongs and pull cover to release it. Whatever you do, never pull so hard that you risk damaging decorative cover.

4. Once cover is removed, look for two, three, or more terminals and wires, depending on how many tones ring in your doorbell system. A standard bell or buzzer has two wires. Detach wires by loosening terminal screws, then connect them to 12-volt circuit tester, or attach them to terminal screws on substitute bell or chime. An inexpensive bell or buzzer or a 12-volt car lamp bulb in a socket with two wires can be used for testing purposes. If test bell or buzzer sounds or bulb lights when you push doorbell button, you will have to install new bell or chime.

5. If you have a chime assembly with three or more wires, tag them with masking tape: "T" for transformer, "2" for front door chime, and "1" for the back door chime. Loosen terminal screws, remove all wires, and connect wires labeled "T" and "2" to screw terminals on test bell or bulb. If test bell rings or bulb lights when you push front door button, old chime set is faulty. To check this conclusion, connect wires labeled "T" and "1" to screw terminals on test bell. If bell rings when you push back door button, then you're certain chimes must be replaced.

6. If bell doesn't ring or bulb doesn't light at button or bell box, both are okay. By process of elimination, you now know problem must be in transformer or wiring. You'll usually find transformer mounted on electrical junction

DOORBELL OR CHIME TROUBLESHOOTING CHART

Problem	Possible Cause	Solution
Bell or chime does not ring	1. Defective button.	1. Remove button and touch wires together. If doorbell rings, button is defective; replace button.
	2. Defective bell or chimes.	2. Detach wires from bell or chimes and connect them to a test bell or light. If bulb lights or doorbell rings when button is depressed, bell is defective; replace bell.
	3. Defective transformer.	3. Connect test bell to transformer and press door button. If bell does not ring, transformer is defective; replace transformer.
	4. Loose connection or break in circuit.	4. Trace and check all wiring; tighten loose connections or replace damaged wiring.
	5. No power at transformer.	5. Check to see that circuit is turned on; check for loose connection at transformer primary. If transformer is defective, replace.

box, subpanel, or main entrance panel. Bell wires are attached to exposed terminal screws on transformer. Connect test bell directly to exposed low-voltage transformer terminals; don't touch any other screws. If bell doesn't ring, transformer is defective or not getting power. **Caution:** Transformer is connected directly to power supply, and it carries current that can hurt you. Before working on transformer, deenergize branch circuit that supplies power to transformer. Remove appropriate fuse, trip correct circuit breaker, or throw main switch to shut off all electricity in your home.

7. Before replacing transformer, check to make sure it's getting power from the 110–120-volt circuit. With circuit deenergized, disconnect transformer from line wires. Then turn circuit back on again and touch probes of 110–120-volt circuit tester to bare wire ends. If tester light glows or indicator reads 110–120 volts, circuit is okay.

8. If transformer is defective, deenergize circuit, and remove transformer. Buy replacement transformer of the same voltage and wattage. You can find electrical information stamped on transformer, and you should find installation instructions on package. Follow instructions carefully. Use crimp-on connectors or wirenuts to attach new transformer to circuit line wires of your electrical system. Then connect bell wires to low-voltage screw terminals on transformer, turn power back on, and press doorbell button. If you've installed transformer properly, you should hear bell or chime.

9. If transformer and its power circuit prove to be working, the only possibility left is a break or loose connection somewhere in bell wiring. Trace bell circuit from transformer to bell or chime to push buttons, searching for loose terminal screw or wire joint. If this proves unsuccessful, you'll have to check each segment of circuit with continuity tester.

10. To test each segment of circuit, disconnect bell wires at transformer to deenergize bell circuit. A continuity tester can never be used on an energized circuit. Disconnect transformer wires at bell or chime, and twist them together so they make contact with one another. Go back to transformer and touch probe leads of continuity tester to bare ends of bell wires. If tester lights up or you get a reading on meter dial, circuit has continuity

and there are no breaks or loose connections in line. That part of the circuit is all right. If tester does not register, there's a break somewhere. If that segment is fault-free, go on to next segment and check it the same way.

11. If there is a break, you must try to locate it and make repairs. Sometimes, however, especially where much of the bell circuit wiring is hidden within walls or is otherwise inaccessible, the easiest course of action is to run new segment of bell wire along whatever path is easiest and forget about old wiring segment.

QUICK CEILING FAN FIXES

Replacing a light fixture with a new ceiling fan is an easy process. With just a little more work you can add a new lighting fixture to the bottom of the fan unit. Only basic tools and skills are needed. Here's how:

1. To deenergize circuit, remove appropriate fuse or trip correct circuit breaker. Alternately, you can throw main switch to shut off all electricity in your home.

2. Remove original light fixture from ceiling. Most fixtures are bolted or screwed into ceiling and can be disconnected once cover is removed.

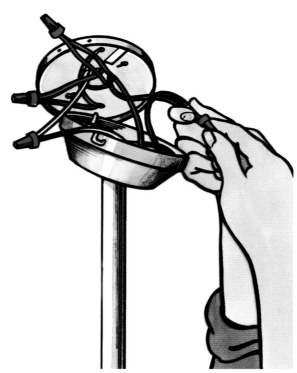

Follow manufacturer's instructions when installing a ceiling fan, but usually you will connect the black wires together, the white wires together, and the bare or green wire to the junction box.

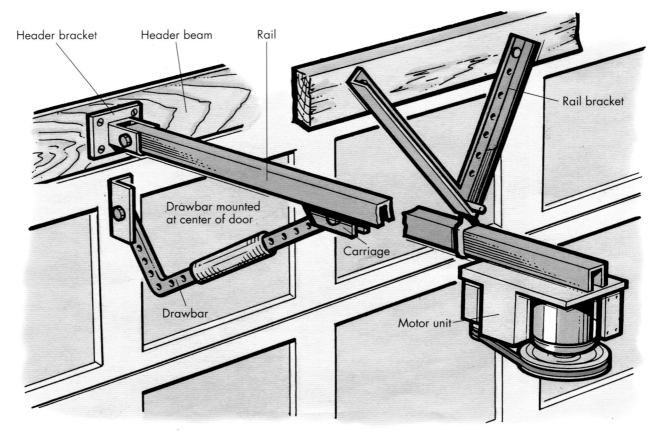

Header bracket   Header beam   Rail

Rail bracket

Drawbar mounted
at center of door

Carriage

Drawbar

Motor unit

The typical garage door opener consists mainly of a reversible motor that drives a carriage along a rail above the door. Attached to the carriage is a drawbar to move the door between its opened and closed positions.

3. Lower fixture, and disconnect wires. Mark each with piece of masking tape for identification later.

4. Review manufacturer's instructions on color coding of wiring and recommended installation procedures. In most homes, there will be two wires in circuit and three in fixture. Connect black wires together and white wires together, then connect remaining ground (bare or green) wire to metal junction box or other location suggested by manufacturer. Use wirenuts to make connections and, once connected, check them for tightness.

5. Check over wiring, reviewing manufacturer's instructions. Then carefully push all wires into junction box.

6. Attach fixture to junction box or hangers as directed by manufacturer.

7. If you're installing light below fan, make sure two parts are of the same brand and designed to work together (this will make process much easier). Remove bottom cover from fan unit, and pull out ends of any loose wires. Follow manufacturer's instructions for connection. Typically that means connect black to black, white to white, and ground to ground.

8. Reenergize circuit and test system.

QUICK GARAGE DOOR OPENER FIXES

Automatic garage door openers are electrical devices that use a motor to move a circular chain that lifts the garage door. The system also has switches and sensors, all electrical devices. Refer to the Garage Door Opener Troubleshooting Chart and the testing and repair methods on page 67.

OTHER QUICK ELECTRICAL FIXES

There are numerous other electrical quick fixes you can perform around your home once you understand how electricity works and how to work safely around it. If you'd like to tackle more electrical repairs, purchase an inexpensive volt-ohmmeter (VOM), and read the instructions. VOMs, also known as multimeters, can test voltage and resistance (measured in ohms). Some also measure electrical current. You can use a VOM to test fuses, batteries, live circuits (carefully), and even fixtures and appliances.

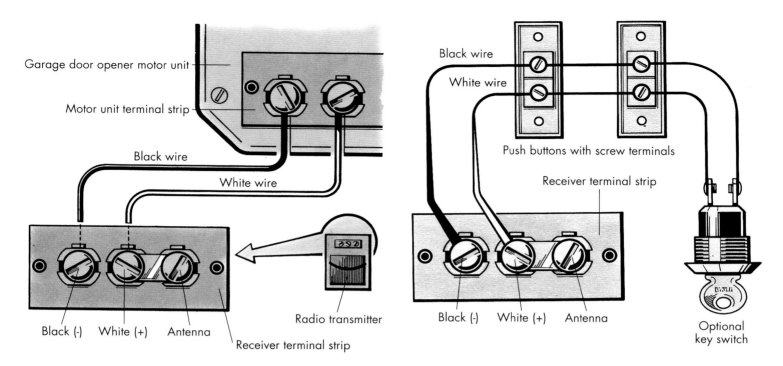

A typical wiring arrangement for connecting a garage door opener's radio receiver to the motor unit.

A typical wiring arrangement for connecting the radio receiver of a garage door opener to one or more manual push buttons and key switch.

GARAGE DOOR OPENER TROUBLESHOOTING CHART

Problem	Possible Cause	Solution
Garage door opener totally inoperative	1. No line power.	1. Test receptacle with a different appliance for power. Check for a blown fuse or a tripped circuit breaker. Make necessary replacement or repairs.
	2. Defective motor.	2. Repair or replace motor.
	3. Motor overload tripped.	3. Reset or wait for automatic reset; check and remedy cause of overload.
Motor hums, but opener will not operate	1. Defective limit reversal operation.	1. Inspect trip mechanism for binding or broken parts. Repair or replace needed parts; relay or switch.
	2. Defective motor capacitor.	2. Replace capacitor.
	3. Damage in carriage drive.	3. Inspect for damage. Make suitable repairs.
Motor runs, but door opener will not operate	1. Broken belt or coupling.	1. Replace belt or coupling.
	2. Broken chain or worm drive.	2. Replace chain or repair worm drive.
	3. Loose setscrew on drive pulley.	3. Tighten setscrew.
Door operates from radio module but not from push button	1. Defective push button.	1. Replace push button.
	2. Defective wiring.	2. Repair wiring to push button.
Door operates from push button but not from radio module	1. Defective receiver.	1. Repair or replace receiver.
	2. Defective module.	2. Repair or replace module.
Door does not completely open or close	1. Incorrect adjustment of limit control device.	1. Adjust the limit control device according to kit instruction.
	2. Door binding.	2. Uncouple door from drawbar. Lower and raise by hand to verify binding. Correct as necessary.
Unit does not shut off when door meets an obstruction (e.g. rock, snow, etc.)	1. Safety limit mechanism inoperative.	1. Inspect unit to determine how safety limit action occurs. Look for defective component or incorrect adjustment. Make necessary repairs or adjustments.

CHAPTER 4

QUICK PLUMBING FIXES

Plumbing follows the basic laws of nature—gravity, pressure, water seeking its own level. Knowing this, you can understand its "mysteries" and make dozens of quick fixes to your home's plumbing system. You can save yourself time, trouble, and money!

UNDERSTANDING THE WATER SUPPLY SYSTEM

The plumbing in your home is composed of two separate subsystems. One subsystem brings freshwater in, and the other takes wastewater out. The water that comes into your home is under pressure. It enters your home under enough pressure to allow it to travel upstairs, around corners, or wherever else it's needed. As water comes into your home, it passes through a meter that registers the amount you use. The main water shutoff, or stop, valve is typically located close to the meter. In a plumbing emergency, it's vital that you quickly close the main shutoff valve. Otherwise, when a pipe bursts, it can flood your house in no time. If the emergency is confined to a sink, tub, or toilet, however, you may not want to turn off your entire water supply. Therefore, most fixtures should have individual stop valves.

Water from the main supply is immediately ready for your cold water needs. The hot water supply, however, requires another step. One pipe carries water from the cold water system to your water heater. From the heater, a hot water line carries the heated water to all the fixtures, out-lets, and appliances that require hot water. A thermostat on the heater maintains the temperature you select by turning the device's heating elements on and off as required. The normal temperature setting for a home water heater is between 140°F and 160°F, but 120°F is usually adequate and is also more economical. Some automatic dishwashers require higher temperature water, though many of these have a water heater within them that boosts the temperature another 20°F.

Whether your home is on a sewer or septic system, the systems within your home are essentially the same. Drainage systems do not depend on pressure, as supply systems do. Instead, waste matter leaves your house because the drainage pipes all pitch, or angle, downward. Gravity pulls the waste along. The sewer line continues this downward flow to a sewage treatment facility or a septic tank.

While the system sounds simple, there's more to it, including vents, traps, and clean outs. The vents sticking up from the roof of your house allow air to enter the drainpipes. If there were no air supply coming from the vents, wastewater would not flow out properly and the water in the traps would need to be be siphoned away.

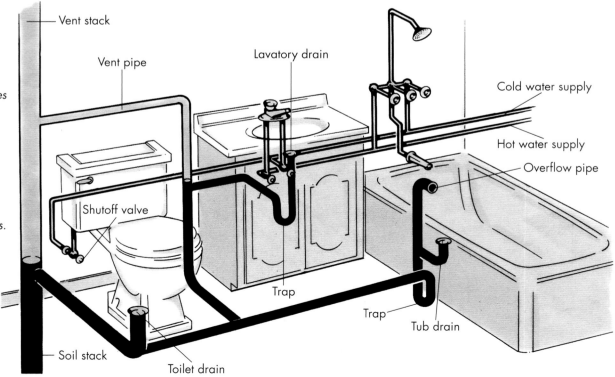

Your home's supply and drainage system must always be two distinct subsystems, with no overlapping. At the fixtures (bridges between the two systems), the air admitted by the vent stack and vent pipes keeps the traps sealed and prevents sewer gases from backing up through the drains.

Vent stack

Vent pipe

Lavatory drain

Cold water supply

Hot water supply

Overflow pipe

Shutoff valve

Trap

Trap

Tub drain

Soil stack

Toilet drain

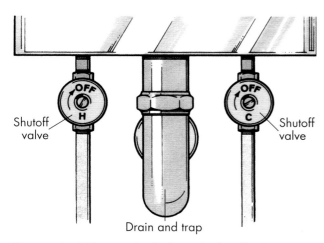

Drain and trap

Shutoff valve

Fixtures should have individual supply shutoff valves so you don't need to close the main shutoff to make repairs at the fixture.

Traps are vital components of the drainage system. You can see a trap under every sink. It is the curved or S-shape section of pipe under a drain. Water flows from the basin with enough force to go through the trap and out through the drainpipe, but enough water stays in the trap afterward to form a seal that prevents sewer gas from backing up into your home. Every fixture must have a trap. Toilets are self-trapped and don't require an additional trap at the drain. Bathtubs frequently have drum traps, not only to form a seal against sewer gas but also to collect hair and dirt in order to prevent clogged drains. Some kitchen sinks have grease traps to collect grease that might otherwise cause clogging. Because grease and hair are generally the causes of drain clogs, traps often have clean-out plugs that give you easier access to remove or break up any blockage.

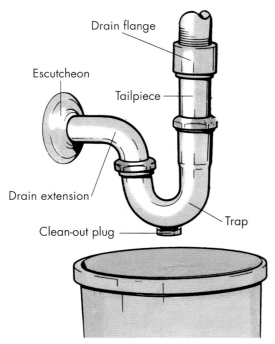

Drain flange

Escutcheon

Tailpiece

Drain extension

Clean-out plug

Trap

Some sink traps have a clean-out plug that enables you to clean the trap without having to remove it from the drain.

Since a drainage system involves all of these components, it is usually referred to as the DWV: the drain-waste-vent system. If water is to flow out freely and waste is to exit properly, all components of the DWV must be present and in good working order. Examine the pipes in the basement or crawl space under your house to help you understand the system better.

The supply and drainage subsystems are two distinct operations, with no overlapping between them. There are bridges between the two, however, and the bridges are what make the plumbing system worth having. In plumbing jargon, any bridge between the supply and drainage systems is a fixture.

Toilets, sinks, and tubs are fixtures. In addition, an outside faucet is a fixture and so is a washing machine. All devices that draw freshwater and discharge wastewater are fixtures, and all are designed to keep the supply and drainage systems strictly segregated.

Some fixtures have individual supply shutoff valves so you don't need to close the main shutoff to repair them. It's a good idea to make sure everyone in the family knows the location of the main shutoff valve in your house as well as how to use it. You may want to tag the main shutoff valve so anyone can easily find it.

Before you embark on any quick plumbing fixes, always turn off the water supply to the fixture or the main shutoff. In addition, check with your local plumbing code official before you add or change any pipe in your house. You will learn what is allowed and what is prohibited and whether or not a homeowner is allowed to do his or her own work.

Troubleshooting plumbing problems is relatively easy. To help you determine the cause of a plumbing problem, review the troubleshooting charts on pages 70, 71, and 83 for assistance. Once you've found the probable causes of the problem, refer to the corresponding quick fixes in this chapter.

QUICK CLOG FIXES

There's no magic involved in clearing a slow drain. You can easily perform this and other quick plumbing fixes using basic tools and knowledge. But it's best to clear a drain as soon as you notice it is slowing down so you don't end up with a totally stopped-up system. Besides, who wants to wait for a slow drain to empty?

SINK, TUB, AND DRAIN TROUBLESHOOTING CHART

Problem	Possible Cause	Solution
Faucet drips	1. Faulty washer.	1. Replace washer. For single-handled faucet, install all parts in repair kit.
	2. Uneven valve seat.	2. Use valve seat grinder to even seat, or replace seat.
	3. Worn stem or cartridge parts.	3. Replace stem assembly.
Hot water slows to trickle	1. Washer expands when hot.	1. Replace with proper nonexpanding washer.
Leaks around faucet handle	1. Packing nut loose.	1. Tighten packing unit.
	2. Inadequate packing.	2. Replace packing.
Leaks around faucet spout	1. Faulty O-ring.	1. Replace O-ring.
Faucet makes noise	1. Wrong size washer.	1. Replace washer with one of proper size.
	2. Washer loose.	2. Tighten washer on stem.
	3. Valve seat clogged.	3. Clean residue from valve seat.
	4. Pipes too small or clogged.	4. Replace or clear pipes.
	5. Stem threads binding against threads in faucet body.	5. Lubricate stem threads or replace stem.
	6. Stem or body threads damaged.	6. Replace stem or faucet.
Moisture under fixture	1. Leaking trap joints.	1. Tighten trap slip nuts or clean-out plug.
	2. Leaking trap.	2. Replace trap.
	3. Leaking connections at fixture.	3. Tighten, or disassemble and repair.
	4. Leaking connections at shutoff valves.	4. Tighten, or disassemble and repair.
	5. Leaking seal at fixture drain.	5. Remove, clean, and reseal drain flange.
	6. Caulking seal around fixture rim faulty— splash water seeping.	6. Remove fixture as necessary and recaulk.
Spray hose does not function properly	1. Spray head body or level malfunction.	1. Replace spray head.
	2. Spray head aerator clogged.	2. Disassemble and clean aerator.
	3. Hose damaged or connection loose.	3. Repair or replace hose; tighten connections.
	4. Hose clogged.	4. Remove blockage; replace hose, if necessary.
	5. Diverter valve clogged or damaged.	5. Disassemble and clean valve; if necessary, replace valve.
Showerhead leaks	1. Connection at arm loose or corroded.	1. Tighten; or remove head from arm, clean, coat with plumbers' joint compound, and retighten.
	2. Swivel connection O-ring or other seal in poor condition.	2. Replace O-ring or other seal and retighten.
Showerhead water flow restricted	1. Showerhead clogged.	1. Disassemble and clean head.
Showerhead adjustment handle binds or does not operate	1. Internal cam broken or other mechanical damage.	1. Replace showerhead.
Drain overflowing	1. Pipes or trap clogged.	1. Use plunger or auger to clear pipes or trap.
Drain sluggish, with sucking noises	1. Drain flow restricted.	1. Clean drain.
	2. Vent restricted.	2. Clean vent.
	3. Improper venting.	3. Install new vent or larger vent.

CLEARING CLOGGED DRAINS

Clogged drains need quick attention. Everyone knows the inconvenience and mess that accompany a sluggish drain. Even so, many people wait until the drain stops completely before they take corrective action. Sometimes a clog can be cleared with a simple homemade remedy.

If you have a moderately clogged drain, try this homemade drain cleaner: Pour ½ cup of baking soda down the drain followed by ½ cup of vinegar. Be careful. The two ingredients interact with foaming and fumes, so replace the drain cover loosely. Let the concoction set for about three hours before running water.

If you know the slow drain is from grease, try this treatment: Pour in ½ cup of salt and ½ cup of baking soda followed by a teakettle of boiling water. Allow to sit overnight.

If the homemade drain cleaners don't work, try the following steps.

1. Cover overflow opening in basin or tub with wet cloth. Most kitchen sinks don't have an overflow vent, but, if you're working on one of two side-by-side basins, plug the other basin's drain opening with wet cloths. In homes that have two bathrooms back to back in adjacent rooms, both may be connected to the same drain. In such cases you must block the other basin at both its drain and overflow vent. Shower facilities seldom have overflow vents; bathtubs do. Cover all of them with wet cloths for plunger to work properly.

2. Fill clogged basin with enough water to cover head of plunger. Coat lip of plunger with petroleum jelly (this helps create better seal). Slide plunger's cup over drain opening, then rapidly pump plunger up and down. You

What You'll Need
Wet cloths
Plunger
Petroleum jelly
Commercial drain opener
Drain-and-trap auger
Bucket
Wire coat hanger
Stiff brush

PIPE TROUBLESHOOTING CHART

Problem	Possible Cause	Solution
Leaking pipe	1. Joint not watertight.	1. Tighten threaded joint, if possible. Apply epoxy paste to joint. Have a plumber disassemble and resolder sweat-soldered joint in copper pipe or tubing or cut out and replace joint in plastic pipe.
	2. Hole in pipe.	2. Repair by patching hole, using best available method, or replace section of pipe. If section is inaccessible, a plumber can disconnect it from system and route new section of pipe.
	3. Burst pipe.	3. Immediately turn off water at main shutoff. Repair or replace pipe or joint. Avoid electrical shock due to contact between electrical devices or equipment and water.
Pipe drips, but there is no leak	1. Condensation.	1. Apply insulation to pipe.
Noise in pipes—hot water only	1. Steam causing rumbling in hot water pipes.	1. Turn down thermostat setting on water heater or replace thermostat.
	2. Pipe creaks against surroundings from expansion and contraction.	2. Rehang pipe on slip hangers or in larger notches or holes.
Water makes sucking noise when draining	1. Improper venting.	1. Clean roof vent. If there is no vent, add antisiphon trap.
Hammering noise when water is shut off	1. Air chambers waterlogged.	1. Shut off and drain supply line to allow air to reenter air chambers.
	2. No air chamber.	2. Install air chamber.
Banging noise while water is running	1. Loose pipe.	1. Track down loose pipe and brace, cushion, or strap it.
No water supply	1. Frozen pipes.	1. Open faucets. Start thawing at closest point to faucet and work back.
	2. Main shutoff valve closed.	2. Open main shutoff valve.
	3. Broken or closed main.	3. Call water department.
	4. Well pump failure.	4. Check and repair pump.

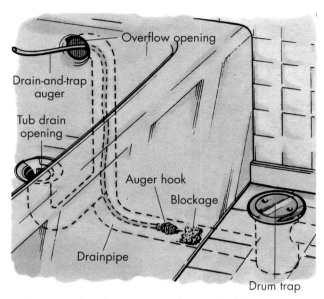

should feel water move in and out of drain. It is this back-and-forth water pressure that can eventually build up enough force to dislodge whatever is blocking drain. After about a dozen firm strikes, jerk plunger up quickly. Water should rush out. If it doesn't, try same procedure two or three more times before attempting another method.

To unclog a sink drain, cover the plunger's rubber cup with water and plug the fixture's vent opening with wet rags.

3. If plunger doesn't remove clog, consider using chemical drain opener. For drain that's completely blocked, however, it's best not to use chemicals, as they contain caustic agents that can actually harm some fixtures. Instead, use drain-and-trap auger. To use it, remove pop-up stopper or strainer from clogged drain and insert auger wire into opening. As you feed flexible wire in, crank handle of device, loosening and then tightening thumbscrew on handle as you advance wire. If wire encounters something, move it back and forth while you turn auger handle. Then continue to turn handle while slowly withdrawing auger.

4. If auger doesn't clear drain, remove clean-out plug from under sink, catching water from trap in bucket. You can use wire coat hanger with hook shape in one end to try to reach clog. If this fails, insert wire of drain-and-trap auger through clean out. Work wire toward basin and drainpipe to remove blockage.

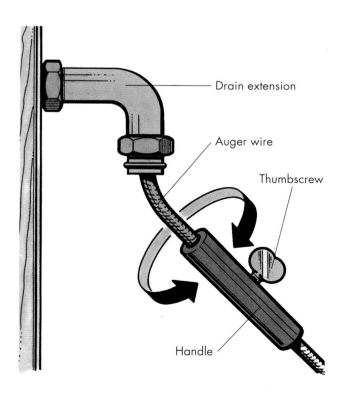

If the clog is not in the fixture's trap, insert a drain-and-trap auger into the drain extension that goes into the wall, and work the auger into the drainpipe.

5. If trap does not have clean out, remove trap following procedure outlined on page 74. With trap removed, clean it out with wire coat hanger and then with stiff brush and hot soapy water; replace trap. If clog wasn't in trap, insert drain-and-trap auger into drain extension that goes into wall and continue working auger down into drainpipe itself. You should be able to reach blockage, unless it's in section of main drain.

A clog near the tub's drain can be attacked from several places—the overflow opening (as shown), the tub drain opening, or the drum trap. Start working at the tub drain. If you can't remove the obstruction there, move onto the overflow and then the drum trap.

6. If bathtub drain is clogged and plunger doesn't clear it, use drain-and-trap auger first through tub drain opening. If this doesn't work, remove overflow plate and insert auger directly into overflow pipe and down into drainpipe.

For floor drains, such as those in basements and showers, a garden hose can be effective in unclogging drains, especially if the clog is not close to the opening. Attach the hose to a faucet, feed the hose into the drain as far as it will go, and jam rags around the hose at the opening. Then turn the water on full force for a few moments.

If you suspect a clog is in the main drainpipe, locate the main clean out. This is a Y-shape fitting near the bottom of your home's soil stack or where the drain leaves the building. Set a large pail or container under the clean out, and spread plenty of papers and rags around the site to soak up the backed-up water. Using a pipe wrench, slowly unscrew the clean-out plug counterclockwise, trying to control the flow of water that will seep from the clean out. Once the flow has stopped and you've cleaned up the flooded site, insert the auger to remove the debris.

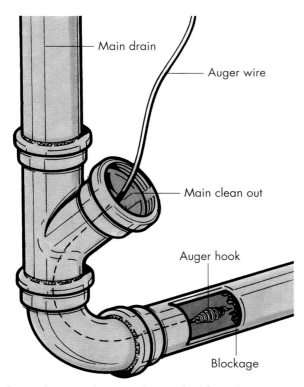

A clog in the main drain can be reached from the main clean out, which is the Y-shape fitting near the bottom of your home's soil stack or where the drain leaves the building.

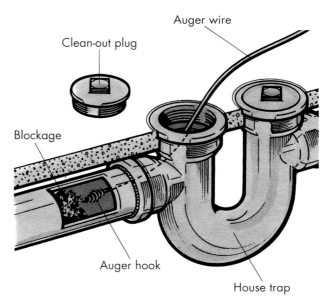

The house trap is a U-shape fitting installed underground. You can locate it by finding two adjacent clean-out plugs in the basement floor. A blockage between the trap and the main clean out can be reached by removing the plug closest to the main clean out.

If you still haven't located the blockage, another place you can try is the house trap. This is a U-shape fitting installed underground. You can locate it by finding two adjacent clean-out plugs in the floor, if the main drain runs under the floor. Again, place papers and rags around the site before opening the clean out nearest to the sewer outside. If the clog is in the house trap or between the trap and the main clean out, you should be able to remove it. But if the water starts to flow out of the trap as you unscrew it, check quickly beyond the house trap with an auger. If you can remove the clog rapidly, do so. Otherwise, replace the trap plug and call in a professional to do the job.

There is one type of drain clog that will not respond satisfactorily to a plunger or an auger. This is when the main drain outside the building or a floor drain in the basement gets stopped up from tree roots that have grown in at the joints. The most effective solution in this case is a power auger or an electric rooter, which is inserted into the pipe and cuts away roots from the pipe walls as it moves along. You can rent a power auger at a home improvement or tool rental store. Feed the auger cable into the clean-out opening closest to the blockage. When the device's cutting head encounters roots, you should be able to feel the cable strain. Keep feeding the cable slowly until you feel a breakthrough, then go over the area once again.

Remove the cable slowly, and run water from a garden hose through the pipe to wash away the root cuttings. Before you return the power auger to the rental firm, replace the clean-out plug, and flush a toilet several times. When you're sure the drain is clear of tree roots, clean the cable.

PREVENTING CLOGGED DRAINS

You can keep your drains clog-free and odorless by using the following homemade noncorrosive drain cleaner weekly. Combine 1 cup baking soda, 1 cup table salt, and ¼ cup cream of tartar. Stir ingredients together thoroughly and pour into a clean, covered jar. Pour ¼ cup of mixture into drain, and immediately add 1 cup boiling water. Wait 10 seconds, then flush with cold water. Flushing weekly with a generous amount of boiling water also works well.

REPLACING TRAP

Directly beneath the drain outlet of every kitchen sink and every bathroom lavatory is a trap. This element is vital not only to the proper functioning of the drainage system but also to your health and safety. Each trap contains and maintains a plug of water within its curved section that seals against the entrance of harmful sewer gases. If the trap leaks, this water barrier may disappear and create a hazardous situation. All traps must be kept in proper working order. Restrictions and clogging are immediately noticeable because the drainage flow is slowed or stopped. Clearing the blockage takes care of the problem. Leakage or seepage can often go undetected for a while, so check your traps from time to time and make quick repairs if anything seems wrong.

Trap assemblies have several parts. The short piece of pipe that extends downward from the drain outlet flange in the sink or lavatory is called the tailpiece. The curved section of pipe connected to the tailpiece is the trap itself. The trap may be either one piece or two coupled sections. The piece of pipe extending from the end of the trap to the drainpipe outlet in the wall or floor is the drain extension. All of these pieces may be made of rather thin metal that is subject to corrosion, seal failure, and mechanical damage. Damage can also result from reaming with a plumbers' auger. Whatever the reason for failure, a malfunctioning trap should be repaired immediately.

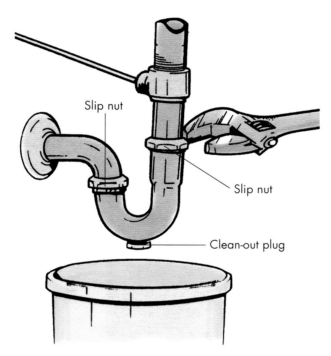

To remove the drain trap, unscrew the slip nuts with a wrench and slide them out of the way.

Sometimes the problem is simply that the slip nuts holding the trap assembly to the drain and the drainpipe have loosened. Tightening them may solve the problem. But if the metal has corroded through, if the slip-nut threads are damaged, or if other damage has occurred, the only solution is replacement. Trap assemblies and parts to fit just about any possible installation requirement are readily available at most hardware and all plumbing supply stores. Chrome-plated thin-wall brass traps are popular, especially where appearance is important. Polypropylene (PP)

plastic traps, notable for their ruggedness and longevity, will outperform all other types. ABS plastic traps are also in use, but they become deformed and eventually fail when forced to handle frequent passage of boiling water and caustic household chemicals. In addition, they may not be allowed by your local plumbing code. Ask the plumbing clerk at your local building materials retailer for recommendations.

Whatever the material, there are typically two trap diameters: 1½-inch traps for kitchen sinks and 1¼-inch traps for lavatories. Take the old trap with you when you buy the new one; if possible, also take the old tailpiece and drain extension. In most cases, trap replacement is simple. Here's how:

1. If trap is equipped with clean-out plug on bottom of curved section, remove plug with wrench and let water in trap drain into bucket. Otherwise, unscrew slip nuts and slide them out of the way.

> **What You'll Need**
> Wrench
> Bucket
> Screwdriver
> Replacement trap
>   or other parts
> Plumbers' joint
>   compound or tape

2. If trap is a swivel type, curved trap section(s) will come free. However, keep trap upright as you remove it, and pour water out after part is free. If trap is fixed and does not swivel, remove tailpiece slip nut at drain flange and slip nut at top of trap. Shove tailpiece down into trap itself, then twist trap clockwise until you can drain water in trap. Pull tailpiece free, and unscrew trap from drain extension or drainpipe.

3. Buy trap of proper diameter, new tailpiece, drain extension, or other fittings, as necessary. A swivel trap is the easiest to work with because it can be easily adjusted for angled or misaligned drainpipe/fixture installations. A clean-out plug on a trap is handy so trap can be cleaned out without removing it.

4. Replace parts in appropriate order, making sure you have slip nuts and compression seals, or large washers, lined up on the proper pipe sections. Couple parts together loosely with slip nuts, make final adjustments for correct pipe alignment, and tighten nuts snugly but not too tight. Plumbers' joint tape or compound is not usually necessary, but you can use either.

5. Run water into new trap immediately, both to check for leaks and to fill trap with water to provide that all-important barrier against sewer gases.

QUICK LEAK FIXES

A dripping faucet is the most common plumbing problem as well as one of the easiest to repair. Yet many people ignore it and leave the dripping faucet unrepaired. That costs money! A steady drip can waste $20 or more in water in a short time. Multiply that figure by the number of faucet drips in your home, and you can calculate how much of your money is literally going down the drain. The waste from a dripping hot water faucet is even more because you're also paying to heat the water before it goes down the drain.

What's the solution? A drip is caused by seepage from the water supply. Remember the water supply enters your home under pressure, so there must be a watertight seal holding back the incoming water when the faucet handle is in the OFF position. That seal is usually created by a washer pressed tightly against the faucet seat. Obviously, when the washer or the seat is not functioning properly, a little water can seep through and drip out of the faucet spout. To stop the drip, all you usually have to do is replace the washer or repair the seat.

The first thing to do when fixing a faucet drip is to turn off the water supply. You should be able to turn off the supply at a nearby shutoff, but, if your house is not equipped with shutoffs for individual fixtures, you'll have to go to the main shutoff and turn off the entire water supply to your home.

COMPRESSION-TYPE FAUCETS

No matter what the faucet looks like, whether it has separate handles for hot and cold water or just one that operates both hot and cold, it operates according to certain basic principles. Here's how to disassemble a faucet and stop a drip:

1. Shut off water supply, and remove faucet handle held to main body of faucet by unscrewing tiny screw on top or at back of handle. Some screws are hidden by metal or plastic button or disc that snaps out or is threaded. Once you get button out, you'll see top-mounted handle screw. If necessary, use penetrating oil, such as WD-40, to help loosen it.

What You'll Need
Screwdriver
Penetrating oil
Slip-joint pliers or
    adjustable wrench
Replacement washers

2. Remove handle, and look at faucet assembly. Remove packing nut with large pair of slip-

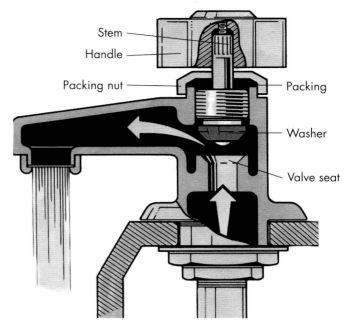

A typical compression-type stem faucet is closed by a washer when the handle is turned. Most leaks are caused by faulty washers.

joint pliers or adjustable wrench, being careful not to scar metal. Twist out stem or spindle by turning it in the same direction you would to turn on faucet.

3. Remove screw that holds washer. Use penetrating oil, if necessary, to loosen screw. Examine screw and stem, replacing if damaged.

4. Replace old washer with an exact replacement. Washers that almost fit will almost stop the drip. Also note whether old washer is beveled or flat, and replace it with one that is identical. Washers designed only for cold water expand greatly when they get hot, thereby closing the opening and slowing the flow of hot water. Some washers will work for either, but you should make sure the ones you buy are exact replacements.

5. Fasten new washer to the stem, and reinstall assembly in faucet. Turn stem clockwise. With stem in place, put packing nut back on. Be careful not to scar metal with wrench.

6. Reinstall handle and replace button or disc. Turn water supply back on, and check for leaks.

REPAIRING FAUCET VALVE SEAT

If a faucet still drips after you've replaced a washer, there may be something wrong with the faucet valve seat. A defective washer may have allowed the metal stem to grind against the seat and leave it uneven, or chemicals in the water may have built up a residue that now prevents the washer from fitting tightly against the valve seat.

What do you do to repair a bad faucet seat? Of course, you can replace the entire faucet. Another option is to replace the seat. Removal of the old valve seat is fairly simple if you have the right tool, called a seat wrench. Insert the seat wrench into the seat and turn it counterclockwise. Once you get the old seat out, be sure the replacement seat you buy is an exact duplicate. If the valve seat is impossible to remove, insert a seat sleeve that slides into place in the old seat and provides a tight seal.

Two types of seat grinders, or dressers, for evening out a worn valve seat.

Another option is to use a valve seat grinder, or dresser, which is an inexpensive tool that will even out a worn seat. Be careful not to use this tool too long or with too much force because the seat is made of soft metal, and you can grind too much of it away quite easily.

To use a dresser, remove the faucet stem and insert the seat grinder down to the valve seat in the faucet body. Using moderate pressure, turn the tool clockwise a few times. Then clean the valve seat with a cloth to remove any metal shavings.

REPLACING FAUCET PACKING

A drip occurs when the faucet is turned off; a faucet leak occurs when the water is running. If you see water coming out around the handle, you have a faucet leak. The first thing to do is make sure the faucet's packing nut is tight, but be careful not to scratch the nut with pliers or a wrench. If you find that a loose nut is not causing the leak, you should replace the packing. Faucet packing can be a solid piece of packing consisting of one or more rubber O-rings, or it can resemble string or soft wire wrapped around the stem under the packing nut. To replace faucet packing:

1. Shut off water supply; remove faucet handle.

2. Loosen packing nut and slip both nut and old packing up off stem.

What You'll Need
Adjustable wrenches
Replacement faucet
  packing
Petroleum jelly

3. Install new packing. If you use stringlike packing material, wrap a few turns around stem. Packing that resembles soft wire is wrapped around stem only once. Before you finish reassembling faucet, smear light coat of petroleum jelly on threads of stem and on threads of packing nut.

REPLACING O-RING

Kitchen faucets have one or more O-rings to prevent water from oozing out around the spout. If the ring wears out, you'll see water at the base of the spout every time you turn on the water. To replace an O-ring:

1. Shut off water supply, and remove threaded coupling nut that holds spout in place by turning it counterclockwise. Be sure to wrap nut with tape to prevent it from being scratched by pliers or wrench.

What You'll Need
Adjustable wrenches
Plumbers' joint tape
Replacement
  O-ring(s)

2. With coupling nut removed, work spout up and out of its socket, where you will find ring(s).

3. Replace any defective rings with new rings of the exact same size. Reassemble faucet.

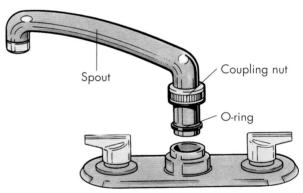

Spout

Coupling nut

O-ring

Kitchen faucets contain one or more O-rings to prevent water from oozing out around the spout. Worn O-rings can be replaced easily.

OTHER TYPES OF FAUCETS

Some faucets use rubber diaphragms instead of washers to control the flow of water. If you have this type of faucet, you may have to remove the faucet stem from the faucet body with a pair of pliers. Be sure to wrap the top of the stem with plumbers' joint tape to protect it from the teeth of the pliers. The rubber diaphragm covers the bottom of the stem, and you may have to pry it off with a screwdriver. Make sure the replacement diaphragm fits snugly over the base of the stem before you reassemble the faucet.

Another type of faucet uses a rubber seat ring that acts like a washer. To remove the ring from the stem, hold the end of the faucet stem with pliers while you unscrew the threaded center piece that holds the seat ring in place. Remove the sleeve to insert the new seat ring, but be sure the seat ring's lettering faces the threaded part of the stem.

Cartridge-type stem faucets may have a spring and a rubber washer. To replace these, lift the cartridge out of the faucet body and remove the washer and spring. Insert the new spring and washer, and carefully align the cartridge so it fits correctly into the slots in the faucet body when reassembling it.

There are also faucets with washers that have the faucet seat built into the stem itself. This type of assembly lifts off the base in a removable sleeve, which contains the valve seat. Unscrew the stem nut from the base of the stem and remove the metal washer and the washer retainer, which contains a rubber washer. Insert the new washer—bevel side up—into the washer retainer.

One type of faucet doesn't have washers at all. It works by means of two metal discs. Turning the faucet on aligns holes in the discs and allows water to flow through the faucet. If something goes wrong with this type of faucet, the valve assembly usually must be replaced.

Single-lever faucets are easy to fix, too, but there are so many different types that you must buy a specific repair kit for the faucet you have. Generally, a faucet company makes repair kits for its products and includes detailed instructions and diagrams with the replacement parts. The most difficult part of repairing a single-lever faucet may be tracking down the hardware dealer or plumbing supply store that carries the appropriate kit. Once you have the kit, however, you should have little difficulty eliminating the leak. Make sure the water supply is shut off before disassembling the faucet, and follow the kit's instructions carefully.

You can avoid having the teeth of the wrench scar a chrome-plated plumbing fixture during installation or repair by wrapping the fixture with a double layer of plastic electrical tape.

If a dripping faucet is getting on your nerves before the plumber arrives or before you have time to fix it yourself, tie a 2-foot-long string around the nozzle, and drop the string's end into the drain. As the faucet drips, the drops will run silently down the string.

SILENCING NOISY FAUCETS

Faucets can scream, whistle, or chatter when you turn them on or off. There are several possible causes for these ear-shattering phenomena. If your house is newly built, you may have pipes that are too small to allow the water to pass through them properly. Similarly, pipes in older homes can become restricted by the formation of scale, indicated by a noisy faucet. In either case, you must replace the pipes to get rid of the noise, which is not really a quick fix.

Most likely, however, your noisy faucet is caused by a washer that is either the wrong size or is not held securely to the stem. Turn off the water supply before starting on this or any other faucet repair job. Replacing the washer or tightening it should eliminate the noise. If the faucet still makes noise, check the washer seat. The seat can become partially closed with residue, and the restricted water flow can cause whistling or chattering. If this is the case, clean the seat.

A squealing noise heard when you turn the faucet handle means the metal threads of the stem are binding against the faucet's threads. Remove the stem, and coat both sets of threads with petroleum jelly. The lubrication should stop the noise and make the handle easier to turn. Of course, if the stem threads or faucet body threads have become worn, the resulting play between them causes vibration and noise in the faucet. In this case, you'll need more than just lubrication to quiet the faucet. Install a new stem, and see if the noise stops. If not, the faucet body threads are worn, and the only solution is a completely new faucet. Fortunately, the stem usually wears first. But even if you must replace the entire faucet, the job is fairly easy.

REPLACING FAUCETS

Replacing a faucet requires a little more work than just changing a washer or putting in a new faucet valve seat. Fortunately, new faucet units are made for do-it-yourself installation with easy-to-follow instructions included. A new faucet can work wonders for the appearance of your fixtures and will also eliminate all the leaks, drips, and other problems you may have had with your old faucet.

Make sure whatever faucet unit you choose will completely cover the old faucet's mounting holes. If you have an unusual sink in your home, look for an adjustable faucet unit that is designed to fit many types of sinks. Once you select the faucet model you want, follow these steps to install it properly:

What You'll Need
Adjustable or basin wrenches
Plumbers' putty
Replacement faucet or other parts

1. Turn off hot and cold water supplies to sink faucets. Loosen nuts with adjustable wrench or basin wrench, and disconnect faucets from water supply pipes under sink.

2. If old assembly has spray head and hose, remove spray head mounting nut under sink. Also disconnect hose from its spout connection.

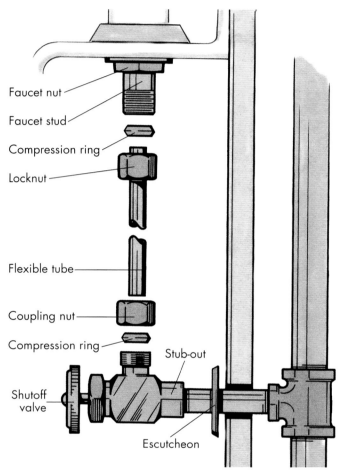

Faucet nut
Faucet stud
Compression ring
Locknut
Flexible tube
Coupling nut
Compression ring
Stub-out
Shutoff valve
Escutcheon

The faucet is secured to the sink by a nut under the basin. The water supply line is usually connected to the faucet with a threaded compression fitting.

3. Remove old faucet assembly from sink, then clean sink around faucet mounting area.

4. Before you install new faucet, apply plumbers' putty around its base. If gaskets are supplied with faucet for this purpose, putty is not necessary.

5. If new faucet has spray hose, attach hose. Run spray hose down through its opening in faucet assembly, through its opening in sink, and up through sink's center opening. Then attach hose to supply stub on faucet.

6. Install new faucet assembly into mounting holes in sink. With new faucet assembly in

position, place washers and nuts on assembly's mounting studs under sink and hand-tighten them, making sure assembly is in proper position and any gaskets are correctly aligned. Then further tighten nuts with basin wrench.

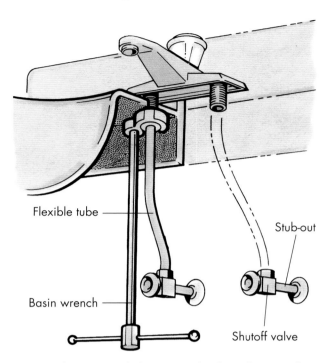

Flexible tube
Stub-out
Basin wrench
Shutoff valve

Because there is very little room under the sink, you will probably need a basin wrench to tighten the coupling nuts.

7. Align and connect original water supply lines with flexible supply tubes coming from new faucet. Make sure hot water and cold water lines are connected to proper supply tubes on faucet assembly. When you attach lines, be sure to use two wrenches. One holds fitting while the other turns nut on water supply line.

8. Turn on hot and cold water supplies to fixture. Run both hot and cold water full force to clear supply lines and to check fixture for leaks. If there's any evidence of leakage, go back over procedure to check for loose or improper connections.

A bathroom sink faucet can be replaced using the same procedures. One difference may be the presence of a pop-up drain plug that's connected by a linkage to a knob or plunger on the old faucet assembly. There should be one or two places in the linkage where it can be easily disconnected from the faucet before removing the original unit from the basin. Instructions provided with the new faucet will tell you exactly how to connect the new drain assembly. Be sure to reconnect the drain linkage when installing the new faucet.

Replacing a shower or tub faucet is not usually a quick fix because the connections are made

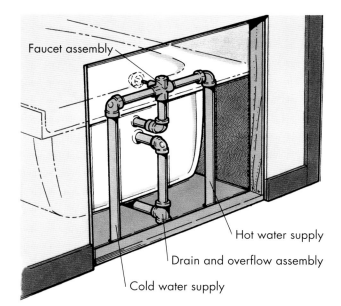

Faccet assembly

Hot water supply

Drain and overflow assembly

Cold water supply

Replacing tub faucets can be complicated because the connections are behind a wall. However, there may be an access panel so you can reach the connections.

1. Remove aerator, and disassemble it.

2. Backflush screens and perforated disc with strong stream of water, being careful not to let parts get washed down drain.

3. Dry all parts, then brush them gently with fine-bristled but fairly stiff brush. Mineral deposits can sometimes be removed by soaking parts in vinegar or by scraping deposits with penknife.

4. Reassemble aerator, making sure you get all parts positioned in proper order and direction.

behind a wall. However, there may be an access panel so you can get at the pipes without ripping the wall apart. If you have to cut into the wall and want to tackle this project, be sure to add an access panel for future pipe and faucet repairs.

Once you get to the tub faucet connections behind the wall, the job is no harder than working on your kitchen sink. Shut off the water supply, remove the faucet handle on the tub side, then disconnect the old faucet unit from the back. If there's an old showerhead pipe, unscrew it from its pipe inside the wall; do the same thing with the tub spout. Now you're ready to install all the new parts. Follow the directions that are included with the new assembly.

REPAIRING SPRAY HOSE

Many modern sink faucets are fitted with spray hose units, and these units occasionally leak or malfunction. The assembly has a diverter valve within the spout body, a flexible hose connected to the spout under the sink, and a spray head with an activating lever and an aerator assembly. The spray head body and lever are part of a sealed unit; if it malfunctions, the unit must be replaced with an identical unit. Other parts of the spray system, however, can be repaired.

REPAIRING AERATOR The aerator portion of the spray head is similar to a faucet aerator. If aeration is inadequate or water squirts off at various angles, the aerator screen has become clogged with sediment or mineral deposits and must be cleaned. To repair an aerator:

What You'll Need
Adjustable wrenches
Clean cloth
Fine-bristled
 stiff brush
Vinegar
Penknife

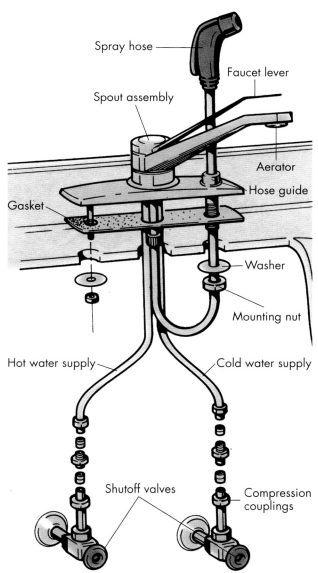

Spray hose

Faucet lever

Spout assembly

Aerator

Hose guide

Gasket

Washer

Mounting nut

Hot water supply

Cold water supply

Shutoff valves

Compression couplings

A spray hose is attached under the sink at the base of the spout assembly. The entire spray assembly can be removed from the top of the sink by unscrewing it and pulling it out through the hose guide.

REPAIRING FLEXIBLE HOSE Water dripping off the flexible hose beneath the sink indicates a leak at the hose-to-spout connection, the hose-to-spray-head connection, or somewhere in the hose itself. To repair the hose:

1. Dry hose thoroughly, and check head connection. If leak is at this point, tighten connec-

What You'll Need
Clean cloth
Adjustable wrenches
Plumbers' joint
 compound or tape
Vinyl electrical tape

tion, disassemble and make repairs, or replace head and hose assembly.

2. Check spout connection under sink. Tightening may stop leak here.

3. If leak continues, disconnect hose, apply plumbers' joint compound or wrap plumbers' joint tape around threads, and reconnect hose. The easiest way to spot leak in hose is to inspect it inch by inch under strong light while water is running through it. Look particularly for tiny cracks, chafes, or indications of some mechanical damage. Temporary repairs can be made by wrapping slightly damaged section of hose with vinyl electrical tape, but replacement of the hose will probably be necessary eventually.

CHECKING DIVERTER VALVE Uneven water flow, low pressure when the pressure at other faucets seems all right, or troublesome switching back and forth from spray head to sink spout can be caused by a malfunctioning diverter valve or by a restricted hose. To check the diverter valve:

1. Remove spray head at coupling, and disconnect coupling from hose by prying off snapring retainer.

What You'll Need
Adjustable wrenches
Wire coat hanger
Replacement hose

2. Turn on water and let strong stream of water flow into hose. If strong stream of water flows out of open end of hose, then you know diverter valve is the source of the trouble. A weak stream flowing from open end of hose may indicate blockage in hose itself. Briefly running water full force may clear hose.

3. If above steps don't locate problem, remove hose from spout attachment, stretch it out straight, and look through it while aiming it toward strong light source. If hose appears to be clear, problem lies in diverter valve. If hose is blocked, clear it with wire coat hanger or length of wire.

4. As needed, replace hose. If you can't get exact replacement, adapters are available for connecting other types and sizes.

SERVICING DIVERTER VALVE

1. Remove sink spout by loosening screw on top, unscrewing threaded spout ring or nut, and lifting spout out of its socket to expose valve. Some valves are just set in place and can be lifted straight out by gripping them with pliers; others are secured by screw. If there is a screw, turn it enough to free valve. If possible, disassemble valve.

What You'll Need
Screwdriver
Pliers
Pipe wrench
Toothpicks
Replacement valve

2. Flush all parts with water, and clean all surfaces and apertures with toothpicks. Don't use metal tools, as they could damage the unit.

3. Reassemble and reinstall valve, then test unit. If it still operates poorly, you will probably have to replace valve. Replacement must be exact, so take faucet manufacturer's name and unit model number or old valve with you when you buy new valve.

FIXING SHOWERHEAD

Showerheads are subject to several problems. Leaks can occur where the head connects to the shower arm or between the showerhead body and the swivel ball. If the arm connection leaks:

1. Unscrew shower arm from pipe with strap wrenches. If you use different wrench, tape pipe to avoid scratching it.

What You'll Need
Adjustable wrenches
or strap wrenches
Plumbers' joint
compound or tape

2. Clean arm threads and coat them with plumbers' joint compound or wrap plumbers' joint tape around them.

3. Screw head back on and hand-tighten it. Remove any excess compound or tape.

FIXING LEAK AT SWIVEL

1. Unscrew showerhead from swivel-ball ring.

What You'll Need
Adjustable wrenches
Replacement O-ring
or other seal

2. Find O-ring or similar seal inside. Replace it, and screw showerhead back into place.

Problems can also be caused by grit or sediment lodged in the showerhead or by a buildup of scale or mineral deposits. The solution is to remove the showerhead at the swivel ball and start cleaning. It may be necessary to soak some parts in vinegar and scrape others, but be careful not to scratch or gouge anything. If the showerhead is of the adjustable-spray type, examine all of the moving parts carefully for signs of excessive wear. If the adjustment handle binds or does not work smoothly, or if the internal cam is fouled up, usually the only solution is to replace the entire head.

QUICK TOILET FIXES

The toilet is one of the most important fixtures in your home. Although toilets are sturdy and reliable components of the plumbing system, it's a rare homeowner or apartment-dweller who never has any problems with a toilet. Clogging is perhaps the most common toilet trouble, but it is far from the only one. The tank, for example, can make all sorts of strange noises, or water can run continuously. Fortunately, most toilet troubles are quick fixes for a do-it-yourself plumber.

REPLACING TOILET SEAT

The easiest toilet repair task is replacing the lid and seat. There are so many styles of replacement seats available that you should have no trouble finding one to match any bathroom color scheme or motif. Most modern toilets are manufactured in two standard sizes (regular and elongated), and replacement seats are made to fit them.

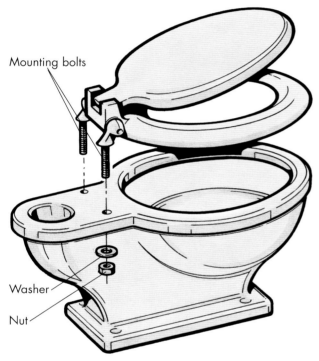

Mounting bolts

Washer

Nut

A new toilet seat can be installed by inserting the two bolts, slipping on the washers, and tightening the nuts. Be careful not to overtighten the nuts, or the seat might be hard to remove later.

Once you have the right size replacement seat, take off the old one by removing the two nuts on the hinge and lifting the old seat up and out. A common problem is that the nuts securing the toilet seat are rusted or corroded. To make the job even more difficult, the nuts on some toilet seats are recessed and practically inaccessible.

What's the solution? If you can get to the fasteners relatively easily, apply some penetrating oil to help loosen them. Give the oil plenty of time to soak in. Use a wrench, or, if you can't reach the nuts with a regular wrench, a deep socket wrench. Be sure you don't use too much force; if the wrench slips off a stubborn nut, it could strike and crack the tank or the bowl or anything else it happens to hit.

If all else fails, cut off the bolts with a hacksaw. To protect the bowl's finish, apply tape to the bowl at the spots the hacksaw blade is likely to rub against. Then insert the blade under the hinge and saw through the bolts. Be extremely cautious in using the saw—a careless slip with a hacksaw can crack the fixture just as easily as a blow with a wrench.

With the nuts removed or the bolts cut, you can remove the old seat without further difficulty. Clean the area before installing the new seat. The new one can be installed by inserting the bolts and tightening the nuts. Be careful not to overtighten the nuts, as you may want to replace this seat someday as well. If you live in a rented apartment and install a new seat that you paid for yourself, be sure to keep the old one. When you're ready to leave, you can replace the new one with the original and take the new seat with you.

If the toilet lid and seat are still in good condition but the small plastic or rubber bumpers on the bottom are in bad shape, you can buy replacement bumpers at the hardware store. Some bumpers screw in; others must be nailed or glued into place. Whichever type you have, try to install the new ones in holes that are close enough to conceal the original holes.

CLEARING CLOGGED TOILETS

You can generally clear a clogged toilet with a plunger, otherwise known as a plumber's helper. Make sure there's enough water in the toilet bowl to cover the rubber suction cup, then work the handle of the plunger up and down. If there isn't enough water in the bowl, do not flush the toilet; flushing a clogged toilet will just cause the bowl to overflow. Instead, bring a pan or pot of water from another source to supply the water you need to cover the plunger cup. There are two types of plungers, and the one with a bulb-type head is especially effective for toilets. Some types have a fold-out head that's also designed for toilet use.

Usually, whatever is blocking the toilet drain is not very far away. If the plunger's action doesn't dislodge the clog, you can try to hook the blockage and pull it free. A wire coat hanger can sometimes do the job, but it is really a substitute for the closet, or toilet, auger. The auger has a long sleeve or tube to guide the snake and auger hook into the trap. A crank on the end enables you to turn the hook in the drain or trap. Here's how to use it:

1. Insert auger into toilet trap and turn crank until it feels tight. This means snake has twisted its way to and into blockage.

2. When you pull in auger, you should be able to remove whatever is clogging toilet. If you aren't successful, try closet auger several more times. In some cases, you may have to resort to pushing regular plumbers' snake through blockage.

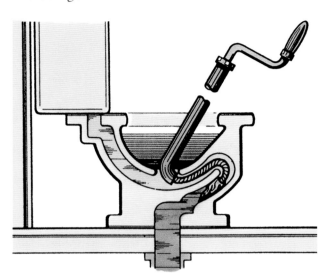

The closet auger has a long sleeve to guide the snake and auger hook into the trap. A crank enables you to turn the hook and dislodge the blockage.

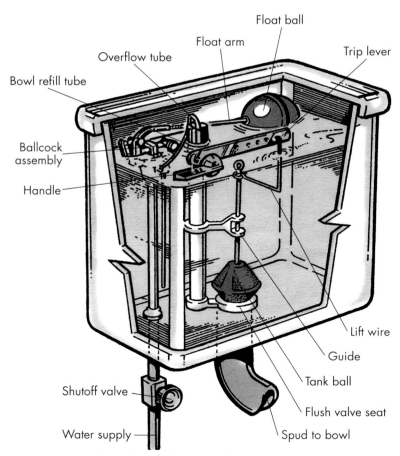

Toilet tank troubles are both common and annoying, and they could be costing you money in wasted water. Most problems, however, can be eliminated quickly and easily. This is a cross section of a typical toilet tank and its components.

3. When all else fails, toilet may have to be removed from floor and turned upside down so you can get at blockage. This is not what anyone would call an easy job, so you should give the simpler methods as good a try as you can before calling a plumber to remove toilet.

TOILET TANK PROBLEMS

Compared with a clogged toilet, tank troubles can seem relatively insignificant. Yet strange noises or continuous water running can be more than annoying—it can cost you money in wasted water. Fortunately, you can eliminate most tank troubles quickly and easily.

Once you know how the toilet works, you can start to look for the source of your toilet tank problems. First, lift the lid off your toilet tank. When you trip the handle on the tank to flush the toilet, a trip lever is raised inside the tank. This lever lifts wires, which, in turn, raise the tank ball or rubber flap at the bottom of the tank. When the flush valve opening is clear, the water in the tank rushes out past the raised tank ball and into the toilet bowl below. This raises the level of water in the bowl above the level of water in the toilet trap.

While the water is rushing out of the tank, the float ball, which floats on top of the water in the tank, drops down. This pulls down on the float arm, raising the valve plunger in the ballcock assembly and allowing fresh water to flow into the tank. Since water seeks its own level, the water from the tank pushes the bowl water out into the drain, causing a siphoning action that cleans everything out of the bowl. When all the water is gone from the toilet bowl and air is drawn into the trap, the siphoning stops. Meanwhile, the tank ball falls back into place, closing the flush valve opening.

As the water level rises in the tank, the float ball rises until the float arm is high enough to lower the valve plunger in the ballcock assembly and shut off the incoming water. If the water fails to shut off, there is an overflow tube that carries excess water down into the bowl to prevent the tank from overflowing. If water flows continuously out of the tank to the bowl and down the drain:

1. Lift up on float arm. If water stops, you know problem is the float ball doesn't rise far enough to lower valve plunger in ballcock assembly. One reason could be float ball is rubbing against

side of tank. If this is the case, bend float arm slightly to move ball away from tank side.

2. If ball doesn't touch tank, continue to hold float arm and remove ball from end of arm by turning it counterclockwise. Then shake ball to see if there's water inside it, as weight of water inside could be preventing ball from rising normally. If there is water in ball, shake it out and put ball back on float arm. If ball is damaged or corroded, replace it with new one. If there is no water in ball, put ball back on, and gently bend float rod down to lower the level float ball must reach to shut off flow of fresh water into tank.

3. If the above steps don't solve the problem, check tank ball at flush valve seat. Chemical residue from water can prevent this ball from seating properly, or ball itself may have decayed. Water will seep through flush valve

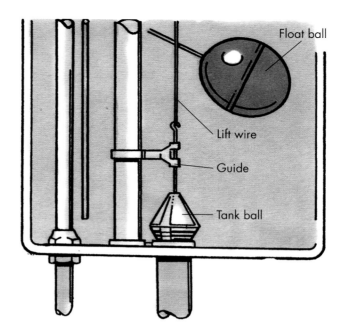

If your toilet runs continuously, check the guide and the lift wire that raises and lowers the tank ball to be sure they are aligned properly.

TOILET TROUBLESHOOTING CHART

Problem	Possible Cause	Solution
Water in tank runs constantly	1. Float ball or rod is misaligned.	1. Bend float rod carefully to move ball so it will not rub against side of tank.
	2. Float ball contains water.	2. Empty or replace float ball.
	3. Float ball not rising high enough.	3. Carefully bend float rod down, but only slightly.
	4. Tank ball not sealing properly at bottom of tank.	4. Remove any corrosion from lip of valve seat. Replace tank ball if worn. Adjust lift wire and guide.
	5. Ballcock valve does not shut off water.	5. Replace washers in ballcock assembly or, if necessary, replace entire assembly.
Toilet does not flush or flushes inadequately	1. Drain is clogged.	1. Remove blockage in drain.
	2. Not enough water in tank.	2. Raise water level in tank by bending float rod up slightly.
	3. Tank ball falls back before enough water leaves tank.	3. Move guide up so tank ball can rise higher.
	4. Leak where tank joins toilet bowl.	4. Tighten nuts on spud pipe; replace spud washers, if necessary.
	5. Ports around bowl rim clogged.	5. Ream out residue from ports.
Tank whines while filling	1. Ballcock valve not operating properly.	1. Replace washers or install new ballcock assembly.
	2. Water supply is restricted.	2. Check shutoff to make sure it's completely open. Check for scale or corrosion at entry into tank and on valve.
Moisture around fixture	1. Condensation.	1. Install foam liner, tank cover, drip catcher, or temperature valve.
	2. Leak at flange wax seal.	2. Remove toilet and install new wax ring seal.
	3. Leak at bowl-tank connection.	3. Tighten spud pipe nuts; replace worn spud washers, if necessary.
	4. Leak at water inlet connection.	4. Tighten locknut and coupling nut; replace washers and gasket, if necessary.
	5. Crack in bowl or tank.	5. Replace bowl, tank, or entire fixture.

opening into toilet bowl below. Turn off water at toilet shutoff valve, and flush toilet to empty tank. You can now examine tank ball for signs of wear and install new ball if necessary. If problem is chemical residue on lip of flush valve opening, take some wet-dry emery cloth, steel wool, or even a knife and clean away debris.

4. If excess water still flows through toilet, guide or lift wire that raises and lowers tank ball may be out of line or bent. Make sure guide is in place so wire is directly above flush valve opening. Rotate guide until tank ball falls straight down into opening. If lift wire is bent, try to bend it back to correct position, or install new one. Make sure trip lever rod is not rubbing against anything and lift wire is not installed in wrong hole of rod; either situation could cause tank ball to fall at an angle and not block opening as it should.

5. If neither float ball nor tank ball is at fault, then problem must be in ballcock assembly (see below).

FIXING BALLCOCK ASSEMBLY The ballcock assembly looks more complicated than it really is. When you go to a hardware or plumbing supply store to buy a new ballcock assembly, you'll find that both plastic and metal units are available. Plastic costs less and will not corrode, but plastic assemblies are not as sturdy as metal ones. In addition, plastic units usually cannot be repaired because many of them are sealed. Nevertheless, you can purchase a type of unit different from the one you're replacing as long as the new assembly has a threaded shank the same size as the old one. If possible, bring the old assembly with you when you go to buy the replacement. Here's how to fix an older-style ballcock assembly:

What You'll Need
Screwdriver
Replacement parts
Adjustable plumbers' wrenches
Penetrating oil

1. Make sure water shutoff valve for toilet is in OFF position. Flush toilet to empty tank. On many older ballcock assemblies, a pair of thumbscrews holds valve plunger. You will have to unscrew them to remove valve.

2. Remove valve plunger, and you'll see one or two washers or O-rings. If any of these parts is faulty, water will flow out past plunger continuously and toilet will run constantly. Examine all washers, and replace any defective ones.

3. If ballcock assembly is sealed, replace it as a unit. Shut off toilet water supply at shutoff valve, and flush tank. Unscrew float arm from old ballcock unit, and remove refill tube from overflow tube.

4. Look under tank for coupling or slip nut where water inlet pipe enters base of tank. Loosen coupling nut to free water inlet pipe. Then use adjustable wrench to grip retaining nut or locknut immediately above slip nut under tank. Use another wrench to grip base of ballcock assembly shaft inside tank.

5. Unscrew locknut under tank to remove ballcock assembly. If nut is stubborn, use penetrating oil to loosen it.

6. Lift old assembly out of tank, saving washers from all connections, both inside and outside tank. New ones will probably be included with replacement unit, but keep old parts until you've installed new ballcock assembly in case new parts are damaged during installation.

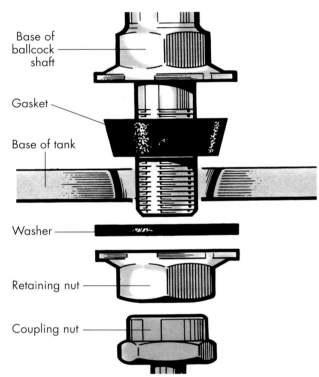

Base of ballcock shaft

Gasket

Base of tank

Washer

Retaining nut

Coupling nut

When installing a new ballcock assembly, make sure the gasket and the washer are properly seated and firmly secured by the retaining nut.

7. Insert new ballcock assembly into hole in tank. With inside washer in place, tighten locknut on outside sufficiently to make inside washer fit watertight against hole. Don't overtighten it.

8. Replace coupling nut and water inlet pipe, reinstall float arm, and set refill tube into overflow tube.

9. Turn water back on at toilet shutoff valve, and check for leaks at all points. Of course, another thing to check is that float ball does not rub against back of tank.

Newer types of ballcock assemblies eliminate the float arm and the float ball. One kind features a plastic cup that floats up to cut off the water as the tank fills. You can set the water level in the tank by adjusting the position of the plastic cup on a pull rod. One advantage to this type of ballcock assembly is it lets the water run full force until the tank is filled. It then shuts the water off immediately, eliminating the groaning noises some toilets make as a float arm gradually closes the valve.

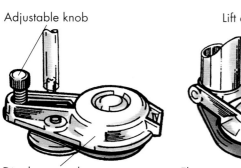
Adjustable knob

Diaphragm valve cover

Lift chain

Flapper-type valve cover

One type of diaphragm-powered valve rests close to the bottom of the tank (left); it eliminates the float ball and float arm. Another type (right) uses a flapper cover, lifted by a chain.

Another type of ballcock also eliminates the float ball and float arm. This is a small unit that rests almost on the bottom of the tank; its diaphragm-powered valve senses the level of the water from down there. Moreover, since it requires no tools, this assembly is an easy unit to install. To install these newer ballcock assemblies:

What You'll Need
Sponge
Adjustable plumbers' wrenches
Replacement ballcock assembly

1. Turn off tank's water supply shutoff valve. Then flush toilet to drain tank. Sponge up any water remaining in tank before proceeding.

2. Remove old ballcock assembly, following procedure outlined above. Slip parts over water inlet pipe under tank in this order: coupling nut, friction washer, cone washer, and retaining or mounting nut.

3. Install new unit inside tank, fitting threaded shank down through hole over water supply pipe and making sure gasket fits into hole. Start hand-tightening retaining or mounting nut under tank onto threaded shank. Push washers into place, and hand-tighten coupling nut under tank; be careful not to overtighten it.

4. Inside tank, attach one end of refill tube to tank's overflow pipe, and place other end on stem of replacement unit.

5. Open water supply valve to fill tank. Water level in tank can be adjusted by knob on new valve unit.

FIXING SWEATING TOILET

Toilet tanks can sweat and drip onto your floors just like pipes can. There are jackets designed specifically to fit over the tank and absorb the moisture as well as drip pans that fit under the tank to catch the dripping condensation so it doesn't damage your bathroom floor. A device called a temperator valve is another way to combat tank sweating. This valve provides a regulated mixture of hot and cold water, which lessens the difference between the temperature inside the tank and the temperature of the surrounding air. It is this difference in temperature that causes condensation, or sweating. Consider installing a temperator valve if the water in the tank is usually below 50°F.

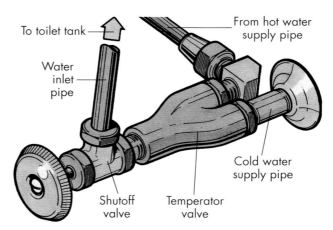
To toilet tank

Water inlet pipe

From hot water supply pipe

Cold water supply pipe

Shutoff valve

Temperator valve

The temperator valve, which requires both hot water and cold water supply connections, can reduce toilet tank sweating.

A temperator valve requires you to hook up a hot water line to the valve, which may be quite inconvenient if there is no such line relatively close to the toilet. Moreover, the temperator valve does not prevent the water inside the tank from cooling between flushings; thus, condensation can still occur even on a temperator-equipped toilet.

A leak may be due to loose connections or defective washers on the spud pipe or where the water inlet pipe and ballcock assembly are attached to the tank. Replace any worn gaskets or washers and tighten all nuts, then test by dropping food coloring in the water and visually inspecting to see if it continues to leak.

It is also possible that water is seeping out from under the toilet bowl. The wax ring seal that joins the bowl to the drain outlet may be defective. If this is the case, the bowl must be removed and a new gasket installed. If the leak is due to a crack in the tank or bowl, the whole toilet must be replaced.

SOLVING OTHER COMMON TOILET PROBLEMS

What can you do if too little water comes from the tank to flush the toilet bowl clean?

- Check water level in tank. It's probably too low. If the water level doesn't reach within 1½ inches of the top of the overflow tube, slightly bend up the float arm to let more water enter the tank.

- If water level is correct but there's still not enough water coming from the tank to clean the bowl properly, the problem may be the tank ball on the flush valve seat at the bottom of the tank. The ball is probably dropping too soon because the guide is set too low. Raise the guide, but make sure it stays in line with the lift wire. If the guide and wire are out of alignment, the tank ball will not drop straight into the valve seat opening and the toilet will run continuously.

- Look for other causes of inadequate flushing. The small ports around the underside of the toilet bowl's rim can get clogged with residue from chemicals in the water and prevent a sufficient amount of tank water from running out into the bowl. A small mirror can help you examine the holes, and a piece of wire coat hanger can ream out any clogged debris.

OTHER QUICK PLUMBING FIXES

Still having problems with your home's plumbing? Not to worry; here are some additional quick fixes.

PIPE PROBLEMS

Most plumbing problems occur at or near such fixtures as sinks, tubs, and toilets. Less often the pipes themselves can leak, sweat, freeze, or bang. Here's how to deal with these difficulties.

STOPPING LEAKS IN PIPES AND JOINTS There are all kinds of plumbing leaks. Some can flood your home, while others are not nearly so damaging. Your approach to stopping a leak depends on the type of leak it is. If the leak is at a joint, tighten the joint. If the leak is in a pipe, remove the section that is leaking and replace it with a new section. Unfortunately, this is more easily said than done. For example, when you turn a threaded galvanized steel pipe to unscrew it from

its fitting at one end, you tighten the pipe into its fitting at the other end. With copper pipe, the new section must be sweat-soldered in place. Most pipe replacement jobs are best left to a plumber, but, as a do-it-yourselfer, you may consider an alternative: the pipe patch.

You'll find patch kits for plumbing leaks at the hardware store, or you can make your own with a piece of heavy rubber from an old inner tube and a C-clamp. Another possibility is to use a hose clamp with a rubber patch. Factory-made kits contain a rubber pad that goes over the hole in the pipe and metal plates that compress the rubber pad over the hole. A quick and easy way to stop a leak, the patch kit can even be used on a permanent basis if the pipe is otherwise sound.

Other quick and easy temporary measures for stopping pipe leaks include wrapping waterproof tape over the bad spot or rubbing the hole with a stick of special compound. Applying epoxy paste or inserting a self-tapping plug into the hole are other alternatives. When using waterproof tape, be sure to dry the pipe thoroughly before you start wrapping. Start the tape about 2 to 3 inches from the hole and extend it the same distance beyond. For tiny leaks in pipes, use a compound stick available at most hardware stores. Simply rub the stick over the hole to stop the leak. The compound stick can even stop small leaks while the water is still running in the pipe. Epoxy paste can be applied only to dry pipes, and the water must be turned off.

There are several ways to stop a leak in a pipe. For a temporary patch, use a piece of heavy rubber and hose clamps (top) or a rubber pad and two plates that bolt together (bottom).

The problem with all of these solutions is that a pipe that's bad enough to spring one leak often starts leaking in other places too. You may fix one spot only to see the pipe burst somewhere else. Especially in cases where the leak results from corrosion, the whole section of pipe will probably need replacing. This is typically a job for a professional plumber.

STOPPING PIPES FROM SWEATING Sometimes there's so much water dripping from a pipe that you're sure there must be a leak somewhere. On closer examination, however, you may discover there is no leak but rather sweating, or condensation. Sweating occurs when the water inside the pipe is much colder than surrounding humid air. During the summer, the surrounding air is naturally hot; in winter, the air is heated by the furnace. In either case, when warm, humid air reaches cold pipes, drops of moisture form and drip as if there was a tiny hole in the pipe.

One effective way to control the moisture problem of a sweating pipe is to insulate the pipes. There are several types of self-adhesive thick "drip" tape designed to easily adhere to problem pipes. Before applying the tape, wipe the pipes as dry as you can. Wind the tape so that it completely covers the pipe and the fittings. You should see no further signs of sweating.

THAWING FROZEN PIPES You may think your entire plumbing system is in perfect working order and there is little or no chance of a pipe bursting and flooding your house. There is one situation, however, you may not have considered. Water that freezes during the winter in an unprotected pipe expands, and that expansion can rupture an otherwise sound pipe. A frozen pipe is always an inconvenience, but it can actually result in a much more serious situation than just a temporary loss of water. By taking the proper preventive steps, you may never need to worry about thawing frozen pipes, or, worse, repairing a pipe that bursts when the water in it freezes solid.

Here's what to do if you wake up some frigid winter morning to find a water pipe frozen solid:

1. Open faucet so steam produced by your thawing activities will be able to escape.

2. Start thawing pipe (see following thawing options) at faucet, and work back toward other end of frozen section. As you melt ice, water and

What You'll Need
Heavy towel or burlap bag and hot or boiling water
Propane torch
Heat lamp, hair dryer, or electric iron

steam will come out open faucet. If you started in the middle, steam produced by melting ice could get trapped and build up enough pressure to burst pipe.

Thawing options:

- Probably the most popular and safest pipe-thawing option is to use hot water. Wrap and secure heavy towel or burlap bag around pipe to concentrate and hold heat against it. Place bucket under pipe to catch runoff water, then pour hot or boiling water over towel.

- A less messy but far more dangerous heat source for thawing frozen pipes is a propane torch equipped with a flame-spreader nozzle. With this heat source, you must be extremely careful to prevent torch flame from damaging or igniting wall behind pipe. A scrap of fireproof material between pipe and wall is a good precautionary measure, but the way you use the torch is the main element in safe pipe thawing. Keep flame moving back and forth. Never leave it in one spot very long. Be especially careful if you're near any soldered pipe joints. Pass over them very quickly or else they may melt and cause leaks, and you'll find that you have a much more serious plumbing problem on your hands than a frozen pipe. **Caution:** Never use torch or other direct high heat on plastic pipe.

- If you want to avoid the messiness of thawing with hot water and the danger of melting soldered joints with propane torch, try heat lamp or hair dryer as heat source. These work less quickly but are much safer.

To thaw a frozen drainpipe, remove trap, and insert length of garden hose into pipe. When you can't push hose any farther, it has probably reached the ice. Raise your end of the hose and feed hot water in through a funnel. This way, the hot water is sure to get to the problem area. You must be careful when using this technique. Until the ice melts and drains down the pipe, the hot water you pour in will back up toward you. Have a bucket ready to catch the overflow, and be careful not to scald yourself.

QUIETING NOISY PIPES

The sound of banging pipes is sometimes called water hammer, but water hammer is only one of several different noises that can come from your plumbing system. If you hear the sound whenever you turn on the water, the pipes are probably striking against something.

Banging pipes are much easier to cure if you can see them. Turn on the water and start looking for movement. Once you find the trouble, you can stop the pipe or pipes from hitting against whatever is in the vicinity. Even if the moving pipe is between the walls, you may be able to silence it without tearing your house apart. Just place padding or foam insulation at each end where the pipe emerges from behind the wall.

A pipe banging against a masonry wall can be silenced by wedging a wood block behind it, fastening the block to the wall, and securing the pipe to the wood.

In many cases, the moving pipe is loose within its strap or U-clamp and is banging against the wall it's supposed to be secured to. To eliminate the noise, slit a piece of old garden hose or cut a patch of rubber and insert it behind the strap or clamp to fill in the gap. Pipes that strike against a masonry wall can be silenced by wedging a block of wood between the pipe and the wall. Nail the block to the wall with masonry nails or screws and attach the pipe to the block with a pipe strap.

In a basement or crawl space, galvanized steel pipes are typically suspended from the joists by perforated pipe straps. A long run of suspended pipe may move within the straps, strike against something, and create a racket. A block of wood strategically wedged along the run can eliminate the pipe's movement and the resulting noise. If you secure a pipe, don't anchor it so tightly that it can't expand and contract with changes in temperature. If you place a bracket on a pipe, install a rubber buffer between the pipe and the bracket. You can make such buffers from garden hose, foam rubber, rubber cut from old inner tubes, or even kitchen sponges.

You may find that supply pipes and drainpipes that run right next to each other are striking one another and creating a clatter. One solution to this problem is to solder the two pipes together.

Another solution is to wedge a piece of rubber between them. If the vibration and noises are caused by water pressure that's too high, try reducing the water pressure.

If the knocking sound occurs only when you turn on the hot water, it means that the water heater is set too high. The noise is steam rumbling through the hot water system. Turning the heat setting down may silence the pipes. A pipe that's too small to begin with or that has become clogged with scale or mineral deposits can be a big noise problem. It's almost impossible to clean clogged supply pipes, and you must replace pipe that's too small if you want to stop the noise. You can diminish the sound level of clogged pipes considerably by wrapping them with sound-dampening insulation.

Drainpipes rarely clatter, but they can make a sucking noise as the water leaves the sink or basin. This sound means that a vent, such as the hole at the top edge of a bathroom sink, is restricted, or perhaps there's no vent at all attached to the drain. In either case, you have a potentially serious plumbing problem on your hands because a nonfunctioning or nonexistent vent can eliminate the water seal and allow sewer gas to back up into your home. If possible, run a plumbers' snake through the vent from the fixture or from the roof vent to eliminate any clogging. If there is no vent on the drain, install an antisiphon trap to quiet the noise and to prevent any problem with sewer gas. An anti-siphon trap is available at a hardware or plumbing supply store.

STOPPING WATER HAMMER Water hammer is a specific plumbing noise, not a generic name for pipe clatter. It occurs when you shut off the water suddenly and the fast-moving water rushing through the pipe is brought to a quick halt, creating a sort of shock wave and a hammering noise. Plumbing that's properly installed has air chambers, or cushions, that compress when the shock wave hits, softening the blow and preventing this hammering. The chambers can fail, though, because water under pressure gradually absorbs the air. If you never had hammering and then it suddenly starts, most likely your plumbing system's air chambers have become waterlogged.

You can cure water hammer by turning off the water behind the waterlogged chamber, opening the offending faucet and permitting the faucet to drain thoroughly. Once all the water drains from the chamber, air will fill it again and restore the cushion. If the air chamber is located below the a workable one, you can reduce pressure by installing a pressure-reducing valve in the supply line that comes into the house. The same purpose is served by installing a globe valve at the head of the affected pipeline. But this too may result in pressure too low for proper operation when other faucets are open.

If pressure reduction is not feasible or is ineffective, install the necessary air chambers to prevent water hammer. If you have no room to make the installation without tearing into a wall, go to a plumbing supply dealer and find out about the substitute devices designed for such problem areas. Many of these devices have a valve that makes it easy for air to reenter the system.

RECAULKING FIXTURES

Because tubs and sinks are used practically every day, the caulking between the fixture and the wall often cracks or pulls loose. When this happens, water seeps into the opening and damages the joint and the surrounding wall. Use silicone caulk or bathtub caulk to make the repair. To recaulk kitchen and bathroom fixtures:

1. Use putty knife or utility knife to remove all old caulk from joint.

2. Clean joint thoroughly with strong household cleaner. If joint is mildewed, scrub it with chlorine bleach. Dry joint thoroughly with clean rag wrapped over blade of putty knife.

3. Apply caulk to joint. Cut nozzle of caulk tube at an angle so opening is a little larger than open joint. If you're caulking several joints, start with the smallest joint and work up, recutting tube nozzle as necessary for larger joints.

4. Let new caulk dry for several hours. Don't let it get wet during drying period. Let caulk cure completely (see manufacturer's instructions) before using fixture.

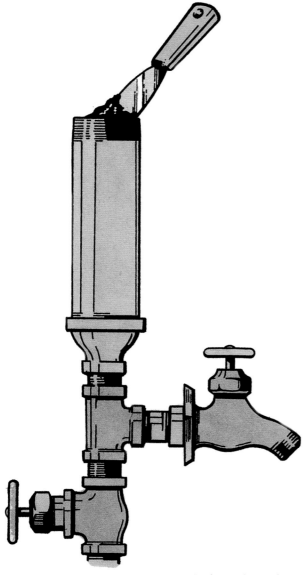

An air chamber will not drain properly if it is clogged. Remove its cap and ream out the accumulated scale inside the chamber.

What You'll Need
Putty or utility knife
Strong household cleaner
Clean rags
Chlorine bleach
Silicone caulk or bathtub caulk
Scissors

outlet, you may have to drain the main supply lines to allow the chamber to fill with air again.

The air chamber will not drain properly if it's clogged with scale or residue from chemicals or minerals in the water. The chamber always should be larger than the supply pipe to preclude such clogging. Since the chamber is simply a capped length of pipe, however, all you have to do to clear it is remove the cap and clean out the residue.

What do you do if there are no air chambers built into your plumbing system? You must do something, because water hammer pressures may eventually cause damage—failure of fittings or burst pipes, for example. Because water hammer is most often caused by water pressure that's too high, the first step is to reduce the water pressure if possible. Sometimes this isn't feasible because a reduction in pressure may result in only a dribble of water at an upper-floor faucet if one on the first floor is turned on. Where the idea is

CHAPTER 5

QUICK HEATING AND COOLING FIXES

Most of us take heating and cooling for granted. We expect our heating systems to keep us warm during the winter, and we depend on air-conditioning to keep us cool during the summer. When the house is cold in winter or hot in summer, the natural reaction is to call for professional service. Fortunately, there is an alternative. You can cut service costs drastically and keep your heating and cooling systems working efficiently by doing some maintenance and quick fixes yourself.

ABOUT HEATING AND COOLING SYSTEMS

All climate-control devices or systems have three basic components: a source of warmed or cooled air, a means of distributing the air to the rooms being heated or cooled, and a control used to regulate the system (e.g., thermostat). The sources of warm air, such as a furnace, and cool air, such as an air conditioner, in a house often use the same distribution and control systems. If your house has central air conditioning, cool air probably flows through the same ducts that heat does and is regulated by the same thermostat. When a heating or cooling system malfunctions, any of these three basic components may be causing the problem.

Both heating and air conditioning work on the principle that heat always moves from a warm object to a cooler one, just as water flows from a higher to a lower level. Furnaces and heaters put heat into the air to make your home warmer; air conditioners remove heat to make your home cooler.

Forced-air heating systems use a fan to move warm air.

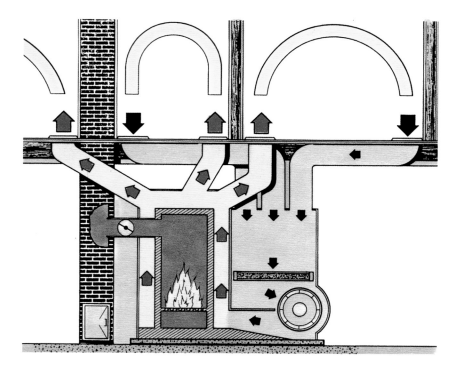

All heating and cooling units burn fuel. Air conditioners use electricity. Most home heating systems use gas or fuel oil; other systems use electricity. The heat pump—an electrically powered climate control unit—both heats and cools air. In summer it extracts heat from the air inside your home. In winter it pulls heat from the air outside and uses this heat to warm the air inside.

When the furnace is turned on, it consumes the fuel that powers it, whether it be gas, oil, or electricity. As fuel is burned, heat is produced and channeled to the living areas of your home through ducts, pipes, or wires and then is blown out of registers, radiators, or heating panels. Older systems use the heat they produce to heat water, which in turn heats the air in your home. These systems use a boiler to store and heat the water supply, which is then circulated as hot water through pipes embedded in the wall, floor, or ceiling.

When an air conditioner is turned on, electrical power is used to cool a gas in a coil to its liquid state. Warm air in your home is cooled by contact with the cooling coil, and this cooled air is channeled to the rooms of your home through ducts and out registers or—in the case of room air conditioners—directly from the unit itself. Heating and cooling system sources are discussed in more detail later in this chapter.

DISTRIBUTION SYSTEMS

Once air is warmed or cooled at the heat/cold source, it must be distributed to the various rooms of your home. This can be accomplished with forced-air, gravity, or radiant heating systems.

FORCED-AIR SYSTEMS A forced-air system distributes the heat produced by the furnace or the coolness produced by a central air conditioner through an electrically powered fan, called a blower, which forces the air through a system of metal ducts to the rooms in your home. As the warm air from the furnace flows into the rooms, colder air in the rooms flows down through another set of ducts, called the cold air return system, to the furnace to be warmed. This system is adjustable: You can increase or decrease the amount of air flowing through your home. Central air conditioning systems use the same forced-air system, including the blower, to distribute cool air to the rooms and to bring warmer air back to be cooled.

Problems with forced-air systems usually involve blower malfunctions. The blower may also be noisy, and it adds the cost of electrical power to the cost of furnace fuel. But because it employs a blower, a forced-air system is an effective way to channel airborne heat or cool air throughout a house.

GRAVITY SYSTEMS Gravity systems are based on the principle that hot air rises and cold air sinks. Gravity systems, therefore, cannot be used to distribute cool air from an air conditioner. In a gravity system, the furnace is located near or below the floor. The warmed air rises and flows through ducts to registers in the floor throughout the house. If the furnace is located on the main floor of the house, the heat registers are usually positioned high on the walls because the registers must always be higher than the furnace. The warmed air rises toward the ceiling. As the air cools, it sinks, enters the return air ducts, and flows back to the furnace to be reheated.

RADIANT SYSTEMS Radiant systems function by warming the walls, floors, or ceilings of rooms or, more commonly, by warming radiators in the rooms. These objects then warm the air in the room. The heat source is usually hot water, which is heated by the furnace and circulated

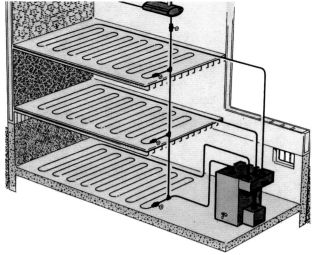

A radiant heating system functions by warming walls, floors, or ceilings, which then warm the surrounding air.

through pipes embedded in the wall, floor, or ceiling. Some systems use electric heating panels to generate heat, which is radiated into rooms. Like gravity wall heaters, these panels are usually installed in warm climates or where electricity is relatively inexpensive. Radiant systems cannot be used to distribute cool air from an air conditioner.

Radiators and convectors, the most common means of radiant heat distribution in older homes, are used with hot water heating systems. These systems may depend on gravity or on a circulator pump to circulate heated water from the boiler to the radiators or convectors. A system that uses a pump, or circulator, is called a hydronic system.

Modern radiant heating systems are often built into houses constructed on a concrete slab foundation. A network of hot water pipes is laid under the surface of the concrete slab. When the concrete is warmed by the pipes, it warms the air that contacts the floor surface. The slab need not get very hot; it will eventually contact and heat the air throughout the house.

Radiant systems—especially when they depend on gravity— are prone to several problems. The pipes used to distribute the heated water can become clogged with mineral deposits or become slanted at the wrong angle. The boiler in which water is heated at the heat source may also malfunction. Hot water systems are seldom installed in new homes.

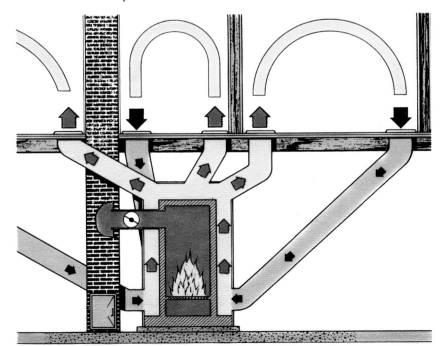

A gravity systems relies on warm air rising naturally.

CONTROLS

The thermostat, a heat-sensitive switch, is the basic control that regulates the temperature of your home. It responds to changes in the temperature of the air where it is located and turns the furnace or air conditioner on or off as needed to maintain the temperature at a set level, called the set point. The key component of the thermostat is a bimetallic element that expands or contracts as the temperature increases or decreases in a house.

QUICK HEATING AND COOLING MAINTENANCE

How can you quickly fix common heating and cooling system problems? By troubleshooting or finding a description of the problem on a troubleshooting chart and then trying the offered solutions. Because systems operate differently, first turn to the section of this chapter on your home's heating/cooling system, then check the corresponding troubleshooting chart.

Heating and cooling systems are usually trouble-free and easy to maintain. Efficient operation is a function of good regular maintenance. No matter what type of heating and cooling system you have, there are several things you can do to keep the system in top condition. You will need a few tools and materials, including screwdrivers, a flashlight, pliers, wrenches, a hammer, a level, newspapers, rags, brushes, and a vacuum cleaner. A few specialized materials are also required: motor oil, fan-belt dressing, refractory cement, and duct tape. These materials are available at most hardware stores and home improvement centers.

When a heating or cooling system malfunctions, any one of its three components—heat/cold source, distribution system, or thermostat—may be causing the problem. If the furnace or air conditioner doesn't run, the malfunction is probably at the source. The furnace or air conditioner may have lost power. Fuel may not be reaching the unit. If the fuel is gas or oil, it may not be igniting. If the furnace or air conditioner turns on but the warm or cool air isn't reaching the rooms of your home, the problem is likely to be the blower or distribution system. And a faulty control, or thermostat, could keep the system from turning on or could cause it to turn on and off repeatedly. Whatever the problem, start with the simplest procedures. In most cases, all it takes is patience and common sense.

Before you start work on a heating or cooling system, take these preliminary steps:

- Make sure the unit is receiving power. Look for blown fuses or tripped circuit breakers at the main entrance panel. Some furnaces have a separate power entrance, usually located at a different panel near the main entrance panel. Some furnaces have fuses mounted in or on the unit.

- If the unit has a reset button, marked RESET and near the motor housing, wait 30 minutes to let the motor cool, then press the button. If the unit still doesn't start, wait 30 minutes and press the reset button again. Repeat at least once more.

- If the unit has a separate power switch, make sure the switch is turned on.

- Check to make sure the thermostat is properly set. If necessary, raise (or, for an air conditioner, lower) the setting 5°.

- If the unit uses gas, check to make sure the gas supply is turned on and the pilot light is lit. If it uses oil, check to make sure there is an adequate supply of oil.

There are also several important safety factors to remember:

- Before doing any work on any type of heating or cooling system, make sure all power to the system is turned off. At the main electrical entrance panel, trip the circuit breaker or remove the fuse that controls the power to the unit. If you're not sure which circuit the system is on, remove the main fuse or trip the main circuit breaker to cut off all power to the house. Some furnaces have a separate power entrance, usually at a different panel near the main entrance panel. If a separate panel is present, remove the fuse or trip the breaker there.

- If the fuse blows or the circuit trips repeatedly when the furnace or air conditioner turns on, there is a problem in the electrical system. In this case, do not try to fix the furnace. Call a professional service person.

- If the unit uses gas and there is a smell of gas in your home, do not try to shut off the gas or turn any lights on or off. Get out of the house, leaving the door open, and immediately call the gas company or the fire department to report a leak. Do not reenter your home.

- To keep your heating and cooling systems in top shape, have them professionally serviced once a year. The best time to have a furnace serviced is at the end of the heating season. Because this is the off-season, you can often get a discount, and service is likely to be prompt. Have your air conditioner checked at the same time.

Dirt is the biggest enemy of your home's heating and cooling system. It can waste fuel and drastically lower efficiency. Dirt affects all three basic components of the system, so cleaning is the most important part of regular maintenance. Lubrication and belt adjustment at the furnace are also important. To keep your system working properly, use the following general procedures. Specific procedures for each type of system are detailed later in this chapter.

The heat/cold source is the most complicated part of the heating and cooling system, and it's the part most likely to suffer from neglect. Problems in this area may also lead to distribution problems. Whatever heat/cold source your system uses, give it regular attention to prevent problems.

CLEANING A FURNACE

Three parts of the furnace should be cleaned: the filter system, the blower, and the motor.

REPLACING FURNACE FILTER The furnace filter should be replaced or cleaned at the beginning of the heating season and about once a month during periods of continuous use. To check the filter, take it out and hold it up to the light. If it looks clogged, replace it with a new filter of the same type and size regardless of the length of time it has been used. A disposable furnace filter consists of a fiber mesh in a cardboard frame. The size of the filter is printed on the edge of the frame. An arrow on the edge of the frame indicates the correct direction of airflow through the filter. Air flows from the return-air duct toward the blower, so the arrow on the filter should point away from the return-air duct and toward the blower. A permanent filter is usually sprayed with a special filter-coating chemical, available at hardware stores and home centers. Clean this type of filter according to the manufacturer's instructions, which are usually attached to the furnace housing. To replace a filter:

What You'll Need
Screwdriver
Replacement filter
Toothbrush
Vacuum cleaner
Clean rags

1. Look for metal panel on front of furnace below return-air duct, between duct and blower system. Panel may be marked

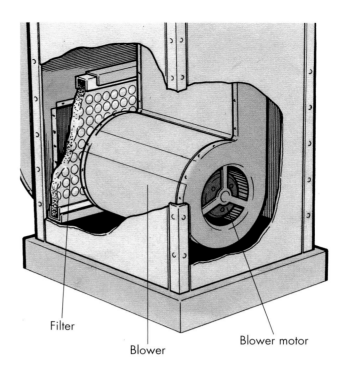

Three parts of the air-moving system should be kept clean: the filter, the blower, and the blower motor.

Filter

Blower

Blower motor

FILTER, or it may form lid or front of boxlike projection on furnace housing.

2. Slip panel off its holding hooks, or unscrew panel from box or furnace housing. On some heating units, filters are exposed; just slip filter up and out of U-shape tracks that hold it in place.

3. Inspect and replace or clean filter, depending on type.

4. Clean blower assembly, belts and pulleys to blower, and motor housing. Cleaning blower is critical if furnace has a squirrel-cage fan, because openings in this type of blower often become clogged with dirt. To clean blower, remove panel that covers filter to gain access to blower or panel on front of furnace. This panel may be slip-fit on hooks or held by series of retaining screws. Access to inside of blower is usually gained by sliding out fan unit, which is held on track by screws. If power cord to fan assembly is not long enough to permit fan unit to slide all the way out, disconnect cord. Mark wire connections first so you'll be able to reassemble unit correctly. With toothbrush, clean each fan blade and spaces between blades. Then, with vacuum cleaner hose, remove all dirt and debris loosened by brushing. Vacuum belts and pulleys. Wipe motor housing clean to prevent heat buildup in motor.

LUBRICATING HEATING AND COOLING MOTOR

To keep the motor running cool, make sure it's clean. Most motors are permanently lubricated and sealed by the manufacturer and, therefore, require no further attention. Some motors, however, have covered oil ports above the bearings near the motor shaft. If the motor has oil ports, it should be lubricated annually. Apply two or three drops of 10-weight nondetergent motor oil (not all-purpose oil) to each port. Do not overlubricate. If the blower shaft has oil ports, it, too, should be lubricated annually, following the same procedure. You'll probably have to remove an access plate to get at the ports. If the blower has grease cups instead of oil ports, remove the screw caps that cover the cups and fill the cups with bearing lubricant, which is available at automotive and hardware stores.

BELT ADJUSTMENT AND REPLACEMENT

On furnaces that have a blower, inspect the belts on the blower and motor when you clean and lubricate the furnace. If the belts are worn or frayed, replace them with new ones of the same type and size. To replace a worn belt:

What You'll Need
Wrench
Replacement belt

1. Loosen mounting bolts on motor, and slide motor forward toward blower unit. This releases worn belt.

2. Remove old belt, and stretch new one into place on pulleys. Then slide motor back and tighten motor mounting bolts to increase tension.

3. Adjust bolts so there's about ½-inch deflection when you press on belt at its center point between the two pulleys.

If a belt squeaks when the blower is running, spray it with fan belt dressing, which is available at automotive and hardware stores and at some home centers.

THERMOSTAT MAINTENANCE

A thermostat is a highly sensitive control instrument that responds to even the slightest changes in temperature. While it has fewer parts to malfunction than the other components of your heating and cooling system, it can be a source of problems. A thermostat cover that's improperly installed or inadvertently bumped can cause the heater or air conditioner to fail to start. Or the thermostat base may slip out of level, causing it to operate incorrectly. A far more common problem, however, is dirt. Dirt can affect the thermostat's calibration and interfere with its operation. If a thermostat set for 70°F, for exam-

ple, is really maintaining the temperature at 73°F, the additional energy used can increase your fuel bill by as much as 7 percent. To prevent this, check your thermostat for accuracy every year before the heating season begins.

Other problems with a thermostat can often be traced to switches on the base and wires near the bimetallic element that loosen and become corroded. Tighten loose connections with a screwdriver, and use a cotton swab to clean away corrosion.

CHECKING THERMOSTAT'S CALIBRATION To check a thermostat's accuracy and clean it if necessary:

1. Tape glass tube thermometer to wall a few inches away from thermostat. Pad thermometer with paper towel to prevent it from touching wall. Make sure neither thermometer nor thermostat is affected by any outside temperature influences. In some homes, hole in wall behind thermostat through which wires enter is too large, allowing cold air to reach thermostat and affect its reading.

What You'll Need
Glass tube
    thermometer
Tape
Paper towel
New dollar bill
    or soft brush
Level
Screwdriver

2. Wait about 15 minutes for mercury to stabilize. Then compare reading on thermometer with reading of thermostat needle.

3. If variation is more than a degree, check to see if thermostat is dirty. To examine thermostat, remove faceplate, usually held by a snap or friction catch. Blow away any dust inside it. Do not use a vacuum cleaner; its suction is too great. If thermostat has accessible contact points, rub new dollar bill between them to clean these spots. Do not use sandpaper or emery cloth. If element is coiled, use soft brush for cleaning.

4. If thermostat has mercury vial inside, use level to make sure unit is straight. If thermostat is not straight, loosen mounting screws and adjust thermostat until it is level. Then retighten screws.

5. After cleaning thermostat, check it again with glass thermometer, as detailed in steps 1 and 2. If thermostat is still not calibrated properly, it should be replaced as detailed below.

REPLACING THERMOSTAT Replace a faulty thermostat with a new one of the same voltage. The thermostat must be compatible with the heating system. To replace a thermostat:

1. Remove old thermostat. Take faceplate off old unit, and look for mounting screws. Remove screws to release thermostat from wall. Remove wires from back of old thermostat by turning connection screws counterclockwise. Be careful not to let loose wires fall down between walls.

2. Clean exposed wires by scraping them with utility knife until wire ends shine. Attach wires to new thermostat. New thermostat must have the same electrical rating as old one.

3. Once wires are attached to replacement thermostat, push wires back into wall, and tape up opening to prevent cold air inside walls from affecting thermostat.

4. Install mounting screws to secure new thermostat to wall. If thermostat has mercury tube, set unit against level during installation; mercury tube thermostats must be exactly level.

5. Snap faceplate back into place. Make sure new thermostat turns heating/cooling system on and off when temperature setting is adjusted.

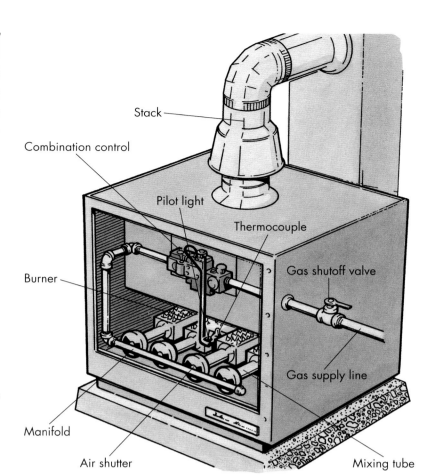

Stack
Combination control
Pilot light
Thermocouple
Burner
Gas shutoff valve
Gas supply line
Manifold
Air shutter
Mixing tube

QUICK HEATING SYSTEM FIXES

Several types of heating plants are commonly used, including oil, gas, and electric furnaces; gas or electric wall or baseboard heaters; and heat pumps. These plants all have their own problems, depending on how they're designed and how they work. In any system, the method of distributing the heat is as important as the means of generating it. Specific procedures are provided below for maintaining and repairing each type of heat source, followed by information about the systems they use to distribute heat.

GAS FURNACES AND HEATERS

Natural gas and propane burn cleaner than fuel oil, and most gas furnaces present fewer operational difficulties than oil burners do. In fact, the problems that affect gas furnaces typically involve the furnace's thermocouple, the pilot light, or some component of the electrical system. Gas furnaces and heaters have control shutoffs to prevent gas leaks, but they are not fail-safe. If you smell gas in your house, do not turn any lights on or off, and do not try to shut off the gas leading to the furnace. Get out of the house, leaving the door open, and immediately call the gas company or the fire department to report a leak. Do not reenter your home.

On some gas furnaces and heaters, a plug-type door covers the pilot light assembly. To gain access to the pilot burner, pull the door out of the furnace housing. On other units, remove the panel that covers the pilot and gas burners.

The pilot light controls, reset buttons, gas valves, and thermocouple are usually contained in an assembly at the front of the furnace. The furnace limit switch is located on the plenum (main chamber) or main duct junction on the upper housing of the furnace.

PILOT LIGHT The pilot light on a gas furnace can go out because of drafts. To relight the pilot, follow the manufacturer's instructions exactly; they are usually fastened to the furnace. If instructions for relighting the pilot are not provided, follow this general procedure:

1. Find pilot light assembly. It typically has a gas valve with ON, OFF, and PILOT settings.

2. Turn valve to OFF and wait three minutes.

3. Switch valve to PILOT setting. Hold lighted match to pilot opening while you push reset button on pilot control panel. Keep this button depressed until pilot flame burns brightly, then set valve to ON position.

Most natural gas furnaces have few operational difficulties. Problems typically involve the pilot light, the thermocouple, or some part of the electrical system.

4. If pilot flame won't stay lit, opening may be clogged. Turn gas valve off, and clean opening with piece of fine wire. If it won't stay lit after several attempts, you may have faulty thermocouple (see below for how to replace thermocouple). If pilot flame still won't stay lit, call professional service person.

Some furnaces have an electrical system to ignite the gas; in these systems there is no pilot light. Instead, an electric element heats up and ignites the burners. If this electric ignition system malfunctions, call a professional service person.

THERMOCOUPLE The thermocouple is a gas furnace component located near the pilot light burner. It is a safety device that shuts off the gas if the pilot light goes out or the electric igniter fails. If the pilot light won't stay lit, the thermocouple may be faulty and should be adjusted or replaced. To adjust the thermocouple, you must tighten the thermocouple nut with a wrench. Take care not to apply too much pressure to the nut—just tighten it slightly. Then try lighting the pilot. If the pilot won't stay lit, replace the thermocouple with a new one of the same type. To replace a thermocouple:

What You'll Need
Wrench
Replacement
    thermocouple

1. Unscrew copper lead and connection nut inside threaded connection to gas line. Under mounting bracket at thermocouple tube, unscrew bracket nut that holds tube in place.

2. Insert new thermocouple into hole in bracket. Be sure steel tube is up and copper lead is down. Under bracket, screw bracket nut over tube. Push connection nut to threaded connection where copper lead connects to gas line. Make sure connection is clean and dry.

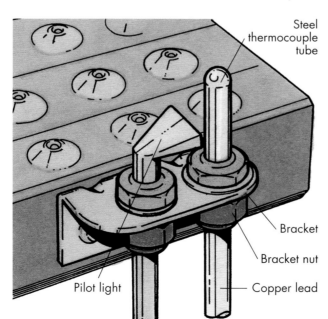

The thermocouple is installed next to the pilot light. A bracket holds it in place, steel tube up and copper lead down.

3. Tightly screw nut into place, but do not overtighten. Both bracket nut and connection nut should be only a little tighter than if hand-tightened.

LIMIT SWITCH The limit switch is a safety control switch located on the furnace just below the plenum. If the plenum gets too hot, the limit switch shuts off the burner. It also shuts off the blower when the temperature drops to a certain level after the burner has shut off. If the blower runs continuously, either the blower control on the thermostat has been set to the ON position or the limit control switch needs adjustment. Check the thermostat first. If the blower control has been set to ON, change it to AUTO; if the blower control is already on AUTO, the limit switch needs adjusting.

To adjust the switch, remove the control's cover. Under it is a toothed dial with one side marked LIMIT; don't touch this side. The other side of the control is marked FAN. There are two pointers on the fan side; the blower goes on at the upper pointer setting and turns off at the lower pointer setting. The pointers should be set about 25° apart. Set the upper pointer at about 115°F and the lower one at about 90°F.

BURNER ADJUSTMENT The flames on the gas burner should be full and steady, with no sputtering and no trace of yellow. To adjust the flame height on the main burners, call a professional service person. To adjust the height of the pilot flame, turn the flame adjustment screw until the flame is from 1½ to 2 inches high. The adjustment screw is located near the gas valve on the pilot assembly, if the control has this adjustment feature.

GAS LEAKS If you suspect leaks around the furnace unit, stir up a mixture of liquid detergent and water. Paint this mixture on the gas supply line along its connections and valves; the soapy water will bubble at any point where there's a leak. If you find a leak, try tightening the leaking connection with a pipe wrench, but be careful not to overtighten the connection. If the pipe connections or valves still leak, call a professional service person.

OIL FURNACES

Oil-fired burners are used in many parts of the country as the basic heat source for warm air and hot water heating systems. Most of the home oil systems in use today are called pressure burners. In this type of system, oil is sprayed into a com-

GAS FURNACE AND HEATER TROUBLESHOOTING CHART

Problem	Possible Cause	Solution
Furnace won't run	1. No power.	1. Check for blown fuses or tripped circuit breakers at main entrance panel or at separate entrance panel; restore circuit.
	2. Switch off.	2. Turn on separate power switch on or near furnace.
	3. Motor overload.	3. Wait 30 minutes; press reset button. Repeat if necessary.
	4. Pilot light out.	4. Relight pilot.
	5. No gas.	5. Make sure gas valve to furnace is fully open.
Not enough heat	1. Thermostat set too low.	1. Raise thermostat setting 5°.
	2. Filter dirty.	2. Clean or replace filter.
	3. Blower clogged.	3. Clean blower assembly.
	4. Registers closed or blocked.	4. Make sure all registers are open and aren't blocked by rugs, drapes, or furniture.
	5. System out of balance.	5. Balance system; see section on forced-air systems.
	6. Blower belt loose or broken.	6. Adjust or replace belt.
	7. Burner dirty.	7. Call a professional.
Pilot won't light	1. Pilot opening blocked.	1. Clean pilot opening.
	2. No gas.	2. Make sure pilot light button is fully depressed; make sure gas valve to furnace is fully open.
Pilot won't stay lit	1. Loose or faulty thermocouple.	1. Tighten thermocouple nut slightly; if no results, replace thermocouple.
	2. Pilot flame set too low.	2. Adjust pilot so flame is about 2 inches long.
	3. Electric pilot faulty.	3. Call a professional.
Furnace turns on and off repeatedly	1. Filter dirty.	1. Clean or replace filter.
	2. Motor and/or blower needs lubrication.	2. If motor and blower have oil ports, lubricate.
	3. Blower clogged.	3. Clean blower assembly.
Blower won't stop running	1. Blower control set wrong.	1. Reset thermostat from ON to AUTO.
	2. Limit switch set wrong.	2. Reset limit switch for stop/start cycling.
	3. Limit control needs adjustment.	3. Call a professional.
Furnace noisy	1. Access panels loose.	1. Mount and fasten access panels correctly.
	2. Belts sticking, worn, or damaged.	2. Spray squeaking drive belts with belt dressing; replace worn or damaged belts.
	3. Blower belt too loose or too tight.	3. Adjust belt.
	4. Motor and/or blower needs lubrication.	4. If motor and blower have oil ports, lubricate.
	5. Burner dirty.	5. Call a professional.

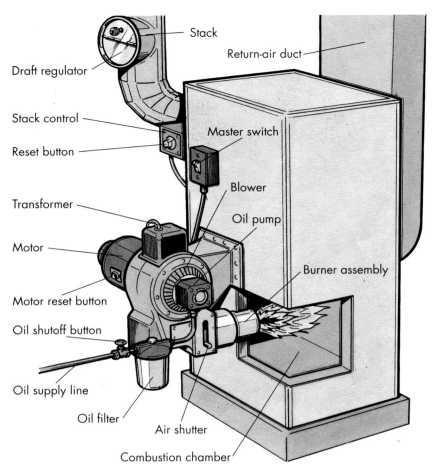

Draft regulator
Stack
Return-air duct
Stack control
Master switch
Reset button
Transformer
Blower
Oil pump
Motor
Motor reset button
Burner assembly
Oil shutoff button
Oil supply line
Oil filter
Air shutter
Combustion chamber

Most oil furnaces in use today are called pressure burners. In this type of system, oil is sprayed into a combustion chamber at high pressure.

An oil furnace is a complex assembly. The maintenance and repair work for this type of furnace is limited to simple parts—the filters, the blower, the motor belts, the switches, and the thermostat. Electrodes, an oil nozzle, air tubes, a transformer, a pump, and other components require special tools and testing equipment and are best left to a professional for service.

To become familiar with your oil furnace, remove the access panel covering the burner blower by removing the retaining screws around the rim of the housing. You can access the air blower and filter through a metal panel on one side of the furnace. The panel is held by either hooks or retaining bolts; slip the panel up and off the hooks or remove the bolts and lift the panel off. Most furnaces have switches and reset buttons located on the motor or in a switch box outside the furnace housing. These are usually identified with stampings or labels, such as DIS-CONNECT SWITCH, RESET, and so on. The stack control sensor, a safety device that monitors burner operation, is positioned in the stack and held with a series of retaining bolts.

OIL FILTERS The oil filter should be changed or cleaned at the start of the heating season and about midway through the season. To clean or replace the filter:

1. Close oil shutoff valve between fuel tank and filter.

2. Unscrew bottom or cup of filter housing, and remove filter.

> **What You'll Need**
> Wrench
> Screwdriver
> Replacement filter and gaskets

3. If filter is disposable, insert new one of same size and type. If furnace has permanent filter, clean filter according to furnace manufacturer's recommendations.

4. Replace old filter gaskets with new ones.

5. Screw in bottom of housing, and open oil shutoff valve.

Some oil furnaces have a pump strainer, which is located on the pump attached to the burner/blower unit. Clean this strainer when you clean the oil filter. Here's how:

1. Unbolt cover of pump housing (where oil line enters burner), and lift off cover.

> **What You'll Need**
> Wrench
> Kerosene
> Old, soft toothbrush
> Replacement pump strainer and gasket

2. Remove thin gasket around rim. Find and remove strainer, which is a cylindrical or cup-shape wire mesh screen.

bustion chamber at high pressure, propelled by a blower, and ignited by an electric spark. The oil continues to burn as the mist is sprayed. While there aren't many quick fixes you can undertake yourself on these types of furnaces, good regular maintenance can help eliminate many problems. Here are a few tips:

- During the heating season, check the smoke from the chimney. If the smoke is black, the furnace is not burning the oil completely and fuel is being wasted. Call a professional service person for adjustments.

- Clean the blower at the beginning of the heating season and again about midway through the season.

- Clean soot from the stack control about midway through the heating season.

- If the blower motor has grease or oil fittings, lubricate the fittings midway through the heating season with cup grease or 10-weight nondetergent motor oil (not all-purpose oil), available at hardware stores.

- Clean the thermostat before each heating season.

OIL FURNACE TROUBLESHOOTING CHART

Problem	Possible Cause	Solution
Furnace won't run	1. No power.	1. Check for blown fuses or tripped circuit breakers at main entrance panel or at separate entrance panel; restore circuit.
	2. Switch off.	2. Turn on separate power switch on or near furnace.
	3. Motor overload.	3. Wait 30 minutes; press reset button. Repeat if necessary.
	4. No fuel.	4. Check tank; if necessary, refill tank.
	5. Fuel line blockage.	5. Clean oil filter and oil pump strainer. If problem persists, call a professional.
Burner won't fire	1. No fuel.	1. Check tank; if necessary, refill tank.
	2. No ignition spark.	2. Press reset button on stack control; if necessary, clean stack control. If no result, call a professional. If furnace has electric-eye safety, clean safety; if no result, call a professional.
Not enough heat	1. Thermostat set too low.	1. Raise thermostat setting 5°.
	2. Air filter dirty.	2. Clean or replace air filter.
	3. Blower clogged.	3. Clean blower assembly.
	4. Registers closed or blocked.	4. Make sure all registers are open; make sure they are not blocked by rugs, drapes, or furniture.
	5. System out of balance.	5. Balance system; see section on forced-air system.
	6. Blower belt loose or broken.	6. Adjust or replace belt.
	7. Burner dirty.	7. Call a professional.
Furnace turns on and off repeatedly	1. Air filter dirty.	1. Clean or replace air filter.
	2. Oil filter dirty.	2. Clean or replace oil filter.
	3. Motor and/or blower needs lubrication.	3. If motor and blower have oil ports, lubricate.
	4. Blower clogged.	4. Clean blower assembly.
	5. Stack control faulty.	5. Call a professional.
Blower won't stop running	1. Blower control set wrong.	1. Reset thermostat from ON to AUTO.
	2. Limit switch set wrong.	2. Reset limit switch.
Furnace noisy	1. Access panels loose.	1. Mount and fasten access panels correctly.
	2. Belts sticking, worn, or damaged.	2. Spray squeaking belts with fan belt dressing; replace worn or damaged belts.
	3. Blower belt too loose or too tight.	3. Adjust belt.
	4. Motor and/or blower needs lubrication.	4. If motor and blower have oil ports, lubricate.
	5. Burner dirty.	5. Call a professional.

3. Soak strainer in kerosene for several minutes to loosen any built-up sludge. Carefully clean strainer with old, soft toothbrush.

4. Inspect strainer. If it's torn or badly bent, replace it with new pump strainer of the same type.

5. Set strainer into place on pump, place new gasket on rim, and bolt cover of pump housing back on.

SWITCHES Some oil furnaces have two master switches. One is located near the burner unit, and the other is near the furnace housing or even at a distance from the furnace. Make sure these master switches are both turned to the ON position.

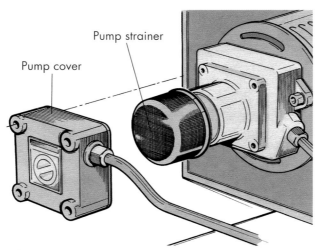

Clean the pump strainer after cleaning the oil filter. To reach the strainer, unbolt the cover of the pump housing and lift off the cover.

STACK CONTROL The stack control, located in the stack, is a safety device that monitors the operation of the oil burner. If the burner fails to ignite, the stack control shuts off the motor. Frequently, however, a furnace shutdown is caused by a malfunctioning stack control rather than by the burner. If the burner fails to ignite, first check the fuel tank and refill it if necessary. If the tank doesn't need to be refilled, press the reset button on the stack control. If the burner doesn't ignite after you've pressed the button once, clean the control, as detailed below. Then press the reset button again. If the burner still doesn't operate, call a professional service person.

The stack control gradually becomes coated with soot during the heating season. To keep it working properly, clean the control every month or as soon as it becomes soot-covered. To clean the stack control:

1. Remove bolts that hold control in stack. Pull out sensor and its housing.

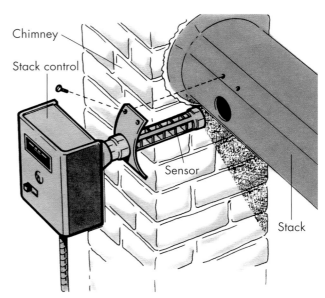

Clean the stack control every month. To remove the control, turn off the power to the furnace, then back out the bolts that hold it in the stack.

2. With brush dipped in soapy water, remove all soot from control. Wipe control dry with soft cloth.

3. Before replacing control, clean stack. Spread newspaper to protect floor, then disassemble stack. As you work, remove soot and debris from each section by tapping them firmly on newspaper-covered floor.

4. After cleaning sections, reassemble them in reverse order. Make sure stack sections are properly aligned and firmly connected.

5. Finally, reposition stack control in stack, and reseal connection to chimney with refractory cement.

Some oil furnaces have an electric-eye safety switch instead of a stack control. This switch serves the same function as the stack control. If the burner has an electric-eye safety, remove the access cover over the photocell; it is held by hooks or retaining screws. Wipe the cover clean to remove accumulated soot. Reassemble the switch, replace the cover, and turn the power back on. If the burner still doesn't ignite, call a professional service person.

If the stack control or electric-eye safety switch is especially dirty, the furnace may not be properly set to burn the fuel completely. In this case, call a professional service person for adjustment. **Caution:** Do not attempt to replace these controls yourself.

DRAFT REGULATOR The draft regulator, located on the stack, is closed when the burner is off but opens automatically to let air into the chimney when the burner is turned on. Accumulated soot and rattling are signs that the draft regulator needs to be adjusted. Too much air in the chimney wastes heat; too little air wastes fuel by failing to burn it completely. To increase the airflow, screw the counterweight inward. To decrease airflow, turn the counterweight outward. The draft regulator should be adjusted by a professional service person as part of regular annual maintenance.

LIMIT SWITCH The limit switch is a safety control switch and is located on the furnace just below the plenum. If the plenum gets too hot, the limit switch shuts off the burner. It also shuts off the blower when the temperature drops to a certain level after the burner has shut off. If the blower runs continuously, either the blower control on the thermostat has been set to the ON position, or the limit control switch needs adjustment. To determine the problem, check the thermostat. If the blower control has been set to ON, change it to AUTO; if blower control is already on AUTO, the limit switch needs adjusting. To do this, remove the control's cover and find the toothed dial underneath. One side is marked LIMIT; don't touch this side. The other side is marked FAN. There are two pointers on the fan side; the blower turns on at the upper pointer setting and shuts off at the lower pointer setting. Pointers should be set about 25° apart. Set the upper pointer at about 115°F and the lower one at about 90°F.

BURNER ADJUSTMENTS Do not try to adjust the burner of an oil furnace; call a professional service person.

ELECTRIC FURNACES AND HEATERS

Although an electric heating system does have advantages, its operating cost generally makes it less desirable than any of the other furnace systems available today. The high cost means that minimizing heat loss caused by improperly installed ducts or inadequate insulation is even more important than with other types of systems.

For maximum energy efficiency, have a professional service person clean and adjust your electric furnace every year before the beginning of the heating season. Do not attempt any repairs to the heating elements, electrical connections, relays, transformers, or similar components of an electric furnace; repairs to these components must be made by a professional service person.

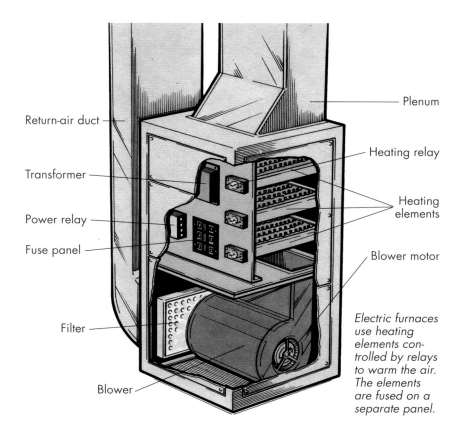

Return-air duct

Transformer

Power relay

Fuse panel

Filter

Blower

Plenum

Heating relay

Heating elements

Blower motor

Electric furnaces use heating elements controlled by relays to warm the air. The elements are fused on a separate panel.

The controls of an electric furnace may be mounted on the surface of the housing or installed behind an access panel on the front of the furnace. The access panel may be slip-fit on hooks fastened to the furnace housing with a series of sheet-metal screws. To remove the access panel to the blower, filter, and blower motor, slip the panel up off hooks or remove a series of sheet-metal screws.

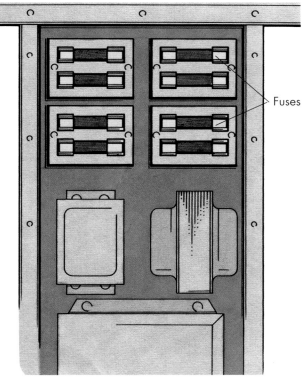

Fuses

The heating elements on an electric furnace are fused on a separate panel located on or inside the furnace housing.

ELECTRIC FURNACE TROUBLESHOOTING CHART

Problem	Possible Cause	Solution
Furnace won't run	1. No power.	1. Check for blown fuses or tripped circuit breakers at main entrance panel, at separate entrance panel, and on or in furnace; restore circuit.
	2. Switch off.	2. Turn on separate power switch on or near furnace.
	3. Motor overload.	3. Wait 30 minutes; press reset button. Repeat if necessary.
Not enough heat	1. Thermostat set too low.	1. Raise thermostat setting 5°.
	2. Filter dirty.	2. Clean or replace filter.
	3. Blower clogged.	3. Clean blower assembly.
	4. Registers closed or blocked.	4. Make sure all registers are open; make sure they are not blocked by rugs, drapes, or furniture.
	5. System out of balance.	5. Balance system; see section on forced-air systems.
	6. Blower belt loose or broken.	6. Adjust or replace belt.
	7. Element faulty.	7. Call a professional.
Furnace turns on and off repeatedly	1. Filter dirty.	1. Clean or replace filter.
	2. Motor and/or blower needs lubrication.	2. If motor and blower have oil ports, lubricate.
	3. Blower clogged.	3. Clean blower assembly.
Blower won't stop running	1. Blower control set wrong.	1. Reset thermostat from ON to AUTO.
	2. Relays faulty.	2. Call a professional.
Furnace noisy	1. Access panels loose.	1. Mount and fasten access panels correctly.
	2. Belts sticking, worn, or damaged.	2. Spray squeaking belts with fan belt dressing; replace worn or damaged belts.
	3. Blower belt too loose or too tight.	3. Adjust belt.
	4. Motor and/or blower needs lubrication.	4. If motor and blower have oil ports, lubricate.

FUSES Electric furnaces are fused at a building's main electrical service entrance. Many electric furnaces are on separate circuits, sometimes located in a separate fuse box away from the main panel. The heating elements of the furnace are also fused, and these fuses are located on a panel that is on or inside the furnace housing. If changing the fuses or resetting the breakers does not restore power to the furnace, call a professional service person. Do not attempt to repair heating elements, the transformer, heating relays, or power relays. Repairs to these components must be made by a professional service person.

HEAT PUMPS

A heat pump not only heats your home during the winter, it also cools it during the summer. It does not burn fuel to produce heat nor does the electricity it consumes go through an element. The heat pump functions on the same principle as refrigerators and air conditioners: A liquid absorbs heat as it turns into a gas and releases heat as it returns to a liquid state.

During the summer, the heat pump operates as a standard central air conditioner: It removes heat from the house and vents it to the outside. A liquid refrigerant is pumped through an evaporator coil of tubing. The liquid expands as it moves through the coil, changing to its gaseous state as it absorbs heat from the air surrounding the coil. A blower then pushes air around the cooled coil through ducts and into the house. The gas, now carrying considerable heat, moves through a compressor and begins the liquefying process. It then moves to a condensor coil outside the house, where the compressed gas releases its heat and returns to a liquid state.

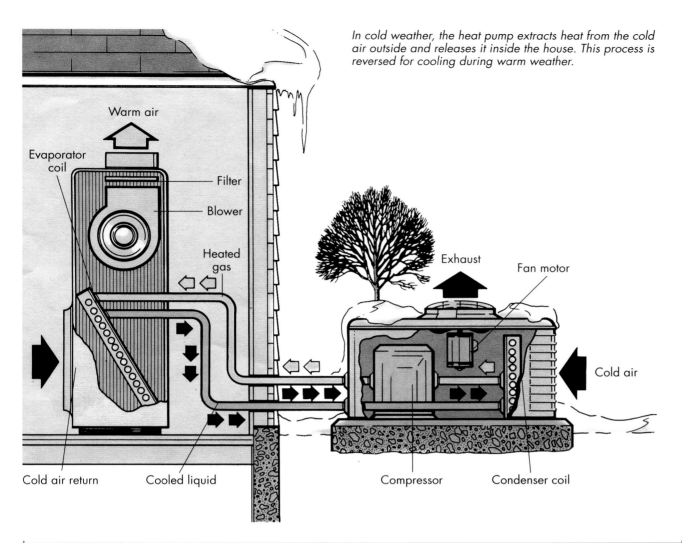

In cold weather, the heat pump extracts heat from the cold air outside and releases it inside the house. This process is reversed for cooling during warm weather.

Warm air

Evaporator coil

Filter

Blower

Heated gas

Cold air return

Cooled liquid

Exhaust

Fan motor

Cold air

Compressor

Condenser coil

HEAT PUMP TROUBLESHOOTING CHART

Problem	Possible Cause	Solution
Pump won't run	1. No power.	1. Check for blown fuses or tripped circuit breakers at main entrance panel or at separate entrance panel; restore circuit.
	2. Switch off.	2. Make sure switch is turned on.
	3. Pump overloaded.	3. Wait 30 minutes; press reset button on outside cabinet. Repeat if necessary.
	4. Coil blocked with dirt or ice.	4. Remove debris from around coil.
	5. Reversing valve stuck.	5. Set on emergency heat and call a professional.
Ice on coil	1. Coil blocked with dirt.	1. Remove debris from around coil.
	2. Reversing valve stuck.	2. Set on emergency heat and call a professional.
Not enough heat	1. Thermostat set too low.	1. Raise temperature setting of thermostat 5° to 10°.
	2. Filter dirty.	2. Clean or replace filter.
	3. Problems in distribution system.	3. See sections on electric furnaces and forced-air systems.
	4. Problems in auxiliary heater.	4. See section on electric furnaces.
Pump goes on and off repeatedly	1. Coil blocked with dirt.	1. Remove dirt and debris from around coil.
	2. Filter dirty.	2. Clean or replace filter.
	3. Problems in distribution system.	3. See sections on electric furnaces and forced-air systems.

During the winter, the heat pump reverses this process, extracting heat from the cold air outside and releasing it inside the house. The heat pump is very efficient when the outside temperature is around 45°F to 50°F, but it becomes less efficient as the temperature drops. When the outside air temperature is very low, an auxilery electric heater must be used to supplement the heat pump's output. Like standard electric heating systems, this auxilery unit is more expensive to operate. Thus, in areas where the winter temperature is below freezing, a heat pump is not practical. It has few advantages over conventional heating systems in areas where air conditioning is not necessary, but it is very efficient in warm to hot climates.

Heat pump maintenance is important. Small problems that are not addressed early can lead to very expensive compressor problems later. And since maintaining a heat pump is more technical than caring for the average heating system, you should call a professional service person when the pump malfunctions. You can, however, keep the system free of dirt by keeping the filter clean and by removing any other obstacles to the flow of air.

GENERAL MAINTENANCE Replace filters and clean and lubricate the components of a heat pump regularly. Use the procedures detailed for electric furnaces on pages 101–102.

OUTDOOR MAINTENANCE Heat pumps, like central air conditioners, have an outdoor unit that contains a compressor, a coil, a fan, and other components. To function properly, this unit should be kept free of debris such as leaves and dirt. The unit should be level on its concrete support pad.

Clean pine needles, leaves, and dirt out of updraft fans by removing the grille, which is held to the frame by a series of retaining screws. Make sure the power to the unit is off before tackling this type of cleaning. A vacuum cleaner hose can sometimes be inserted between the fan blades to remove debris from the sides and bottom of the unit.

At the beginning of each heating season, set a carpenters' level across the top of the metal cabinet and check the level from side to side and from front to back. If the unit is no longer level on the pad, lift the pad back to level by prying it up with a pry bar or a piece of 2×4. Build up the ground under it with stone or crushed rock. Also check the piping insulation for deterioration. If this insulation is faulty, replace it with new insulation, available at heating supply stores. Installation instructions are usually provided by the manufacturer.

POWER INTERRUPTION If a heat pump has been off for more than an hour because of a blown fuse, a tripped circuit breaker, or a utility power failure, the unit should not be operated for about six to eight hours—especially if the temperature is 50°F or lower. The lubricant in the pump's oil reservoir may be too cool to circulate properly and may cause damage to the valves of the unit. Instead, set the pump on emergency heat. This turns the pump off and keeps it from running. Leave the pump in this mode for about six to eight hours, then switch the pump to its normal heating setting. If little or no heat is generated at this point, call a professional service person for repairs.

QUICK DISTRIBUTION SYSTEM FIXES

The way heat is distributed is as important as how it's generated. Whatever type of system you have, regular maintenance is essential to make the best use of the heat your furnace provides. Forced-air systems are the most common; radiant heat is also widely used. Gravity systems, the simplest of the three types, are not as efficient as forced-air and radiant heat and are not used much today. To maintain the ducts, registers, and returns of a gravity system, follow the procedures detailed for forced-air systems.

FORCED-AIR SYSTEMS

Fueled by gas, electricity, or oil, a forced-air distribution system is just what the name implies. Air is forced from the furnace through ducts to registers in various rooms. Besides warming the air, the blower system that distributes the warmed air also returns the cold air to the furnace so it can be rewarmed and distributed to the rooms again. A forced-air system is also efficient for distributing cool air from a central air conditioner with the same ducts, registers, and blower. There is little that can go wrong with a forced-air system. The big problems typically include noise and blockage of airflow, usually caused by dirt or by furniture or draperies blocking the registers. Forced-air systems should be cleaned and maintained regularly (see procedures in the troubleshooting chart opposite).

FORCED-AIR SYSTEM TROUBLESHOOTING CHART

Problem	Possible Cause	Solution
Motor won't run	1. No power.	1. Check for blown fuses or tripped circuit breakers at main entrance panel, at separate entrance panel, and on furnace; restore circuit. Also see charts for specific furnaces.
	2. Switch off.	2. Turn on separate power switch on or near furnace.
	3. Motor overload.	3. Wait 30 minutes; press reset button. Repeat if necessary.
Not enough heat	1. Thermostat set too low.	1. Raise thermostat setting 5°.
	2. Filter dirty.	2. Clean or replace filter.
	3. Blower clogged.	3. Clean blower assembly.
	4. Registers closed or blocked.	4. Make sure registers are open; make sure they are not blocked by rugs, drapes, or furniture.
	5. Blower running too slow.	5. Increase blower speed.
	6. Blower loose.	6. Tighten nut that holds blower to drive shaft.
	7. Blower belt misaligned or broken.	7. Adjust or replace belt.
	8. Duct joints loose.	8. Trace ducts and wrap leaking joints with duct tape.
	9. Ducts losing heat.	9. Insulate ducts.
Uneven heating	1. System out of balance.	1. Balance system.
Blower won't stop running	1. Blower control set wrong.	1. Reset thermostat from ON to AUTO.
	2. Limit switch set wrong (gas or oil furnace).	2. Reset limit switch; see sections on gas and oil furnaces.
	3. Limit control needs adjustment.	3. Call a professional.
System noisy	1. Access panels loose.	1. Mount and fasten access panels correctly.
	2. Blower running too fast.	2. Decrease blower speed.
	3. Belts sticking, worn, or damaged.	3. Spray squeaking drive belts with belt dressing; replace worn belts.
	4. Blower belt too loose or too tight.	4. Adjust belt.
	5. Blower/motor pulleys loose or misaligned.	5. Tighten pulleys on shafts, and/or realign pulleys.
	6. Blower/motor needs lubrication.	6. Lubricate blower/motor.
	7. Ducting loose.	7. Make sure ducts are tightly fastened to framing with duct hangers; wrap joints with duct tape.

Floor registers are slip-fit into ducts or are held by retaining screws on the frame of the register. Wall and ceiling registers are also held in place by retaining screws on the frame of the register. Duct joints are usually slip-fit and held with sheet-metal screws or duct tape. The ducts are supported by wire or metal strap hangers nailed or screwed to wooden framing members such as studs and rafters. All of these parts are easy to disassemble. Lay them out in order as you work so you'll be able to reassemble them properly.

BALANCING THE SYSTEM Forced-air systems often go out of balance, causing some of the rooms in a home to be too hot or too cold. The furnace is usually not to blame; the problem is caused by ducts and registers that are not properly set. You should balance the system while the furnace is turned on.

To balance a forced-air system, open all the ducts and registers in the system. There may be dampers in various ducts that need to be turned to open the ducts. The damper is open when it's

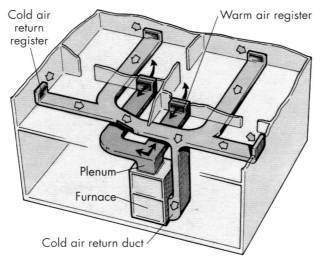

A forced-air distribution system uses a blower to distribute warmed air and to return cold air to the furnace so it can be rewarmed and distributed again.

turned parallel with the top and bottom of the ducting.

Next, gather six or seven thermometers and get them all to have about the same temperature reading. You can do this by laying out the thermometers together for about 30 minutes and then noting any discrepancies. Tape the thermometers on the walls of each room so each thermometer is about 36 inches up from the floor, away from the hot air register or cold air return. Wait one hour, then take a thermometer reading in each room when the heat is on. If one room shows a higher temperature than an adjoining room, close the damper or register slightly in the hotter room.

Follow this procedure for each room in your home, opening and closing dampers and registers until the same temperature is maintained in each room or the temperature balance you want

To check alignment of the motor and blower pulleys, place a carpenters' square against them. The pulleys should be in a straight line at right angles to the motor shaft.

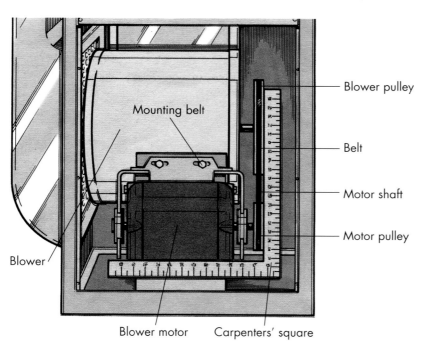

is reached. The thermostat to the furnace should be kept at the same reading while you balance the system.

ADJUSTING BLOWER SPEED An increase in blower speed can sometimes improve the flow of warm air through your home. A decrease can make the system quieter. You can increase or decrease the blower speed by slightly adjusting the pulley on the blower drive motor. To increase blower speed, slightly loosen the setscrew that holds the pulley to the driveshaft. Move or turn the pulley clockwise on the shaft one turn, then tighten setscrew. If more speed is desired, turn the pulley clockwise two turns. For decreasing blower speed, loosen the setscrew that holds the pulley to the driveshaft. Move or turn the pulley counterclockwise on the drive-shaft one turn, then tighten the setscrew. If less speed is desired, turn the pulley counterclock-wise two turns.

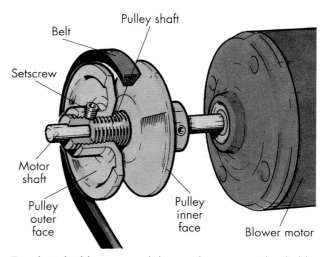

To adjust the blower speed, loosen the setscrew that holds the pulley to the drive shaft, and turn the pulley on the shaft.

The motor and blower pulley may also get out of alignment. This causes the blower to be noisy and cuts down on the efficiency of your distribution system. To check alignment, place a carpenters' square against the outside of the motor and blower pulleys. The pulleys should be in a straight line and at right angles to the motor shaft. If the pulleys are not lined up at right angles to the motor housing, loosen the setscrew holding the motor pulley and move the pulley backward or forward as needed to align it properly. If the setscrew is jammed or rusted and won't loosen or if the pulleys are out of alignment, loosen the mounting bolts on the motor and slide the motor backward or forward until the pulleys are properly aligned.

NOISE PROBLEMS Air forced through the ducts of a forced-air system can cause vibration and noise if the ducts are not firmly connected. The best way to stop this noise is to add duct hangers to the ducting system. The hangers are usually wrapped around or across the ducting and nailed or screwed to the stud or rafter framing. At the elbows of the ducts, where air moving through the ducts changes direction, the duct sections can become loose or separated. Push loose sections back together, and tape the joints firmly with duct tape to stop vibrations.

Noise can also be caused by inadequate lubrication, worn or damaged belts, or too high blower speed. Correct these problems as detailed earlier in this chapter.

HEAT LOSS FROM DUCTS If ducts run through cold basements or exterior crawl spaces, wrap the ducts with fiberglass insulation. Spiral insulation around the ducting and secure it with duct tape, wire, or heavy cord. Or, wrap the ducts with aluminum-face insulating tape, sold in wide rolls and available at heating supply stores.

HOT WATER SYSTEMS

Hot water and steam systems work similarly, but neither are typically installed in newer homes. However, because both are still in existing homes, here are some maintenance and quick fix tips for them.

Because water retains heat, it is used to store and distribute heat in home systems. There are two types of hot water systems: the gravity system and the hydronic or forced hot water type. Hot water heating systems can be powered by gas, oil, or electricity.

Gravity systems depend on the upward flow of hot water to circulate heated water from the boiler through a system of pipes to radiators in the rooms of your home. The better radiators for hot water systems are called convectors. These units employ a series of fans to disperse the heat.

The heat from the water in the radiators or convectors is transferred first to the metal radiators and then to the air. As the water loses its heat, it sinks and flows back to the boiler through return pipes. Most gravity systems heat the water to no more than about 180°F, and cooled water that goes back to the boiler rarely falls below 120°F. Open gravity systems have an overflow outlet to let water escape; this prevents a buildup of excess pressure in the system. Closed systems have a sealed expansion tank; when water pressure builds up in the system, the excess water flows into the expansion tank to prevent damage

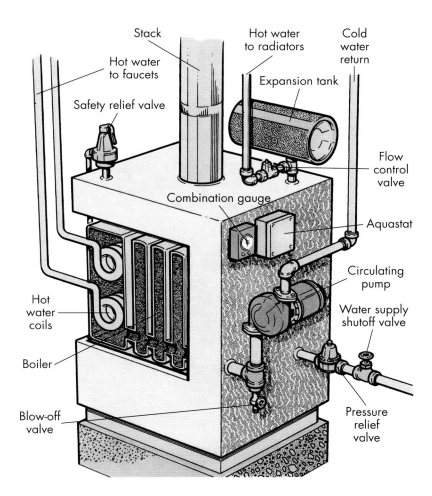

to the pipes or the boiler. Hydronic hot water systems are much like closed gravity systems, except a hydronic system uses a motor-driven circulating pump to move the water. As a result, water in a hydronic system moves more rapidly and arrives at the room radiator with less heat loss than water in a gravity system.

SLOPE Hot water systems depend on proper slope. All pipes and radiators must slope back toward the boiler. Hammering noises and failure to heat indicate incorrect slope. To correct these malfunctions, check the slope of radiators and pipes, and prop radiators or fasten pipes so all components are properly tilted.

WATER LEVEL The water level in a hot water system's boiler should be maintained at about half full. There should be an air space between the surface of the water and the top of the tank. A water level that is too low can cause inadequate heating. In most cases, an automatic filling system keeps the boiler filled with the proper amount of water. However, if the water level of the system is consistently low, check the pipes for leaks. Close the water supply valve and note the water level for two or three days. If the level drops drastically, call a professional service person.

EXPANSION TANK For efficient heating, the water in a hot water system is heated well above

Hydronic hot water systems use a motor-driven circulating pump to move the hot water; the water moves rapidly and arrives at the radiator with little heat loss.

HOT WATER SYSTEM TROUBLESHOOTING CHART

Problem	Possible Cause	Solution
System won't run	1. Problems in boiler/furnace assembly.	1. See sections on specific furnaces.
Not enough heat (entire system)	1. Thermostat set too low.	1. Raise temperature setting on thermostat 5°.
	2. Boiler water level low.	2. Check boiler; if necessary, let boiler cool, and refill half full.
	3. Problems in boiler/furnace assembly.	3. See sections on specific furnaces.
	4. Rust or scale in boiler and/or pipes.	4. Flush boiler system. If problem persists, call a professional.
	5. Aquastat faulty.	5. Call a professional.
	6. Combination gauge faulty.	6. Call a professional.
	7. Problem in boiler.	7. Call a professional.
Not enough heat (radiator)	1. Radiator not sloping properly.	1. Check slope; prop radiator or adjust return pipes to slope toward boiler.
	2. Inlet valve closed or only partially open.	2. Open inlet valve completely.
	3. Air trapped in radiator.	3. Open air vent valve to purge air.
	4. Radiator blocked.	4. Make sure radiators are not blocked by rugs, drapes, or furniture.
Leaks	1. Loose pipe connection.	1. Tighten pipe connection.
	2. Worn stem packing or washer on inlet valve.	2. Replace stem packing or washer on inlet valve.
	3. Circulator seal or impeller faulty.	3. Call a professional.
Relief valve leaks	1. Air in system.	1. Drain expansion tank.
Pipes or radiator noisy	1. Cold water trapped in system.	1. Check slope; prop radiators or adjust return pipes to slope toward boiler.
	2. Circulator coupler broken.	2. Call a professional.

boiling, but it doesn't turn to steam because the expansion tank and a pressure-reducing valve keep the water under pressure. Usually the expansion tank is hung from the basement ceiling, not far from the boiler. In older systems, look for the expansion tank in the attic. If there is not enough air in the expansion tank, the buildup of pressure will force water out of the safety relief valve located above the boiler. Without enough air in the tank, the tank fills with water. The water expands as it heats up and then escapes through the safety relief valve. Check for air in the expansion tank by lightly touching it. Normally, the bottom half of the tank feels warmer than the top; if the tank feels hot all over, it has filled with water and must be drained. To drain an expansion tank:

1. Turn off power to boiler. Close water supply shutoff valve, and let tank cool.

2. A combination drain valve lets water out and air in when it's opened. If there is a combina-tion valve, attach garden hose to valve and drain 2 or 3 gallons of water. If there is no combination valve, shut off valve between expansion tank and boiler, and completely drain expansion tank.

3. Turn water supply back on. Then turn on power to boiler to get system running again. It isn't necessary to refill expansion tank; it will fill up as part of system's normal operation.

RADIATORS If an individual radiator is cold and both it and the pipes leading to it are tilted properly, check the radiator's inlet valve. This valve must be opened all the way for the radiator to function properly. If some radiators get warmer than others, the vents are probably not adjusted properly. Adjust the vents so the ones farthest from the boiler are opened more than the vents closest to the boiler.

Air trapped in a radiator can prevent water from entering and keep it from heating. To remove air trapped in the system, open air vent valve on unit so hissing stops and water comes out. Use screw-driver or key furnished by manufacturer to open vent. If you don't have key, look for one at a heating supply store. Close vent, then reopen it for desired heat.

Some radiators have automatic valves; they don't have to be opened or closed.

CIRCULATOR The circulator is a pump that forces the hot water to radiators throughout a house. Problems with the circulator usually occur when the coupler that separates the motor from the pump breaks. This will generally make a lot of noise. Another source of trouble with the circulator is the pump seal. If water leaks from the pump, chances are the seal is damaged. If the circulator develops either of these problems, call a professional service person.

LEAKS Hot water systems are prone to plumbing leaks in the pipes and at inlet valves. Pipe leaks are frequently caused by loose connections and can be stopped by tightening the connections with a wrench. Leaks around inlet valves, however, are due to deterioration of the stem packing or the washer in the valve.

Radiator inlet valves consist of a packing nut, a valve body or stem, and a washer assembly. To replace the valve packing or the washer:

1. Shut off boiler and let it cool. It isn't necessary to shut off water; as system cools, water will flow back out of radiator to boiler.

2. Remove screw that holds handle in place. Unscrew packing nut, remove handle, and back out valve stem or body.

3. Remove screw and washer at bottom of stem. Replace washer with new one of the same size and type.

4. Install new packing while reassembling valve.

5. Tighten all connections, and then turn system back on.

FLUSHING AND DRAINING SYSTEM Once a year, the entire heating system should be flushed to keep the pipes clear and the water flowing freely. To flush the system, open the blow-off valve and let the water run off into a bucket until it runs clear. If the water still looks rusty after the system has been flushed, call a professional service person.

What You'll Need
Screwdriver
Replacement washers and packing

STEAM SYSTEM TROUBLESHOOTING CHART

Problem	Possible Cause	Solution
System won't run	1. Problems in boiler/furnace assembly.	1. See sections on specific furnaces.
Not enough heat (entire system)	1. Thermostat set too low.	1. Raise thermostat 5°.
	2. Boiler water level low.	2. Check boiler; if necessary, let boiler cool and refill half full.
	3. Problems in boiler/furnace assembly.	3. See sections on specific furnaces.
	4. Rust or scale in boiler and/or pipes.	4. Flush boiler system; add antiscale preparation. If problem persists, call a professional.
	5. Problem in boiler.	5. Call a professional.
Not enough heat (radiator)	1. Radiator or pipes not sloping properly.	1. Check slope; prop radiator or adjust supply pipes to slope toward boiler.
	2. Inlet valve closed or partially open.	2. Open inlet valve completely.
	3. Air trapped in radiator.	3. Clear or replace air vent.
	4. Radiator blocked.	4. Make sure radiators are not blocked by rugs, drapes, or furniture.
Uneven heat	1. Air vents not sized or adjusted properly.	1. Adjust air vents so that those far away from boiler are open more than those close to the boiler.
Leaks	1. Loose pipe connection.	1. Tighten pipe connection.
	2. Worn stem packing or washer on inlet valve.	2. Replace stem packing or washer on inlet valve.
Water level gauge unreadable	1. Rust or scale in system.	1. Flush boiler system; add antiscale preparation. If problem persists, call a professional.
Pipes or radiators noisy	1. Water trapped in system.	1. Check slope; prop radiators or adjust supply pipes to slope toward the boiler.

Hot water systems should be drained to prevent the pipes from freezing during a prolonged cold weather power failure. It may also be necessary to drain the system to make repairs. To drain the pipes:

What You'll Need
Wrench
Garden hose

1. Turn off power to boiler, and let water cool until it's just warm.

2. Turn off water supply valve, and attach length of garden hose to boiler drain.

3. Open drain valve and air vents of all radiators. Water from system will flow out through hose. Give valve plenty of time to drain.

4. To refill system, close air vents on all radiators, and shut drain valve. Turn on water supply to boiler. If boiler has automatic shutoff, refilling is automatic. If there is no automatic shutoff, fill it until combination valve gauge reads 20 pounds of pressure per square inch (psi).

5. Release air from all convectors in system so they'll heat properly. Gauge on boiler should read 12 psi. If pressure on gauge shows less than 12 psi, add more water. If pressure is above 12 psi, drain off some water.

QUICK COOLING SYSTEM FIXES

There are two types of home cooling systems—central air conditioning and individual room air conditioners. Both systems use the same components—a condenser, which uses electricity to cool a refrigerant liquid in a coil, and an evapo-

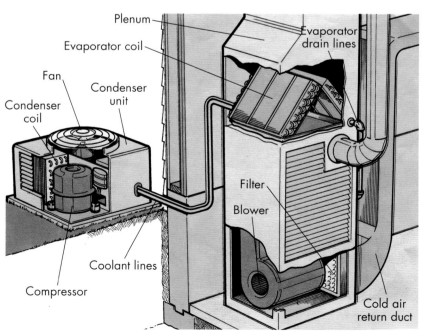

Central air conditioners are made up of two separate components: the condenser unit, located outside the house on a concrete slab, and the evaporator coil above the furnace.

rator, which cools the air in your home. Heat pumps, when operated in their cooling cycle, function as central air conditioners. Procedures for heat pump maintenance and repairs are detailed earlier in this chapter.

CENTRAL AIR CONDITIONING

Central air conditioners have two separate components: the condenser and the evaporator. The condenser unit is usually located outside the house on a concrete slab. The evaporator coil is mounted in the plenum or main duct junction above the furnace.

Most central air conditioners are connected to a home's forced-air distribution system. Thus, the same motor, blower, and ductwork used for heating are used to distribute cool air from the air conditioning system. When a central air conditioner is operating, hot air inside the house flows to the furnace through the return-air duct. The hot air is moved by the blower across the cooled evaporator coil in the plenum and is then delivered through ducts to cool the house. When the air conditioner works but the house doesn't cool, the problem is probably in the distribution system. In this case, refer to the section on troubleshooting forced-air systems on page 105.

Both the evaporator and the condenser are sealed. Therefore, a professional service person should be called for almost any maintenance other than routine cleaning. Central air conditioners should be professionally inspected and adjusted before the beginning of every cooling season. However, don't let your maintenance end with this annual checkup. While there aren't many repairs you can make yourself, there are specific maintenance procedures you can follow to keep your system operating at peak efficiency. **Caution:** Before doing any work on an air conditioning system, make sure the power to the system, both to the condenser and to the evaporator assembly, is turned off.

EVAPORATOR The evaporator is located directly above the furnace in the plenum. The evaporator may not be accessible, but if it is, you should clean it once a year. If the plenum has foil-wrapped insulation at its front, you can clean the evaporator; if the plenum is a sealed sheet metal box, do not attempt to open it. To clean an accessible evaporator:

1. Remove foil-wrapped insulation at front of plenum; it's

What You'll Need
Screwdriver
Stiff brush
Large hand mirror
Household bleach
Wire

CENTRAL AIR CONDITIONER TROUBLESHOOTING CHART

Problem	Possible Cause	Solution
Condenser doesn't run	1. No power.	1. Check for blown fuses or tripped circuit breakers at main entrance panel or at separate entrance panel; restore circuit.
	2. Thermostat set too high.	2. Lower thermostat setting 5°.
	3. Motor faulty.	3. Call a professional.
	4. Compressor faulty.	4. Call a professional.
Uneven cooling	1. Distribution system out of balance.	1. Balance system; see section on forced-air systems.
Inadequate cooling	1. Thermostat set too high.	1. Lower thermostat setting 5°.
	2. Evaporator dirty.	2. Clean evaporator.
	3. Unit too small.	3. Replace with larger unit; call a professional.
	4. Problem in distribution system.	4. See section on forced-air systems.
Unit doesn't cool	1. Thermostat set too high.	1. Lower thermostat setting 5°.
	2. Condenser dirty.	2. Clean condenser coil and fins; if necessary, straighten fins.
	3. Condenser unit blocked.	3. Remove debris blocking condenser; cut down weeds, grass, and vines.
	4. Evaporator dirty.	4. Clean evaporator.
	5. Problem in distribution system.	5. See section on forced-air systems.
	6. Compressor faulty.	6. Call a professional.
	7. Not enough refrigerant in system.	7. Call a professional.
Condenser unit turns on and off repeatedly	1. Condenser dirty.	1. Clean condenser coil and fins.
	2. Condenser unit blocked.	2. Remove debris blocking condenser; cut down weeds, grass, and vines.
	3. Evaporator dirty.	3. Clean evaporator.
	4. Problem in distribution system.	4. See section on forced-air systems.

probably taped in place. Remove tape carefully, because you'll have to replace it later. Behind insulation is access plate, which is held in place by several screws. Remove screws and lift off plate.

2. Clean entire underside of evaporator unit with stiff brush. A large hand mirror can help you see what you're doing. If you can't reach all the way back to clean entire area, slide evaporator out a little. Evaporator can be slid out even if it has rigid pipes connected to it, but be careful not to bend pipes.

3. Clean tray below evaporator unit. This tray carries condensation away from evaporator. Pour 1 tablespoon of household bleach into weep hole in tray to prevent fungus growth. In extremely humid weather, check condensate drain and pan every other day. If there's much moisture in pan, weep hole from pan to drain line may be clogged. Open weep hole with piece of wire.

4. Put unit back into place, reinstall plate, and tape insulation back over it.

5. Turn back on air conditioner, and check for air leaks. Seal any leaks with duct tape.

CONDENSER In most systems, the condenser unit is located outside the house and is prone to accumulated dirt and debris from trees, lawn mowing, and airborne dust. The condenser has a fan that moves air across the condenser coil. You must clean the coil on the intake side, so, before you turn off the power to the air conditioner, check to see which direction the air moves across the coils. To clean the condenser:

1. Cut down any grass, weeds, or vines that have grown around condenser unit; they could be obstructing airflow.

2. Clean condenser with commercial coil cleaner, available at refrigerator supply stores. Instructions for use are included. Flush coil clean (do not use hose); let dry.

What You'll Need
Grass shears or pruners
Spray bottle of coil cleaner
Soft brush
Fin comb
Carpenters' level
Pry bar or piece of 2×4
Gravel or rocks

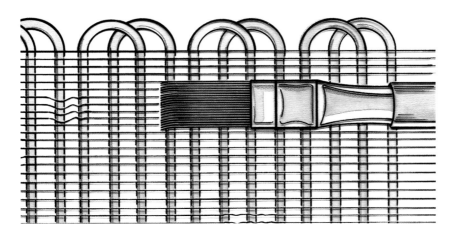

If the fins on a condenser are bent, carefully straighten them with a fin comb.

3. Clean fins with soft brush to remove accumulated dirt. You may have to remove protective grille to reach them. Do not clean fins with garden hose, as water could turn dirt into mud and compact it between fins. Clean fins very carefully: They're made of light-gauge aluminum and are easily damaged. If fins are bent, straighten them with fin comb, sold at most appliance parts stores. A fin comb is designed to slide into spaces between fins. Use it carefully to avoid damaging fins.

4. Check concrete pad on which condenser rests to make sure it's level. Set carpenters' level front to back and side to side on top of unit. If pad has settled, lift pad with pry bar or piece of 2×4, then force gravel or rocks under concrete to level it.

During the fall and winter, outside condenser units should be protected from the elements to prevent leaf blockage and ice damage. Cover the condenser unit with a commercial condenser cover made to fit the shape of the unit or use heavy plastic sheeting secured with sturdy cord.

REFRIGERANT The coolant used in most air conditioning systems is a refrigerant called Freon. If the system does not contain the proper amount of Freon, little or no cooling will take place. If you suspect a Freon problem, call a professional service person to recharge the system. **Caution:** Do not try to charge your system's refrigerant lines.

Here's a quick fix you can make to the system's coolant lines. Examine the lines running from the condenser outside the evaporator inside the house. If the insulation is damaged or worn, it will cut down on the cooling efficiency of the unit and, therefore, should be replaced. Replace damaged or worn coolant line insulation with new insulation of the same type as soon as possible. Follow manufacturer's instructions for installation.

DISTRIBUTION SYSTEM In most cases, circulation problems and noisy operation are caused by problems in your home's heating and cooling distribution system. For instructions on correcting distribution problems, see the section on troubleshooting forced-air systems on page 105.

ROOM AIR CONDITIONERS

Room air conditioners, also called window units, work the same way central air conditioners do. They are smaller than central systems and often more expensive to operate. Depending on its size, a room unit may cool only the room in which it's located, or it may be able to cool adjoining rooms as well.

Sandwiched between the coils are a compressor, two fans, a motor, and thermostat controls. Dirt is the biggest enemy of window air conditioners; it can lower the efficiency of the evaporator coil, block the operation of the fan that blows out the cool air, clog filters, and block drain ports.

The coils, the compressor, and the motor of a room air conditioner are sealed components, so any repairs to them should be left to a professional service person. However, you can make minor repairs, and regular maintenance will keep

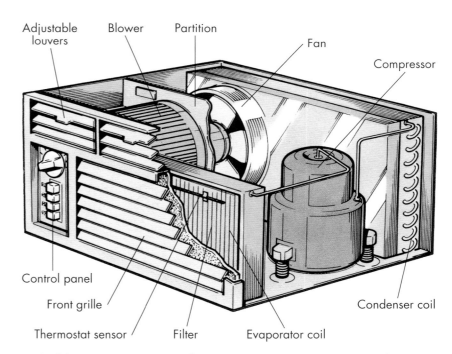

Both of the major components of a room air conditioner are contained in one housing. The condenser coil faces outside, and the evaporator faces inside.

ROOM A/C TROUBLESHOOTING CHART

Problem	Possible Cause	Solution
Unit doesn't run	1. No power.	1. Check cord, plug, and outlet. Check for blown fuse or tripped circuit breaker at main entrance panel; restore circuit.
	2. Motor overload or safety shutoff.	2. Wait 30 minutes; press reset button. Repeat if necessary.
	3. Switch faulty.	3. Check terminals and insulation; if burns are evident, replace switch. If switch looks all right, call a professional.
Fuses blow	1. Circuit overloaded.	1. Put on different circuit.
	2. Voltage low.	2. Call a professional or the power company.
Cooling inadequate	1. Thermostat set too high.	1. Lower thermostat setting 5°.
	2. Filter dirty.	2. Clean or replace filter.
	3. Coils dirty.	3. Clean coils.
	4. Condenser blocked from outside.	4. Make sure outside of unit is not blocked.
	5. Motor faulty.	5. Call a professional.
	6. Compressor faulty.	6. Call a professional.
	7. Coolant leak.	7. Call a professional.
Fan runs, but unit doesn't cool	1. Thermostat set too high.	1. Lower thermostat setting 5°.
	2. Thermostat faulty.	2. Test thermostat; if faulty, replace, or call a professional.
	3. Coils dirty.	3. Clean coils.
	4. Motor faulty.	4. Call a professional.
	5. Compressor faulty.	5. Call a professional.
Unit cools, but fan doesn't run	1. Control switch set wrong.	1. Reset switch; try different settings.
	2. Fan clogged.	2. Clean and tighten fan blades.
	3. Fan blades bent.	3. Straighten fan blades.
	4. Fan motor faulty.	4. Replace fan motor or call a professional.
Unit turns on and off repeatedly	1. Coils dirty.	1. Clean coils.
	2. Filter dirty.	2. Clean or replace filter.

your unit running well. When extensive repairs are needed, you can also save the cost of a service call by removing the air conditioner from its mounting and taking it to the repair shop.

During the winter, room air conditioners should be protected from the elements. Either remove the unit from its mounting and store it or cover the outside portion of the unit with a commercial room air conditioner cover or with heavy plastic sheeting, held in place with duct tape.

Caution: Before doing any work on a room air conditioner, make sure it's unplugged. Room air conditioners have either one or two capacitors, located behind the control panel and near the fan. Capacitors store electricity, even when the power to the unit is turned off. Before you do any work on an air conditioner, unplug it and discharge the capacitor or you could receive a severe shock. The unit's owner's manual will show the location of capacitors and tell how to discharge them. Otherwise, let an air conditioning technician do it.

FILTER At the beginning of every cooling season and once a month during the season, remove the front grille and clean or replace the filter. If you live in a very dusty area, clean or replace the filter more often. Most room air conditioners have a washable filter that looks like sponge rubber. Clean the filter with a solution of mild household detergent and water; rinse well. Let the filter dry completely before reinstalling it. Some units have a throwaway filter, similar to a furnace filter. When this type of filter becomes dirty, replace it with a new one of the same type.

POWER CORD The power cord that connects the air conditioner to the wall outlet may become worn and fail to supply electricity to the unit. To check the cord, remove the control panel. Unscrew the cord terminals and then attach a test wire across the bare lead wires. Hook the clips of a volt-ohm-milliammeter (VOM) set to the RX1 scale to the prongs of the cord's plug. If the meter reads zero, the cord is functioning. If the meter reads higher than zero, replace the cord. For testing and cord/plug replacement procedures, refer to Chapter 3.

EVAPORATOR AND CONDENSER COILS Clean the evaporator and condenser coils at the beginning of the cooling season and every month during the season. If you live in a very dusty area, clean the coils more often. Use a vacuum cleaner on these components. If the fins on the coils are bent, straighten them with a fin comb, sold at most appliance parts outlets. A fin comb is designed to slide into the spaces between the fins. Use it carefully as the fins are made of light-gauge aluminum and are easily damaged.

SWITCH The selector switch, located directly behind the control panel, turns the unit on. If the air conditioner does not run at any setting—and it is receiving power—chances are the switch is faulty. To correct the problem, remove the control panel and locate the switch. Check the switch terminals for burnt insulation or burn marks on the terminals. If you see any indication of burning, replace the switch with a new one of the same type. The switch is held to the control panel or frame with screws; unscrew it and connect the new one the same way. If you determine the problem may not be the switch, call a professional service person.

THERMOSTAT The thermostat is located behind the control panel. To test and/or replace the thermostat:

1. Remove grille and control panel from unit. Thermostat has special sensing bulb attached to it; this part extends from thermostat into evaporator coil area. Its role is to sense temperature, which is controlled by thermostat.

2. Remove thermostat carefully because you must return sensing bulb to identical spot later. To make replacement easier, tag location of bulb before you remove thermostat.

3. Check thermostat with VOM set to RX1 scale. Clip probes of tester to thermostat terminals, and turn temperature control dial to coldest setting. If meter reads zero, thermostat is functioning properly. If reading is higher than zero, replace thermostat with new one of same type. If thermostat is held to control panel or frame with screws, clips, or metal tabs, connect new thermostat the same way the old one was connected.

Note: If the thermostat has more than two lead wires connected to it (not counting the sensing bulb wire) do not try to test or replace it. Instead, call a professional service person.

DRAIN PORTS As the air conditioner operates, condensed moisture and water vapor from the evaporator coil are funneled through drain ports or an opening between the partition in the middle of the evaporator coil and the condenser coil. At this point, the fan blows the moisture against the condenser coil, where the water is dissipated. Drain ports can become clogged with dirt. The result is water leaking from the appliance, usually through the bottom of the grille. To prevent clogging, clean the ports with a short piece of wire hanger or the blade of a pocketknife. Do this at the beginning of every cooling season and every month during the season. Also check the condenser side of the air conditioner. Some models have a drain port along the bottom edge of the cabinet frame. If your air conditioner has this drain port, clean it out when you clean the other ports.

FAN When a fan malfunctions, the problem is usually loose or dirty blades. If the fan won't operate or if it's noisy, cleaning and tightening will usually fix it. To repair a room air conditioner's fan:

1. Open cabinet and locate fan.

2. Clean away any debris with vacuum and soft cloth.

3. Check fan blade on motor shaft for looseness. Blade is fastened to shaft with setscrew at hub of blade. Tighten setscrew with screwdriver or Allen wrench. If air conditioner has round vent fan, tighten fan on motor shaft by inserting long-blade screwdriver through port in fan. Fan is installed in its housing with bolts, and vibration can loosen these fasteners. Tighten them with wrench.

4. If fan has oil ports, apply several drops of 20-weight nondetergent motor oil (not all-purpose oil) to each port at beginning of cooling season.

5. If you suspect fan motor is faulty, test it with VOM set to RX1 scale. Disconnect terminal wires from terminals, and clip probes of VOM to wires. If meter reads between about 3 and 30 ohms, motor is functioning properly. If meter reads either zero or an extremely high number, replace motor.

To remove the fan motor, remove the fan, the power wires, and several mounting bolts. Install the new motor with the reverse procedure. However, if the condenser coil must be moved to get the fan out, do not try to remove the motor. Call a professional service person.

MOTOR AND COMPRESSOR If problems occur in the motor or compressor of the air conditioner, call a professional service person.

QUICK FIREPLACE FIXES

Most fireplaces are made of solid steel, iron, or masonry, requiring few fixes. If your fireplace has glass windows, a periodic cleaning with vinegar and a stiff brush will keep them clean. There are some quick fireplace fixes you can do in just an hour or two once a year. The most practical one is cleaning the chimney.

A straight chimney with a clean-out door at the bottom is relatively easy to clean. Before starting any chimney cleaning job, however, make sure the fireplace doors are fully closed and sealed or, if it's an open fireplace, that it is covered with cloth or cardboard and sealed. You don't want soot in your home.

Chimney cleaning brushes are available at many hardware stores and building material retailers. If you purchase a set, make sure they are the correct size for your chimney. You also can construct your own chimney cleaner by weighting a burlap bag with old rags, sawdust, or some other waste material and lowering it into the chimney from the top. Raise and lower the bag several times and the soot will dislodge from the sides and fall to the bottom of the chimney where it can be removed with a small shovel.

To test the chimney for possible leaks, start a fire in the fireplace and, when it is burning well, throw in some material that will cause smoke. When the smoke begins to billow from the top of the chimney, cover it with a piece of heavy, wet cloth for a short time. This will force the smoke to find some other exit from the chimney, if one exists. Mark any leaks with a piece of chalk and repair them later with a chimney patch product available at larger hardware stores.

QUICK HUMIDIFIER FIXES

Humidity, or moisture in the air, is important not only to your home but also to its inhabitants. Both high and low humidity can be uncomfortable and cause health problems. So many homes have a humidifier either in the heating system or as a stand-alone unit.

What can you do to keep your humidifier running well? Here are a few quick tips:

- Disassemble and clean the unit at least once a year, removing any buildups in the tank.

- Replace the filter once a year or as suggested by the manufacturer.

- If you live in an area of hard water or water that contains contaminants or high concentration of minerals, install a water filter in line with your humidifier.

- If your humidifier is ultrasonic, read the manufacturer's recommendations on maintenance to keep it trouble free.

OTHER QUICK HEATING AND COOLING FIXES

Rising energy costs can make a cold, drafty house a misery that grows increasingly expensive. Sealing your home with tight-fitting weatherstripping can make you feel warm all winter long. You'll also enjoy the lower utility bills!

WEATHERSTRIPPING

If you had a 6-inch-square hole in the middle of your front door, you would certainly do something in order to plug it up. Yet there are thousands of homes in which a 1/8-inch-wide crack exists all the way around the door, and this gap is just about the equivalent air loss of that 6-inch-square hole. Letting these cracks exist is like throwing dollars out the door or window. Fortunately, weatherstripping can reduce your heating/cooling bills by as much as 30 percent while reducing drafts that can cause discomfort.

Your home may or may not need weatherstripping. Luckily, there are some very simple ways to find out. If you can feel cold air coming in around doors and windows on a windy day, you know the answer. If you are uncertain, you can create your own windstorm at the precise spot where you suspect air might be leaking. Go outside with a handheld hair dryer and have a helper inside move his or her hands around the door and/or window frame as you move the hair dryer.

You may discover that all your doors and windows are airtight. Or you may find a door or window that is airtight around three edges but needs help along the fourth edge. What you will probably conclude, however, is that your home has several drafty areas that would benefit from weatherstripping.

TYPES OF WEATHERSTRIPPING There are several types of weatherstripping because different situations call for different types of material. All of the following types are available to homeowners, and most can be used for either doors or windows.

- Pressure-sensitive adhesive-backed foam is the easiest weatherstripping to apply, and it is quite inexpensive. Available in both rubber and plastic, adhesive-backed foam comes in rolls of varying lengths and thicknesses. When compressed by a door or window, the foam seals out the air. As an added advantage, these strips also provide a cushioning effect that silences slamming. Though not permanent, this type of weatherstripping can last from one to three years. Avoid getting paint on the material because paint causes the foam to lose its resiliency.

- Spring-metal strips (V-shape or single) are available in bronze, copper, stainless-steel, and aluminum finishes. Most manufacturers package spring-metal weatherstripping in rolls, and they include the brads necessary for installation. Although this kind of weatherstripping seems like a simple installation, it does require patience.

- Self-sticking spring metal has a peel-and-stick backing. These are like the standard spring-metal strips just described, but they are far easier to install.

- Felt is one of the old standbys and is very economical. It comes in a variety of widths, thicknesses, qualities, and colors (brown, gray, and black). Felt strips are usually nailed in place, but they are also available with a pressure-sensitive adhesive backing.

- Serrated metal is felt- or vinyl-backed weatherstripping that combines the sturdiness of

metal with the application ease of felt. Most manufacturers package serrated-metal weatherstripping in rolls that include brads for installation.

- Tubular gasket weatherstripping is made of extremely flexible vinyl. It is usually applied outside where it easily conforms to uneven places. Available in white and gray, it cannot be painted because paint causes the tube to stiffen and lose its flexibility.

- Foam-filled tubular gasket weatherstripping includes a foam core in the tubular part of the gasket just described. The foam provides extra insulating qualities and extra strength. Moreover, the foam-filled tubular gasket will hold its shape better than the hollow-tube type. It should not be painted.

Interlocking metal weatherstripping can provide a secure seal as long as the separate pieces fit together as they should. Installation is tricky, and maintenance requires careful examination for bent pieces.

- Interlocking metal weatherstripping requires two separate pieces along each edge. One part fits inside the other to form the seal. One piece goes on the door, while the other is attached to the jamb. Because installation generally requires professional-level cutting (rabbeting), no step-by-step installation instructions are provided for this type of weatherstripping. If you already have interlocking metal weatherstripping, keep it working right by straightening any bent pieces with a screwdriver, pliers, or a putty knife. Casement window gaskets are specially made vinyl channels that slip over the lip of the casement frame. No adhesives or tools—except scissors for cutting the gasket to the proper length—are needed. This weatherstripping is generally available only in shades of gray.

- Jalousie gaskets are clear vinyl tracks that can be cut to fit over the edges of jalousie louvers. They snap in place for a friction fit.

Apply pressure-sensitive types of weatherstripping only on the friction-free parts of a wooden window.

PRESSURE-SENSITIVE FOAM Pressure-sensitive types of weatherstripping can be used only on the friction-free parts of a wooden window, such as the lower sash or the top of the upper sash. If the strips were installed snugly against the gap between upper and lower sashes, the movement of the window would pull it loose.

1. Clean entire surface to which weatherstripping is to be attached. Use dishwashing detergent and water, and make certain no dirt or grease remains. If pressure-sensitive weatherstripping had been installed previously, use petroleum jelly to remove any old adhesive. Dry surface with rags.

What You'll Need
Dishwashing detergent
Clean rags
Petroleum jelly
Scissors

2. Use scissors to cut strip to fit, but do not remove backing paper yet. Starting at one end, slowly peel paper backing as you push sticky foam strips into place. If backing proves stubborn at beginning, stretch foam until seal between backing and the foam breaks.

SPRING METAL Spring-metal weatherstripping fits into the tracks around the windows. Each strip should be about 2 inches longer than the sash so the end of the strip is exposed when the windows are closed.

What You'll Need
Tin snips
Hammer
Nails
Awl or ice pick
Nail set
Screwdriver

1. Position vertical strips so flared flange faces outside. Center strip should be mounted to upper sash with flare aimed down, while other horizontal strips are mounted to top of upper sash and bottom of lower sash with flared flange facing out. Using snips, cut spring-metal weatherstripping to size. Be sure to allow for window pulley mechanisms.

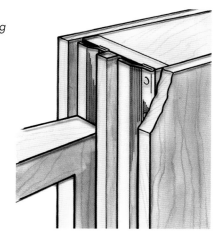

Position the flange on spring metal so the flared edge faces outside.

2. Attach strips to window frame. Position strip properly and note any hinges, locks, or other hardware that might interfere. Trim away metal where needed. Then trim ends of strip at an angle where vertical and horizontal strips meet. Tap in one nail at top and one nail at bottom of strip. Do not put in more nails and do not drive top and bottom nails all the way in. Since some vertical strips do not come with nail holes, you may have to make pilot holes with an ice pick or awl.

3. Check to make sure strips are straight and properly positioned. Then drive nail in center of strip—but, again, only partway. Add more nails between starter nails. To avoid damaging strip, never drive any of the nails all the way in with hammer. Instead, drive nails flush with nail set.

4. Flare out edge of strip with screwdriver to render snug fit.

Flare the edge of a spring-metal strip with a screwdriver to render a snug fit.

SELF-STICKING SPRING METAL This type of weatherstripping works best on wood windows.

1. Measure and cut strips to fit window, then clean surface where strips are to be placed.

2. Put strips in place without removing backing paper, and mark spots for trimming (for example, indicate hardware points and where vertical and horizontal strips meet).

3. Peel off backing at one end, and press strip in place, peeling and pressing as you work toward other end.

FELT Felt strips are somewhat unsightly for sealing gaps on wooden windows. There are places where felt can be used to good advantage, however. Attach felt strips to the bottom of the lower sash, the top of the upper sash, and to the interior side of the upper sash. The strips will then function as horizontal gaskets.

1. Measure and cut felt to fit window. Keep in mind that felt strips can go around corners. Push material snugly against gap.

2. Nail ends of each strip first, but do not drive nails flush; leave room to pry them out. Start at one end and drive a tack every 2 to 3 inches, pulling felt tight as you go. If you find slack when you reach other end, remove nail, pull to tighten, and trim off any excess.

Note: If possible, do this job on a warm day. The adhesive forms a better bond if applied when the temperature is at least 60°F.

PRESSURE-SENSITIVE FELT Follow the same steps as you would to attach pressure-sensitive foam.

TUBULAR AND FOAM-FILLED GASKETS Tubular types of weatherstripping are also unsightly. They are best used when installed on the outside of the window. If the window is easily accessible from outside the house, then tubular weatherstripping is worth considering. It can also be used to improve existing weatherstripping. To install tubular and foam-filled gaskets:

1. Begin by measuring strips and cutting them to size with scissors. Cutting all strips for window at one time will save you trips up and down ladder later on.

2. Position each strip carefully and drive nail into one end. Space nails every 2 to 3 inches, pulling weatherstripping tight before you drive each nail.

Most metal windows are grooved around the edges so the metal flanges will interlock and preclude the need for weatherstripping. Sometimes, though, gaps do exist, and you must apply weatherstripping in such instances.

Generally, the only kind of weatherstripping that can be applied to metal windows is the pressure-sensitive type. Screws would go through the metal and impede movement of the window. To install, apply weatherstripping to top of upper sash (if it is movable) and to bottom of lower sash. These are usually the only spots where metal windows allow for air movement. If you find any other gaps, attach a vinyl tubular gasket to the area with a special adhesive formulated to hold vinyl to metal.

WEATHERSTRIPPING SLIDING WINDOWS Sliding windows, those in which the sash moves laterally, come in both wood and metal frames. Weatherstrip the wooden frames much as you would a double-hung window turned sideways. If only one sash moves, weatherstrip it and caulk the stationary sash. For metal frames, follow the instructions for weatherstripping standard metal windows.

Special gaskets are designed for sealing gaps in jalousie and casement windows. To weatherstrip jalousies, measure the edge of the glass louver, cut the gasket to size with scissors, and snap the gasket in place. To weatherstrip casement windows, measure the edges of the frame, cut strips of gasket to size, miter the ends of the gasket strips where they will intersect, and slip the strips in place over the lip of the frame.

Double-hung wood windows almost always require weatherstripping, although if the top sash is never opened, you can solve an air leak problem by caulking to seal any cracks. You may find it advantageous to use more than one type of weatherstripping to complete the job. Be sure to follow the correct installation procedures for each type of weatherstripping.

WEATHERSTRIPPING DOORS All four edges around a door can permit air to leak in and out of your house. In fact, the average door has more gaps than a loose-fitting window. Doors, moreover, don't run in grooves as windows do, so any crack area around a door is likely to be far greater than the area around a window.

Before you start weatherstripping, inspect the door to be sure it fits properly in the frame opening. Close the door and observe it from the inside. Look to see that the distance between the

What You'll Need
Tape measure
Pencil
Scissors
Dishwashing detergent
Clean rags

What You'll Need
Tape measure
Pencil
Scissors
Hammer
Nails

What You'll Need
Tape measure
Pencil
Scissors
Hammer
Nails

door and the frame is uniform all along both sides and at the top. The distance does not have to be precisely the same all the way around, but, if the door rests crooked in the frame, weatherstripping may make it impossible to open or close. Naturally, if there is great variance in the opening between the door and frame, it will be difficult to fit weatherstripping snugly at all points, and gaps will result.

The cause of most door problems is the hinges. Therefore, the first thing to do is open the door and tighten all the hinge screws. Even slightly loose screws can cause the door to sag. If the screw holes have been reamed out and are now too big to hold the screws, you can use larger screws as long as they will still fit in the hinge's countersunk holes. If even the larger screws won't work, pack the holes with toothpicks dipped in glue, and use a knife to cut off the toothpicks even with the surface. Now the screws have new wood in which to bite.

Sometimes the door must be planed off to prevent binding. If so, you can usually plane the top with the door still in place. Always move the plane toward the center of the door to avoid splintering off the edges. If you must plane wood off the sides, take the door off its hinges, plane the hinge side, and always move toward the edges.

Spring metal is quite popular for door weatherstripping. It works effectively when installed properly and is not visible with the door closed. In the packages designated as door kits, most manufacturers include the triangular piece that fits next to the striker plate on the jamb.

SPRING METAL AROUND DOORS

1. Measure and cut spring-metal strips to size.

2. Position side strips so flared flange almost touches door stop. Trim away metal where needed to accommodate any hinges, locks, or other hardware.

> **What You'll Need**
> Tape measure
> Pencil
> Tin snips
> Hammer
> Nails
> Awl or ice pick
> Nail set
> Screwdriver

3. Tap in one nail at top and one nail at bottom of each side strip. Do not put in any more nails, and don't drive top and bottom nails in all the way. If strips do not have prepunched holes, make pilot holes with ice pick or awl. Check to make sure side strips are straight and properly positioned.

4. Drive nail in center of side strip but only partway in. Then add nails spaced at regular

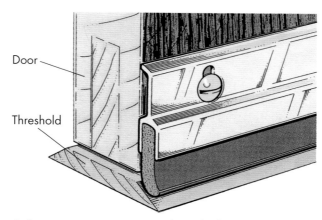

A door sweep can create a tight seal when a gap exists between the bottom of the door and the threshold. Door sweeps can be made of wood and felt, wood and foam, or metal and vinyl. All are effective in sealing out drafts.

intervals between ends. To avoid damaging strip, never drive nails all the way in with hammer. Instead, drive nails flush with nail set. Repeat procedure for other side strip.

5. Put top strip in last, and miter it to fit. Flare out edge of each strip with screwdriver to render snug fit.

SELF-STICKING SPRING METAL AROUND DOORS

Self-sticking spring metal can be used in the same places as regular spring metal.

1. Clean surface where strips are to be placed. Measure and cut strips to size with tin snips.

2. Put strips in place without removing backing paper. Mark spots for trimming (for example, hardware points and where vertical and horizontal strips meet).

3. Peel off backing at one end and press strip in place, peeling and pressing as you work toward other end.

> **What You'll Need**
> Dishwashing detergent
> Clean rags
> Tape measure
> Pencil
> Tin snips

PRESSURE-SENSITIVE FOAM AROUND DOORS

Pressure-sensitive foam weatherstripping is easy to install around most doors. The foams are effective, but they have a shorter life span than other weatherstripping materials. To install pressure-sensitive foam weatherstripping around doors:

1. Select warm day to work, if possible. Adhesive forms a better bond if applied when temperature is at least 60°F.

2. Clean surface where weatherstripping is to be attached with detergent and water. Make sure no dirt or grease remains. If pressure-sensitive weatherstripping had been previously installed, use petroleum jelly to remove any old adhesive. Dry surface with rags.

> **What You'll Need**
> Dishwashing detergent
> Clean rags
> Petroleum jelly
> Scissors

Seal the top and sides of a door with adhesive-backed foam weatherstripping. To install the foam, peel off the backing and stick the strip down.

3. Use scissors to cut strip to fit, but don't remove backing paper yet.

4. Starting at one end, slowly peel paper backing as you push sticky foam strips into place. If backing proves stubborn at beginning, stretch foam until seal between backing and foam breaks.

5. Attach strips on hinge side to doorjamb.

6. Attach other two strips to doorstop. If corner of door catches weatherstripping as you close it, trim top piece of foam on hinge side.

Serrated-metal weatherstripping, usually with a felt-strip insert running the length of the serrated groove, also can be used to seal air gaps around doors. To install this type of weatherstripping, measure the length of strips required, and then use tin snips or heavy-duty scissors to cut the serrated-metal material to the proper lengths. Nail each strip at both ends, add a nail to the center of each strip, and drive additional nails every 2 to 3 inches along the rest of the strip.

WEATHERTIGHT THRESHOLD The gap at the bottom of the door is treated differently from the gaps on the sides and along the top. The wood or metal hump on the floor along the bottom of the door is called the threshold. Many of the metal types feature a flexible vinyl insert that creates a tight seal when the door closes against it. Other thresholds consist of one unit on the floor and a mating piece on the bottom of

the door. These two pieces interlock to form a weathertight barrier.

In most cases, the threshold with a flexible vinyl insert is the easiest to install. Interlock systems are quite effective when properly installed, but they require a perfect fit or they will not work satisfactorily.

Wooden thresholds often wear down to the point where they must be replaced. This is an easy installation, and there are many types of replacement thresholds from which to choose. Most are aluminum and come in standard door widths; however, if your door is not standard width, you can trim the aluminum threshold with a hacksaw. To install a replacement threshold:

1. Remove old threshold. If it is wood, there are two ways to remove it. In most cases, you can pry it up after removing doorstops with small flat pry bar or putty knife, but you must work carefully and slowly. If jamb itself rests on threshold, saw through old threshold at each end. Use backsaw placed right against jamb, and saw down through threshold, being careful not to scar floor. Once you make cuts, threshold should be easy to pry up. If prying doesn't work, use chisel and hammer to split piece. Metal thresholds are frequently held down by screws concealed under vinyl inserts. Once you remove screws, threshold will come up easily.

> **What You'll Need**
> Small flat pry bar or putty knife
> Backsaw
> Chisel
> Hammer
> Screwdriver
> Replacement threshold
> Door sweep
> Tape measure
> Pencil
> Nails
> Drill

2. Install replacement threshold by driving screws through metal unit and into floor. If

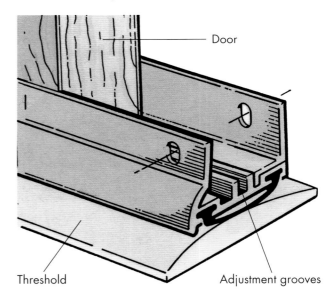

A bottom sweep slides on over the bottom of the door; adjustment grooves adapt it to any door thickness.

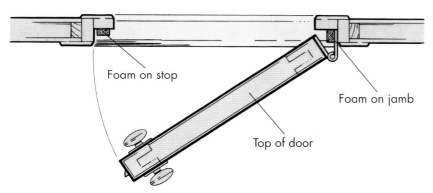

Attach strips of pressure-sensitive foam on the hinge side of the doorjamb and on the doorstop. The adhesive backing on the foam will form a secure bond only when applied to a clean, grease-free surface.

you don't want aluminum threshold, cut replacement from wood, using original one as pattern.

3. Install door sweep to seal gap. Most sweeps are attached to inside of door with nails or screws. Cut sweep to size, and close door. Tack both ends of sweep to door, then install remaining nails or screws. If you are using screws, drill pilot holes first.

Some types of sweeps slip under the door and wrap around the bottom. Still another type fits on the outside, with a section of it flipping upward to miss the threshold when the door is opened. When the door is closed, this section flips back down to provide a seal against the threshold. You can adjust this type of door sweep so it renders a snug fit.

IMPROVING HEATING AND COOLING EFFICIENCY

- Protect the thermostat for your heating or cooling system from anything that would cause it to give a false reading. If the thermostat is in a draft, misplaced on a cold outside wall, or too close to a heat-producing register, its accuracy will be compromised.

- If you won't be home for a few days, turn the thermostat to its lowest setting. If there's no danger of pipes freezing or other household items being damaged, turn the heating system off completely.

- Install a thermostat timer to save fuel and money. The timer can be set to automatically raise and lower the temperature during peak and off-hours.

- Close the draperies over large windows and glass doors to form a barrier against heat loss during the winter and heat gain during the summer.

- If your home has rooms that are seldom or never used, close the vents in these rooms and shut the doors most of the time. Make sure the rooms get enough heat to prevent mildew from growing or contents being damaged.

- Avoid constant thermostat adjustments, as they can waste fuel. When coming into the house after the thermostat has been turned down, don't set it higher than the desired temperature. Setting the thermostat up very high generally will not cause the temperature to reach the desired level any faster.

- One heating adjustment you should make, however, is a reduction in the thermostat setting before you go to bed every night. Cutting back for several hours can make a big difference in fuel consumption.

- Reduce the thermostat setting when you have a large group of people in your home. People generate heat, and a party can quickly raise the temperature.

- Keep the fireplace damper closed except when you have a fire going. Otherwise, updrafts will suck heated air out through the chimney.

- Maintain proper humidity. A house that's too dry can feel uncomfortably cold even when the temperature setting is correct.

- Aim the vents of room air conditioners upward for better air circulation; cold air naturally settles downward. On central air conditioning systems, adjust the registers so the air is blowing up.

- Make sure the outside portion of an air conditioning system is not in direct sunlight or blocked from free airflow.

- If you have room air conditioners, close all heating system vents so the cool air isn't wasted.

CHAPTER 6

QUICK INTERIOR FIXES

Chapter 2 addressed quick fixes to walls, ceilings, floors, doors, and windows—in other words, the structural parts of your home. A house's interior is made up of a lot more, however. Paint, wallpaper, furniture—even pests—often require quick fixes, many of which can be accomplished by a novice do-it-yourselfer.

ABOUT HOME INTERIORS

The inside of your home is more than four walls. It's furniture, decorations, and other things that make a house a home, and sometimes these things need fixing. Fortunately, most are quick fixes that you can tackle yourself with minimal time and effort.

The first step in fixing interior problems is to figure out what the problem is. Then you can look for the quick solution in this chapter, whether it be related to painting, wallpapering, furniture repair, or pest problems.

QUICK INTERIOR PAINTING FIXES

Painting can be a task that takes a couple of hours, a half day, or more. It all depends on what and how much you decide to paint. You can freshen up a room by giving a door or cabinet a new coat of paint in just a few hours. Or you can break it into smaller jobs and spread them out over a week or more. Whatever the size of the job you decide to tackle, the painting techniques remain the same.

PREPPING FOR QUICK PAINTING

If you're painting over a new primed wall, you can safely skip this step. But if you're painting over a previously painted surface, look for rough, peeling, or chipped areas. The best way to find flaws is to remove all the furniture from the room. If this isn't possible, cluster the furniture in one area, and cover it and the floors with drop cloths. Take down the draperies and the drapery hardware. Loosen the light fixtures; let them hang and wrap them with plastic bags. Remove the wall plates from electrical outlets and switches (if you intend to paint them the same color as the wall, do so while they're off the wall). If you find flaws, now is the time to fix them. You don't need to take a weekend or a

INTERIOR PAINTS		
Type	**Characteristics/Use**	**Application**
Acoustic	For acoustic ceiling tile. Water-thinned, water cleanup.	Spray (preferable) or roller.
Alkyd	Solvent-thinned, solvent cleanup. Don't apply over unprimed drywall.	Brush, roller, pad.
Cement	For concrete, brick, stucco. Some contain waterproofing agents. Must be mixed just before use.	Brush.
Dripless	For ceilings. More costly than ordinary paints.	Brush or roller.
Epoxy	For metal, glass, tile, floors, woodwork: high-stress areas. Expensive. May require special mixing; tricky to use.	Brush.
Latex	Most popular. Water-thinned, water cleanup. Gloss, semigloss, flat. May be used over most surfaces but not on wallpaper, wood, or metal.	Brush, roller, pad.
Metal	For bare or primed metal or as a primer for other types of paint. Some water-thinned, most solvent-thinned.	Brush or spray.
Oil	Slow-drying, strong odor. Coverage may not be as good as synthetic paints. Solvent cleanup, solvent-thinned.	Brush, roller, spray.
One-coat	Water- or solvent-thinned. Costs more than regular latex or alkyd. Surface must be sealed first. Excellent covering power.	Brush, roller, pad.
Polyurethane/Urethane	Expensive. Can be used over most finishes, porous surfaces. Extreme durability. Solvents, primers vary.	Brush.
Texture	Good for covering surface defects. Premixed or mix-at-home types. Application slow. Permits surface design of choice.	Brush, roller, pad, trowel, sponge.

Scrub walls with a sponge mop. Squeeze dirty water out of the mop into a separate pail or down the drain.

week to tackle interior fixes. Instead, you can break it down into smaller jobs—quick fixes that take just an hour or two each.

After fixing any flaws, wash down the surfaces to be painted with warm water and a good household detergent or wall-cleaning soap to remove soot, grease, cigarette smoke, and airborne dirt. Using a sponge just slightly less than dripping wet, go over a vertical strip of wall about 2 feet wide. Squeeze the dirty water out of the sponge into a separate pail or down the drain. Go over the wall with the squeezed-out sponge to pick up as much of the remaining dirt as possible. Squeeze out the sponge again, and rinse it in clean water. Then, sponge the same area once more to remove the last of the dirt and detergent residue. This routine sounds tedious, but it actually goes fast, and you'll end up with a wall that is clean and provides a good surface for a new coat of paint.

Don't attempt to paint over a surface that already has a glossy finish, even if it is clean. Glossy surfaces don't provide enough adhesion. And even if the paint goes on, it may not stay on. To cut the gloss on an entire wall, wash it down with a strong solution of trisodium phosphate (TSP), available at hardware or paint stores. Mix the TSP powder into hot water until no more will dissolve. Swab it on the wall, and sponge it dry. Rinse with clear water, then sponge dry again. If TSP is not available (in many communities it has

been banned because of its tendency to pollute water sources), you can use a commercial deglosser, a solution that you swab on glossy surfaces before painting.

You can use deglossing solutions on woodwork, too, or you can give woodwork a light sanding with medium- or fine-grade sandpaper. Wipe off or vacuum the resulting powder before you paint. On baseboards, remove accumulations of floor wax or acrylic floor finish with a wax remover or finish remover.

SCRAPING The older your house, the greater the chance there's an area that needs scraping. A previous paint job may have begun to peel or crack in some places. Windowsills and sash frames may have chipped, or the old paint may have "alliga-

ESTIMATING PAINT JOBS

Estimating the paint you'll need for a job is easy. Take a few minutes at home to measure the area to be painted. A gallon of paint will typically cover 450 square feet according to the manufacturer's calculations. It's safer to figure 400 square feet of coverage per gallon of paint. If you're buying 2 or more gallons of the same color, it's a good idea to mix them all together at home so color variations don't show up in the middle of a wall.

To determine the amount of paint required to cover a wall, multiply the height of the wall by its length, then divide by 400. This means a gallon of paint will cover a 10×15-foot room (two 10-foot walls and two 15-foot walls, 8 feet high) with one coat. Two coats will take 2 gallons. However, there are other factors you should consider when calculating coverage.

When a wall is textured or rough-troweled, it will require more paint than if it were a smooth wall. This is because the texture represents added surface to be covered, even though it does not contribute to the size of the area. Just how much more surface area there is depends on just how textured the surface is, but, for medium-rough, porous, or previously unpainted walls, you can safely estimate 300 to 350 square feet of coverage from a gallon of paint.

Most walls have doors or windows or other areas that are not painted. If the nonpainted area is a single window or door, ignore it in your calculations. Two or three windows, a door and a window, multiple sliding doors, or a fireplace reduce the paint you'll need. By how much? Multiply the lengths by the widths of these nonpaint areas to get the total square footage that you can subtract from your overall surface figures, or you can subtract about 15 square feet for typical windows and 21 square feet for typical doors. (These figures also can be used to estimate the paint you'll need for each if you plan to use a different color or surface finish.) If you're painting the ceiling, figure its square foot area at width times length, too.

Estimating the time you'll have to put in on any given paint project is less precise. Some people work faster than others, so there's no way to estimate individual differences in speed. On the average, you should be able to cover about 120 square feet of flat surface in about an hour. For bare wood or plaster, figure about 100 square feet. In a typical 12×15-foot room, you're likely to spend four or five hours on the job, including trim work, for the first coat. The second coat, if it's necessary, will go faster, but you'll have to wait for the first coat to dry, anywhere from 2 to 36 hours.

tored" into a maze of cracks. If you find these conditions, scrape them gently to remove the loose particles, then sand them smooth to blend with the area around them. If you get down to bare wood on woodwork, prime the spots before you apply the final coat of paint. If it's impossible to blend the scraped areas with the nonscraped areas on walls, go over them with a light coat of drywall joint compound. When walls are dry, sand them smooth, prime, and paint.

MASKING Where two new paint colors come together on a single surface, it's practically impossible to keep a straight line between them while painting freehand with either a brush or a roller. To get a straight line, use a carpenters' level and a pencil to draw a faint line on the wall. Then, align masking tape with the line across the wall. Peel the tape off the roll a little at a time, and press it to the wall with your thumb. Don't pull the tape too tightly as you go, or it may stretch and retract once it's in place. To keep the paint from seeping under the masking tape, use the bowl of a spoon to press the tape tightly to the surface.

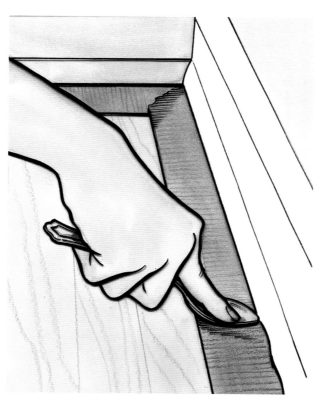

To keep paint from seeping under painter's tape, use the bowl of a spoon to press the tape tightly to the surface.

Don't leave the tape on until the paint is dry. If you do, it may pull the paint away from the surface. With latex paint, you only need to wait a half hour or so before peeling off the tape. With alkyds, two or three hours is enough. The paint can's label will tell you how long it takes for the paint to set completely.

Masking tape is useful for protecting trim around doors, windows, built-ins, baseboards, or bookshelves. When you're brushing or rolling new paint on the wall, you won't have to slow down or worry about sideswiping the trim.

PAINTING EQUIPMENT

The selection of painting tools was covered on pages 13–15. Once you have assembled the materials and completed the prep work, you're ready to resuscitate those old, drab walls with clean, new paint. You'll soon discover how easy it is to use brushes and rollers competently. Even so, there are a few techniques that will help postpone fatigue and provide a neater job.

BRUSHES The grip you use depends on the brush you've chosen. Trim and sash brushes with pencil handles are grasped much as you would a pencil, with the thumb and the first two fingers of the hand. This technique gives you excellent control for intricate painting. With beaver-tail handles on larger brushes, you'll need a stronger grip because the brushes are wider and heavier. Hold the handle with the entire hand, letting the handle span the width of your palm as you would hold a tennis racket. This technique works best when you're painting large, flat surfaces.

Grasp sash and trim brushes as you would a pencil (top). Hold a wall brush with your entire hand (bottom).

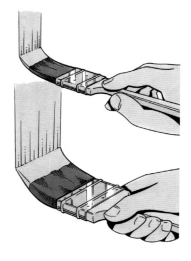

The goal of loading a brush is to get as much paint on the wall as possible without dribbling it all over the floor and yourself in the process. It will take you only a few minutes to be able to gauge accurately how much paint your brush will hold along the way. Meanwhile, start the job by dampening the bristles of the brush (with water for latex or the appropriate thinner for other types of paint) to condition them and make them more efficient. Remove excess moisture by gently striking the metal band around the handle's base against the edge of your palm and into a sink or bucket.

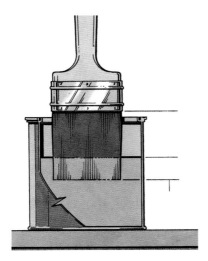  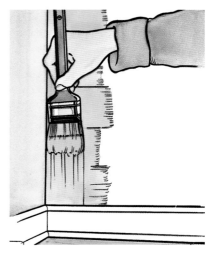

With the first dip, move the brush around a bit in the paint to open the bristles and let the brush fill completely. It will be easier to pick up a full load if you jab the brush gently into the paint with each dip. With most latex paints, you can simply dip the brush and let the excess drip off for a few seconds before moving the brush to the wall. With thinner coatings, however, you may have to gently slap the brush against the inside of the paint can or lightly drag it across the inside edge of the lip to remove excess paint.

To remove excess paint, gently slap the brush against the inside of the paint can or lightly drag it across the inside edge of the lip of the can.

To neatly paint up to a line where two edges or colors meet, called "cutting in," use a trim brush with beveled bristles (the end of the brush resembles a chisel). Paint five or six strokes perpendicular to the edge of the ceiling or the wall. Next, smooth over these strokes with a single, long

stroke, painting out from the corner first, then vertically. Where the wall and ceiling come together, use downward strokes on the wall first followed by smooth horizontal strokes. On the ceiling itself, cut in strokes toward the center of the room, away from the wall. Then paint a smooth horizontal stroke on the ceiling that follows the direction of the wall. Even if you're using the same color of paint on adjoining surfaces, follow this method of cutting in with 2-inch-wide borders rather than just plopping a loaded brush directly into a corner. This will prevent drips, sags, and runs.

Another cutting-in approach, beading, can practically eliminate the need to use masking tape to protect one painted area from another. Use a beveled trim brush with nice long bristles. Hold the brush so that your thumb is on one side of the metal ferrule and your fingers on the other. Press the brush lightly against the surface, then, as you move the brush, add just enough pressure to make the bristles bend away from the direction of your brushstroke. Keep the brush about $\frac{1}{16}$ inch away from the other colored surface. The bent bristles and the pressure will release a fine bead of paint that will spread into the gap.

With both methods of cutting in, but especially when you're dealing with two colors, it's better to have a brush that's too dry than one that's too wet. This is detail work. To do it effectively, go slowly and cut in 4 or 5 inches at a time. It will seem tedious at first, but your speed and accuracy will improve with practice, and even one ordinary-size room will give you lots of practice.

ROLLERS Working with a roller is even less exacting than working with a brush. Even a novice painter can get the feel of it in just a few minutes. As with brushes, moisten the roller first with water for latex paint or the appropriate thinner for other types of paint. Roll out the

excess moisture on a piece of scrap lumber or kraft paper or even on a paper grocery bag. Don't use newspaper because the roller may pick up the ink. Fill the well of the roller pan about half full, and set the roller into the middle of the well. Lift the roller and roll it down the slope of the pan, stopping just short of the well. Do this two or three times to allow the paint to work into the roller. Then, dip the roller into the well once more, and roll it on the slope until the pile is well saturated. You'll know immediately when you've overloaded the roller. It will drip en route to the wall and have a tendency to slide and smear instead of roll across the surface.

With a roller, begin by making an M, a backward N, or a W pattern about 3 feet square. Always start with an upstroke so paint won't run down the wall. Next, fill in the pattern with crosswise strokes. You should be able to paint each 3-square-foot area with one dip of the roller.

The most effective method of painting with a roller is to paint 2- or 3-square-foot areas at a time. Roll the paint on in a zigzag pattern without lifting the roller from the wall, as if you're painting a large M, W, or backward N. Then, still without lifting the roller, fill in the blanks of the letters with more horizontal or vertical zigzag strokes. Finish the area with light strokes that start in the unpainted area and roll into the paint. At the end of the stroke, raise the roller slowly so it does not leave a mark. Go to the next unpainted area, and repeat the zigzag technique, ending it just below or next to the first painted patch. Finally, smooth the new application, and blend it into the previously finished area.

Professional painters also suggest starting with a roller stroke that moves away from you. On walls, that means the first stroke should be up. If you roll down on the first stroke, the paint may puddle under the roller and run down the wall. In addition, be careful not to run the roller so rapidly across the wall that centrifugal force causes it to spray.

Be careful not to run the roller so rapidly that centrifugal force causes it to spray droplets of paint.

AIRLESS SPRAYERS For larger painting jobs, an airless sprayer is the most efficient way to apply paint. An airless sprayer uses an electrically run hydraulic pump to move paint from a bucket or container, through a tube, into a high-pressure hose, to a spray gun, and, finally, to the surface. Once you get the knack of it, an airless sprayer is easy to use, but if you rent one, make sure you get a set of written instructions.

The instructions will tell you how to flush the system with solvent (usually water or mineral spirits, depending on the paint you'll be using) and how to pump the paint through the hose to the spray gun. For cleanup, the procedure is reversed: Pump the leftover paint out and flush with solvent.

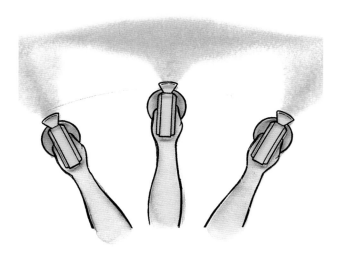

To use a sprayer, hold the gun a constant 6 to 12 inches from the surface. Maintain this distance with each pass of the gun, and keep the gun precisely parallel to the wall. Don't sweep it back and forth (as shown in top illustration) or paint will end up concentrated in the middle of the arc and almost transparent at the ends.

You'll only need the spray rig for a day or two, but plan to spend at least another day beforehand to thoroughly mask off everything you don't want to paint. Tape drop cloths to every floor surface. Drape windows, the fireplace, and doors. Remove all hardware or cover it with masking tape. Mask switches and outlets. Paint from a sprayer travels on the tiniest of air currents and settles a fine mist of overspray on just about every surface in a room.

Proper atomization	Too little thinner	Too low a pressure

Too much or too little thinner, too high or too low a pressure, and the paint won't atomize properly. Follow the manufacturer's instructions for thinning and adjusting pressure.

Plan to keep at least one window in each room open and set up an exhaust fan to draw paint vapor out of the room. Be sure, too, to wear a painters' mask, a hat, and old clothes with long sleeves to protect your arms.

Airless sprayers are equipped with several filters to keep paint particles and foreign matter from clogging the spray tip, but it's a good idea to filter the paint yourself through a nylon stocking or paint filter before you pump the paint through the hose.

Using an airless sprayer effectively takes some getting used to, so plan to practice on some scrap plywood or an inconspicuous part of the room or the house. The object is to cover the surface with a uniform coating of paint. Hold the spray gun a constant 6 to 12 inches from the surface and maintain this distance with each pass of the gun. Keep the gun precisely parallel to the wall. Don't sweep it back and forth or you'll end up with a wide arc of paint on the wall; the paint will be concentrated in the middle of the arc and almost transparent at each end.

Paint about a 3-foot horizontal strip at one time, then release the trigger and drop down to paint another strip of the same length, overlapping the first strip by one-third to one-half. Once you've covered a 3-foot-wide area from the top of the wall to the bottom, go back to the top and start

USING AN AIRLESS SPRAYER SAFELY

Airless sprayers are fast and efficient because they supply pressures of up to 3,000 pounds per square inch. This force moves the paint at 100 to 200 miles an hour through the spray tip. All that power can be dangerous. Consequently, treat an airless sprayer with lots of respect, follow the manufacturer's instructions to the letter, and take the following precautions to prevent accident or injury:

- Keep the spray gun's safety lock on when you're not painting.
- Make sure the spray gun has a trigger guard and a safety shield around its tip.
- If the spray tip becomes clogged, do not try to clear it by pressing your finger on it while the paint is being sprayed. Keep your fingers away from the tip when the sprayer is operating.
- Never point the gun at anyone else or allow anyone to point it at you.
- Always turn the sprayer off and disconnect it from its electrical source before you clean out the gun or the sprayer's filters. Even then, if you have to clean the tip, squeeze the trigger to release any built-up pressure in the hose.
- Only work in a well-ventilated area, wear a painters' mask to avoid inhaling fumes, and don't smoke or work around open flames. If you're working outside, don't leave containers of solvents sitting in the hot sun; put them in the garage or another shady spot.
- Never leave the sprayer within reach of children or pets.

another 3-foot section adjacent to the first, overlapping the edge of the first painted area by several inches as you work your way down the wall again.

Examine the painted areas to make sure the entire surface is receiving a uniform coat of paint. Too much will run or drip; too little will let the old paint show through. If you notice these flaws, it means you are not keeping the spray gun a uniform distance from the wall at all times or that you are tilting it. An upward tilt will deliver excess paint to the bottom of the painted strip. A downward tilt will concentrate paint at the top of the strip.

To prevent paint buildup at the end of each strip, release the trigger on the gun a fraction of a second before the spray gun stops moving at the end of your stroke. When beginning a new strip, start moving the gun a fraction of a second before compressing the trigger. Always keep the gun moving when it's spraying.

Be sure, too, that you've properly thinned the paint and adjusted the pressure control according to the manufacturer's instructions. If there is too much or too little thinner or too high or too low a pressure, the spray of paint won't atomize properly.

PAINTING WALLS

Paint an entire wall before taking a break so the painted portions won't lose their wet edges. Then stand back, scan the wall, and cover any missed spots or smears. Whether you paint in sections from top to bottom or from side to side across the room is up to you. But if you're using an extension handle on your roller, you may find it more convenient to start at one high corner and go all the way across the room with a series of completed zigzag patterns. This way you won't have to constantly change the handle on your roller as you would if you painted in sec-

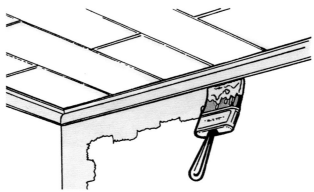

Use a brush to paint along the edge of the ceiling next to moldings and to paint next to corners. This technique is called "cutting in."

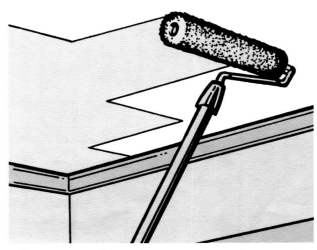

When using a roller, work in strips across, always working over the wet edge of previously painted strips.

tions from the ceiling down to the floor. If you're right-handed, start in the room's left-hand corner; if you're left-handed, start in the room's right-hand corner.

PAINTING CEILINGS

When rolling paint on a ceiling, maintain a wet edge at all times to avoid creating lines and ridges. If you're using fast-drying paint, you may have to work faster than you anticipated and without taking a break. Both speed and ease can be achieved by using an extension handle so you can paint from the floor instead of from a stepladder that has to be moved around the room. Many roller handles are made to accept a screw-in extension that you can buy at the paint store, but you may want to see if the threaded end of your broom or mop handle will work.

PAINTING TIGHT SPOTS

You probably won't have enough room to use the zigzag technique described earlier over and under windows and above doors and doorways. Instead, just roll the paint on horizontally. For areas that are narrower than the standard 7- or 9-inch roller, use a 4-inch roller or a paintbrush. (The little roller is best because it will give you the same surface finish as the rest of the wall.) Brushes apply paint less evenly and tend to leave trails.

PAINTING WOODWORK

Should you paint woodwork first or last? There is wide disagreement even among veteran painters about whether to paint woodwork before or after painting walls. It comes down to personal preference. The argument for painting woodwork first is that any stray drips or spatters that end up on the wall only need to be feathered out, not removed, since the wall's going to get a new coat of paint anyway. If you get all of the slow, detail work out of the way first you'll feel as if you're flying right along when it's time to fill in the big, flat areas. On the other hand, rollers always emit a powder-fine spray of paint into the room. No matter how careful you are, some of it is going to end up on the woodwork.

Whether you decide to paint the woodwork first or last, be sure to inspect it for defects, and make the necessary repairs before you actually get down to painting. If you'll be painting over already-glossy woodwork, sand it lightly with sandpaper or steel wool first to help with adhesion. Or, give it a coat of deglosser.

Painting trim progresses more slowly than cutting in walls and ceilings, and there's more room for error. Following are some tips for painting the specific types of woodwork.

TRIM, BASEBOARDS, AND WAINSCOTING If you're using only one color and one finish on all surfaces, you may want to paint the trim as you come to it in the process of painting the walls. Of course, you'll have to keep alternating between brush and roller if you use this technique, but this shouldn't be difficult in rooms that have only a couple of windows and a single door. If you decide to paint the trim first, mask it off with masking tape or painter's tape when you paint the ceiling and walls.

Use the cutting-in technique discussed on page 125 to paint the top of a baseboard. Then, using a painting shield or a thin piece of cardboard as a movable masker, cut in along the floor. After that, you can fill the unpainted space between with long brush strokes. Paint only 2 or 3 feet of baseboard at a time. Examine the surface for drips, spatters, and overlapped edges, and clean them up immediately. Do not wait until the entire baseboard is painted or the paint flaws will have already set.

Painting wainscoting or paneling requires a similar approach. Cut in along the top and bottom edges where the wainscoting meets the wall and the floor, just as you did with the baseboard. Next, paint the indented panels and the molding around them. Paint tends to collect in the corners of these panels, so your brush strokes should be toward the center of the panel. On the raised surfaces around and between panels, work from the top down, and use up-and-down strokes on the verticals, back-and-forth strokes on the horizontals.

WINDOWS, DOORS, AND SHUTTERS Flush doors—those with smooth, flat surfaces—are easy to paint with either a brush or a roller, but doors with inset panels can be tricky. No matter what type of door you're dealing with, paint the entire door without stopping. Otherwise the lap marks may show. Before you start, remove the doorknobs, the plates behind them, and the latch plate on the edge of the door.

On ornate doors, start by painting the inset panels at the top of the door. As with wainscoting, paint all the panels and the molding around them. Then work your way down from the top to the bottom, painting the top rail, middle rail, and bottom rail (the horizontals) with back-and-forth strokes. Next, paint the vertical stiles (the sides) with up-and-down strokes. If you're painting both sides of the door, repeat this procedure. If you're painting only one side, paint the top edge of the door with a light coat. Over time, paint can build up on the top edge and cause the door to stick. Finally, paint the door's hinge edge and latch edge.

The job of painting windows will go faster if you purchase a 2- or 2½-inch sash trim brush, angled slightly across the bottom to make it easier to get into 90° corners and tight spaces.

To paint wood-frame windows, first raise the bottom sash more than halfway up and lower the top sash until its bottom rail is several inches below the bottom sash. Paint the bottom rail of

PAINTING PRECAUTIONS

Except for the danger of falling off a ladder or scaffold, painting may not seem to pose much risk to the painter or other members of the family, but paint itself is a substance that can be hazardous to a person's health. Paint is a combination of chemicals and requires careful handling and proper precautions.

- Water-thinned or solvent-thinned, paint ingredients are poisonous and should be kept away from children and pets. Antidotes are listed on can labels.

- Work in well-ventilated areas at all times, even if you're using odorless paints. They still contain fumes that may be harmful if inhaled. Wear a paper painters' mask when painting indoors. Also wear one outdoors if you're using an airless sprayer. Do not sleep in a room until the odor has dissipated.

- Do not smoke while painting and, if possible, extinguish pilot lights on gas appliances. Shut off gas to the unit first.

- Toxic paint chemicals can be absorbed through the skin. Wash up as soon as possible.

- When painting overhead, wear goggles to keep paint out of your eyes. Chemical ingredients can cause burns to sensitive eye tissue.

- Never drink alcohol while you're painting. Combined with paint fumes it can be deadly.

When painting a door, paint the panels first. Then paint the rails, the stiles, and finally the edges, working from the top to the bottom.

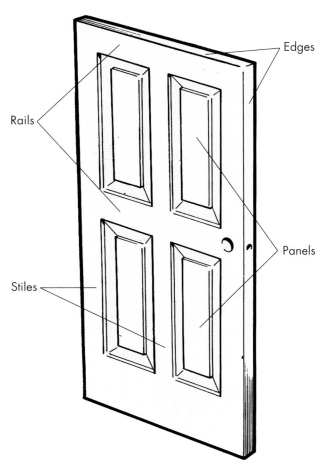

Edges

Rails

Stiles

Panels

same time. Otherwise, stand them upright or lay them out on the floor to paint one side at a time.

Keep your brush on the dry side. An excessively wet brush will result in runs and drips and, if the louvers are adjustable, sticking problems. Paint the window side of the shutter first. That way, if you do miss a run, it won't show. On adjustable shutters, put a wood matchstick or a little wood wedge between the adjusting rod and one or two of its staples to keep the rod away from the louvers. Paint the louvers first with a ½-inch or 1-inch trim brush. Then paint the frame with a 2-inch brush. Leave the shutter edges until last so you can periodically turn the shutter over to check for runs. If you find any, smooth them out with an almost-dry brush before they set. When the front is dry, paint the back.

CABINETS Painting cabinets and cupboards will be easier if you remove all obstructions first, including shelves, drawers, handles, pulls, knobs,

the top sash and up the stiles as far as you can go. Paint all the surfaces of the bottom sash except the top edge. Reverse the position of the sashes: top sash up to within an inch of the window frame, bottom sash down to within an inch of the windowsill. Then, paint the formerly obstructed surfaces of the top sash and the top edges of both sashes.

Don't paint the wood jambs in which the sashes move up and down yet. Instead, paint the window frame, working from top to bottom, including the sill. When the paint on the sashes is dry to the touch, move them both down as far as they will go. Paint the exposed jambs. Let the paint dry, raise both sashes all the way, and paint the lower jambs. To keep the sashes from sticking in the jambs, put on only as much paint as is necessary to cover the old coat. Wait for the paint to dry, then lubricate the channels with paraffin or a silicone spray.

The best way to paint shutters, both interior and exterior types, is to spray them, using either canned spray paint or an airless power sprayer. But, because that's not always possible, you can still get a quality finish on old shutters by using a brush. Take them down and scrape, sand, and clean them as needed. Then, if you can hang them from an open ceiling joist—in the garage, for example—you can paint both sides at the

1

2

3

4

Paint double-hung windows in the sequence shown, moving the top and bottom sashes for access to all surfaces.

and latches. If the hinges on the doors have pins you can remove easily, take off the doors until the cabinet and cupboard interiors and surfaces have been painted.

The most difficult part of painting cabinets is reaching the barely accessible interior surfaces. Consider shortening the handles on your trim brushes to make things easier. Paint the inside back walls; inside top; side walls; and bottoms, tops, and edges of shelves. Then paint all the exterior surfaces, working from the top down. If the doors are still in place, swing them open and paint the inside surfaces. Then close them partway and paint the outside. Finally, stand the drawers up on newspapers and paint only their fronts. Do not paint the exterior sides or bottoms of the drawers.

FLOORS Once reserved for porches, paint is turning up on wood floors with increasing frequency, particularly in vacation homes. You can do a small floor in just a couple of hours once everything is prepared.

The techniques for painting floors are the same as for painting any other large flat surface. Be sure to remove all traces of wax, and sand the floor lightly to roughen its surface, improving its paint-holding ability. You can use ordinary porch and deck paint, but the color selection may be limited. You can also use a good-quality oilbase enamel. In either case, follow up with two to four coats of clear polyurethane to protect the painted finish.

First, remove all the furniture from the area, and cut in the paint around the baseboards with a brush. Then you can use either a wide wall brush or a medium-pile roller for the rest of the floor. If you use an extension handle on a roller, you will be able to do the job standing up. Paint your way out of the room. On most wood floors, plan on applying at least two coats of paint, then two, three, or four coats of polyurethane. Let each coat dry to absolute hardness before reentering the room, and wear rubber-soled shoes until after the very last coat to avoid marring or scarring the surface.

Painting masonry floors is easier, faster, less expensive, and more common than painting wood floors. Moisture is a major cause of masonry painting problems. Most masonry is porous, and water that comes through it pushes at the paint, causing small particles to come off. In addition, the alkalinity in masonry affects the adhesiveness of some paints and attacks the

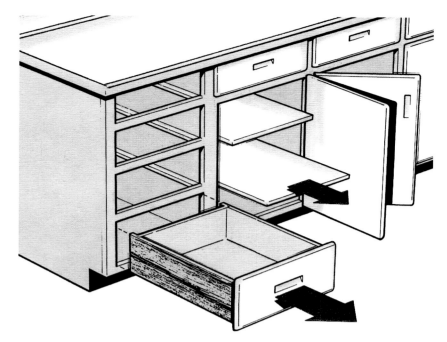

With cabinets, paint in this sequence, starting inside and working out. Paint drawers last. Don't be in too much of a rush to put everything back together again; doors and drawers can stick to tacky surfaces.

pigments in others. Paint designed for masonry surfaces can handle rough treatment.

There are a number of latex-base masonry paints that offer the advantages of easy application and easy cleanup. They can be used in damp conditions without adhesion problems. Cement-base paints are frequently used on previously unpainted concrete where very low-pressure moisture is a problem. Epoxy paints are often applied where a hard finish is needed to resist moisture and chemicals. Just make sure the paint you use is compatible with any existing paint and with the type of masonry you'll be covering. A paint dealer can help you select the appropriate coating.

Before you get down to painting, repair and patch all cracks and holes and allow the patch compounds to cure fully. Then, wearing rubber gloves and goggles, use a 10 percent muriatic acid solution to remove efflorescence, the whitish powder that appears in spots on concrete. Mop up the solution, let the area dry, rinse it thoroughly, and let it dry again. Wash the entire floor with a strong detergent or a concrete degreaser. Then, once the floor is dry and just before painting, vacuum it to get rid of any leftover dirt.

On most masonry floors you can paint with a long-napped roller fitted with an extension handle so you can paint standing up, but you may need a brush for very rough areas. Depending on the surface conditions and the kind of paint you use, you may have to apply a second coat. If so, read the label on the paint can to find out how long you should wait between coats.

CLEANING UP

One of the most important aspects of a successful paint job is keeping things clean as you're working. It's also important to clean equipment as soon as you're finished and to wipe up any spatters or drips as soon as they occur. Here are some specific tips on keeping things clean while painting.

MINIMIZING DRIPS AND SPATTERS Even if you have already cut in around the room, avoid bumping the roller into the walls as you paint the ceiling or into the ceiling as you paint the walls, even if you're using the same color paint on both surfaces. The roller may deposit a visible ridge of paint each time it touches the ceiling or the wall.

No matter how slowly and steadily you move the roller across a surface, it will emit a fine spray of paint. Wear a scarf or cap (inexpensive painters' caps are available at paint stores), and make sure the floor and furniture are covered with drop cloths. Canvas drop cloths are best because they're durable, washable, and reusable. Plastic drop cloths, however, are far less expensive and, if you tape them down so they won't slide around, just as effective.

If you choose not to mask around windows, doors, and woodwork, minimize the risk of spatters by using a paint shield, either homemade or purchased from a paint dealer. The store-bought shields come in several sizes and materials (plastic or aluminum). Do-it-yourself shields can be made from thin cardboard or the slats of an old venetian blind. The paint shield works like a moving masker. Holding the shield in one hand, place it perpendicular to the surface being painted. Then, with the other hand, apply the paint. Paint shields are ideal for painting window frames because they can be used to keep paint off the glass, eliminating the need to scrape off dried paint later.

Because some spatters and spills are inevitable, keep a moist sponge and a pail of water handy when you're using latex paints. If you're using a solvent-thinned paint, keep some thinner and a supply of rags nearby to wipe up spatters and drips before they dry into bumps.

CLEANING WINDOWPANES, SPATTERS, AND DRIPS The best time to clean up paint drips and spatters is when they're still wet and will wipe away easily. If you do miss them, you can clean them up later with some extra effort.

If you used masking tape around windows, peel it off right after painting. Otherwise it may pull off some of the paint. If you painted with a painting shield or freehand, there will most likely be a few errant drops or smudges on the glass. A razor blade scraper, available at paint or hardware stores, will scrape the paint off the glass easily. Avoid breaking the seal between the new paint and the windowpane when you're cleaning up ragged edges around the sash.

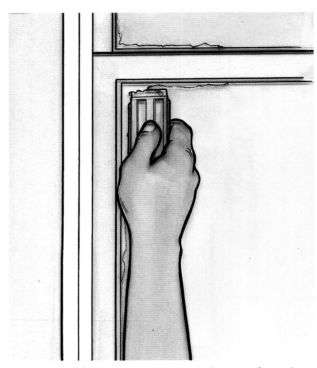

Use a razor blade scraper to remove dry paint from glass. Avoid breaking the seal between the paint and windowpane.

Cleaning up drips and spatters on most other surfaces is easier and less time consuming. For latex paint, a soft cloth combined with household detergent and warm water should do the trick. Don't scrub a freshly painted finish, though, even if it is dry to the touch. Many paints don't cure for 30 days or more. For solvent-thinned paints, use a soft cloth and turpentine or mineral spirits to soften and remove dried-on paint droplets. Then, go over the area again with warm water and detergent.

To get paint drips off hardwood, ceramic tile, or resilient flooring, wrap a cloth around a putty knife and gently scrape them up. Then wash the areas with warm, soapy water. Don't use solvent if you can avoid it, as it can damage the finish on the floor.

CLEANING PAINTING EQUIPMENT Cleaning painting equipment includes not only brushes and rollers but also reusable drop cloths, paint cans, containers, and roller pans. Don't delay cleaning your equipment one minute longer than necessary. Fresh paint comes out of brushes, rollers, and pans easily; let paint dry for a while and you'll have to put a lot more time and effort into getting it out.

Inexpensive roller covers don't respond well even to thorough cleaning. Some paint residue will remain in the nap of the roller cover. When the roller is exposed to fresh paint later, the dried-in paint can soften and cause streaks in the new finish. If you use inexpensive roller covers, buy a new one for each job and save yourself the time and effort of trying to clean them. If you invest in a professional quality roller cover, it will clean thoroughly and can be used repeatedly.

If you used latex paint, drag the brushes across the lip of the paint can to remove most of the paint. Then rinse the brushes and rollers under warm tap water and wash with dishwashing detergent. A paintbrush comb can help remove paint residue from the bristles. To get out the excess water, gently squeeze the bristles or take the brush outside and give it a few vigorous flicks. Squeeze the water out of the roller covers. Use paper towels to soak up any remaining water in both brushes and rollers.

When the brush is clean, shake out the excess solvent or water, and comb out the bristles.

With solvent-thinned paints, use the appropriate solvent as identified on the paint can's label. Agitate brushes and rollers in a container of the solvent. Repeat this process to get out all the paint. To clean brushes, pour the solvent into an old coffee can. For rollers, use an inexpensive aluminum foil loaf pan or a clean roller pan. Solvents are toxic and flammable, so don't smoke or work near a water heater or furnace, and make sure there's plenty of ventilation. Use paper towels to blot out the excess solvent from brushes and rollers, then wash everything in warm, soapy water. Hang up brushes until they're dry; set roller covers on end.

Wipe out, wash, and dry roller pans and paint containers. Wipe off the lips of paint cans and hammer down the lids to preserve leftover paint. Store paint and solvent cans away from extreme heat or cold and out of the reach of children. If you have less than a quart of paint left, store it in a tightly capped glass jar and save it for touch-ups. Brushes and rollers that have been cleaned and dried should be wrapped up before they're stored away. Brushes can go back in the plastic or paper packages they came in, or you can wrap them in aluminum foil. Rollers can be wrapped in kraft paper, foil, or perforated plastic sandwich bags.

To clean reusable drop cloths of heavy-duty plastic or canvas, wipe off major paint splotches with soap and water and paper towels. Don't use solvent on drop cloths, as it may cause them to dissolve. Let them dry thoroughly, fold them up, and store them with your other equipment for the next project.

QUICK WALLPAPER FIXES

Despite the remarkable durability of today's wallcoverings, they are not indestructible. When damage occurs or flaws turn up, it's best to fix them as soon as possible. The longer you wait, the larger they get; the larger the defect, the tougher the repair job.

REPAIRING BLISTERS

Blisters, which result from excess adhesive or air trapped in bubbles between the wall and the backside of the wallcovering, can show up within minutes, days, weeks, or even years after a project is finished. The easiest way to deal with blisters is to prevent them in the first place. Smooth out a newly applied strip of paper thoroughly with a smoothing brush, a straightedge, or a sponge. If you encounter blisters, work them toward the nearest edge of the strip to release trapped air or excess adhesive.

Blisters located in inconspicuous places won't be noticed. If you're using an untreated printed paper, small blisters may go away by themselves as the paste dries and the paper contracts. However, if a blister is still there an hour after the strip has been applied to the wall, it's not likely it will disappear on its own. Blisters that are only an hour or two old can often be repaired following these steps:

What You'll Need
Straight pin
Single-edge
    razor blade
    or utility knife
Artists' brush
Wallpaper adhesive

1. Use straight pin to puncture blister.

2. With your thumbs, gently squeeze out trapped blob of still-wet adhesive or trapped air through hole, being careful not to tear paper.

3. If that doesn't work, use single-edge razor blade or utility knife to slit small X in wallcovering, and peel back tips of slit.

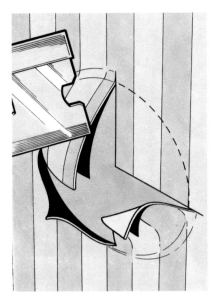

To repair a blister in wallpaper, slit it twice to form an X. Peel back the tips of the slit, brush paste into the blister, and smooth the paper down.

4. If there's a lump of adhesive underneath, gently scrape it out. If air was the cause, use artists' brush to apply small amount of adhesive behind flaps, then press flaps back down. Edges may overlap a little, but this overlapping is seldom detectable later.

REPAIRING LOOSE SEAMS

Loose seams are even easier to repair. Here's how:

What You'll Need
Artists' brush
Wallpaper adhesive
Wallpaper seam roller
Straight pins

1. Lifting seam slightly, use brush to work adhesive under seam. Press seam back down and go over it with seam roller. If you find loose seam in overlapped vinyl wallcovering, use vinyl-to-vinyl adhesive to stick it back down.

To repair loose seams in wallpaper, lift the seam and use an artists' brush to apply adhesive under the seam.

2. If seam shows any tendency to pull away, tack it in place with two or three straight pins stuck through paper and into wall until adhesive is dry. Tiny holes won't show.

REPAIRING HOLES AND TEARS

Holes and tears in wallcoverings require more effort to repair, but, if done carefully, the repairs will be nearly invisible. Here's how:

1. Use single-edge razor blade or utility knife to trim off any ragged edges around damaged area.

What You'll Need
Single-edge
    razor blade
    or utility knife
Scrap wallcovering
Wallpaper adhesive

2. Tear out patch from piece of scrap wallcovering that is slightly bigger than damaged area. Hold scrap printed side up with one hand, and rotate scrap as you gently tear out a round patch. With practice, you'll have patch with intact design on printed side of paper and slightly feathered edge on backside.

3. Spread thin coating of adhesive on back of patch, and place it over damaged area.

4. Line up pattern on patch with pattern on wall as best you can. A perfect pattern alignment may not be possible, but match should be close enough to escape detection.

Another technique for repairing holes is called double cutting. With this method you create a patch that is perfectly sized to fit the damaged area.

1. Cut out square scrap of wallcovering about an inch larger all the way around than damaged section.

What You'll Need
Single-edge
    razor blade
    or utility knife
Scrap wallcovering
Masking tape or
    thumbtacks
Metal ruler
Wallpaper adhesive

2. Place scrap over hole, and align pattern with pattern on wall. Hold scrap in place with masking tape or thumbtacks, whichever is the least likely to damage wallcovering.

3. Hold metal ruler firmly against wall over scrap, then use very sharp utility knife to cut square slightly bigger than hole itself through both layers of wallcovering.

4. Remove scrap and square patch you've just made; set aside. Use end of utility knife to lift one corner of original wallpaper square with hole, and peel this square off wall.

5. Apply adhesive to back of new patch, and press it into cleaned-out area on wall, making sure patterns are once again aligned.

QUICK FURNITURE FIXES

Unlike most of the other components that make up your home, your furniture is movable. It goes with you when you move, it's rearranged or shifted periodically, and it may be handed down for generations. You add to your furniture collection gradually, and you may end up with more old pieces than new. Because it gets moved around, and because it takes a lot of abuse over years of service, your wood furniture needs regular care to keep it looking good. And when it needs repairing, you should know how to do the job yourself.

FURNITURE CONSTRUCTION

Like all other components of your home, furniture is easy to work with when you know how it's put together. Essentially, all furniture is made to provide comfort and convenience and is judged on the basis of how well it succeeds in providing them. To function well, all wood furniture—no matter what type and age—must be sturdy, steady, and securely joined. Of course, there's no more to good furniture than sturdy legs. Good wood and crafting made good furniture, age enhances its value, and style is also important. All of these factors affect the quality and usefulness of your furniture as well as the techniques you need to know.

FURNITURE FINISHES

Furniture finishes can be classified into several basic types: varnish, penetrating resin, shellac, lacquer, wax, and oil. All of these finishes are designed to protect the wood and to bring out its natural beauty, and all of them can be assessed in terms of how well they accomplish these objectives. Choosing a finish comes down to two essential factors: how you want the wood to look and how durable you want the finished surface to be.

Of the six most common finishes, all can be beautiful, but when it comes to durability, two types outperform all the others: varnish and penetrating resin. Varnish, the most durable of all finishes, is available in high-gloss, satin, and flat forms, for whatever surface shine you want. Applying varnish can be difficult, but the results are worth the work. Penetrating resin sinks into the wood to give it a natural look and feel; it is easy to apply and durable. The other furniture finishes do have their advantages. Oil produces a very natural finish, and shellac dries fast and is

easy to use. But for most refinishing, varnish or penetrating resin is often the best choice.

Whatever finish you choose, it's important to know exactly what you're working with. Some finishes can be mixed and some cannot. Each finish has its own preferred application techniques, and each finish requires different tools and materials. Before you buy and apply a finish, always read the ingredient and application information on the container. In addition, always follow the manufacturer's instructions and recommendations.

The one requirement common to all finishes is a dust-free environment during application. Providing this environment isn't easy, but it can be done. Consider using a finish that dries with a matte or flat surface. This type of finish gives you the opportunity to remove dirt and lint with rubbing abrasives. Before starting to work, clean your work area thoroughly and let the dust settle for about 24 hours. Keep doors and windows closed. Don't work near heating/cooling registers or next to open windows, and never work outside. Be sure to wear lint-free clothes, and don't wear gloves.

Before applying any finish, make sure you have all the materials you need. Set up your work space so the piece of furniture will be between you and the light to make it easy to see dust and lint on the newly finished surfaces. Work with clean tools and new finishing materials, and make sure you have adequate light and ventilation. Clean all surfaces carefully with a tack cloth before applying the finish; if necessary, give the piece of furniture a final going-over with mineral spirits to remove dirt and fingerprints. Let the wood dry thoroughly before applying the finish. To keep the finish smooth, remove specks of dust and lint from the wet surfaces with an artists' brush or lint picker.

In most cases, how a piece of furniture stands up to wear is as important as how it looks. The first step in giving wood furniture long life is to take care of needed repairs. This means repairing veneer (the top surface of laminated wood) and hardware. After this is done, surfaces can be refinished if necessary to enhance the function and beauty of wood furniture.

REPAIRING VENEER

Most wood furniture is constructed of veneer rather than solid wood to keep costs down. Because veneer is only a thin layer of wood attached with glue to a solid base, it is very vulnerable to damage. On old furniture, the glue that holds the veneer is often not water resistant. Prolonged humidity or exposure to water can soften the glue, letting the veneer blister, crack, or peel. Veneer is easily damaged from the surface, and old veneers are often cracked, buckled, or broken, with chips or entire pieces missing.

In most cases, as long as the veneer layer is in good shape, the thinness that makes it damage-prone also makes it easy to repair. Undamaged veneer can be reglued; chips and bare spots can be filled with matching veneer. If you're careful to match the grain, the repairs will hardly show.

SMALL BLISTERS Small blisters in veneer can usually be flattened with heat. Here's how:

1. Set smooth cardboard on veneer surface to protect it, and cover cardboard with clean cloth.

2. Press blistered area firmly with medium-hot iron; if there are several blisters, move iron slowly and evenly back and forth. Be careful not to touch exposed surface with iron. Check surface every few minutes or so as you work, and stop pressing as soon as blisters have flattened.

3. Put weight on cardboard for 24 hours. Remove cardboard; wax and polish surface.

LARGE BLISTERS Large blisters must usually be slit because the veneer has swelled. To repair:

1. Using sharp craft knife or single-edge razor blade, carefully cut blister open down middle, along wood grain. Be very careful not to cut into or damage base wood.

2. Cover surface with smooth cardboard, and press blistered area with medium-hot iron. Check surface every few seconds to see if glue has softened. If the glue has deteriorated and does not soften, carefully scrape it out, and insert small amount of carpenters' glue under

To repair a large blister in veneer, slit it and insert a little glue under the edges, then flatten it with heat.

What You'll Need
Smooth cardboard
Clean, soft cloths
Iron
Books or other
   objects for weight
Furniture wax

What You'll Need
Craft knife or single-
   edge razor blade
Smooth cardboard
Iron
Carpenters' glue
Clean, soft cloths
Books or other
   objects for weight
Furniture wax

slit edges of bubble with tip of knife. Be careful not to use too much glue; wipe off any excess as blister flattens.

3. As soon as one edge of slit bubble overlaps the other, carefully shave off overlapping edge with craft knife or razor blade.

4. Heat blister again. If edges overlap further, shave overlapping edge again.

5. When blister is completely flattened, weight repair area for 24 hours.

6. Wax and polish entire surface.

LOOSE VENEER Lifted veneer occurs most often at the corners of tabletops and on cabinet and dresser edges, legs, and drawer fronts. If the loose veneer is undamaged, it can be reglued. Here's how:

1. With sharp craft knife or razor blade, carefully scrape off residue of old glue left on back of veneer and on base wood. Don't lift veneer any further; if you bend it up, you'll damage it.

2. Clean bonding surfaces with mineral spirits or benzene and clean cloth to remove any residue; glue left under loose area will interfere with new adhesive. If any glue still remains, sand bonding surfaces lightly with fine-grade sandpaper; wipe clean with soft cloth moistened with mineral spirits. If more than one veneer layer is loose, clean each layer the same way.

What You'll Need
Craft knife or single-
   edge razor blade
Mineral spirits or
   benzene
Clean, soft cloths
Fine-grade
   sandpaper
Contact cement or
   carpenters' glue
Small paintbrush
Thumbtacks
Wax paper
Scrap wood
C-clamps
Furniture wax

3. To reglue veneer, apply contact cement to both bonding surfaces, and let it set as directed by manufacturer. If necessary, set small tack or two between layers to keep them from touching. Or apply carpenters' glue to base wood, spreading it on along grain with small brush. Then, starting at solidly attached veneer and working out toward loose edge, smooth loose veneer carefully into place. Contact cement bonds immediately, so make sure veneer is exactly matched; if you're using carpenters' glue, press from center out to force out any excess, and wipe excess off immediately. If more than one veneer layer is loose, work from bottom up to reglue each layer. Press reglued layers together to align them properly, and wipe off excess glue.

Loose veneer can be reglued. Apply glue to the base wood, press the veneer into place, and clamp it firmly.

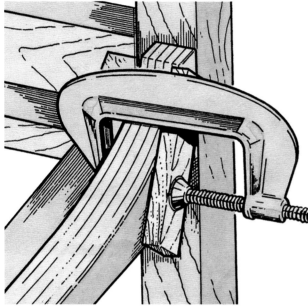

Press the reglued layers together to align them properly, wipe off excess glue, and clamp the mended part securely.

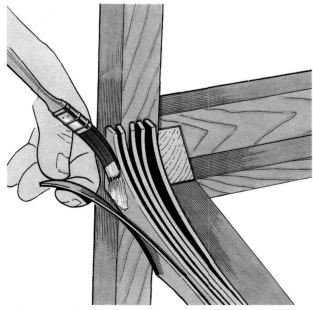

When more than one layer has separated, work from the bottom up and from the inside out to reglue each layer.

4. To protect surface, cover it with sheet of wax paper after all excess glue is removed. Set buffer block of scrap wood over newly glued area, and use another block or soft cloth to protect opposite edge or side of surface. Clamp glued and protected surface firmly with C-clamps for one to two days.

5. Remove clamps and buffers, then wax and polish the entire surface.

CRACKED OR BROKEN VENEER If the veneer is lifted and cracked but not broken completely through, it can be reglued; large areas may be easier to repair if you break the veneer off along the cracks. Broken veneer can be reglued, but you must be very careful not to damage the edges of the break. Do not trim ragged edges; an irregular mend line will not be as visible as a perfectly straight line.

Before applying glue to the veneer, clean the bonding surfaces carefully. Fit the broken edges together to make sure they match perfectly. Then apply contact cement to both surfaces or spread carpenters' glue on the base wood. Set the broken veneer into place, matching the edges together. Clamp the mended area. Refinishing may be necessary when the mend is complete.

CHIPPED OR MISSING VENEER Replacing veneer is easy, but finding a new piece to replace it may not be. If the piece of furniture is not valuable, you may be able to take the patch from a part of it that won't show. The patch area must be along an edge so you can lift the veneer with a craft knife or a stiff-bladed putty knife.

In cases in which patch veneer should not be taken from the same piece of furniture, you'll have to buy matching veneer to make the repair. If only a small piece is missing, you may be able to fill in the hole with veneer edging tape, sold at many home centers and lumberyards. Or, if you have access to junk furniture, you may be able to salvage a similar veneer from another piece of furniture. For larger patches or if you can't find a scrap piece of matching veneer, buy a sheet of matching veneer from a specialized wood supplier.

To fit a chip or very small patch:

1. Set sheet of bond paper over damaged veneer. Gently rub very soft, dull lead pencil over paper; edges of damaged area will be exactly marked on paper. Cut out pattern.

2. Tape pattern to replacement veneer, matching grain of new veneer to grain of damaged area. Cut patch firmly and carefully with sharp craft

What You'll Need
Bond paper
Soft, dull pencil
Scissors
Replacement veneer
Masking tape
Craft knife

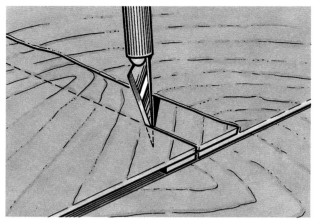

With the patch veneer held firmly to the surface, cut through the patching sheet and the veneer below it.

knife; it's better to make it too big than too small.

To make a larger patch:

What You'll Need
Replacement veneer
Masking tape
Craft knife
Mineral spirits
Clean, soft cloth
Fine-grade
    sandpaper
Contact cement or
    carpenters' glue
C-clamps or books
    or other objects
    for weight

1. Tape replacement veneer firmly over damaged area with masking tape, with grain and pattern of patch matching grain and pattern of damaged veneer. Make sure patch is flat against surface and secure.

2. Cut patch carefully with craft knife, scoring through patching veneer and damaged veneer layer below it. Cut patch in irregular shape or in boat or shield shape; these shapes will be less visible than square or rectangular patch.

3. Untape patching sheet and pop out patch. With tip of craft knife, remove cutout patch of damaged veneer. If necessary, score it and remove it in pieces. Be very careful not to damage edges of patch area. Remove only top veneer layer; do not cut into base wood. Remove any old glue, and clean base wood with mineral spirits.

4. Test fit of patch in hole. It should fit exactly, flush with surrounding surface, with no gaps or overlaps. If patch is too big or too thick, do not force it in. Carefully sand edges or back with fine-grade sandpaper to fit.

To mend veneer, cut a patch in an irregular shape; any of these shapes will be less visible than a square.

5. Glue fitted patch into place with contact cement or carpenters' glue, and clamp or weight it solidly. Let repair dry for one to two days; then very lightly sand patch and surrounding veneer.

6. Refinish damaged area or, if necessary, entire surface or piece of furniture.

REPAIRING HARDWARE

Drawer pulls, handles, hinges, locks, protective corners, decorative bands and escutcheons, and other furniture hardware often begin to show signs of use. Sometimes hardware is missing; other times it's loose, broken, or bent. Loose hardware can be repaired; missing or damaged pieces should be replaced. Replacement is also the solution if you don't like the existing hardware.

Many pieces of furniture are made with very common types of hardware, and matching these basic designs is simple. If the hardware is more distinctive or unusual, it may be easier to replace all the hardware than to find a matching piece. In this case, make sure the new hardware's bases are at least as large as the old bases. If the piece of furniture is very valuable or an antique, however, or if the hardware is very attractive, the old hardware should not be removed. In this case, missing parts should be replaced with matching or similar hardware; a slight difference in design usually is acceptable. Hardware stores, home centers, and similar stores offer a wide selection of furniture hardware. Specialty hardware outlets and craft suppliers are also good sources.

DRAWER PULLS AND HANDLES To tighten a loosely attached drawer pull, remove the pull and replace the screw with a longer one. If the screw is part of the pull, you'll have to make the hole in the wood smaller. When the hole is only slightly enlarged, you can tighten the pull by using a hollow fiber plug with the screw; for metal pulls, fit a piece of solid-core solder into the hole and then replace the screw. When the hole is much too big:

1. Insert wood toothpicks or thin shavings of wood, dipped in glue, into hole.

2. Let glue dry, then use utility knife to carefully trim shavings flush with wood surface.

3. Dip pull's screw into glue, replace pull, and tighten screw firmly.

What You'll Need
Wood toothpicks
    or thin wood
    shavings
Wood or carpenters'
    glue
Utility knife
Screwdriver

Make the hole in the wood of a drawer smaller by inserting a toothpick dipped in glue into the hole.

For a more substantial repair, enlarge the hole with an electric drill, glue a piece of dowel into it, and drill a new screw hole in the dowel.

HINGES Hinges that don't work properly usually have bent hinge pins that should be replaced. If the hinges are loose, try using slightly longer screws to attach them. When the screw holes are greatly enlarged, adjust them using one of the methods detailed above for repairing a drawer pull or handle when the screw hole has become enlarged. If the hinge leaves are damaged and the hinges cannot be replaced, glue the hinges into position with epoxy or a rubber- or silicone-base adhesive.

LOCKS Locks on old pieces are often damaged, and keys are often missing. If the piece of furniture is antique or the lock is very unusual, have it repaired by a professional. Otherwise, remove the damaged lock and take it to a locksmith so they can order a matching or similar lock to replace it. Install the new lock the same way the old one was secured.

COVERUP HARDWARE If old hardware holes are impossible to repair or if you want to change the look of a piece entirely, the damage can be covered with new wood or metal escutcheon plates. Escutcheons are mostly used under drawer pulls or handles; many handles are made with escutcheon-type backers. Attach the escutcheons with adhesive or screws, matched metal to metal.

If you're using escutcheon-type handles, no other treatment is necessary. If you're using an escutcheon under other hardware, drill new mounting holes as required.

REMOVING STAINS AND DISCOLORATION

Over years of use, furniture can become stained or discolored. Spills happen. Water glasses are forgotten. Children color. Fortunately, many of these accidents have easy solutions.

WHITE SPOTS Shellac and lacquer finishes are not resistant to water and alcohol. Spills and condensation from glasses can leave permanent white spots or rings on these finishes. To remove these white spots, first polish the surface with liquid furniture polish, firmly buffing the surface. If this doesn't work, lightly wipe the stained surface with denatured alcohol. Use as little alcohol as possible; too much will damage the finish.

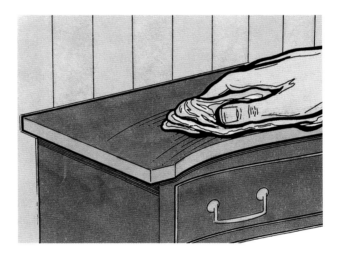

Rubbing with oil and fine abrasives is often effective in removing spots and blushing. Rub along the grain of the wood, then wipe the surface clean.

If neither polishing or alcohol treatment removes the white spots, the damaged finish must be treated with abrasives. Gentle wood abrasive pastes are available at larger building supply stores and woodworking shops. Rub the paste over the stained area, along the grain of the wood, then wipe the surface clean with a soft cloth. If necessary, repeat the procedure. Stubborn spots may require several applications. Then wax and polish the entire surface.

If this doesn't work, use a coarser abrasive paste, rubbing carefully to control the removal. As soon as the white spots disappear, stop rubbing and wipe the wood clean with a soft cloth. Then apply two coats of hard furniture wax and buff the wood to a shine.

BLUSHING Blushing, a white haze over a large surface or an entire piece of furniture, is a common problem with old shellac and lacquer finishes. The discoloration is caused by moisture, and it can be removed following these steps:

What You'll Need
No. 0000 steel wool
Linseed oil
Clean, soft rags
Furniture wax

1. Buff surface slightly and evenly with no. 0000 steel wool dipped in boiled linseed oil; work with grain of wood, rubbing evenly on entire surface until white haze disappears.

2. Wipe wood clean with soft cloth.

3. Apply two coats of hard furniture wax, and buff surface to a shine.

BLACK SPOTS Black spots are caused by water that has penetrated the finish completely and entered the wood. They cannot be removed without damage to the finish. If the spots are on a clearly defined surface, you may be able to remove the finish from this surface only; otherwise, the entire piece of furniture will have to be refinished. When the finish has been removed, bleach the entire stained surface with a solution of oxalic acid as directed by the manufacturer. Then refinish the piece.

INK STAINS Ink stains that have penetrated the finish, like black water spots, cannot be removed without refinishing. Less serious ink stains can be removed following these steps:

What You'll Need
Mineral spirits
Clean, soft rags
Furniture polish
No. 0000 steel wool

1. Lightly buff stained area with cloth moistened with mineral spirits.

2. Rinse wood with clean water on soft cloth.

3. Dry surface thoroughly, then wax and polish it.

4. If this does not work, lightly rub stained area along grain of wood with no. 0000 steel wool moistened with mineral spirits. Wipe surface clean, then wax and polish it.

The last step may damage the finish. If necessary, refinish the damaged spot (see Touch-up Refinishing on this page). If the area is badly damaged, the entire surface or piece of furniture will have to be refinished.

GREASE, TAR, PAINT, CRAYON, AND LIPSTICK SPOTS These spots usually affect only the surface of the finish. To remove wet paint, use the appropriate solvent on a soft cloth—mineral spirits for oilbase paint, water for latex paint. To remove dry paint or other materials, very carefully lift the surface residue with the edge of a putty knife. Do not scrape the wood, or you'll scratch the finish. When the surface material has been removed, buff the area very lightly along the grain of the wood with no. 0000 steel wool moistened with mineral spirits. Then wax and polish the entire surface.

WAX AND GUM SPOTS Wax and gum usually come off quickly, but they must be removed carefully to prevent damage to the finish. To remove wax or gum, press the spot with an ice pack wrapped in a towel or paper towel until deposit hardens, then lift it off with your thumbnail. The hardened wax or gum should pop off the surface with very little pressure. If necessary, repeat the ice application. Do not scrape the deposit off, or you'll scratch the finish. When the wax or gum is completely removed, buff the area very lightly along the wood grain with no. 0000 steel wool moistened with mineral spirits. Wax and polish the entire surface.

TOUCH-UP REFINISHING

Deep scratches, gouges, burns, or any other surface damage requires refinishing the repair area. Spot refinishing is not always easy and not always successful, especially on stained surfaces. But, if the damage isn't too bad, it's worth trying. If you have to touch up several areas on one surface, consider completely refinishing the surface or the piece of furniture. Here's how to refinish a spot:

1. Select stain. To stain one area on a surface, use oilbase stain that matches surrounding stain. You may have to mix stains to get a good match. Test stain on inconspicuous unfinished part of wood before working on finished surface.

What You'll Need
Stain
Fine-grade sandpaper
Clean, soft cloths
Artists' brush
No. 0000 steel wool
Tack cloth
Varnish, penetrating resin, shellac, or lacquer (depending on existing finish)
Hard paste wax

2. Sand damaged area smooth with fine-grade sandpaper, and wipe surface clean.

3. Apply stain to damaged area with artists' brush or clean cloth, covering entire bare area.

Spot-staining is tricky, but it is sometimes successful. Apply stain to the repair area with an artists' brush or a clean cloth.

4. Let stain set for 15 minutes, then wipe it off with clean cloth. If color is too light, apply another coat of stain, wait 15 minutes, and wipe again. Repeat this procedure until you're satisfied with color, then let stain dry according to manufacturer's instructions.

5. Lightly buff stained surface with no. 0000 steel wool, and wipe it clean with tack cloth.

6. Apply new coat of same finish (varnish, penetrating resin, shellac, or lacquer) over newly stained area, smoothing out new finish into surrounding old finish.

7. Let new finish dry for one or two days, then lightly buff patched area with no. 0000 steel wool.

8. Wax entire surface with hard paste wax, and polish it to a shine.

REPAIRING SURFACE DAMAGE

Scratches, dings, dents, cracks and gouges, burns, and other maladies can also mar furniture surfaces. Here's how to treat these afflictions:

SCRATCHES To hide a small scratch, rub oil from the meat of a walnut, pecan, or Brazil nut along the scratch. The oil in the nut meat will darken the raw scratch, making it less conspicuous. These oils are available at woodworker's stores or from the nut itself. They're the main ingredient in many scratch-removal products. When many shallow scratches are present, apply hard paste wax to the surface with No. 0000 steel wool, stroking very lightly along the grain of the wood. Then buff the surface with a soft cloth. If the scratches still show, apply one or two more coats of hard paste wax to the surface. Let each coat dry thoroughly, and buff it to a shine before applying the next coat.

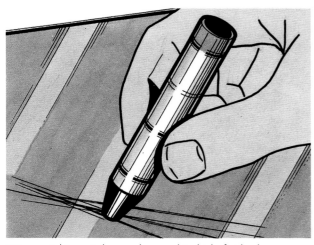

Wax patching sticks can be used to hide fairly deep scratches. Press firmly to fill the scratch. Level with the edge of a piece of thin plastic or a credit card.

For one or two deeper scratches, wax furniture-patching sticks are usually effective. These retouching sticks, made in several wood colors, are available at hardware and, sometimes, grocery stores. Choose a stick to match the finish. To use the wax stick, run it firmly along the scratch, applying enough pressure to fill the scratch with wax. Remove any excess wax with the edge of a credit card or other thin plastic card. Let the wax dry; then buff the surface with a soft cloth.

DINGS Dings are tiny chips in the finish, usually caused by a sharp blow. The wood may not be affected. To repair a ding:

1. Use craft knife to remove any loose finish in or around ding. Work carefully, scraping damaged spot with flat, sharp edge of knife blade; do not scratch spot.

2. Carefully smooth edges of ding with no. 0000 steel wool.

3. Clean damaged area with soft cloth moistened in mineral spirits. Let dry completely.

4. Apply new finish to spot using artists' brush to match rest of finish. Spot will be very noticeable at first. Let finish dry; it will be glossy.

5. Lightly buff spot with no. 0000 steel wool, then wax and polish entire piece of furniture. Ding should blend perfectly when job is complete.

DENTS Small shallow dents in pine and other soft woods are usually easy to remove; large and deep dents, especially in hard wood, are harder to repair. Dents are easiest to remove from bare wood. Very large, shallow dents are probably best left untreated. Very deep dents should be filled, as detailed later for cracks and gouges.

1. Using fine-grade sandpaper, carefully remove finish about ½ inch around damaged area.

2. Raise wood in the dent by applying few drops of water to dent. Do not wet entire surface. Let water penetrate wood for day or so. This treatment may be enough to raise dent, especially if it's shallow and wood is soft.

3. If this doesn't raise dent, soak cloth in water and wring it out. Place damp cloth, folded in several layers, over dent; then press cloth firmly with warm iron. Be careful not to touch iron directly to wood. This moist heat may be enough to swell wood and raise dent. If not, apply commercial wood-swelling liquid to area, and give it time to work—about a day or so, as directed by manufacturer.

What You'll Need
Craft knife
No. 0000 steel wool
Clean, soft cloths
Mineral spirits
Artists' brush
Varnish, penetrating resin, shellac, or lacquer (depending on existing finish)
Furniture polish

What You'll Need
Fine-grade sandpaper
Water
Clean, soft cloths
Iron
Commercial wood-swelling liquid
Fine straight pin or needle
Hammer
Pliers
No. 0000 steel wool
Furniture polish

4. For deep dents that can't be raised with water, heat, or wood sweller, use fine straight pin or needle to drive series of holes in dent. Pound straight pin in about ¼ inch and carefully pull it out with pliers. Holes should be as small as possible. Then treat dent as previously described. Pinholes help water penetrate wood's surface.

Use a fine pin or needle to drive a series of small holes in a stubborn dent, then swell the wood to raise the dent.

5. After dent has been raised, let wood dry for about a week. Refinish damaged area as previously described on pages 140–141. Let finish dry completely. Lightly buff new finish with no. 0000 steel wool, then wax and polish entire surface.

CRACKS AND GOUGES Cracks and gouges should be filled so they're level with the wood surface. For very small holes, like staple holes, woodtone putty sticks can be used. If you can't match the wood, several colors can be mixed together. To use a putty stick, wipe it across the hole and smooth the surface with your finger. If you plan to finish or refinish the wood, let the putty dry for at least a week before proceeding further.

For larger holes, wood plastic and water putty are the easiest fillers. They can be used on bare or finished wood; wood plastic is available in several colors, and water putty can be tinted with oil or water stain. However, wood plastic and water putty patches are usually noticeable and may look darker than the wood. For the best results, test the patch on an inconspicuous surface to make sure the color is right. To use wood plastic:

1. Clean crack or gouge with tip of craft knife.

2. Press wood plastic firmly in with tip of craft knife or edge of putty knife. Wood plastic shrinks slightly as it dries, so press it in tightly and leave it mounded slightly above wood surface. Let wood plastic set for at least two days.

3. Smooth patch lightly with fine-grade sandpaper, and buff the area with no. 0000 steel wool. If surrounding finish is involved, smooth edges so new patch blends in with rest of finish.

4. If necessary, stain patch, and buff it lightly with no. 0000 steel wool. Apply finish to match rest of surface, using artists' brush and feathering edges. Let finish dry, then lightly buff it with no. 0000 steel wool.

5. Clean area of any residue and wax, and polish surface.

> **What You'll Need**
> Craft knife
> Wood plastic
> Putty knife
> Fine-grade sandpaper
> No. 0000 steel wool
> Wood stain
> Artists' brush
> Varnish, penetrating resin, shellac, or lacquer (depending on existing finish)
> Clean, soft cloth
> Hard paste wax

Fill deep cracks and gouges with wood plastic or water putty; leave the filler slightly high to allow for shrinkage as it dries. When the patch is dry, sand it smooth.

Water putty dries flint-hard, usually harder than the wood being patched and is best used on bare wood. It can be toned with oil and water stains, but you'll have to experiment to come up with a perfect match. To use water putty, mix the powder with water to the consistency of putty, then trowel it into the break with a putty knife, leaving the patch slightly high. Let the patch dry completely, then sand and steel wool the area smooth and level with the surrounding surface. Finish the patch area as mentioned on pages 140–141, or finish the entire piece of furniture.

For the most professional patching job, use shellac sticks to fill cracks and gouges. Shellac sticks leave the least conspicuous patch and are very effective on finished wood that's in good condition. Shellac sticks are available in several woodtone colors; use a stick that matches the finish as closely as possible. Practice on scrap wood before working on a piece of furniture. To use a shellac stick:

1. Carefully clean crack or gouge with tip of craft knife.

2. Shellac sticks must be heated and melted to fill crack. The best heat source for this is alcohol lamp or propane torch turned to low setting. Do not use match to soften stick; smoke from match may discolor shellac. Do not use range burner as liquid shellac could damage either gas or electric ranges. Hold stick to heat source over blade of a palette knife or putty knife to prevent it from dripping. Stick should soften to about consistency of glazing compound or putty.

3. Use heated putty knife blade to trowel shellac smooth. Make sure soft shellac fills break completely; it hardens quickly, so you'll have to work fast. Leave patch slightly high.

4. Let patch set for one to two hours. When shellac is hard, sand surface smooth and level. Finish surrounding break usually doesn't have to be retouched, but surface can be coated with shellac, if desired.

5. Rub surface smooth with no. 0000 steel wool and linseed oil.

To fill very deep holes, use wood plastic or water putty to fill the hole almost level. Let the filler dry completely, then fill the indentation with a shellac stick. If a hole or split is very large, consider filling it with a piece of wood cut and trimmed to fit perfectly. If the patching wood can be taken from the piece of furniture in a spot that won't show, the repair may be almost impossible to detect.

Fit the wood patch into the hole or split; use carpenters' glue to bond it to the surrounding

What You'll Need
Craft knife
Alcohol lamp or propane torch
Putty knife or palette knife
Fine-grade sandpaper
Shellac
No. 0000 steel wool
Linseed oil

wood. Leave the patch slightly high. When the glue is completely dry, sand the plug smoothly level with the surface of the surrounding wood. Then refinish the piece of furniture.

BURNS Burns on furniture can range from scorches to deep char, but the usual problem is cigarette burns. Scorches from cigarettes or cigars are usually very easy to remove. Buff the scorched area with a fine steel wool pad moistened with mineral spirits until the scorch disappears. Then wipe it clean and wax and polish the surface.

More serious burns require the removal of the charred wood. Shallow burns, when repaired, will always leave a slight indentation in the wood, but this depression will be inconspicuous. To repair a burn hole:

1. With flat, sharp edge of a craft knife, very carefully scrape away charred area to bare wood, smoothing out edges. Work carefully to avoid scratching wood with point of knife. Any burned or scorched spots will show, so all burn crust must be removed. For deep burns, it's best to use curved blade.

2. Level groove as much as possible with fine-grade sandpaper, but stay close to edges of groove. If you sand too far out from burned area, damage will be very visible as a wide

What You'll Need
Craft knife
Fine-grade sandpaper
Water
No. 0000 steel wool
Hard paste wax
Clean, soft cloth

PROFESSIONAL FURNITURE STRIPPERS

Professional furniture strippers can help you reduce the labor of refinishing wood furniture. These services use huge tubs of methylene chloride or other wash-away chemicals. Your chest of drawers, table, or chair is dipped into the solution, which eats off the old finish right down to the bare wood. The furniture item is then dipped into a neutralizing chemical and/or sprayed with water to remove the chemicals.

The cost of commercial finish removal usually depends on the size of the item to be cleaned. A chair, for example, would cost less to clean than a dresser. The cost for most items, however, is not prohibitive. Professional strippers will remove the finish from almost any item, including woodwork or railings; their work isn't limited to furniture.

There are some advantages and some disadvantages to professional strippers.

Pros: The item you have stripped comes out extremely clean. If there are several layers of finish on the item, a commercial stripper can definitely save you hours of labor. It is probably less expensive to have the piece stripped than to buy the remover to strip it yourself.

Cons: The chemicals used by commercial strippers are thought by some furniture buffs to take the "life" or oil out of the wood and render it "deadwood." Moreover, the chemicals sometimes soften or destroy the adhesive that holds the furniture together.

Professional strippers are a good investment for most projects, but you will want to make sure the service is bonded in case your antique furniture is damaged in the process. Better yet, strip antiques yourself by hand.

After removing the char, sand the burn area lightly to smooth it and level it out to the surrounding surface.

saucer-shape indentation. Be careful not to damage surrounding finish. If you're not sure all burn has been removed, wet sanded area. If water makes burned area look burned again, you haven't removed all the char. If depression isn't too deep, try swelling wood as detailed on page 141 for dents. If you're left with a deep gouge, burn area can be filled with wood plastic or shellac stick.

3. Refinish damaged area as detailed on pages 140–141. Let new finish dry for one or two days, then lightly buff patch with no. 0000 steel wool to blend edges into old finish.

4. Wax and polish entire piece.

CLEANING OLD FINISH

Refinishing is a long, slow, messy job. Before you consider stripping the old finish off any piece of furniture, take a good look at it. A complete refinishing job may not be necessary. Instead, you can use a few simple restoration techniques to revive the old finish. Restoration doesn't always work, but it's well worth trying before you resort to more drastic means. Start with the simplest techniques and work up; the easiest way is often best.

After identifying the finish, you're ready to restore it. Whether the problem is dirt, cracks, discoloration, or overall wear, it can often be solved by these restoration techniques. The easiest restoration process is cleaning. What first appears to be a beat-up finish may be just dirt. Over a period of years, even well-cared-for furniture can acquire a dull, sticky coating of wax and dust. In many cases, this coating can be removed with an oilbase commercial wood cleaner/conditioner, which can often dig through layers of dirt and wax. They are available at furniture stores, some supermarkets, and paint stores. Here's how to restore a surface by cleaning it:

1. Apply cleaner generously with soft cloth, and let it stand for an hour or two.

2. Wipe off cleaner with another cloth. Repeat process, using plenty of cleaner, until wood is clean and lustrous. This may take up to four or five applications.

3. Lightly buff clean wood to remove excess oil. Let wood dry completely. If there's a haze on finish, buff surface lightly along wood grain with no. 0000 steel wool. Then apply commercial cleaner/conditioner, and gently buff wood again.

If detergent cleaning doesn't work, use a solvent to clean the wood. Solvent cleaning is the last resort to consider, because it may damage the finish, but it is worth a try. Use mineral spirits or turpentine on any finish; use denatured alcohol on varnish or lacquer. Do not use alcohol on shellac or on a shellac/lacquer mixture. Working in a well-ventilated area or outdoors, apply the solvent with a rough cloth, such as burlap or an old towel. Then wipe the wood clean with another cloth. Finally, apply a commercial cleaner/conditioner and buff the wood lightly.

COVERING WORN FINISH

All materials wear down over a period of time, and furniture is no exception. Sometimes the entire finish is worn; other times only heavy-use areas need repair. Worn spots are most common around doors and drawers. On an antique, wear is part of the patina of the piece and is used to date and determine the value of the furniture. It should not be covered or restored. The same consideration applies to almost any piece of furniture: Wear and tear adds a certain character. But a thin, old finish can be recoated. And where refinishing is the only alternative, you may be able to repair the worn spots. Here's how to cover a worn finish:

1. Clean entire worn surface, then sand worn spots very lightly with fine-grade sandpaper. Be careful not to exert much pressure.

2. To touch up worn spot, use oilbase stain that matches stain on piece of furniture. You may have to mix stains to get a good match. Test stain on an inconspicuous unfinished part of wood before working on worn spots. Apply stain to dam-

aged area with artists' brush or clean cloth, covering entire bare area.

3. Let stain set for 15 minutes, then wipe it off with clean cloth. If color is too light, apply another coat of stain, wait 15 minutes, and wipe again. Repeat procedure until you're satisfied with color. Let stain dry according to manufacturer's instructions.

4. Lightly buff stained surface with no. 0000 steel wool, and wipe it clean with tack cloth.

5. Apply new coat of same finish already on surface (lacquer, shellac, penetrating resin, or varnish) over newly stained areas, feathering out new finish into surrounding old finish.

6. Let new finish dry for one or two days, then lightly buff patched areas with no. 0000 steel wool.

7. Wax entire surface with hard paste wax, and polish it to a shine.

QUICK PEST BANISHMENTS

Are bugs bugging you? Are other pests pestering you? Fortunately, there are some quick fixes to these problems.

ANTS

Keep ants away from your home with a mixture of equal amounts of borax and sugar. Mix in a jar, label the contents, punch holes in the jar's lid, and sprinkle outdoors around the foundation of your home and inside around the baseboards of your house. Avoid sprinkling where children and pets could be affected. Ants are attracted by the sugar and poisoned by the borax. Alternatively,

Sprinkle a mixture of borax and sugar around your home's foundation to keep ants away.

wiping or spraying areas where ants enter or wherever you see them will help discourage them from invading your home. Even ordinary table salt sprinkled in areas where ants congregate may help deter them.

COCKROACHES

If cockroaches are a problem, sprinkle borax powder in the kitchen and bathroom cabinets. Avoid sprinkling where children and pets could be affected. A squirt of pure vinegar from a spray bottle may stop a cockroach long enough to be captured and disposed of properly.

FLEAS

If your home becomes infested with fleas, try any or all of the following suggestions. Vacuum rugs thoroughly before spraying, and throw out the dust bag at once. Sprinkle carpet or rugs with salt to help kill any flea eggs. Let stand a few hours, then vacuum. Repeat weekly for six weeks. Put salt, flea powder, or a piece of a flea collar in your vacuum cleaner bag to help kill fleas and flea eggs that may have been vacuumed up.

MICE AND OTHER RODENTS

Carefully wrap all food in containers so mice cannot get to it. Raw bacon or peanut butter makes good bait for a mousetrap; so does a cotton ball saturated with bacon grease. Make sure a mouse will have to tug the trap to remove the bait. If you're using peanut butter, dab some on the triggering device and let it harden before setting the trap. If bacon is your bait, tie it around the triggering device. To keep rodents out of your house, seal every opening they could squeeze through. Some need less than ¼ inch of space. Put poison in deep cracks or holes, and stuff these with steel wool or scouring pads pushed in with a screwdriver. Close the spaces with spackling compound mixed with steel wool fragments.

RACCOONS

If a raccoon sets up house in your attic or chimney, chemical repellents, such as oil of mustard, are temporarily effective. The smell may bother you as much as it does the raccoon, however. Your best bet is to let the animal leave and then cover its entrance hole with wire mesh so it cannot return. If pest is away from the house, such as in a shed, use rotten eggs, available in powder form to keep raccoons, deer, and other pests away from gardens and plants.

CHAPTER 7

QUICK EXTERIOR FIXES

The outside of your home is just as important as the inside—you just don't see it all the time. Because of this, minor repairs often get overlooked. This chapter will not only show you where to look for exterior problems but also how to fix them. Fortunately, most outside quick fixes are neither expensive nor difficult. All that's required are a few tools and materials, some know-how, and a few weekend mornings when the weather is pleasant. In fact, outside jobs can actually be fun!

ABOUT HOME EXTERIORS

Your home exterior is not just made up of paint and siding. It also includes all the other components that serve your home and your living space. On some homes that means a front porch a back deck, or a fence. On all homes this means a roof. The fixes included in this chapter are quick—you can tackle most of them in just a few hours or less. Others you may need to start one day and finish another, but they are all relatively easy. In addition, as you learn more about the exterior of your home, you'll feel more confident about estimating the time and money needed to tackle other quick fixes to your home's exterior.

Visually inspect your home exterior to come up with a list of things that need to be done. Because many of the problems you will find involve painting, this chapter addresses painting problems first.

IDENTIFYING PAINT PROBLEMS

Inspect your house thoroughly before you paint, and take corrective action to prevent the root causes of paint failure. Following are some common paint problems and their causes:

PEELING

Peeling is often the result of painting over wet wood. It can also result from moisture within the house pushing its way out. If you cannot control the moisture with exhaust fans, use latex primer and latex paint. Latex allows some moisture to pass right through the paint.

Another cause of peeling is a dirty or a glossy surface. To undo the damage, all loose paint flakes must be scraped off with a wire brush and the surface must be sanded to smooth sharp edges. Bare spots should be primed before painting.

ALLIGATORING

This problem looks just like its name suggests: the hide of an alligator. Paint shrinks into individual islands, exposing the previous surface, usually because the top coat is not adhering to the paint below. Perhaps the paints are not compatible or the second coat was applied before the first coat had dried. To get rid of this problem, scrape off the old paint and then sand, prime, and repaint the surface.

BLISTERING

Paint that rises from the surface and forms blisters is usually due to moisture or improper painting. To fix the problem, first scrape off the blisters. If you can see dry wood behind them, the problem is due to moisture. If you find paint, then it is a solvent blister and is probably caused by painting with an oilbase or alkyd-base coating in hot weather. The heat forms a skin on the paint and traps solvent in a bubble.

WRINKLING

New paint can run and sag into a series of slack, skinlike droops. This occurs when the paint you are using is too thick and forms a surface film over the still-liquid paint below. It can also happen if you paint in cold weather; the cold surface slows drying underneath. To recoat, make sure the new paint is the proper consistency and be sure to brush it out as you apply. Before doing this, though, you will have to sand the wrinkled area smooth and, if necessary, remove the paint altogether.

CHALKING

This is paint that has a dusty surface. Some oilbase and alkyd-base paints are designed to "chalk" when it rains. When this happens, a very fine powdery layer is removed, automatically cleaning the surface. In most cases, this is desirable. But if foundations, sidewalks, and shrubs become stained, too much chalking is occurring.

PAINT TROUBLESHOOTING CHART

Problem	Possible Cause	Solution
Peeling	Paint curls due to wet wood, interior moisture vapor, dirty, glossy surface.	Scrape, sand, prime, repaint. Install siding/soffit vents outside, exhaust fans inside.
Wrinkling	New paint sags and droops. Paint applied too thickly.	Scrape, sand, prime, and repaint. Stir new paint and brush out thoroughly.
Alligatoring	Paint dries into islands. Either due to incompatible paints or painting too soon over still-wet coat.	Scrape, sand, prime, and repaint with a compatible coating.
Blistering	Surface blisters caused by underlying moisture or solvent from paint applied on hot day.	Sand smooth, repaint. Install vents. Paint on mild days.
Chalking	Powdery residue stains on sidewalks, foundations. Inferior paint or porous undercoat to blame.	Wash down surface, let dry, repaint with nonchalking coating.
Mildew	Discoloration of exterior surface due to growth of fungus, usually black/green stains.	Scrub off with chlorine bleach or fungicide, let dry, repaint with mildew-resistant formula. Trim tree branches, shrubs.
Running sags	Wavy paint surface. Paint applied too heavily.	Sand smooth, repaint. Brush out paint to a consistent thickness.
Paint won't dry	Inferior paint.	Patience or removing and repainting. Test paints on small areas before painting entire house.
Efflorescence	Whitish deposits on masonry caused by moisture-induced oxidation.	Scrub off deposits with 10:1 water-muriatic acid solution, followed by 2:1 water-ammonia, water rinse, dry, repaint with appropriate masonry paint. Check downspouts, eliminate damp conditions.
Rust-stained siding/shingles	Rusting nail heads, gutters sealed insufficiently.	Seal rusting nail heads with rust-resistant sealer and paint entire surface.
Rusted metal	Deteriorated paint combined with moisture.	Scrape, sand, recoat with metal primer, metal paint.
Bleeding knots	Knot resin dissolved by paint solvent from improperly sealed, primed knots.	Scrape, sand to bare wood, coat with shellac, prime, repaint.

This is likely due to painting over a too-porous surface that has absorbed too much of the paint's binding agents. A chemical imbalance in an inferior paint may also be the cause of excessive chalking. The best solution is to wash down the chalking surfaces as thoroughly as possible, then paint over them with a nonchalking paint.

MILDEW

This moldy growth appears where dampness and shade prevail. And, if you paint over it, it's likely to come right through the new paint. Use a fungicide such as chlorine bleach or a commercial solution to kill patches of mildew before repainting.

RUNNING SAGS

Using a paintbrush incorrectly (e.g., too much paint on the brush) can create a wavy, irregular surface. To correct it after the paint is dry, sand and repaint surface, smoothing out the new coat to an even thickness.

PAINT WON'T DRY

This is perhaps the best reason to buy high-quality paint. Prolonged tackiness is an indication of inferior paint. If you apply poor-quality paint too thickly or during high humidity, it will stay tacky for a long time. Good paint, on the other hand, dries quickly. If you think you may have an inferior paint, first experiment on an inconspicuous portion of the house.

QUICK EXTERIOR PAINTING FIXES

Painting the whole outside of your house is not a quick fix. It's a major job. But your home may not need a whole paint job. You may be able to spiff up the appearance of your home and extend the life of an entire paint job by several years with regular maintenance and some quick repairs. Whether you decide to paint a porch, the most weathered side of your house, or an outbuilding or two, the general process is the same as painting your whole house. You'll need to clean and prep the surface, decide what type of paint to use, and apply the paint. The best time to paint is in late spring or early fall on a dry day that is not too sunny. Temperatures below 40°F and direct hot sun can ruin paint jobs.

REMOVING OLD PAINT

If you're lucky, all your house may need before repainting is a good, healthy bath. Wash it down with a hose, and go over stubborn dirt with a scrub brush and warm, soapy water. Or wash it down with a power washer (see page 150). If you're not so lucky, then you just have to face the fact that a time-consuming and dirty job lies ahead of you. Do the job well, and your paint job will not only look better, but it will last for five to eight years on average.

Start by thoroughly examining the outside of the house or outbuilding—not just the exterior walls but under the eaves, around windows and doors, and along the foundation. Look for split shingles and siding, popped nails, peeling or blistering paint, mildew, and rust stains. Once you've identified the areas that need attention, roll up your sleeves and make the repairs.

Remove small areas of defective paint with a wire brush and/or a wide-blade putty knife. Scrub under the laps of clapboard siding and on downspouts and gutters.

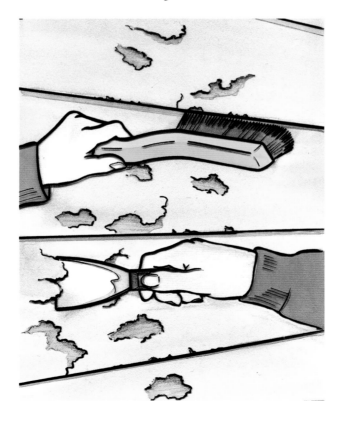

SCRAPING Use a wire brush and a wide-blade putty knife to remove small areas of defective paint. Scrub under the laps of clapboard siding as well as on downspouts and gutters. For speedier work on metal, a wire brush attachment on an electric drill will remove rust and paint with less effort. For more extensive paint removal, invest in a sharp pull scraper—a tool with a replaceable blade that's capable of stripping old paint all the way down to bare wood with a single scrape. Hold the scraper so the blade is perpendicular to the wood, apply moderate to firm pressure, and drag it along the surface. Keep the blade flat against the wood so it doesn't gouge the surface.

SANDING For smoothing the edges of scraped spots here and there, you can wrap a piece of sandpaper around a wood block. For larger areas, it's less tiring and more effective to use an electric orbital sander. Move it up and down or back and forth across the surface to remove old paint and smooth rough edges at the same time. Don't use an electric disc sander or a belt sander. Both can leave swirls or dips in the wood that will show through a new coat of paint.

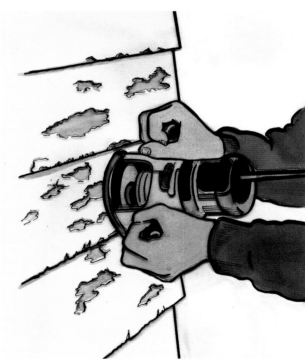

Move an electric orbital sander up and down or back and forth to remove old paint and feather rough edges.

MELTING For particularly heavy deposits of paint, heat may be more effective than muscle. One way to apply heat is with an electric paint remover, which is a device with a platelike heating element that "cooks" the paint and has a built-in scraper to pull it off. Wearing heavy gloves, hold the heating element against the surface until the paint sizzles. Pull the remover

Another way to remove old paint is with an electric paint remover—a device with a platelike heating element that softens the paint and has a built-in scraper.

firmly over the surface. The attached scraper will pull off the cooked paint as you go.

LIQUID PAINT REMOVERS Use liquid paint removers only as a last resort. They work well, but they're expensive, especially on big jobs. Also, they can slop onto perfectly good paint, giving you one more problem to deal with.

PRIMING

Once you have removed all the loose paint, you should apply an appropriate primer to some of the distressed areas, especially if your paint-removal system has exposed raw wood or bare metal. The kind of primer you use depends on the kind of paint you'll be using later. For latex paint, use latex primers; for solvent-thinned paints, use solvent-base primers; and for metals, use metal primers. Not only do these coatings provide extra protection against the elements, they also form a firm foundation for finishing paints. Also, priming is always required when you're working on new wood.

OTHER PREP WORK

Even if you're fortunate enough to skip spot-scraping, sanding, and repriming, there are still some prepainting chores to attend to. They're much less laborious than removing peeling paint but no less vital to a successful job.

Rust stains on siding, overhangs, and foundations need to be removed. Leaks in gutters and downspouts have to be repaired. Loose caulking

should be replaced, along with split shingles. Cracks in siding must be filled, sanded, and primed. Mildew must be scrubbed off, and steps should be taken to eliminate its return.

Also, to make painting easier, storm windows, screens, shutters, awnings, wall-mounted light fixtures (be sure to turn the power supply off), the mailbox, and even the street address numbers should be taken down, cleaned, and painted separately. You may even want to remove downspouts, as it's sometimes difficult to get a paintbrush behind them.

To make painting easier, remove light fixtures and other accessories.

You can typically complete all of these preparations for an entire house in a single day or over a weekend. If you're painting a porch or an outbuilding, it may only take an hour. If you're painting with latex, you can start the following day; solvent-base paint does not adhere well to moist surfaces so wait several days until all the washed surfaces are absolutely dry before applying this type of paint.

WASHING Not only will this process get the outside of your house clean and provide a dirt-free foundation for the new coating, it will also help you find surface flaws that have to be dealt with.

Depending on just how dirty the outside of your house is and on the house's size, there are two ways to approach this job. If you live in an average-size house, use a garden hose with a carwash brush attachment to bathe the big areas. For caked-on dirt, use a scrub brush or a sponge and a pail of warm water with a good, strong household detergent in it. Work from the top

To remove caked-on dirt, use a scrub brush or a sponge and a pail of warm water with a good, strong household detergent in it. Work from the top down and rinse all areas where you scrubbed.

down, and rinse all areas where you scrubbed with water.

For bigger houses or for faster work on smaller ones, rent a high-pressure spray cleaner. This device attaches to your home's water-supply system and puts out a jet of water at a pressure of about 600 pounds per square inch. It is equipped with a handheld wand tipped with a trigger-activated nozzle. The pressure is high enough to dislodge not only stubborn dirt, mildew, stains, and dried-on sea-spray salt, it's enough to remove peeling paint. In fact, if the jet nozzle is held too close to the surface it can even peel off perfectly sound paint, split open shingles, and drill a hole in siding. So follow the manufacturer's directions and wear goggles and protective clothing.

You can use the spray cleaner while working from a ladder— although scaffolding is better— but practice at ground level first; the force of the spray against the house could knock you off a ladder if you're not careful. Some of these machines come with separate containers you can fill with cleaning solutions or anti-mildew solutions. Sprayers are so powerful that ordinarily you probably won't need to use a cleaning solution; if you do, remember to rinse the surface with clean water afterward.

RESETTING POPPED NAILS The house bath may reveal nails that have popped out of the siding or rusting nail heads that have left streaks of rust on exterior walls. If so, use sandpaper or steel wool to clean the nail heads. On clapboard siding, use a nail set to recess the nail head about ⅛ inch below the surface of the wood. Dab on a coat of rust-inhibiting primer (unless the nail is aluminum or nonrusting galvanized steel), and let it dry. Then fill the nail hole with spackle or putty. When the filler is dry, give it a coat of primer. For flathead nails, which cannot be recessed, sand the heads until they're shiny, and coat with primer.

COVERING SHRUBS Trees, bushes, and orna-mental shrubs can also get in the way of your painting. Prune any branches that hang over the house or brush up against walls. Evergreen trees and tall bushes growing close to the house can be wrapped with canvas drop cloths. Tie one end of a rope around the trunk at least halfway up. Pull the top of the tree out and away from the house, and tie the other end of the rope to a stake placed farther out in the yard. Cover smaller shrubs, flower beds, sidewalks, and driveways with drop cloths to protect them from paint drips and spills.

PAINTING SIDING

With the surface preparations out of the way, you're almost ready to brush, roll, or spray on a new coat of paint. First, because paint colors tend to vary slightly from batch to batch, mix all

To keep trees out of the way while you're painting, tie a rope around the trunk, and pull the tree out away from the house. Stake the other end of the rope out in the yard.

At the sides of window and door casings, jab your brush into joints, then smooth out the paint.

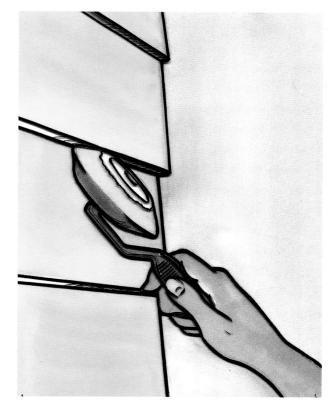

A corner roller makes short work of the undersides of shingles or clapboards.

the paint together in one or two large containers. Leftover paint should go back in the original paint cans and be resealed.

Plan your painting day so you follow the sun, working in the shade after the sun has dried off the early morning moisture. Try not to let the setting sun catch you in the middle of an exterior wall at the end of the day. If you have to stop, try to finish painting an entire course of siding all the way across the house. Otherwise, you may leave lap marks in the middle of the course.

Also, plan to paint high places in horizontal sections across the top of the exterior wall. Never lean away from an extension ladder or reach more than an arm's length to either side. Paint one high section, move the ladder, and paint another, creating a painted band as you go. Repeat the process all the way across the exterior wall. Then, lower the ladder to work on a lower section. An extension ladder can be perilous. Make sure it's on firm footing about one-quarter of its length out from the foundation of the house. Also make sure it doesn't tilt to the left or right. Always check both extension hooks to ensure they are firmly locked on the supporting rungs. The two sections of the ladder should overlap at least three rungs. When moving the ladder, watch out for power lines. Here's another tip: Hang your paint bucket on a rung with an S-shape bucket hook so you can hang onto the ladder with one hand while painting with the other.

If your house has dormers, you may have to paint them from the roof instead of a ladder. If so, the ladder should reach at least 3 feet above the edge of the roof so you can step onto the roof without standing on the top rungs of the ladder.

When painting either clapboard or shingles, pay special attention around door and window casings. At the top of each casing you'll find a drip cap or metal flashing that tucks up under the siding. Paint a tight seal between metal and wood. At the sides of the casings, jab your brush into joints, then smooth out the paint to seal them. At casings and for the undersides of siding laps, you may prefer to use a corner roller. Before dismounting and moving the ladder, check your work for drips, runs, thin areas, and missed spots.

PAINTING TRIM

Painting exterior trim means you're making progress and the job is winding down. Unfortunately, painting trim is a slow process that consumes a considerable amount of time, even if you apply the same color used on the siding. Diligence and patience in dealing with these details pays off. If done carefully and thoroughly, trim painting will keep your house looking fresh and protect it from the elements for a long time. Here are some tips to make the job easier:

- When painting trim, work from the top down; gables, dormers, eaves and gutters, second-

SELECTING THE RIGHT EXTERIOR COATING

Most of the coatings listed below can be applied with an airless sprayer as well as a brush, roller, or painting pad. But if you want to spray, read the labels carefully or ask your paint dealer if you're buying a sprayable coating. Latex paints require only water to thin them enough for spraying. With alkyds, oils, and other types of paints, you'll have to purchase the appropriate solvents to dilute them.

Type	Characteristics/Use	Application
Acrylic	A type of latex; water-thinned and water cleanup. Fast-drying and suitable for any building material, including masonry and primed metal.	Brush, roller, pad, spray. Comparable to regular latex paint.
Alkyd	Similar to oilbase paints but dries faster. Solvent-thinned, solvent cleanup. Use over oil and alkyd coatings.	Brush, roller, pad, spray. Smooths out more readily than latex but more difficult to apply.
Latex	Most popular exterior paint. Excellent durability. Water-thinned, water cleanup. Mildew-proof; may even be applied over damp surfaces. Do not use over oil paints unless specified by the manufacturer.	Brush, roller, pad, spray. Except when spraying, don't thin; apply thickly with little spreadout.
Oil	Extremely durable but dries slowly. Solvents must be used for cleanup. Least popular.	Brush, roller, pad, spray on very dry surfaces. Insects and rain are dangers because of lengthy drying time.
Marine	Excellent durability on wood, some metals. Expensive. Solvent cleanup.	Brush recommended due to thick, gooey consistency.
Masonry	May be latex, alkyd, epoxy, Portland cement, or rubber. Some contain their own primers.	Brush, roller. Latex types easiest to apply.
Metal	Water-thinned or solvent-thinned, usually with rust-resistant ingredients.	Brush, roller, pad, spray. Prime bare metals first.
Primers	Seals raw wood, bare metal. Also use over old, worn finishes. Provides good bonding for top coating. Use primer formulated for top coat.	Brush, roller, pad, spray. Easier than top-coat painting. Porous surfaces may drink up lots of primer.
Porch/Deck	Alkyd, latex, epoxy, rubber, oil, or polyurethane types. Synthetics dry quickly; oilbase types dry slowly, but are very durable. Limited color selection.	Brush, roller, pad, or wax applicator. For floors, pour on, smooth out. For decks, dip applicator and apply.
Shingle	Alkyd-base, oilbase, or latex-base. For wood siding shingles. Permits escape of moisture behind shingles.	Brush, roller, pad, spray. Do not use on creosote-treated wood that is less than eight years old.
Stains	Water- or solvent-thinned; both types durable. Choice of transparent, semi-transparent, solid-stain pigmentation. May contain preservatives.	Brush, roller, pad, spray.
Preservatives	Moisture-, rot-, and insect-resistant for decks, fences, wood siding, and shingles.	Dipping, brush, spray.
Varnish	Moisture-cured urethane, alkyd, or spar types for exterior wood; acrylic for metal.	Brush, roller, or pad. Limited durability; one to two years. Won't dramatically alter natural appearance and color of woods.

story windows, porches and stairs, and foundations. If you don't want to mask around window panes, use a paint shield as you work. Scrape off any spatters and drips later.

- If you've replaced the caulking around doors, windows, and joints, make sure caulking is dry before painting over it. Use enough paint to form a tight seal between the siding and the trim to keep out moisture, wind, and insects.

- Paint exterior windows, sashes, sills, and jambs in the same order as the interior ones, working from the sashes out to the frames. Be sure to pay close attention to the windowsills. They bear the brunt of rain, snow, and accumulated dirt. If the windowsills look particularly weather beaten, take the time to give them two or even three coats of paint, including the underside edges.

- Screens and storm windows should be removed and painted separately. If the screens have holes, this is a good time to mend them or replace the screening. If the screening is sound but needs painting, coat it first (using a pad applicator), then paint the frame. Don't forget to do both sides and all edges of screens and storms.

- Doors are easier to paint if you remove the knobs, latch plates, and door knocker. If possible, also remove the door from its frame, lay it flat, and paint one side at a time, working on recessed panels first, then raised areas. Sand the bottom and top edges, then apply a thin coat of paint to keep out moisture and prevent rot. While the door is open or off its hinges, paint the jambs and the frame and give the wooden threshold a coat of urethane varnish. Do not paint the hinges.

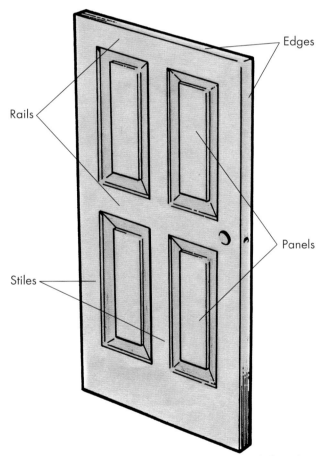

When painting an exterior door, paint the panels first, then the rails, the stiles, and finally the edges, working from top to bottom.

- Gutters and downspouts made of galvanized metal should be scraped with a wire brush to remove loose paint and then primed and painted again. On downspouts, paint in the direction of the flutes, usually up and down, to prevent runs, drips, and sags. Because some downspouts are flat on all four sides and are attached closely to the house, you may want to

ESTIMATING EXTERIOR PAINT

The size of the house, the condition of the surfaces, the type of coating you select, and the method of application are all factors that will determine the amount of paint you need to buy.

Narrow lap siding, shingles or shakes, masonry, or stucco exterior walls can take 10 to 50 percent more paint than smooth, flat walls.

Airless sprayers, which apply the equivalent of two coats of paint at one time, may require twice as much paint as brushes, rollers, or pads for the same surface dimensions.

You can get more standard, premixed paint if you run out. Or, if you buy too much, many stores will give credit or refunds for unopened gallons. With custom-colored paints, however, it may be difficult to get a precise match if you run short. Calculate your needs carefully, then buy an extra gallon for insurance.

To determine how much paint your house needs, measure the house's perimeter. Then multiply that figure by the height, excluding gable ends. Take the measurements with a steel tape measure, or reel out a ball of twine around the house and mark and measure the twine. If you will use a different paint on your home's trim, subtract 21 square feet for every door and 15 square feet for each typical window. Divide the final figure by the square-foot coverage specified on the can of paint to determine the number of gallons you will need for one coat.

If your house has gables, you can estimate by just adding 2 feet to the height when making your calculations. For more precision, measure the width of the gable wall and multiply that figure by its height. Divide the final figure by 2 to determine the gable's square-foot dimensions.

For trim paint, the rule of thumb is 1 gallon for every 6 gallons of wall paint. To be more accurate, you'll have to figure the areas of doors, windows, and shutters. For gutters, a linear foot is about equal to a square foot, so for 50 feet of gutter, buy sufficient paint to cover 50 square feet.

take them down to paint them. Consider coating the inside of gutters with an asphalt-base paint, which waterproofs the gutters and seals tiny holes and joints.

- On ornamental metal work and porch railings, use a lamb's wool applicator instead of a trim brush. The mitten applicator, which can be

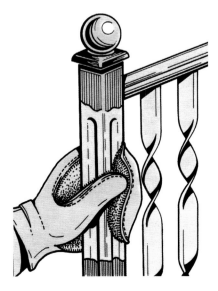

For railing and ornamental metal work, use a lamb's wool mitten applicator instead of a trim brush.

used on either hand and is cleanable and reusable, allows you to grasp a railing support, smearing on the paint as you move your hand from top to bottom.

QUICK FENCE FIXES

Sun, wind, rain, snow, rot, and below-ground frost subject fences to a terrific beating. The following pages explain how to keep your fences mended. As you work with fences, keep nature in mind. Wood is vulnerable to nature's punishments, especially rotting. This means you should always repair fencing with the most rot-resistant lumber you can afford. Pressure-treated lumber has been saturated with preservatives and lasts almost indefinitely, even with wood that has been buried in the ground. This type of wood is expensive, however. Cedar and redwood stand up well underground and are also costly. Exterior paints and stains work well above ground but are almost useless below or on parts of fences in frequent contact with water.

WOOD FENCES

The components of a wood fence include vertical posts, rails that run horizontally from post to post, and screening material such as boards or pickets. Examine your fence, no matter what its type, and you can probably identify each of these elements.

Rot is a wood fence's biggest enemy. Posts that weren't properly treated or set in concrete typically rot away at ground level. Bottom rails and the bottoms of screening can suffer, too, especially if vegetation has been rubbing against them and trapping water. Carefully inspect fences at least once a year, paying particular attention to these areas. When you find a problem, correct it before the damage spreads. One weak post, for example, could pull down an entire fence.

RAILS A rail that's pulled loose from one or more of its posts may or may not be salvageable, depending on how badly rotted the joint is. You may be able to mend the break with a 2×4 scrap or a couple of metal T-braces, or you may have to replace the entire rail. To repair a rail with a 2×4:

1. Before you make repair, saturate damaged areas and 2×4 liberally with wood preservative. This keeps rot from spreading.

2. To make cleat to support rail, make sure rail is level, then fit 2×4 snugly underneath. Nail

What You'll Need
Wood preservative
Clean rags
2×4 lumber scraps
Level
Hammer
Galvanized nails
Caulk

One way to mend a broken fence rail is to shore it up with a 2×4 scrap and secure it with galvanized nails.

2×4 to post with galvanized nails. Drive couple of nails down through rail into cleat.

3. Carefully caulk top and sides of repair to keep out moisture.

Galvanized steel T-braces, available at most hardware stores and home improvement centers, are somewhat less conspicuous and often make a more lasting repair. To use T-braces in rail repair:

1. Level rail, then drill pilot holes into post and rail.

2. Secure T-braces to rail with galvanized screws.

3. Caulk joint.

4. Paint T-braces to match fence.

What You'll Need
Level
Electric drill
Metal T-braces
Galvanized screws
Caulk
Paint and paintbrush

For a less conspicuous and more lasting repair, use a galvanized T-brace; the screws should be galvanized, too.

SECTIONS If the entire rail needs to be replaced, dismantle that section of fence and rebuild it as explained below.

1. Cut 2×4 rails to fit flat along tops of posts. Rails can extend from post to post, or a rail can span two sections. Measure and cut each rail individually to allow for slight variations in fence post spacing. Butt ends of rails tightly together. Then, beginning at one end of fence line, nail rails in place with two 10d galvanized common nails at ends of each rail.

2. Measure and cut 2×4 bottom rail to fit snugly between each pair of posts. Position rails flat between posts, anywhere from slightly above grade level to 12 inches up. Nail bottom rails into place with 10d galvanized nail driven at an angle through fence post and into end of rail on each side. Use level to keep rails even.

3. Measure and cut fence boards. They should be of uniform length, as long as the distance from bottom of bottom rail to top of top rail, as measured at one of the posts. Starting at one end, nail boards to one side of rails, leaving space equal to single board width between each. Secure each board to rails with two 8d galvanized nails at top and two at bottom. Nail tops first, flush with top, then nail bottoms, pulling or pushing bottom rail into alignment as you go. If your fence will have boards on both sides, nail up all boards on one side first, then nail alternate boards to other side of rails, positioning boards to cover spaces left by boards on opposite side.

SCREENING Replacing broken or rotted screening takes only a few hours and simple carpentry skills. To replace rotted screening:

1. Measure unbroken piece to get correct length and width for new piece or pieces you'll need. Use lumber the same width as old screening, or rip boards to proper width with handsaw or power saw. Check all cuts with carpenters' square before you make them.

2. If you're replacing pickets or other curve-top screening, set cut board against unbroken picket and trace top onto new board. Make these cuts with saber, coping, or keyhole saw.

What You'll Need
2×4 lumber
Tape measure
Power saw or handsaw
Hammer
10d galvanized nails
Level
8d galvanized nails

What You'll Need
Tape measure
Lumber
Handsaw or power saw
Carpenters' square
Pencil
Saber, coping, or keyhole saw
Primer
Paint or stain
Paintbrushes
Hammer
8d galvanized nails

If fence is painted, give new screening coat of top-quality exterior primer; for natural wood fences, stain new boards to match.

3. Remove broken pieces by hammering and prying them away from rails. Pull out any nails.

4. Set new board or picket against rails, align it, and nail it firmly into place with galvanized 8d nails.

5. Paint new pieces to match rest of fence.

POSTS When a post begins to wobble, determine the cause before you make the repair. If the post is rotted or broken, you may be able to repair it with a pair of splints or you may have to replace the entire post. If the post seems intact but has come loose in its hole, a pair of stakes or, better yet, a new concrete base can steady the post. To stake a post:

1. Select pair of 2×4s long enough to reach below frost line for your region and that extend at least 18 inches above ground. Use only pressure-treated lumber, cedar, or clear all-heart redwood.

2. Bevel cut one end of each 2×4, and drive them into ground along opposite sides of post.

3. Bore two holes through both 2×4s and post, then bolt everything together with galvanized carriage bolts.

For a more permanent cure, dig out around the post, plumb it with temporary braces, and pour concrete around the post's base. Prepare pre-

What You'll Need
2×4 lumber
Handsaw
Electric drill
Galvanized carriage bolts
Wrench

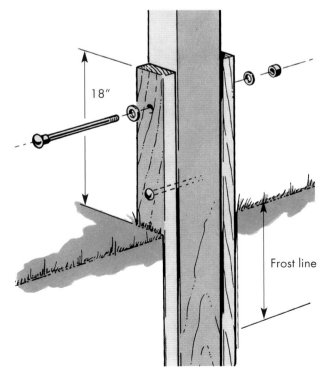

18"

Frost line

A pair of stakes can steady a wobbly post. Drive them into the ground on either side of the post and bolt them to it.

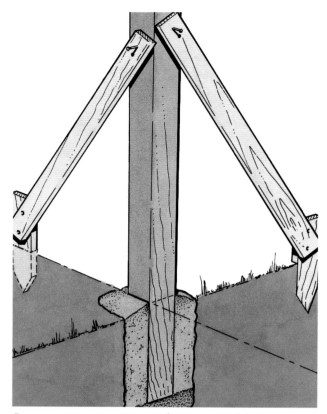

For a more permanent cure, dig out around the post, plumb it with temporary braces, and pour concrete around the post's base.

Straighten a slightly sagging gate by removing screws from the bottom hinge and shimming it with a cedar shingle.

mixed concrete, stir it well, and pour it into the hole around the post. Slice the concrete mix periodically with a spade as you pour to eliminate any air pockets. At the top of the hole, mound concrete around the base of the post to shed water.

GATES When a gate sags or won't close properly, the first thing you should do is check its hinges. If they're bent, replace them with a heavier type of hinge. If the hinge screws are pulling loose, remove them and plug the holes by gluing in short pieces of dowel. Then drill new holes and install longer screws or carriage bolts. Use only galvanized steel hardware.

With a gate that's sagging only slightly, you may be able to straighten it up by shimming under the bottom hinge. Prop the gate open, remove the screws from the post side of the hinge, and cut a thin piece of cedar shake to fit into the hinge mortise. Reattach the screw by driving longer screws through the shim.

Sometimes a gate sags because its own weight has pulled it out of alignment with the fence. One quick way to square up a gate is to drive a screw eye into the upper corner of the gate on the hinge side and another into the lower corner on the gate side. Run wire and a heavy-duty turnbuckle from one screw eye to the other, and tighten the turnbuckle until the gate frame is square.

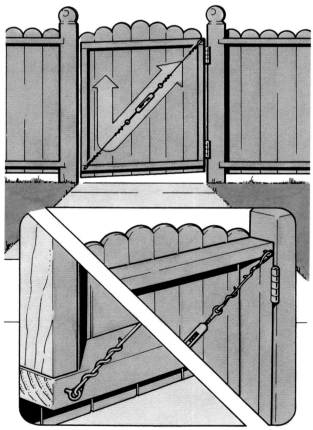

To square up a gate, drive screw eyes into opposite corners, run wire and a turnbuckle between them, and tighten the turnbuckle.

MASONRY FENCES

Brick, stone, and concrete fences typically require little maintenance or repair for many years. With simple maintenance and quick fixes you can keep your masonry fence or wall in great shape for many years.

TUCK-POINTING Tuck-pointing involves cutting out all loose and disintegrated mortar to a depth of at least ½ inch and replacing it with new mortar. Tuck-pointing is done as routine maintenance only; therefore, to stop any leaks, all the mortar in the affected area should be cut out and replaced with new mortar.

To prepare the mortar joint, remove all dirt and loose material by brush or water jet. Make sure the joint is thoroughly wet before applying new mortar. The mortar needed for tuck-pointing should be portland-cement-lime, prehydrated type-S mortar, or prehydrated prepared mortar made from Type II masonry cement. The prehydrated (premoistened) mortar greatly reduces shrinkage.

Allow sufficient time for moisture absorption before filling the joint with mortar, called repointing. Using a pointing trowel, pack the mortar tightly into the joint in thin layers about ¼-inch thick. Finish to a smooth concave surface with a pointing tool. Push the mortar into the joint from one direction to reduce the possibility of air pockets.

QUICK DECK FIXES

Most deck fixes that can be tackled by a do-it-yourselfer involve cleaning and routine maintenance. Here are just a few tips:

- Inspect your deck frequently for popped nails and loose railings or boards. Remove and replace any nails that have popped with coated screws, and immediately repair or replace loose railings to avoid hazards.

- To clean everyday dirt from a wood deck, use a mild household detergent in water to wash it. Rinse thoroughly.

- Use mineral spirits to remove stains caused by tree sap. Rinse thoroughly.

- To remove mildew, wash the deck with a bleach and water solution (1 cup bleach to 1 gallon warm water). Flush the area with water and allow it to dry. Commercial brighteners are also available; follow the manufacturer's

instructions. If mildew is a continued problem, you probably have too much shade on your deck. Check to see if you can trim some tree branches or bushes to expose more of the deck to the sun's drying effects.

- Deck stains make routine cleanup much easier and preserve the life of the wood. Apply stains specially formulated for decks immediately over new wood, except for pressure-treated lumber, which should age for six months before being stained. The deck will benefit from a new coat of stain every one to two years (be sure the stain contains commercial sealant). Follow the manufacturer's instructions for applying the stain. If your deck has been painted, you will have to remove the paint before a stain can be applied.

- Avoid applying clear finishes, such as varnish or shellac, to wood decks. They don't withstand sun and moisture, and they must be removed if they start to peel.

QUICK ROOF AND GUTTER FIXES

Although replacing or doing a major repair on a roof isn't a quick fix, there are many fixes you can perform in a short time.

LEAKY ROOFS

Sometimes roofs develop leaks years before the entire roof needs replacing. Usually these leaks are caused by localized damage, such as cracked or missing shingles or shakes, or, on a flat roof, a blistered or cracked area. The hardest part to repairing this kind of damage is locating it.

Locating the leak will greatly simplify the actual repairs. It's best to look for a leak when it's raining. If you have an unfinished attic or crawl space below a leaky roof, finding the leak is easy. Climb into this space and look around with a flashlight. Don't turn on a light, as it's easier to see a leak in the dark. Water coming in through the roof at one point often runs down the beams or along the ceiling joists before dripping into the space below; it may travel quite a distance from the actual point of entry to the apparent leak point. Watch for the gleam of water in your flashlight beam, and try to trace the water to its highest point on the roof, where it's coming into the house. When you find the leak, outline the wet area with chalk. If you can, push a piece of stiff wire up through the bad spot so it sticks out

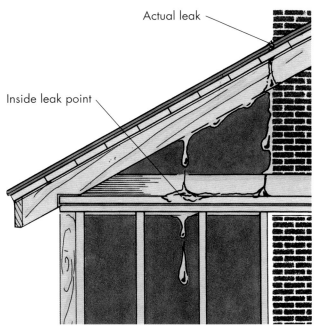

Actual leak

Inside leak point

Water leaking in at one point may travel quite a distance before dripping into a room below. While it's still raining, use a flashlight to trace the leak.

on the roof above. This will make it easier to find the bad spot when you're working outside.

If there's a finished ceiling directly under the leak, it will be harder to locate the problem but you can make an educated guess. Draw a rough plan of the roof in that area, marking chimneys, vent pipes, ridges, and wall intersections. Every place where two surfaces meet or where the roof changes pitch is a potential trouble spot; any one of these spots close to the leak is a good place to start looking.

Adequate safety measures must be taken for any roof repairs. Always use safety ropes, and on steep roofs, use a ladder framework to provide secure anchoring.

Caution: Never work on a roof while it's still wet. It must dry out completely before you can fix the leak. When working on a roof, wear rubber-soled shoes and old clothes. On gentle pitches, tie a rope to the chimney for use as a

safety rope. On a steep roof, you'll need an anchor hook or framework for the ladder. Don't try to make repairs unless the ladder is secured to the ridge of the roof. Use an extension ladder to get up to the roof, bracing the ladder firmly against the house, with the top of the ladder extending above the roof. Don't rest the ladder on a gutter. Always work away from power lines.

SHINGLE ROOFS Shingle roofs are usually easy to fix. At the marked leak point, look for damaged, curled, or missing shingles. At every place where two surfaces meet and around every chimney or vent, look for breaks in the flashing or caulking or for gaps in the lines of roof cement. If you can't see any damage to the shingles or flashing in the leak area, you'll have to call a professional roofer; the problem may be inadequate flashing or simply deterioration of the shingles.

If you find evidence of shingle problems, repairs are fairly simple. Curled-back shingles can be reattached with asphalt roof cement or compound in tubes for use with a caulking gun. In warm weather, you can easily straighten out the curled shingle. In cold weather, shingles become very brittle and must be softened before they can be flattened out. To soften a brittle shingle, carefully use a propane torch with a flame-spreader nozzle. Apply the flame carefully to the curled edges of the shingle; it should get just warm enough to soften but not hot enough to catch fire. Then flatten the edges of the shingle. To reattach the shingle, apply roof cement generously to the bottom; a good dollop of cement at each corner is usually enough. Press the shingle firmly into place.

If shingles are torn, rotten, or missing, they should be replaced with new ones. Any shingle that lifts right off the roof with no effort is rotten and should be replaced. If you find a large area of rotten shingles, you may need a whole new roof. If so, consider calling a professional roofer. Otherwise, replace the damaged shingles with shingles left over from the previous roof installation. If you can't get matching shingles, you can make do with nonmatching ones. In an emergency, cut shingle-size patches from sheet aluminum or copper. To replace damaged shingles:

1. To remove damaged shingle, lift edges of surrounding shingles, and carefully remove nails with pry bar. Slide out old shingle. If there's loose or brittle roof cement left under

What You'll Need
Pry bar
Scraper
Replacement shingle
Utility knife
6d galvanized roofing nails
Hammer
Asphalt roof cement
Trowel

it, scrape opening clean. When shingles are blown off by a storm, remove any protruding nails left in roof. Nails that don't stick up can be left in place.

2. To make it easier to slide new shingle into place, slightly round its back corners with sharp utility knife.

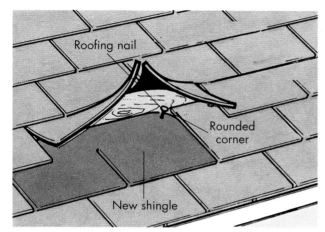

Round the corners of the new shingle and slide it up into the gap. Lift the corners of the overlapping shingles and drive a roofing nail at each corner of the new shingle.

3. Slide new shingle into gap, with its front edge aligned with shingles on each side and its back edge under shingles in row above it.

4. Lift corners of overlapping shingles and fasten top of new shingle with 6d galvanized roofing nails driven through each corner. Cover nail heads with roof cement, then smooth down overlapping shingle edges.

If you're replacing rows of shingles, you only need to round the back corners where the top row meets the row above. Ridge shingles, the tent-shape shingles along the peak of a roof, can be replaced the same way. Overlap them along the ridge and over the shingles on both sides. Do not try to use flat shingles; you must use new ridge shingles. Cover the back of each new ridge shingle with roof cement before setting it into place.

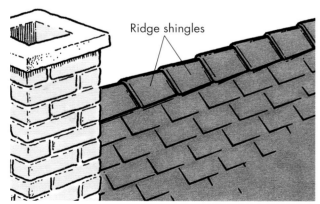

For repairs on the peak of the roof, use ridge shingles, overlapping along the ridge and over the shingles on both sides of the peak. Don't try to adapt ordinary shingles for the peak.

Secure each corner of the shingle with a roofing nail, and cover the nail heads with roof cement.

After replacing the damaged shingles or if the shingles are undamaged, inspect the chimney flashing, the flashing around vents or vent pipes, and any line of roof cement where two surfaces meet. If the metal flashing around a chimney or dormer is not thoroughly caulked, fill the joints with roof cement in a caulking gun. Along joints sealed with a line of roof cement, apply roof cement with a putty knife to areas that look worn or cracked. Apply the cement liberally, covering the questionable areas completely. If there are any exposed nail heads in the flashing, cover them with roof cement.

FLAT ROOFS Flat roofs are built up of layers of roofing felt and tar. Leaks usually occur at low spots or where the roofing felt has been damaged. In most cases, the leak is directly below the damaged spot and the damage to the roofing felt is easy to see. If there's still water pooled in the leak area, mop it up or soak it up with rags, and let the surface dry. Brush off any gravel. Look for cracks in the felt or for large blisters where the top layer has separated. To mend a blister:

1. Use sharp utility knife to slice blister open down middle. Cut should penetrate to full depth of blistered layer but should not reach sound roofing felt beneath it.

2. Lift cut edges of blister. If there's water inside blister, press from edges in toward center to squeeze out water from between roofing layers. Soak up all the water you can with rags; then prop edges up to let layers dry. In cold weather or if layers are thoroughly saturated, use propane torch with flame-spreader nozzle to dry out felt (be sure to wear safety goggles). Carefully move flame back and forth over inside layers of blister. Roofing felt and tar are very flammable, so don't let layers get hot enough to burn or bubble. **Caution:** If there's water under a large area of the roof, the problem is more than a simple blister; water may be running in from an adjoining pitched roof surface. In this case, it's best to call a professional roofer.

3. Spread thick coating of roof cement on bottom edges of loose felt and firmly press down sides of blister.

4. Close blister permanently with row of 6d galvanized roofing nails along each side of slit, then spread roof cement over entire blister, making sure nail heads are well covered.

What You'll Need
Utility knife
Clean rags
Propane torch with flame-spreader nozzle
Safety goggles
Asphalt roof cement or compound
Trowel
6d galvanized roofing nails
Hammer

WOODEN SHAKE ROOFS Repairing a wooden shake roof is similar to repairing a shingle roof, although it can be a little more difficult. Use the same type of shakes or shingles to replace the damaged ones. If a ridge shingle is damaged, use a new specially cut ridge shingle instead of trying to make do with regular shingles. To repair a wooden shake roof:

1. Use hammer and sharp chisel to split damaged shake. Slant chisel up into shake at same angle as pitch of roof. Be careful not to gouge surrounding shakes. Pull out pieces of damaged shake. Since shakes aren't flexible like shingles, it isn't possible to pry out nails. Use hacksaw to cut off nail heads as far down nail shaft as you can. You may want to wrap electrical tape around one end of hacksaw blade to protect your fingers. If you can't reach nails without damaging other shakes, you'll have to work around them.

2. Measure gap left by old shake, and cut new one about ⅜ inch smaller than this measurement, using fine-tooth hacksaw. You must allow this ⅜-inch clearance because shake will swell the first time it rains.

3. Install new shake. If you were able to cut off nails that held old shake, just slide new one up into place, with its top edge under overlapping shingles. Nail shake down with two galvanized roofing nails, one at each side of exposed top edge. If you weren't able to cut off nails, you'll have to notch new shake to fit around them. Push shake up into gap, hard enough so edge is marked by old nails. Then carefully cut slots at marked points with coping saw. If possible, clamp shake in vise so it doesn't split. Slide notched shake into place, and nail it with two roofing nails.

4. Set heads of nails with nail set, and seal them with caulking compound.

FLASHING Metal flashing is used to seal out water around the chimney, at vent pipes, along the valleys where two roof pitches meet, and sometimes over exposed windows. To prevent leaks at the flashing, inspect it every spring. If you see thin spots or gaps along a flashing joint, spread roof cement over the entire joint, applying it generously with a trowel. The flashing edge should be covered completely. At the chimney, examine the flashing carefully. Chimney flashing is installed in two parts: the base, which covers the bottom of the chimney and extends onto the roof; and the cap, which is mortared into the chimney bricks. If the mortar holding the cap flashing is crumbling or if the flashing has pulled loose, you'll have to resecure the flashing. To resecure the flashing around a chimney:

Remove a damaged shake by splitting it with a chisel slanted up into the shake along the roof pitch. Then cut off the nails with a hacksaw blade.

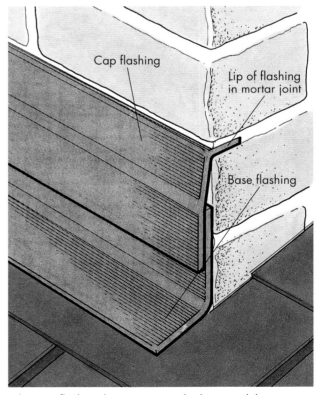

Chimney flashing has two parts, the base and the cap. The lip of the cap is embedded in mortar between the chimney bricks.

Cap flashing

Lip of flashing in mortar joint

Base flashing

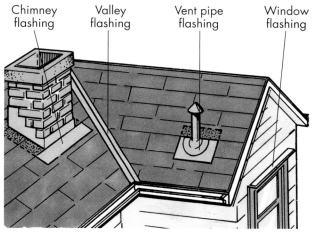

Chimney flashing   Valley flashing   Vent pipe flashing   Window flashing

Metal flashing is used to seal out water around the chimney, at vent pipes, along the valleys where two roof pitches meet, and sometimes over exposed windows. Inspect flashing annually.

1. Pull lip of cap flashing out of mortar joint, only as far as it comes easily. Do not yank entire flashing out or pull it completely away from chimney. The less you have to separate it, the easier it will be to fix.

2. With flashing out of mortar joint, clean out old mortar with hammer and chisel, wearing safety goggles to protect your eyes. Then, being careful not to damage flashing, use wire brush on joint to clean out debris.

3. Wet joint with paintbrush dipped in water. With small trowel, fill joint firmly with cement mortar.

4. When joint is full, press lip of flashing into mortar, in same position it was in before. Press flashing in firmly, but don't push too far or it may pop back out and you'll have to start all over again. Let mortar dry as directed.

5. When joint is completely cured, caulk around joint and over lip of cap flashing with butyl rubber caulk.

In a closed valley, the flashing is covered by shingles; no exposed metal is visible. This type should be professionally repaired.

At vent pipes or metal chimneys, make sure the joint at the base of the pipe or chimney is sealed. If you can see gaps at the roof line, caulk around the base of the pipe or chimney with roof cement in a caulking gun. Vent pipes on pitched roofs usually have a protective collar; if the collar is loose, tap it back into place, and then caulk the collar base joint with roof caulk.

OPEN ROOF VALLEYS Because closed valleys aren't visible from the roof, the only sign of damage is usually a leak directly under the valley. This kind of valley should be repaired by a professional roofer. An open valley, however, is easy to access and repair. To repair an open valley:

1. Inspect valley for holes all along joint. You can patch small holes with the same type of sheet metal valley is made of. Most valleys use either aluminum or copper. Using different metal to patch valley will cause corrosion.

2. Clean surface of valley with wire brush.

3. Cut sheet metal patch about 2 inches bigger all around than hole.

4. Spread thick coating of roof cement on damaged area and press patch into place, bending it to shape of valley. Spread more roof cement over edges of patch to seal out water.

What You'll Need
Sheet metal
Wire brush
Metal shears
Roof cement
Trowel

In an open valley, the flashing strip is exposed; a strip of metal is visible along the joint where two roof pitches meet. Repair this type yourself.

VENT PIPES Vent pipes and appliance chimneys are sealed with metal flashing to prevent leaks, but the flashing may eventually need replacement. Pitched roof vents are usually flashed with a flat metal sheet cut to fit around the pipe and a protective collar that fits around its base. Flashing for flat roofs usually covers the entire vent, with a flat base and a pipe casing that slides on over the chimney. Replacing either type of flashing is fairly easy. Make sure your replacement

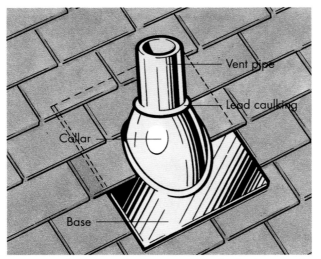

Pitched-roof vent pipe flashing consists of a flat base and protective collar that fits around the pipe.

flashing is exactly the same type and diameter as the old one. Follow the roof safety procedures detailed below. **Caution:** Wear work gloves when working with metal flashing because the edges of the flashing are sharp.

On a pitched roof, the base of the flashing is covered with shingles on the side above the chimney and left exposed on the side below it. To reflash a vent pipe on a pitched roof:

What You'll Need
Work gloves
Pry bar
Scrap wood
Hammer
Replacement
    flashing
6d galvanized
    roofing nails
Asphalt roof cement
Trowel

1. Remove shingles on part of roof above chimney. Lift shingles with pry bar, but be careful not to damage them, as you will have to put them back to cover new flashing. If you break a shingle, you'll need a new one to replace it.

2. Remove flashing by inserting blade of pry bar under its edge, and lever bar on block of scrap wood to lift flashing.

3. Lift flashing up over vent pipe, being careful not to knock pipe out of place. Then pull out any nails left around pipe, and fill holes with roof cement.

SAFE ROOF REPAIRS

Working on a roof can be dangerous. Keep these safety precautions in mind before tackling a quick roof fix:

• Roof repairs should be done on a sunny day when the roof is completely dry. A wet roof is slippery and very dangerous.

• Adequate safety measures must be taken for any roof repairs. Always use safety ropes.

• On steep roofs, use a ladder framework to provide secure anchoring.

• Rubber-soled shoes provide the best traction when working on a roof.

• The location of power lines should be kept in mind when working on a roof.

4. Set new flashing over pipe, with its protective collar aligned same way as old one. Nail down flashing with 6d galvanized roofing nails, and cover nail heads with roof cement. Apply more roof cement to seal base of protective collar.

5. Put shingles back over top of flashing. Starting with bottom row and working up, nail each shingle into place at top. Use two 6d galvanized roofing nails for small shingles, four nails for large ones. As you work, cover nail heads with roof cement. Slide top edges of top row of shingles under overlapping bottom edges of the row above.

To reflash a vent pipe on a flat roof:

1. If there's gravel on roof, sweep it away from vent pipe to clear 4-foot-square area.

2. Locate edge of flashing base, and use sharp utility knife to cut slit through roofing felt along one side of it.

3. Insert blade of pry bar into slit and under edge of flashing. Lever bar over block of scrap wood, working along slit in roofing, to release flashing. Cut around remaining three sides to free flashing completely. Lift old flashing out and over pipe.

What You'll Need
Work gloves
Broom
Utility knife
Pry bar
Scrap wood
Replacement
    flashing
15-pound roofing
    felt
Asphalt roof cement
Trowel
6d galvanized
    roofing nails
Hammer
Pliers

4. Set new flashing on top of roof to determine how to fill hole. For each layer of roofing you can see in hole, cut patch of 15-pound roofing felt with utility knife. Use base of old flashing as pattern to cut out felt. On each piece of roofing felt, mark location of vent pipe and cut hole at that point so patch will fit snugly over pipe.

5. Spread thick layer of roof cement on bottom of hole, set first patch over pipe, and press it firmly into hole. Then spread more roof cement on top. Fill entire hole this way, building up layers of roofing felt and roof cement, until top patch is level with roof surface. Spread thick layer of roof cement over top patch, and fill any gaps around vent pipe with more cement.

6. Set new flashing carefully into place over vent pipe, and press it down firmly so vent pipe is encased in flashing pipe and base is aligned in exactly the same way old flashing was.

7. Nail down flashing with 6d galvanized roofing nails, and cover nail heads with roof cement.

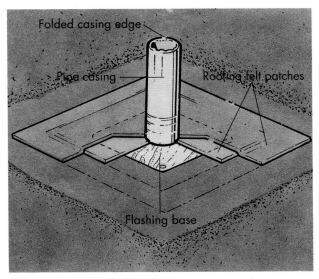

Flat-roof vent pipe flashing has a casing pipe that covers the entire pipe; the edge of the casing folds down to seal it. The base is covered by roofing.

Using pliers, fold top edge of casing pipe down over top edge of vent pipe to seal new flashing.

8. Cover base of flashing with two more layers of roofing felt—the first layer 3 inches larger and the second 6 inches larger all around than flashing. As you did with first patches, cut hole in center of each piece so it will fit over vent pipe. Spread another thick layer of roof cement over base of flashing, extending it 3 inches onto roof all around. Set smaller piece of roofing felt over pipe, and press it into place. Cover this piece of felt with another layer of roof cement, again extending it 3 inches onto roof all around; set larger patch into place. Press this final patch down, and nail it into place with 6d galvanized roofing nails, about 1 inch apart. Cover nail heads with roof cement.

9. If you removed gravel from patch area, you can spread it back over bare spot, but this isn't necessary.

MAINTAINING GUTTERS

Good drainage is very important to your home's structural well-being. Gutters and downspouts, the main components of your drainage system, must be kept clear to prevent storm water from overflowing or backing up. Blocked gutters can cause erosion around the house, damage to the exterior walls, basement leaks, and—eventually—uneven settling of the foundation. To prevent these drainage problems, regularly maintain your gutters and downspouts, and repair them at the first sign of trouble. When you work on your gutters, follow the roof safety procedures outlined earlier in this chapter.

Clean gutters at least twice a year to prevent clogging. Shovel out leaves and other debris with a plastic scoop.

At the minimum, clean your gutters twice a year, in late spring and late fall. If you live in a wooded area, clean them more frequently. A plastic scoop is an ideal gutter-cleaning tool. Wear work gloves to protect your hands. To clean the gutters shovel out leaves and other debris with the plastic scoop. Work from a ladder that's tall enough to let you reach the gutters comfortably. As you work, move the ladder frequently. Don't lean or bend to reach to either side or you might lose your balance. After cleaning out all the loose debris, flush the gutters with a garden hose. Check the downspouts by flushing them with the hose. If a downspout is clogged, you can break up the clog with a plumbers' snake fed down through the opening in the gutter. Clear out any remaining debris with the hose.

To keep the downspouts clear, use a wire leaf strainer at each one. Insert a leaf strainer into each downspout opening along the gutters, then push it in just far enough to hold it steady. The

To keep downspouts clear, flush them with a hose. If necessary, remove clogs with a plumbers' snake. Use a wire leaf strainer at each downspout.

strainer will prevent sticks and other debris from entering the downspout and clogging it.

Many homeowners use plastic or metal screening leaf guards on their gutters to keep leaves from building up. Leaf guards are not effective against leaf fragments, leaf cases, and other small debris that can go right through the screening. Gutters covered by leaf guards must still be cleaned regularly, and leaf guards may make the cleaning much more difficult.

REPAIRING HOLES IN GUTTERS

After cleaning out the gutters, let them dry thoroughly, and inspect them for signs of damage. Rust spots and holes can be mended with scrap wire screening and asphalt roof cement. First, wire-brush the damaged area to remove dirt and loosen rust. Clean the area well with a rag soaked in mineral spirits. If the hole is small, or if the metal isn't rusted all the way through, a screening patch isn't needed; just spread roof cement over the damaged area. To repair an open hole in a gutter:

What You'll Need
Wire cutters
Scrap wire screening
Roof cement
Trowel

1. Cut piece of scrap wire screening, ½ to 1 inch bigger all around than hole.

2. Using trowel, spread roof cement around hole, and press wire screening patch down into hole. Spread thin layer of cement over screening. Let dry.

3. If holes of screening are still open, spread another layer of cement over patch to close it completely.

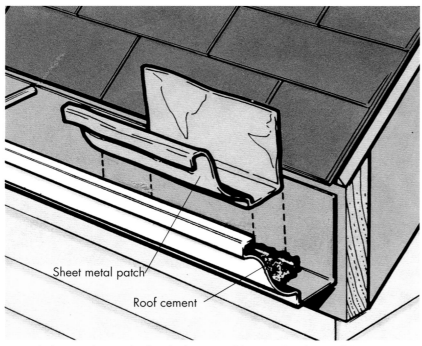

Sheet metal patch

Roof cement

Large holes can be patched with sheet metal bent to the shape of the gutter. Spread roof cement on the damaged gutter before installing the patch.

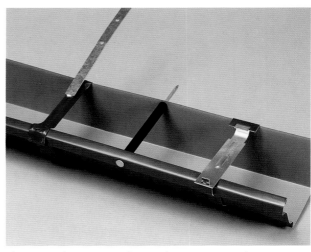

There are three types of gutter hangers: strap hangers (left), sleeve-and-spike supports (center), and fascia brackets (right). Gutter hangers should be used about every 2½ feet.

If the gutter is extensively damaged or has a large hole in it, patch it with sheet metal instead of wire screening. If the gutters are copper, use copper for this repair. Use sheet aluminum for other types of gutters. Here's how:

1. Cut piece of sheet metal big enough to cover inside of gutter completely and wrap around outside edges. Patch should extend at least 1 inch beyond damage each way along gutter.

What You'll Need
Sheet metal
Sheet metal cutters
Roof cement
Trowel
Pliers

2. Bend patch to exact shape of inside of gutter.

3. Use roof cement to coat entire area inside gutter where patch will go, then press patch down into cemented gutter to cover hole.

4. Bend edges back over gutter lips with pliers, then coat entire patch inside gutter with roof cement. Make sure edges of patch are well covered.

Besides patching obvious damage, inspect gutters for sags, loose sections, and loose hangers. Gutters are held by sleeve-and-spike supports, fascia brackets nailed to the face of the wall, or strap hangers nailed to the roof. Loose hangers can be adjusted or renailed; use 6d galvanized roofing nails to reset them. Cover the nail heads with roof cement to prevent leaks. If you can't get at a fascia bracket to renail it or if the gutter sags even though all its supports are solid, add supports. There should be a support about every 2½ feet along the gutter. Make sure you cover all nail heads with roof cement.

If a section of downspout or an elbow is loose, reattach it with pop rivets using an inexpensive pop rivet tool. Pop rivets can be installed from the outside, so it isn't necessary to take the sections of downspout apart. To install pop rivets:

1. Hold loose section up in proper position. Use electric drill and bit the size of the pop rivets to drill through overlapping sections. Make one hole on each exposed side of downspout.

What You'll Need
Electric drill
Pop rivets
Pop rivet tool

2. To set pop rivet through each drilled hole, place rivet in pop rivet tool, insert tip of tool into hole, and squeeze handles of tool until rivet pops off. Pop rivets will hold section of downspout in place permanently.

QUICK BARBECUE FIXES

Most fixes to charcoal and gas grills are simply parts replacements. Larger hardware stores will have replacement grates, burners, lighters, tanks, control knobs, and other components near where the barbecues are sold. Before shopping for replacement parts, make sure you have the part that needs to be replaced or its measurements as well as model numbers. Fortunately, many of the components are universal and fit many brands of barbecues.

Before you take those old parts in or finish your quick fix, make sure you clean the grill. Here are some quick cleaning tips:

- You can loosen burned-on foods from barbecue grill racks by enclosing racks in a large plastic bag. Mix 1 cup baking soda and ½ cup ammonia, and pour over racks. Close bag, and

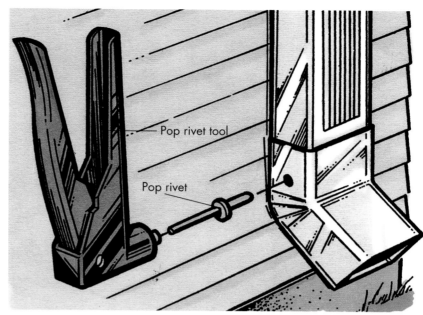

Reattach loose sections with pop rivets. Drill through the overlapping sections, then set one rivet through each exposed side.

let sit overnight. Rinse thoroughly before placing food on racks.

- A grill will steam-clean itself if wrapped in wet newspapers or sprayed with window cleaner while it's still hot.

- Wipe a grill with crumpled aluminum foil while it's still warm to clean it.

- To provide a protective coating to the grill before cooking, use vegetable oil and wipe it off as soon as the grill is cool enough to touch.

- A beer can opener makes a great scraper for cleaning barbecue grills. File a notch in the end of the opener opposite the sharp point.

CHAPTER 8

QUICK CLEANING TIPS

Routine inside and outside cleaning of your home will mean less fixing in the future. For example, furniture that is cleaned of spills quickly will seldom need serious stain removal. Drains that are routinely treated with noncorrosive cleaners shouldn't need to be dismantled for clogs. Tile and grout won't need replacement nearly so soon if water is wiped away and mildew not allowed to form. This chapter suggests ways to handle many of the common cleaning chores in your home, from polishing furniture to cleaning your chimney. And most of these tasks can be completed quickly and easily without specialty products or harsh chemicals.

TROUBLESHOOTING DIRT AND GRIME

Getting rid of dirt and grime is largely a matter of inspecting your home for those very elements. Soap scum and mildew can lurk in showers and tubs, around windows, and in damp corners anywhere, including closets. Grease and germs hide in kitchen sink drains and on countertops. Walls collect fingerprints, crayon marks, and cooking grease. Carpets absorb glue, wine, and anything else that is spilled. Creosote builds up in fireplace chimneys, making the chimney opening smaller and smaller and posing a real fire hazard. So move the furniture, pull back the drapes and shower curtains, shine a flashlight up the chimney, and ferret out all those dirt devils!

Basic cleaning supplies

Cleaning around your house can be fast and easy, giving you time for other things. That's because there are only a few common cleaning problems and proven ways to tackle them. Cleaning materials you will need include brushes, buckets or other containers, rags, and mops as well as cleaners. Fortunately, you can make many handy cleaners with recipes in this chapter.

QUICK ROOM CLEANING

The rooms in your home all hold furniture to sit on and put things on. Those pieces of furniture get dusty, smudged, and spilled on. Following are some ways to clean and revitalize that furniture, including a recipe for Basic Furniture Polish that can safely be used on wood surfaces.

WOOD FURNITURE

- Waxy buildup of grease and cleaners on wood tabletops can be removed by applying a solution of equal parts water and vinegar. Wipe onto area, then rub and dry immediately using a soft cloth.

- Remove alcohol stains from a wood table with a paste of baking soda and mineral, linseed, or lemon oil. Rub in the direction of the grain, then wipe with linseed oil.

- Rub out white rings on wood tables with equal amounts of toothpaste and baking soda.

- Labels, decals, tape, or any sticky paper product can be removed from wood furniture by dampening the piece with straight vinegar. Let sit for a few minutes, then peel or gently scrape off.

BASIC FURNITURE POLISH

1. Mix ingredients in small bowl. Pour mixture into clean, resealable jar, and label clearly.

2. When ready to use, give jar good shake, then apply polish

What You'll Need
½ teaspoon light olive oil
¼ cup white vinegar
Small bowl
Resealable jar
Clean, soft cloth

To remove alcohol stains from wood, rub paste in the same direction of the wood grain, then wipe paste away with linseed oil.

liberally to wood surfaces with soft cloth. Wipe away excess.

UPHOLSTERY

- A fresh stain of oily or greasy food on a fabric chair or sofa can be absorbed with equal parts baking soda and salt. Sprinkle mixture on stain, rub lightly, leave on a few hours, then vacuum.

- Clean old grease stains with 3 parts baking soda and 1 part water. Rub paste into the stain, let dry, then brush away.

- Leather furniture can develop a waxy buildup from polish. Remove buildup with a solution of 1 tablespoon vinegar in 1 cup warm water. Wipe on with a soft cloth, then buff dry.

- Spots on vinyl furniture can be removed by wiping with a cloth dipped in straight vinegar. If any spots remain, try a baking soda paste rubbed on, dried, then wiped off.

OTHER FURNITURE CLEANING TIPS

- Whiten the ivory keys of a piano by rubbing them with a little white vinegar on a soft white cloth. Do not saturate.

- Keep white wicker furniture from yellowing by scrubbing it with a stiff brush moistened with saltwater. Scrub, then let piece dry in full sunlight.

QUICK KITCHEN CLEANING

The kitchen is probably the most difficult room in a home to keep clean. Spills, drips, greasy pans, dirty dishes, and foot traffic can make kitchen cleanup feel endless. The following cleaners, most made from things on your kitchen or pantry shelves, will keep your kitchen looking, smelling, and feeling clean and will cut down on the use of strong commercial cleaners that can be harmful to your skin, your respiratory system, your kitchen surfaces, and the environment. Keep each mixture in a spray bottle clearly labeled with a list of its contents. Protect your hands by wearing rubber gloves, and avoid breathing ammonia fumes by making sure your work area is well ventilated.

GENERAL KITCHEN CLEANING

What follows are some handy solutions to help you quickly and easily keep your kitchen sparkling clean.

DAILY KITCHEN CLEANER

1. Add oil, vinegar, and dish soap to bottle, then fill rest of bottle with water.

2. Shake well before each use. Spray cleaner on countertops and appliances, then wipe off with damp cloth or sponge.

ALL-SURFACE KITCHEN CLEANER

1. Combine ingredients in spray bottle.

2. Use on virtually any surface in your kitchen for daily cleaning. It is especially good for cleaning stovetops and ovens. For caked-on stains on your stovetop, spray on mixture and let it sit 15 minutes before wiping surface clean. You can even use to clean inside of your oven; just spray on cleaner, leave overnight, and wipe clean.

The All-Surface Kitchen Cleaner can be used to clean bathroom counters, utility room surfaces, even some garage surfaces. You may decide to try one of the all-purpose cleaners for several rooms in your home. And for efficient use, you may want to make a large batch and keep some in the kitchen, some in each bathroom, some in the utility room, and some in the garage.

What You'll Need
5 drops peppermint oil or any essential oil fragrance
¼ cup vinegar
1 squirt liquid dish soap
Water
32-ounce spray bottle
Cloth or sponge

What You'll Need
1 teaspoon borax
½ teaspoon washing or baking soda
2 teaspoons vinegar
1 squirt liquid dish soap
2 cups hot water
32-ounce spray bottle
Cloth or sponge

GOODBYE GREASE

1. Combine mixture in bucket or other container.

2. Wipe mixture on greasy surfaces, making sure room is well ventilated. Rinse well.

KITCHEN BRIGHTENER

1. Combine mixture in bucket or other container.

2. Use to revitalize white appliances or enamel sinks that are yellowing.

COUNTERTOPS

• Wipe countertops with straight vinegar once a day. Cider vinegar will smell particularly nice. Your counters will shine, grease will be gone, and your kitchen will smell fresh.

• Instead of using abrasive cleansers that may scratch surfaces, try the All-Surface Kitchen Cleaner (see page 167). Just spray on, let sit briefly, then wipe off with a clean damp cloth.

• If your laminated countertops become stained, try a paste of baking soda and water. Apply with a sponge or cloth, let dry, then rub off and rinse.

• For very tough stains on grout or tile, use a paste made of 1 part bleach to 3 parts baking soda.

COUNTER AND TILE CLEANER

1. Combine ingredients in bucket (add more soda to make thicker mixture for extra cleaning power on grout).

2. Apply cleaner with sponge. Scrub with old toothbrush if grout is heavily soiled.

A toothbrush is a handy tool for removing dirt and mildew from tile grout.

OVENS

• For a thorough oven cleaning, leave 1 cup of ammonia in a closed, cold oven overnight to loosen baked-on food and grease. In the morning, wipe away ammonia, then wipe surfaces with baking soda. Or finish by sponging with a mixture of half vinegar and half water to help prevent grease buildup.

• If you choose to use a commercial oven cleaner, you may notice that an odor lingers after the cleaning is supposedly finished. To eliminate that odor, mix 2 cups vinegar and 3 quarts warm water. Dip a sponge into mixture and wring it out well, then wipe the oven's inside surfaces. There's no need to rinse.

• Stained areas in your oven can be washed away with a combination of ½ cup vinegar and ½ cup hot water. Use this solution and a sponge to rub away stains.

• Twice a year you should "degrease" the vents of your oven hood. To do this, wipe vents with a sponge and undiluted vinegar or remove vents and soak them for 15 minutes in 1 cup vinegar and 3 cups water.

STOVETOPS

• Any spill on a conventional stovetop can be cleaned up easily if first sprinkled with salt. The mildly abrasive quality of salt removes stuck-on food, but it won't mar the surface.

• Clean burned-on food from a stovetop burner by sprinkling it with a mixture of salt and cinnamon, then wipe away immediately. The mixture will give off a pleasant smell and cover up any burnt odor the next time you turn on the burner.

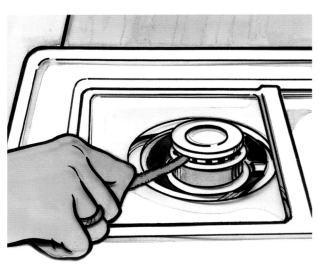

Clean the holes of a gas burner with a chenille stem or fine wire.

- General stovetop cleaning can be handled by the Daily Kitchen Cleaner, All-Surface Kitchen Cleaner, or Goodbye Grease (see pages 167–168). Or you can use baking soda as a mild abrasive and deodorizer for your stovetop. Just make a paste and apply with a sponge or cloth. Follow with a thorough rinsing.

REFRIGERATORS

- To clean and refresh the inside of your refrigerator, sprinkle equal amounts salt and baking soda on a damp sponge and wipe refrigerator surfaces.

- Remove any mildew spots in or on your refrigerator by scrubbing with an old toothbrush dipped in vinegar. A toothbrush is an excellent tool for reaching inside the folds of the rubber seals. There's no need to rinse afterward.

- To remove any unpleasant taste in ice cubes from an automatic ice cube maker, clean removable parts of the unit with baking soda and water.

DISHWASHERS

- Add ½ cup vinegar to an empty dishwasher, and run the rinse cycle. This will open up any clogs in the dishwasher drain lines and deodorize the machine.

- Remove hard-water stains from the inside of an automatic dishwasher by loading the dishwasher with glassware and china and then adding ¾ cup household bleach. Run a complete wash cycle, then put 1 cup vinegar in a glass bowl and place the bowl in the dishwasher. Run another complete wash cycle.

- If you're waiting for a full load before running your dishwasher, avoid odor buildup by sprinkling a small amount of baking soda onto the dishes or in the bottom of the machine.

MICROWAVES

- If your microwave is splattered with old sauces and greasy buildup, place a glass measuring cup with 1 cup water and ¼ cup vinegar inside microwave. Boil for 3 minutes, then remove measuring cup and wipe inside of oven with a damp sponge. You'll be surprised how easily it will wipe away.

- Deodorize your microwave by keeping a dish of vinegar inside overnight. If smells continue, change vinegar and repeat procedure nightly until the odor is gone.

- Store an open cup of baking soda in your microwave between uses to absorb odors.

COFFEEMAKERS AND TEAPOTS

- Remove coffee and mineral stains from the glass pot of an automatic drip coffeemaker by adding 1 cup crushed ice, 1 tablespoon water, and 4 teaspoons salt to carafe when it is at room temperature. Gently swirl mixture, rinse, and then wash as usual.

- Buildup in a coffeemaker's brewing system can affect coffee flavor. Get rid of buildup by running 1 brewing cycle of cold water and ¼ cup vinegar. Follow with a cycle of clean water. If you can still smell vinegar, run another cycle using fresh water.

- Clean a teapot by boiling a 50/50 mixture of vinegar and water for several minutes; let stand for 1 hour. Rinse with water. Or fill with water, add 2 or 3 tablespoons of baking soda, and boil 10 to 15 minutes. After cooling, scrub and rinse thoroughly.

UNCLOGGING SINK DRAINS

- If your kitchen sink is draining slowly, try a mixture of equal parts vinegar, salt, and baking soda. Pour solution down the drain, let it sit at least 1 hour, then pour boiling or very hot water down the drain.

- If it's grease that has slowed or stopped your sink drain, try ½ cup salt and ½ cup baking soda. Sprinkle this solution into the drain, then flush with hot tap water.

ELIMINATING SINK DRAIN ODORS

- Pour a solution of 1 cup salt and 2 cups hot water down kitchen sink. This will also help break up grease deposits. Or pour ¼ cup each baking soda, salt, and dishwasher detergent into your garbage disposal. Turn on hot water, then run garbage disposal for a few seconds to clean out any debris and clear odors.

- The rubber seal on garbage disposals can retain odors. To deodorize it, remove the seal and let it soak in a pan of white vinegar for 1 hour.

HANDY DRAIN CLEANER

1. Blend ingredients well, and keep mixture in airtight container.

What You'll Need
2 cups baking soda (use old box from refrigerator)
2 cups salt
Airtight container

2. Pour 1 cup of cleaner down drain, let it sit several hours or overnight, then flush with hot water for 1 minute. Use weekly to keep drains clean and clog free.

MAKING SINKS SPARKLE

- Undiluted vinegar will reduce or eliminate mineral deposits around your sink's faucets. Squirt vinegar on deposits, let sit 15 minutes or more, then scrub away deposits with an old toothbrush.

- Clean minor stains in a white porcelain sink with a sprinkling of baking soda and a sponge dampened in vinegar. Stains are best tackled immediately.

- For tough or aged stains in a white porcelain sink, cover the stained areas with paper towels saturated in household bleach. Leave the paper towels for $1/2$ hour or until they dry out. Remove the towels, and then rinse the area thoroughly. Follow this treatment by cleaning the sink with pure vinegar to remove the bleach smell.

QUICK BATHROOM CLEANING

As in the kitchen, much of your bathroom cleaning can be accomplished without expensive, harsh chemical cleaners. For everyday cleaning in the bathroom, a sprinkling of baking soda on a damp sponge can often do the trick. Baking soda mixed with the right ingredients can clean mildew stains that plague tubs and showers and make your powder room smell clean and look shiny at all times without much effort. Vinegar and ammonia are other key ingredients to keeping your bathroom beautiful.

GENERAL BATHROOM CLEANING

General bathroom cleaners can be made out of simple ingredients that work just as well as harsh chemical cleaners. Here are a few for you to try. (Again, protect your hands by wearing rubber gloves, and be sure to work in a well-ventilated area.)

What You'll Need
3 tablespoons baking soda
½ cup ammonia
2 cups warm water
Bucket
Cloth or sponge

BASIC BATHROOM CLEANER WITH AMMONIA

1. For everyday cleaning, mix ingredients together in bucket or other container.

2. Use for cleaning on bathroom surfaces.

NO AMMONIA BASIC BATHROOM CLEANER

1. Mix all ingredients together in a squeeze bottle.

2. Use for everyday bathroom cleaning.

What You'll Need
16 ounces baking soda
4 tablespoons dishwashing liquid
1 cup warm water
Squeeze bottle
Cloth or sponge

SOAP SCUM CLEANER

1. Mix ingredients together in a bucket or other container.

2. Apply liberally to soap scum; rinse well.

What You'll Need
½ cup baking soda
½ cup vinegar
1 cup ammonia
1 gallon warm water
Bucket
Cloth or sponge

TOILETS

- Use ½ cup baking soda in the toilet bowl for light cleaning. Let baking soda sit 30 minutes, then brush.

- Pour vinegar into the toilet, and let sit 30 minutes. Then sprinkle baking soda on a toilet bowl brush and scour any remaining stained areas. Flush.

- Once a week, pour 2 cups vinegar into toilet, and let it sit overnight. Brush toilet well; flush. This regular treatment will keep hard-water stains at bay and clean and freshen your bowl between major cleanings.

- Clean and disinfect your toilet bowl with ½ cup chlorine bleach. Pour it into the bowl, and let it stand for 10 minutes. Then scrub with the toilet brush and flush. Do not mix chlorine bleach with any other cleaner.

- Rust stains under a toilet bowl rim will sometimes yield to laundry bleach. Rub off truly stubborn stains with extra-fine steel wool or with wet-dry sandpaper.

- Clean the exterior of a toilet with the same products you use for tubs and sinks.

TUBS

- Try one of the homemade cleaners above for cleaning your tub, shower, and bathroom basin. They are nonabrasive and will not harm even a fiberglass or marble tub, shower, or basin. Or you can simply spray the fixture with vinegar and wipe it down.

- A light ring around the tub can be rubbed away without using any cleaners with a nylon net ball or pad. Cover a stubborn ring with a paste of cream of tartar and hydrogen peroxide. When the paste dries, wipe it off—along with the ring.

- Tackle stains on a porcelain tub with a paste of baking soda and hydrogen peroxide, then cover with damp paper towels. The towels keep the paste from sliding down into the tub. Let sit 30 minutes, then scrub.

- To remove discoloration from a yellowed bathtub, rub the tub with a solution of salt and turpentine. Rinse until all residue of salt and turpentine is gone.

- Stains on nonskid strips or appliqués in the tub can be removed by dampening the area, then sprinkling with baking soda. Let sit 20 minutes, then scrub and rinse.

SHOWERS

- Shower curtains can become dulled by soap film or plagued with mildew. Keep vinegar in a spray bottle near shower, and squirt shower curtains once or twice a week. There's no need to rinse.

- You can also clean mildew stains on shower curtains by sprinkling baking soda on a sponge and scrubbing. Rinse well. If mildew remains, mix a light bleach and water solution and spray on. Scrub well and rinse thoroughly.

- Most shower curtains can be washed in your washing machine, which will also kill mildew and germs.

- If none of these solutions gets rid of mildew stains on your shower curtain, mix borax with enough vinegar to make a paste, then scrub the stained area. Rinse well.

- Remove mineral buildup and improve performance of your showerhead with ½ cup baking soda and 1 cup vinegar mixed in a sturdy plastic bag. Secure the bag around the showerhead with a rubber band so the showerhead is submerged in the solution. Soak for 1 hour. Remove bag, and run very hot water through the showerhead for several minutes.

- Plastic showerheads can be soaked for 1 hour in a mixture of 1 pint vinegar and 1 pint hot water.

- Keep mildew from taking hold by wiping your shower walls with a towel after each shower while you are still in the tub or the shower stall.

- If the shower area is subject to mildew, periodically spray it with a mildew inhibitor and disinfectant.

- Leave the shower door slightly open to allow air to circulate; this will discourage the growth of mildew.

TOUGH JOB SHOWER CLEANER

1. When shower walls need a thorough cleaning, run shower water at its hottest temperature so steam will loosen dirt.

2. Mix together ingredients in bucket or other container. Use sponge mop on shower walls and floor; rinse with clear water.

What You'll Need
½ cup vinegar
1 cup clear ammonia
¼ cup baking soda
1 gallon warm water
Bucket
Sponge mop

SINKS

- For routine cleaning of sink and tub drains, pour in ½ cup baking soda followed by 1 cup vinegar. Let sit 10 to 20 minutes, then flush with very hot water.

- Hard-water stains and mineral deposits around sink and tub faucets can be removed by covering stained area with paper towels soaked in vinegar. Cover and leave on for 1 hour, then rinse with a damp sponge.

- You can also clean discolored porcelain fixtures with a paste of cream of tartar moistened with hydrogen peroxide or a paste of borax moistened with lemon juice. Scrub the paste into lightly stained areas with a brush, and rinse well.

- You may have to use a commercial rust remover to eliminate some rust stains. Be sure to wear rubber gloves when you work with these products because they contain acid.

- Mix equal amounts of white vinegar and water in a spray bottle. Spray onto moldy or mildewed areas and let sit for 15 minutes. Wipe clean. Use solution occasionally as a preventative measure in any area of your home that is prone to being damp, such as under the sink or in the cellar.

COUNTERS AND VANITIES

- Clean marble surfaces with a paste of baking soda and white vinegar. Wipe clean, and buff.

- A simple baking soda paste will attack hard water or rust stains on ceramic tile. Use a nylon scrubber, then rinse.

- To clean plastic laminate counters, use a two-sided scrubbing pad with fiber on one side and a sponge on the other. Moistened slightly with water, the fiber side is just abrasive enough to loosen greasy smears and other soil. Use the sponge side to wipe the surface damp-dry.

- When a spot or stain persists, first sprinkle baking soda on the spot, then scrub gently. If this doesn't take care of the problem, apply a polishing cleanser with a wet sponge.

COUNTER AND TILE CLEANER

What You'll Need
½ cup vinegar
1 cup clear ammonia
¼ cup baking soda
1 gallon warm water
Bucket
Cloth or sponge

1. Combine ingredients in bucket.

2. Use when your bathroom counters need a thorough cleaning.

FLOORS

- A tile or no-wax bathroom floor can be cleaned effectively with ½ cup baking soda in a bucket of warm water. Use the solution with a mop, then rinse well.

- To remove odors from floors, sprinkle the area with baking soda, let it sit, then vacuum or sweep up. The stronger the odor, the more soda you should use and the longer you should leave it on.

MIRRORS

- Mix ⅓ cup clear ammonia in 1 gallon warm water. Apply solution with a sponge/squeegee, or pour the solution into a spray container and spray it directly on the mirror. Buff with a lint-free cloth, chamois, or paper towel. Vinegar may be substituted for ammonia.

- Pour vinegar into a shallow bowl or pan, then crumple a sheet of newspaper, dip it in vinegar, and apply to mirror. Wipe the glass several times with the same newspaper until the mirror is almost dry. Then shine it with a soft clean cloth.

- Mix 2 cups of isopropyl rubbing alcohol (70 percent solution), 2 tablespoons of liquid dishwashing detergent, and 2 cups of water. Stir until thoroughly mixed, then pour solution into a spray bottle. Spray directly on the mirror. Buff with a lint-free cloth, chamois, or paper towel.

QUICK WALL AND FLOOR CLEANING

Walls, ceilings, and floors get touched, walked on, spilled on, and splashed on. But most marks, soils, and stains can be cleaned quickly and easily. Be sure to wear rubber gloves and work in a well-ventilated area when using cleaners that contain ammonia.

Attach a sponge or washcloth to your wrist with a rubber band to stop water from running down your arm when cleaning.

WALLS AND CEILINGS

BASIC WALL CLEANER

1. Mix thoroughly in bucket.

2. Wash ceilings and walls with cleaning solution from top to bottom, using clean sponge (or sponge mop for ceilings and high walls) and rinsing often. Stir mixture occasionally during use.

What You'll Need
1 cup ammonia
½ cup baking soda
½ cup vinegar
1 gallon water
Bucket
Sponge or
    sponge mop

LEMON FRESH WALLS

1. Combine ingredients in spray bottle.

2. Shake well before each use. Spray on trouble areas about once a week. This solution is especially good for cleaning dirty fingerprints off walls and door frames.

What You'll Need
1 teaspoon baking
    soda
1 teaspoon borax
2 teaspoons lemon
    juice or white
    vinegar
3 teaspoons liquid
    dish soap
2 cups hot water
Spray bottle
Cloth or sponge

WALLPAPER

- To wash large sections or whole walls of washable wallpaper, mix ½ cup vinegar and 1 quart water; apply mixture with a sponge. Be careful not to saturate, especially at seams and corners, or you could loosen wallpaper.

- Remove ordinary soil from washable wallpaper by rubbing spots with an art gum eraser.

- Get rid of crayon marks by rubbing carefully with a dry soap-filled fine-grade steel wool pad or by delicately sponging the area with a wad of white paper towels moistened with dry-cleaning solvent. Carefully blot small areas to prevent the solvent from spreading and discoloring the paper.

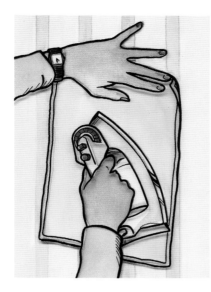

Soak up a grease stain on wallpaper by placing a clean cloth over the stain and ironing it.

Wash door and window frames from the bottom up.

- Remove transparent tape from a wall without marring the wallpaper (or paint) by pressing the tape—through a protective cloth—with a warm iron to soften and loosen the tape's adhesive backing.

- To remove grease from nonwashable wallpaper, place a blotter, such as a clean cloth, over the grease spot and press it with a moderately hot iron. The blotter will soak up the grease. Repeat as required.

- You can also remove grease by dusting talcum powder on the spot with a powder puff. Leave it for an hour, then brush it off. Repeat if necessary.

- Get rid of grease stains by applying a paste of cornstarch and water or by rubbing dry borax over stains.

WOOD PANELING

- Wood paneling can have a natural, stained, oil, or waxed finish. Routine care includes occasional vacuuming with a brush attachment. Many commercial oil and wax finishes are available. For best results follow the manufacturer's instructions.

- You can remove white water marks from wood paneling by rubbing mayonnaise into them. Wipe off the mayonnaise 12 hours later. The marks will have vanished.

WOODWORK

- Woodwork is either painted, stained, or left natural with an oil finish or a varnish finish. Like walls, it benefits from a regular cleaning routine. Vacuum or dust the woodwork in your home regularly. Don't forget the tops of doorjambs, window frames, cornices, ledges, and baseboards. Keep a small container of matching paint or stain handy to touch up nicks and scratches.

- Clean stained and natural woodwork with a wood cleaner/polish. Do not use water or waterbase cleaners on stained or natural woodwork except for light touchups that you buff-dry quickly. Spray the cleaner on a cloth instead of directly on the woodwork to prevent staining adjoining surfaces.

CARPETING

- The first rule of carpet cleaning is to wipe up any spill immediately. Often undiluted vinegar can be your best bet for removing a new stain.

- If you don't like using commercial carpet cleaners, you can shampoo your carpet with 1 cup baking soda mixed with 1 gallon warm water. Scrub by hand with a brush, or use this mixture in a carpet cleaning machine. If you use a steam cleaner and commercial shampoo, try rinsing with ¼ cup vinegar and 1 gallon water after shampooing. You can use it in the steam cleaner just like you used the shampoo. Because it removes shampoo residue, the carpet rinse will keep your carpet fresh and clean longer between shampoos.

- Spills on your carpet need to be dealt with as soon as you see them. As mentioned above, many carpet spills can be cleaned efficiently and effectively with plain undiluted vinegar or a solution of vinegar and water. Test a small area first for color fastness. Always blot up (don't rub) as much of the spill as possible. Then sponge undiluted or water-diluted vinegar onto the spot. Wring out the sponge. Repeat until the spot disappears. This will work well with ketchup, chewing gum, chocolate, soda, white glue, and many other common spills.

- You can remove crayon stains from carpeting or any other fabric or surface by scrubbing the area with a toothbrush dipped in vinegar.

- Ink stains may come up if you immediately blot and spray stained area with hair spray. Once ink spot is gone, work a solution of half vinegar, half water into the area to remove sticky spray.

- For pet accidents, rinse the stained area immediately with warm water. Then mix 3 tablespoons of white vinegar and 1 teaspoon of liquid soap. Apply the solution to the stained area and leave on 15 minutes. Rinse, and rub dry. If you have to use a commercial cleaner to remove the stain, follow that treatment with a rinse of vinegar and water to remove any lingering odors.

- Coffee should come out of carpets easily with plain water if you attack it immediately. If not, mix 1 part vinegar to 2 parts water and sponge solution into rug. Blot up any excess, and rinse until brown color is gone.

- Red wine spills must be immediately blotted up. Then sprinkle area with salt. Let sit 15 minutes. The salt should absorb any remaining wine in the carpet (turning pink as a result). Then clean entire area with a mixture of ⅓ cup vinegar and ⅔ cup water.

- If gravy has been spilled, remove as much liquid as possible by covering the spot with salt to prevent the greasy stain from spreading. Then follow rug manufacturer's instructions. You may need a dry-cleaning solution or an enzyme detergent.

- Grease spots can be cleaned with a mixture of 1 part salt to 4 parts rubbing alcohol. Rub hard, going the same direction as carpet nap, then rinse with water.

- If using salt for absorbing a stain has left a salt residue in your rug or carpet, mix equal amounts of vinegar and water, and apply the solution with a sponge. Do not saturate. Let dry, then vacuum.

CARPET FRESHENER

1. Combine ingredients in glass jar or airtight container.

2. Sprinkle over carpet. Allow to sit for a few minutes, then vacuum.

What You'll Need
1 cup crushed dried herbs
1 teaspoon each ground cloves, cinnamon, baking soda
Glass jar or airtight container
Vacuum

CARPET FRESHENER VARIATION

1. Combine ingredients in glass jar or airtight container.

2. Sprinkle over carpet. Let sit for 10 to 20 minutes, then vacuum.

What You'll Need
1 cup baking soda
1 cup cornstarch
15 drops essential oil fragrance
Glass jar or airtight container
Vacuum

TILE, VINYL, AND LINOLEUM

- Ceramic tile floors will sparkle if cleaned with 1 cup vinegar and 1 gallon warm water. Simply mop on.

- Wash grout between tiles with straight vinegar to clean and prevent smudges.

- Linoleum and vinyl floors can be scrubbed with the same mixture of 1 cup vinegar and 1 gallon water. If the floor needs a polish after this, use straight club soda.

- If you've stripped the wax from a floor using ammonia, finish the project by rinsing entire floor with a solution of 1 gallon water and ½ cup vinegar. The vinegar will remove lingering wax and the ammonia smell.

- If you use detergent on your no-wax vinyl or linoleum floor, rinse afterward with a solution of 1 cup vinegar to 1 gallon water.

- A damp sponge or scrubber dipped in baking soda will remove black heel marks on linoleum or vinyl floors.

- Mop up salt deposits from winter boots with a mixture of half vinegar, half water.

HARDWOOD

- Add a cup of plain vinegar to a gallon bucket of water, and mop lightly onto hardwood floors (do not saturate). There's no need to rinse. This will keep floors shiny and remove any greasy buildup.

- A closet with bare wood floors can begin to smell stale. To freshen, lightly mop with a mixture of 1 cup baking soda and ½ cup vinegar in 1 gallon warm water.

QUICK WINDOW AND WINDOW COVERING CLEANING

It's a joy to gaze out streak-free, clean windows, but they can seem hard to achieve. The following hints will help. Use a commercial cleaner, or try the following recipes and washing techniques below.

Clean the corners of a window with a cotton swab or toothbrush.

To prevent drips, wash windows from the top down.

WINDOWS

- Wash windows on a cloudy day to avoid streaks.

- Work from the top down to prevent drips.

- Use a soft toothbrush or cotton swab to clean corners.

- To give an extra shine to window glass, polish it with well-washed cotton T-shirts or old diapers. Or rub a clean blackboard eraser over a freshly washed and dried window to give it a diamond-bright shine.

- Wash one side of the window with horizontal strokes and the other side with vertical strokes so you can pinpoint which side of the window has a streak. Use a squeegee on a long handle or a sponge/squeegee combination to prevent streaks on large windows.

VINEGAR WINDOW WASHER

1. Combine ingredients in spray bottle.

2. Spray on windows and wipe clean with rags.

What You'll Need
2 tablespoons vinegar
1 cup water
Spray bottle
Cotton rags

VINEGAR AND ALCOHOL WINDOW CLEANER

1. Combine vinegar and rubbing alcohol in spray bottle. Fill rest of bottle with water.

2. Spray on windows and clean with rags.

What You'll Need
½ cup vinegar
¼ cup rubbing alcohol
Water
Spray bottle

BLINDS

- Vacuum blinds regularly with the brush attachment of your vacuum. Close adjustable slats when vacuuming so you can reach more of their surface. You can remove finger marks with a sponge.

- When blinds require a thorough cleaning, immerse plastic, metal, and painted blinds in

To locate a streak in a window, wash one side of the window with vertical strokes, horizontal on the other side.

water (add ½ cup baking soda if you wish). Wash them in the bathtub or outdoors by hanging them on the clothesline for scrubbing. Natural wood blinds with decorative yarn tapes should not be immersed.

- Touch up dingy white tapes on venetian blinds with white shoe polish. Rub the cords with baking soda to whiten them.

SHADES

- Light-diffusing or opaque shades are usually made of fabric that is washable, and some shades have a protective vinyl coating that makes them easy to clean. Other shades are not washable and must be dry-cleaned.

- Vacuum shades regularly using the brush attachment. Lower the shades completely before vacuuming to clean the full length; don't forget the tops and valances.

- Remove finger marks on shades with a sponge or a quick spray of one of the all-purpose spray cleaners on pages 167.

- To thoroughly clean shades, remove them from the window and spread them out on a flat surface. Test a corner of the shade with a detergent to see if the color bleeds. If the color does not bleed, wash the entire shade with an all-purpose cleaner. Rinse and allow to dry thoroughly before rehanging.

QUICK EXTERIOR CLEANING

Done cleaning inside? There are lots of easy cleaning tips for outside, too!

HOUSES, DECKS, AND SIDEWALKS

- A yearly wash will keep your house looking fresh and bright between paintings. And when it is time to paint, a thorough washing will help ensure proper adhesion of new paint.

- Depending on the size of the house and on just how dirty it is, there are two ways to approach this job. If you live in an average-size house that isn't terribly dirty, use a garden hose with a carwash brush attachment to bathe the big areas. For caked-on dirt, use a scrub brush or a sponge and a pail of warm water with a strong household detergent in it. Work

from the top down, and rinse all areas thoroughly with water.

- For bigger houses or for faster work on smaller ones, rent a pressure washer. This device attaches to your home's water-supply system and puts out a jet of water at a pressure of several hundred pounds per square inch. It is equipped with a hand-held wand tipped with a trigger-activated nozzle. The pressure is high enough to dislodge not only stubborn dirt, mildew, stains, and dried-on sea-spray salt, it's enough to remove peeling paint. In fact, if the jet nozzle is held too close to the surface it can even peel off perfectly sound paint, split open shingles, and drill a hole in siding. So follow the manufacturer's directions and wear goggles and protective clothing. You may want to purchase a special cleaning agent from your local paint store. For example, if you live in a damp climate, you may want a product that includes a mildew killer.

- You can use the pressure sprayer while working from a ladder—although scaffolding is better—but practice at ground level first; the force of the spray against the house could knock you off a ladder if you're not careful. Some of these machines come with separate containers you can fill with cleaning solutions or anti-mildew solutions. Sprayers are so powerful that you may not need to use a cleaning solution; if you do, remember to rinse the surface with clean water afterward.

- The same techniques will work on any outbuildings, decks, and concrete driveways, leaving the whole exterior of your building looking clean and bright.

CHIMNEYS

If you have a wood-burning fireplace, you know how much soot is produced by a fire. Over the years, soot can build up in a chimney, blocking it and creating a fire hazard. To prevent this, clean the chimney every year or two. The job is a messy one, but it's not hard, and cleaning the chimney will make the fireplace operate more efficiently. Work on a warm, dry day, wear work gloves and safety goggles, and follow the roof safety procedures detailed in chapter 7. To clean a chimney:

1. Open damper to fireplace. Seal off fireplace opening to

What You'll Need
Heavy plastic sheet
    or scrap plywood
Masking tape
Burlap bag
Straw or paper
Bricks
Chimney brush
Rope
Hand mirror
Flashlight
Shop vacuum

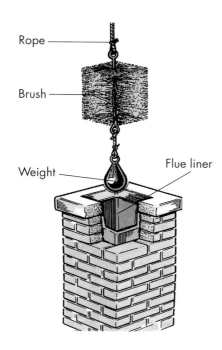

For chimneys with flue liners, a chimney brush is the best cleaning tool. Use a brush the same shape, round or square, as the flue liner.

Rope

Brush

Weight

Flue liner

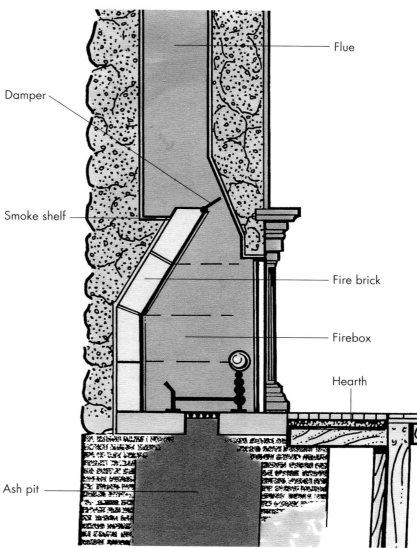

Damper

Smoke shelf

Ash pit

Flue

Fire brick

Firebox

Hearth

As the fireplace is used, soot builds up in the firebox and on the sides of the flue. To prevent problems, clean the chimney and the ash pit regularly.

room with heavy plastic sheet taped into place or piece of scrap plywood. Make sure there are no leaks or cracks around edges.

2. Check to see if chimney has a flue. If not, use burlap bag filled with straw or wadded paper, weighted with a brick or two, as cleaning tool. If chimney is lined with a flue, use chimney brush to do the cleaning. Chimney brushes are available at larger hardware stores.

3. Fasten bag or brush securely to rope. Working from roof, lower bag or brush down chimney until it hits bottom. Lower and raise brush several times to dislodge caked soot. If you're using bag, start at one corner of chimney. Lower bag, pull it up, and repeat, lowering and raising it several times. Move bag around perimeter of opening, moving it about a foot each time, and repeat this procedure until you've cleaned entire chimney area.

4. If fireplace has an outside door, open it and remove soot that's fallen through. Wait an hour or so for dust to settle, then remove plastic sheet or plywood from fireplace opening.

5. Use large hand mirror and flashlight to inspect chimney. Look for any obstructions. If there are any, repeat cleaning procedure. If there are no obstructions, reach over damper to smoke shelf. Gently clean away debris with shop vacuum.

Soiled fireplace bricks can be cleaned with a stiff bristled brush dipped in white vinegar. Or scour soot and ash from fireplace bricks with a baking soda solution. Rub into brick with a stiff brush. Rinse as necessary.

Rope

Burlap bag

Brick

A burlap bag, filled with crumpled newspaper and weighted with a brick, makes a good cleaning tool for unlined chimneys.

MONTH-TO-MONTH ROUTINE MAINTENANCE SCHEDULE

Some homeowners like to schedule routine maintenance on a seasonal basis; others prefer to tackle quick fixes each month. The following monthly schedule is a guide that should be adjusted for your climate, your home, and your lifestyle. If your fall schedule will be packed with football games, children's soccer games, music lessons, and other weekend activities, you may want to start your activities earlier. Likewise, if you're planning major gardening, you may want to hurry up the spring chores so that you have lots of time to garden. Notice that periodic chores can be done any time relegated to the least active months. The important thing about a routine maintenance schedule is to get your chores completed so that minor maintenance doesn't become a major problem.

January

- Change disposable filters on forced-air furnaces; wash permanent filters.
- Give major appliances a thorough dusting. Clean dust from behind refrigerator compressor panel and move refrigerator away from wall to clean behind back panel; clean range thoroughly according to manufacturer's instructions.
- Check wood ladders for loose rungs; repair or replace any defective ladders.

February

- Change disposable filters on forced-air furnaces; wash permanent filters.
- Check cords on appliances and extension cords for wear and/or fraying. Repair or replace defective cords.

March

- Change disposable filters on forced-air furnaces; wash permanent filters.
- Turn on outside faucets after the threat of a hard freeze has passed.
- Check window and storm door screens for holes. Patch them now or have them rescreened.
- Inspect roof shingles or shakes for damage from winter storms; replace any missing shingles.
- Inspect siding for popped nails and weathering; check brick for crumbling mortar.

April

- Change disposable filters on forced-air furnaces; wash permanent filters.
- If needed, paint or stain the exterior of your home when it gets warm enough, but avoid postponing the job until the summer when paint and stain dry too quickly.
- Wash windows and put up screens.
- Change batteries in smoke alarms on the weekend that daylight savings time begins.
- Check the exterior of your home for insect infestations; plug any small holes where wasps and hornets could try to make a nest. Inspect for termite tunnels.
- Inspect caulked areas; recaulk, if necessary.

May

- Inspect outdoor furniture and barbecue for wear; make necessary repairs.
- Check deck, patio, walkway, and driveway for split wood, cracks, etc.

June

- Call a professional service person to inspect and adjust the central air conditioning. Install window air conditioners; clean the filter with a solution of mild household detergent and water; and clean the evaporator and condenser coils with a vacuum cleaner.

July

- Flush the hot water tank to remove sediment that accumulates and can eventually deteriorate the inside of the tank. Follow manufacturer's instructions for draining.

August

- Check your home's exterior for signs of weathering and to see if you need to make time to touch up peeling paint when cooler weather arrives.

September

- Have your furnace and chimney cleaned.
- Inspect the roof for any problems. If you have skylights, make sure to check that the flashing is intact.
- Store outside furniture.

October

- Change disposable filters on forced-air furnaces; wash permanent filters.
- Change batteries in smoke alarms on the weekend that daylight savings time ends.
- Remove or cover window air conditioners.
- Check thermostat. Remove faceplate and blow away any lint that's collected.
- Remove and clean screens before storing them for the winter.

November

- Change disposable filters on forced-air furnaces; wash permanent filters.
- Clean gutters and downspouts, preferably after the last leaves have fallen.
- Put up storm windows.
- Put weatherstripping on windows and doors that require additional help in keeping out cold air.
- Get your humidifier ready. Clean filters and use a humidifier cleaning solution to clean the reservoir.

December

- Change disposable filters on forced-air furnaces; wash permanent filters.
- Make sure your electrical system is operating well before using holiday lights.

GLOSSARY

ABS (acrylonitrile-butadine-styrene)—Material used for rigid black plastic pipe in DWV systems.

air-dried lumber—Lumber that has been dried naturally by air with a minimum moisture content of 15 to 20 percent.

alternating current (AC)—Electric current in which the direction of flow is reversed at frequent intervals, usually 100 or 120 times per second (50 or 60 cycles per second or 50/60 Hz).

ambient temperature—Temperature of the surroundings.

American Wire Gauge (AWG)—A standard system for designating the size of electrical wire (the higher the number, the smaller the wire). Most house wiring is AWG 12 or 14.

ammeter—A device used for measuring current flow at any point in an electrical circuit.

ampere or amp (A)—The unit for the electric current; the flow of electrons. One amp is 1 coulomb passing in 1 second. One amp is produced by an electric force of 1 volt acting across a resistance of 1 ohm.

amp hour—The quantity of electrical energy corresponding to the flow of current of 1 ampere for 1 hour.

apron—The flat piece of inside trim that is placed against the wall directly under the stool of a window.

armored cable—A flexible metal-sheathed cable used for indoor wiring. Commonly called BX cable.

ballast—A circuit used to stabilize an electric current, for example, in a fluorescent light.

baseboard—A trim board placed at the base of a wall next to the floor.

base molding—A strip of wood used to trim the upper edge of a baseboard.

bearing wall—A wall that supports any vertical load in addition to its own weight.

blind nailing—Nailing in such a way that the nail heads are not visible on the face of the work.

board foot—A unit of lumber equal to a piece 1 foot square and 1 inch thick (144 cubic inches of wood).

board lumber—Yard lumber less than 2 inches thick and 2 or more inches wide.

box—See *junction box*.

branch—Any part of the supply pipes connected to a fixture in a plumbing system.

British Thermal Unit (BTU)—The amount of heat energy required to raise 1 pound of water from a temperature of 60°F to 61°F at 1 atmosphere pressure. One watt hour equals 3,413 BTU.

building drain—The lowest horizontal drainpipe in a structure. Carries all waste out to the sewer.

cable—An electricity conductor made up of two or more wires contained in an overall covering.

casement—A window sash on hinges attached to the sides of a window frame. Such windows are called casement windows.

casing—Moldings of various widths and forms; used to trim door and window openings between the jambs and the walls.

caulk—Viscous material used to seal joints and make them watertight and airtight.

caulk gun—A tool used to apply caulk.

check valve—A valve that lets water flow in only one direction in a pipe system.

circuit—The path of electric current as it travels from the source to the appliance or fixture and back to the source.

circuit breaker—A safety device used to interrupt the flow of power when the electricity exceeds a predetermined amount. Unlike a fuse, you can reset a circuit breaker.

clean out—An easy-to-reach and easy-to-open place in a DWV system where obstructions can be removed or a snake inserted.

compact fluorescent lights—Lights that use a lot less energy than regular light bulbs. Often used as reading lights and ceiling lights.

conductor—Any low-resistance material, such as copper wire, through which electricity flows easily.

conduit—A metal, fiber, or plastic pipe or tube used to enclose electric wires or cables.

countersinking—Boring the end of a hole for a screw or bolt so the head can be brought flush with or below the surface. Also, sinking or setting a nail or screw so the head is flush with or below the surface.

cove molding—A molding with a concave face. Usually used to trim or finish interior corners.

CPVC (chlorinated polyvinyl chloride)—The rigid white or pastel-color plastic pipe used for supply lines.

crawl space—A shallow space between the floor joists and the ground; usually enclosed by the foundation wall.

cripple studs—Short studs surrounding a window or between the top plate and end rafter in a gable end or between the foundation and subfloor. Also called *jack studs*.

crown molding—A convex molding used horizontally wherever an interior angle is to be covered (usually at the top of a wall, next to the ceiling).

current—The movement or flow of electrons, which provides electric power. The rate of electron flow is measured in amperes.

d—See *penny*.

dado joint—A joint where a dado is cut in one piece of wood to accept the end of another piece.

dimension lumber—Yard lumber from 2 inches to, but not including, 5 inches thick and 2 or more inches wide. Includes joists, rafters, studs, planks, and small timbers.

diode—Electronic device that allows current flow only in one direction.

direct current (DC)—Electrical current that flows only in one direction, although it may vary in magnitude. Contrasts with alternating current.

direct nailing—Driving nails so they are perpendicular to the surface or joint of two pieces of wood. Also called *face nailing*.

doorjamb—The case that surrounds a door. Consists of two upright side pieces called side jambs and a top horizontal piece called a head jamb.

drywall—Panels consisting of a layer of gypsum plaster covered on both sides with paper. Used for finishing interior walls and ceilings. Also called *wallboard*, *gypsum wallboard*, and Sheetrock.

ducts—Pipes that carry air from a furnace or an air conditioner to the living areas of a structure.

DWV (drain-waste-vent)—An acronym referring to all or part of the plumbing system that carries wastewater from fixtures to the sewer and gases to the roof.

electric circuit—Path followed by electrons from a power source (generator or battery) through an external line (including devices that use the electricity) and returning through a different line to the source.

electricity—The movement of electrons (a subatomic particle), produced by a voltage, through a conductor.

face nailing—See *direct nailing*.

finish carpentry—The fine work, such as that for doors, stairways, and moldings, required to complete a building.

finish electrical work—The installation of the visible parts of the electrical system, such as the fixtures, switches, plugs, and wall plates.

finish plumbing—The installation of the attractive visible parts of a plumbing system, such as plumbing fixtures and faucets.

fitting—Any device that connects pipe to pipe or pipe to plumbing fixtures.

fixture—Any plumbing device that is permanently attached to the water system of a house or any lighting device attached to the surface of, recessed into, or hanging from the ceiling or walls.

fluorescent light—A form of lighting that uses long thin tubes of glass that contain mercury vapor and various phosphor powders (chemicals based on phosphorus) to produce white light. Generally considered to be the most efficient form of home lighting.

footing—The rectangular concrete base that supports a foundation wall or pier or a retaining wall. Usually wider than the structure it supports.

frame—The enclosing woodwork around doors and windows. Also the skeleton of a building; lies under the interior and exterior wall coverings and roofing.

furring—Narrow strips of wood attached to walls or ceilings; forms a true surface on which to fasten other materials.

fuse—A safety device for electrical circuits; interrupts the flow of current when it exceeds predetermined limits for a specific time period.

ground—Connected to the earth or something serving as the earth, such as a cold water pipe. The ground wire in an electrical circuit is usually bare or has green insulation.

ground loop—An undesirable feedback condition caused by two or more circuits sharing a common electrical line, usually a grounded conductor.

grout—Mortar that can flow into the cavities and joints of any masonry work, especially the filling between tiles and concrete blocks.

gypsum wallboard—See *drywall*.

halogen lamp—A special type of incandescent globe made of quartz glass and a tungsten filament, enabling it to run at a much higher temperature than a conventional incandescent globe. Efficiency is better than a normal incandescent but not as good as a fluorescent light.

hanger—Any of several types of metal devices for supporting pipes, framing members, or other items. Usually referred to by the items they are designed to support, for example, joist hanger or pipe hanger.

hardboard—A synthetic wood panel made by chemically converting wood chips to basic fibers and then forming the panels under heat and pressure. Also called *Masonite*.

header—A horizontal member over a door, window, or other opening; supports the members above it. Usually made of wood, stone, or metal. Also called a *lintel*. Also, in the framing of floor or ceiling openings, a beam used to support the ends of joists.

heat pump—Like an air conditioner or refrigerator, a heat pump moves heat from one location to another. In the cooling mode, heat pumps reduce indoor temperatures in the summer by transferring heat to the ground. Unlike an air-conditioning unit, however, a heat pump's cycle is reversible. In winter, a heat pump can extract heat from the ground and transfer it inside. The energy value of the heat thus moved can be more than three times the cost of the electricity required to perform the transfer process.

hertz (Hz)—The frequency of electrical current described in cycles per second. Appliances in the U.S. use 60 Hz. Appliances in other countries generally use 50 Hz.

hot wire—In an electrical circuit, any wire that carries current from the power source to an electrical device. The hot wire is usually identified with black, blue, or red insulation, but it can be any color but white or green.

incandescent light—An electric lamp that is evacuated or filled with an inert gas and contains a filament (commonly tungsten). The filament emits visible light when heated to extreme temperatures by the passage of electric current through it.

insulation—Any material that resists the conduction of heat, sound, or electricity.

insulation board—A structural building board made of coarse wood or cane fiber in ½- and ²⁵⁄₃₂-inch thicknesses. It can be obtained in various size sheets in various densities and with several treatments.

jack studs—See *cripple studs*.

jamb—The frame surrounding a door to window; consists of two vertical pieces called side jambs and a top horizontal piece called a head jamb.

joist—One of a series of parallel beams, usually 2 inches in thickness, used to support floor and ceiling loads and supported in turn by larger beams, girders, or bearing walls.

junction box—A metal or plastic container for electrical connections. Sometimes just called a *box*.

kiln-dried lumber—Lumber that has been kiln dried, often to a moisture content of 6 to 12 percent. Common varieties of softwood lumber, such as framing lumber, are dried to a somewhat higher moisture content.

kilowatt (kw)—A unit of electrical power (1,000 watts).

kilowatt-hour (kwh)—1,000 watts acting over a period of 1 hour. The kwh is a unit of energy (1 kwh=3,600 kJ).

laminate—To form a panel or sheet by bonding two or more layers of material. Also, a product formed by such a process; plastic laminate used for countertops, for example.

lath—A building material of metal, gypsum, wood, or other material. Used as a base for plaster or stucco.

level—A device used to determine when surfaces are level or plumb.

linear measure—Any measurement along a line.

load—Anything in an electrical circuit that, when the circuit is turned on, draws power from that circuit.

load circuit—Wiring, including switches and fuses, that connects the load to the power source.

load current—The current required to power a given electrical device.

load resistance—The electrical resistance of a given load.

lumber—Wood product manufactured by sawing, resawing, and passing lengthwise through a standard planing machine and then crosscutting to length.

main drain—The pipe that collects the discharge from branch waste lines and carries it to the outer foundation wall, where it connects to the sewer line.

main vent—In plumbing, the largest vent pipe to which branch vents may connect. Also called the *vent stack*.

masonry—Stone, brick, concrete, hollow tile, concrete block, gypsum, block, or other similar building units or materials bonded together with mortar to form a foundation, wall, pier, buttress, or similar mass.

mastic—A viscous material used as an adhesive for setting tile or resilient flooring.

megawatt (mw)—1 million watts (1,000 kilowatts).

megawatt-hour (mwh)—A measurement of power with respect to time (i.e., energy). One megawatt-hour is equal to 1 megawatt being used for a period of 1 hour or 1 kilowatt being used for 1,000 hours.

milliamps (mA)—One-thousandth of an amp.

miter box—A tool that guides a saw in making miter or angle cuts.

mortar—A mixture of sand and portland cement. Used for bonding bricks, blocks, tiles, or stones.

mud sill—See *sill plate*.

neutral wire—In a circuit, any wire that is kept at zero voltage. The neutral wire completes the circuit from source to fixture or appliance to ground. The covering of neutral wires is always white.

nipple—In plumbing, any short length of pipe externally threaded on both ends.

NM cable—Nonmetallic sheathed electric cable used for indoor wiring. Also known by the brand name Romex.

nominal size—The size designation of a piece of lumber before it is planed or surfaced. If the actual size of a piece of surfaced lumber is $1\frac{1}{2} \times 3\frac{1}{2}$ inches, it is referred to by its nominal size: 2×4.

nonbearing wall—A wall supporting no load other than its own weight.

ohm—The resistance between two points of a conductor when a constant potential difference of 1 volt applied between these points produces a current of 1 amp in the conductor.

Ohm's law—A simple mathematical formula that allows either voltage, current, or resistance to be calculated when the other two values are known. The formula is $V = I \times R$, where V is voltage, I is current, and R is resistance.

outlet—See *receptacle*.

panel—A large thin board or sheet of construction material. Also a thin piece of wood or plywood in a frame of thicker pieces, as in a panel door or wainscoting.

particleboard—A form of composite board or panel made of wood chips bonded with adhesive.

partition—A wall that subdivides any room or space within a building.

penny—As applied to nails, it originally indicated the price per 100. The term now serves as a measure of nail length and is abbreviated by the letter *d*.

phillips head—A type of screw and screwdriver on which the driving mechanism is an *X* rather than a slot.

pier—A column of masonry, usually rectangular, used to support other structural members. Often used as a support under decks.

pigtail—A short length of electrical wire or group of wires.

plaster—A mixture of lime, sand, and water plus cement for exterior cement plaster and plaster of paris for interior smooth plaster used to cover the surfaces of a structure.

plasterboard—See *drywall*.

plate—A horizontal framing member, usually at the bottom or top of a wall or other part of a structure, on which other members rest. The mudsill, soleplate, and top plate are examples.

plumb—Exactly perpendicular; vertical.

plywood—A wood product made up of layers of wood veneer bonded together with adhesive. It is usually made up of an odd number of plys set at a right angle to each other.

polyvinyl chloride (PVC)—A plastic used as an insulator on electrical cables. A toxic material, it is being replaced with alternatives made from more benign chemicals.

post—A vertical support member, usually made up of only one piece of lumber or a metal pipe or I beam.

putty—A soft, pliable material used for sealing the edges of glass in a sash or to fill small holes or cracks in wood.

quarter-round—A convex molding shaped like a quarter circle when viewed in cross section; typically used as wall or baseboard trim.

receptacle—In a wall, ceiling, or floor, an electric device into which the plugs on appliance and extension cords are placed to connect them to electric power. Also called an *outlet*.

register—In a wall, floor, or ceiling, the device through which air from the furnace or air conditioner enters a room. Also any device for controlling the flow of heated or cooled air through an opening.

resistance (R)—The property of a material that resists the flow of electric current when a potential difference is applied across it, measured in ohms.

resistor—An electronic component used to restrict the flow of current in a circuit. Sometimes used specifically to produce heat, such as in a water heater element.

ripping—Sawing wood in the direction of the grain.

riser—Each of the vertical boards between the treads of a stairway.

run—The front-to-back width of a single stair or the horizontal measurement from the bottom riser to the back of the top tread.

service panel—The box or panel where electricity is distributed to the house circuits. It contains the circuit breakers and, usually, the main disconnect switch.

shim—A thin wedge of wood, often part of a shingle, used to bring parts of a structure into alignment.

shoe molding—A strip of wood used to trim the bottom edge of a baseboard.

shutoff valve—A fitting to shut off the water supply to a single fixture or branch of pipe.

sill plate—The lowest member in the framing of a structure; usually a board bolted to the foundation wall on which the floor joists rest. Also called a *mudsill*.

soffit—The underside of a stairway, cornice, archway, or similar member of a structure. Usually a small area relative to a ceiling.

soil stack—In the DWV system, the main vertical pipe. Usually extends from the basement to a point above the roof.

span—The distance between structural supports, such as walls, columns, piers, beams, girders, and trusses.

splash block—A small masonry block laid with the top close to the ground surface to receive roof drainage from downspouts and to carry it away from the foundation.

square—A term used to describe an angle of exactly 90°. Also a device to measure such an angle or a unit of measure equaling 100 square feet.

stringer—The supporting member to which the treads and risers of a stairway are fastened. Also called a carriage.

stucco—A plaster of sand, portland cement, and lime used to cover the exterior of buildings.

stud—One of a series of wood or metal vertical framing members that are the main units of walls and partitions.

stud wall—The main framing units for walls and partitions in a building composed of studs; top plates; bottom plates; and the framing of windows, doors, and corner posts.

subfloor—Plywood or oriented strand boards attached to joists. The finish floor is laid over the subfloor. The subfloor also can be made of concrete.

switch—A device for turning the flow of electricity on and off in a circuit or for diverting the current from one circuit to another.

threshold—A shaped piece of wood or metal, usually beveled on both edges, that is placed on the finish floor between the side jamb. Forms the bottom of an exterior doorway.

timber—Pieces of lumber with a cross section greater than 4×6 inches. Usually used as beams, girders, posts, and columns.

toenailing—Driving a nail at a slant to the initial surface in order to permit it to penetrate into a second member.

tongue and groove—A way of milling lumber so it fits together tightly and forms an extremely strong floor or deck. Also boards milled for tongue-and-groove flooring or decking that have one or more tongues on one edge and a matching groove or grooves on the other.

top plate—In a stud wall, the top horizontal member to which the cap plate is nailed when the stud walls are connected and aligned.

transmission lines—Transmit high-voltage electricity from the transformer to the electric distribution system.

trap—In plumbing, a U-shape drain fitting that remains full of water to prevent the entry of air and sewer gas into a building.

tread—In a stairway, the horizontal surface on which a person steps.

trim—Any finish materials in a structure that are placed to provide decoration or to cover the joints between surfaces or contrasting materials. Door and windows casings, baseboards, picture moldings, and cornices are examples of trim.

underlayment—The material placed under the finish coverings of floors to provide waterproofing as well as a smooth, even surface on which to apply finish material.

VAC—Volts alternating current.

vapor barrier—Any material used to prevent the penetration of water vapor into walls or other enclosed parts of a building. Polyethylene sheets, aluminum foil, and building paper are the materials used most.

VDC—Volts direct current.

veneer—A thin layer of wood, usually one that has beauty or value, that is applied for economy or appearance on top of an inferior surface.

vent—Any opening, usually covered with screen or louvers, made to allow the circulation of air, usually into an attic or crawl space. In plumbing, a pipe in the DWV system for the purpose of bringing air into the system.

vent stack—See *main vent*.

VOC—Open-circuit voltage.

volt (V)—A unit of measure of the force, or pressure, given the electrons in an electric circuit. One volt produces 1 ampere of current when acting at a resistance of 1 ohm.

voltage drop—The voltage lost along a length of wire or conductor due to the resistance of that conductor. This also applies to resistors. The voltage drop is calculated by using *Ohm's law*.

voltmeter (VOM)—An electrical or electronic device used to measure voltage, resistance, and current.

wallboard—See *drywall*.

water-repellent preservative—A liquid designed to penetrate into wood and impart water repellency and a moderate preservative protection.

watt (W)—The unit of electric power, or amount of work (J), done in a unit of time. One ampere of current flowing at a potential of 1 volt produces 1 watt of power.

watt hour (Wh)—A unit of energy equal to 1 watt of power being used for 1 hour.

waveform—The shape of a wave or pattern representing a vibration. The shape characterizing an AC current or a voltage output.

weatherstripping—Narrow strips of metal, fiber, plastic foam, or other materials placed around doors and windows. Prevents the entry of air, moisture, and dust.

wirenut—A device that uses mechanical pressure rather than solder to establish a connection between two or more electrical conductors.

INDEX